THE REPUBLIC OF THE LIVING

FORDHAM UNIVERSITY PRESS   NEW YORK 2014

COMMONALITIES
Timothy C. Campbell, series editor

THE REPUBLIC OF THE LIVING

Biopolitics and the Critique of Civil Society

MIGUEL VATTER

Copyright © 2014 Fordham University Press

All rights reserved. No part of this publication may be reproduced, stored in a retrieval system, or transmitted in any form or by any means—electronic, mechanical, photocopy, recording, or any other—except for brief quotations in printed reviews, without the prior permission of the publisher.

Fordham University Press has no responsibility for the persistence or accuracy of URLs for external or third-party Internet websites referred to in this publication and does not guarantee that any content on such websites is, or will remain, accurate or appropriate.

Fordham University Press also publishes its books in a variety of electronic formats. Some content that appears in print may not be available in electronic books.

Library of Congress Cataloging-in-Publication Data

Vatter, Miguel E.
 The republic of the living : biopolitics and the critique of civil society / Miguel Vatter. — First edition.
     pages cm. — (Commonalities)
 Includes bibliographical references and index.
 ISBN 978-0-8232-5601-3 (cloth : alk. paper)
 ISBN 978-0-8232-5602-0 (pbk. : alk. paper)
 1. Civil society. 2. Biopolitics. I. Title.
 JC337.V37 2014
 306.2—dc23
                                            2013050014

Printed in the United States of America

16 15 14   5 4 3 2 1

First edition

CONTENTS

Acknowledgments vii

Introduction 1

Part I Biopolitics of the Economy

1 The Tragedy of Civil Society and Republican Politics in Hegel 17

2 Living Labor and Self-Generative Value in Marx 60

Part II Biopolitics of the Family

3 Reification and Redemption of Bare Life in Adorno and Agamben 99

4 Natality, Fertility, and Mimesis in Arendt's Theory of Freedom 129

5 The Heroism of Sexuality in Benjamin and Foucault 156

Part III Biopolitics of Rights

6 Free Markets and Republican Constitutions
in Hayek and Foucault 195

7 Biopolitical Cosmopolitanism: The Right
to Have Rights in Arendt and Agamben 221

Part IV Biopolitics of Eternal Life

8 Bare Life and Philosophical Life in
Aristotle, Spinoza, and Heidegger. 263

9 Eternal Recurrence and the Now
of Revolution: Nietzsche and Messianic
Marxism 290

Notes 327
Works Cited. 365
Index 387

ACKNOWLEDGMENTS

Chapter 1 is a greatly expanded and revised version of the essay "Hegel y la libertad de los antiguos," in *Hegel pensador de la actualidad*, edited by Vanessa Lemm and Juan Ormeño (Santiago, Chile: Ediciones Universidad Diego Portales, 2010), 235–58. Chapter 3 is a revised version of the article "In Odradek's World: Bare Life and Historical Materialism in Agamben and Benjamin," *Diacritics* 38, no. 3 (2008): 45–70. Chapter 4 is an expanded and revised version of "Natality and Biopolitics in Arendt," in *Revista de Ciencia Política* 26, no. 2 (2006): 137–59. Chapter 5 is an expanded version of "Married Life, Gay Life as a Work of Art, and Eternal Life: Towards a Biopolitical Reading of Benjamin," *Philosophy and Rhetoric* 44, no. 4 (2011): 309–35. An earlier version of Chapter 6 appears in Spanish as "Foucault y la ley: la juridificación de la política en el neoliberalismo," in *Michel Foucault: biopolítica y neoliberalismo*, edited by Vanessa Lemm (Santiago, Chile: Ediciones Universidad Diego Portales, 2010), 199–216, and a shorter version of this chapter is forthcoming in *The Government of Life: Michel Foucault, Biopolitics and Neoliberalism*, edited by Vanessa Lemm and Miguel Vatter (New York: Fordham University Press). A version of Chapter 7 was presented as "Arendt's Right to Have Rights as Natural Right: A Contribution to a Bio-Politics of Rights" at the American Political Science Association Annual Meeting, Seattle, WA, August 2011. Chapter 8 is a slightly revised version of "Eternal Life and Biopower," *The New Centennial Review* 10, no. 3 (2011): 217–49. Parts of Chapter 9 were presented under the title "Reification and Temporality: What Does it Mean to Have Class Consciousness?" at the international conference "A 160 años del *Manifiesto Comunista*: relecturas del pensamiento de Marx," Santiago, Chile, November 2008, and also at the Historical Materialism conference in New York, May 2011; and as

"Revolution and Eternal Return in Benjamin and Altusser" at the international conference "Anthropologischer Materialismus und Materialismus der Begegnung," Deutsch-französische Sommerschule in Potsdam, July 2012. I wish to thank all publishers for permission to reprint and all conference organizers for the opportunity to present and discuss this work.

It would hardly have been possible for me to engage with such a diverse range of authors and themes without the friendly encouragement, discussion, and suggestions I received from other scholars who master this material, in part or as a whole, far better than I, and whom I wish to thank: Wendy Brown, Hauke Brunkhorst, Judith Butler, Massimo de Carolis, Melinda Cooper, Roberto Esposito, Peter Fenves, Simona Forti, Agnes Heller, Thomas Lemke, Vanessa Lemm, Federico Luisetti, Jamie Martel, Sofia Nasstrom, Antonio Negri, Angelica Nuzzo, Michael Pelias, Diego Rossello, Mark C. Taylor, and Sam Weber. Thanks also go to my editor, Helen Tartar, and to the entire team at Fordham University Press, as well as to Jessica Mathiason and Benjamin Stork for cleaning up the manuscript and my English.

As always I am very grateful to Vanessa and to our children, Lou, Esteban, and Alizé, for signaling the way back from writing to life. The book is dedicated to them.

THE REPUBLIC OF THE LIVING

INTRODUCTION

One of the legacies bequeathed by the twentieth century to political language is the confusion of politics with government. Politics today seems to be reduced to the alternative of having more or less government. Liberalism has taught that the less politics we have, the less governed we are, and thus the freer we become. The republican understanding of freedom rejects this basic axiom of liberal government. Republicanism stands for the irreducibility of politics to government; it teaches that more politics may be necessary if we are going to be governed less. The Courses that Michel Foucault delivered at the Collège de France during the late 1970s and early 1980s were intended to provide a "history of governmentality" that distinguishes government from politics. For Foucault, the activity of "governing" is something other than political action: the more civil society governs the life of individuals, the less a people can act politically. The genealogy of governmentality shows that government is not a function of the people's power to give itself a political constitution or form of life in common. Government takes place in the spheres that compose civil society: the economy, the legal system, the family. For liberalism, civil society is where the enterprising individual is "naturally" free to pursue his or her interests. By deregulating civil society, neoliberalism seeks to further unleash its "natural" dynamics in the name of the liberty of enterprise. For Foucault, instead, the "naturality" of the enterprising universe of civil society is the artificial outcome of "technologies" of government and of a "conduct of conducts" that is as "total"—in its extension of governmentality into both the subjective and the natural worlds—as the "totalitarian" state was in its extension of domination.

In his Courses dedicated to elaborate a genealogy of governmentality, Foucault suggests that the government exercised in and by civil society acquires its centrality in late modern political life because of a phenomenon he calls "biopolitics," which he defines as the entrance of biological or species life into the calculations carried out by political rationality. If in the ancient and medieval understanding, political reason oriented itself toward those ethical virtues that allowed individuals and groups to pursue their political or "common good," and in the early modern understanding, political reason oriented itself toward the establishment of sovereignty that allowed for a people to live under the protection of a state, then in late modernity, with the emergence of the idea of civil society, political reason orients itself toward the government of biological life, taking upon itself the care for the well-being, the health, the vitality, and, in our days, even the happiness of a population. To distinguish the kind of rule exercised by biopolitics from the traditional understandings of politics (whether these turn on the city or the sovereign state), Foucault calls it the "police": "The police govern not by the law, but by a specific, a permanent and a positive intervention in the behaviour of individuals" (Foucault 2000, 415). The shift from politics to police is marked by the invention of an entirely new set of "political sciences," which today form the core of our social sciences, that is, of our sciences of civil society: from the science of police (which today ranges from public policy to criminology), through the science of social systems (sociology), to the science of economics (political economy).

From a Foucaultian perspective, one can say that biopolitics is what allows liberalism to replace politics by police government, rule of law by governance, action by normalized conduct. This is why the rise of liberal civil society and its "self-steering" social subsystems places the republican understanding of politics in crisis. The underlying question motivating the chapters of this book is whether this horizon of biopolitics poses a challenge that republican politics is unable to cope with, or whether, to the contrary, a republicanism of the living is both possible and necessary.

The aim of this book is to explain what makes the discourse of biopolitics essential both to the understanding and to the critique of modern civil society. Foucault did not have the time, nor perhaps the inclination, to clear the new field of biopolitics of its conceptual puzzles and stumbling blocks.[1] In the Course entitled *The Birth of Biopolitics*, for instance, Foucault offers a comparative reading of French, German, and North American neoliberal thinkers, which suggests that the "relative autonomy" of family, law, and the free market, with respect to the political control of the state, has its reason in the biopolitical functions carried out by these subsystems. But Foucault does not say exactly what about the configuration of family, law, and economy in a civil society is biopolitical.

This book attempts to fill this lacuna by focusing on the imbrications and crossings between three dimensions of biopolitics that I shall call "natality," "normality," and "normativity." By "natality" I refer to that aspect of political life that is related to the human species as a biological species, what Marx called the *Gattungswesen,* or "species life," the "universal" element of life. Throughout these chapters, I follow the customary designation of this aspect of life with the Greek term *zoe.* Generally speaking, in civil society natality is encountered in the sphere of prepolitical or familial life (Greek: *oikos*) that governs the sexual reproduction of life, and then in the economy that governs living labor. By "normality" I refer to that aspect of political life bound by norms, which adopts a "particular" form of life as a result of rule-following conduct. Throughout these chapters, I follow the customary designation of this aspect of life with the Greek term *bios.* Generally speaking, in civil society normality overlaps with the system of law. By "normativity" I refer to that aspect of political life that is creative of novelty, in which the universal and the particular dimensions of life are indistinguishable because singularity is entirely a feature of the common. There is no customary Greek term for this aspect of life that I am aware. But, again speaking generally, normativity overlaps with the sphere of a philosophical or contemplative life, which the Greeks considered to be a form of life that partakes of eternity, an eternal life. The thrust of this book lies in the argument that civil society can be both described and criticized from the perspective of biopolitics by studying the different relationships established between the components of natality, normality, and normativity, within and between each sphere of civil society.

In Foucault, biopolitics is associated with the creation of a "surplus of life."[2] The "surplus of life" has a negative connotation when it is linked to the government of species life enacted by the police, in Foucault's sense of the term. This is analogous to the negative connotation of "surplus value" as a product of the exploitation of living labor in capitalist relations of production in Marx's discourse. But in Foucault "surplus life" also recovers an affirmative sense, when, for instance, he warns that "life has not been totally integrated into techniques that govern and administer it; it constantly escapes them" (Foucault 1990, 143). Here, the excess of life becomes a source of resistance to governmentality and opens the possibility of a renewal of political life. Following Foucault's scant indications of an affirmative sense of biopolitics, recent Italian philosophy in Negri, Agamben, and Esposito has established the possibility of an affirmative biopolitics. Despite their different paradigms, Negri, Agamben, and Esposito share the belief that biopower contains two radically opposed conceptions of power, one affirmative (*potenza*, potentiality), the other negative (*potere*, power). Anyone today who wishes to make a serious contribution to the study of governmentality and civil society cannot start without taking into consideration the perspective opened up by their theoretical contributions with respect to biopolitics.

In this book, I am interested in teasing out the affirmative possibilities for biopolitics suggested by the work of Negri, Agamben, and Esposito. All of the chapters, in one way or another, seek to illuminate and expand on their often cryptic formulations of an affirmative biopolitics. But the affirmative biopolitics this book is after parts ways with the current reception of Italian theory on one fundamental point. Following a widespread reading of Negri, Agamben, and Esposito, it has become commonplace to think that the connection between law and life must be antinomical, as if the nondomination of life (and therefore an affirmative biopolitics) must entail the exclusion of law and, conversely, the rule of law must entail a "state of exception" over life that leads to a politics of death. By way of contrast, the argument of this book is that an affirmative biopolitics requires overcoming the antinomian opposition between rule of law and politics of life.

Recent Italian theory formulates an affirmative biopolitics within the horizon of a communist form of political life that lies beyond the capitalist exploitation and the liberal government of species life. My approach to affirmative biopolitics shares this orientation insofar as I understand communism to refer to a way of life in common where the normative power of natality lies at the basis of the rule of law and where the "surplus of life" is reappropriated by peoples organized in the political form of communes. In this book I argue that this "commune-ist" orientation of affirmative biopolitics, when it is properly understood, has an elective affinity with the modern tradition of revolutionary republicanism represented by such thinkers as Machiavelli, Spinoza, Milton, Rousseau, Madison, Sieyès, Kant, and others. This tradition understands republicanism, following Arendt's formula, as the rule of law based on the power of the people that brings to an end the government of human beings over each other. For this reason, the forms of commune-ism that this book associates with an affirmative biopolitics stand in tension with the antinomian formulations of communism associated today with the work of Žižek, Badiou, and, to a lesser degree, Agamben.[3]

The critique of liberal civil society needs to be carried out from this dual republican and commune-ist perspective. Civil society was the bone of contention in the struggle between totalitarian and liberal worldviews during the last century. However, both of these ideologies could only emerge thanks to the crisis of republicanism in late modernity. It was republicanism, not liberalism that destroyed the ancien régime and made possible the emergence of a modern civil society. But republicanism proved unable to defend its ideals with the rise of bourgeois civil society, arguably because it often preferred to ally itself with liberalism rather than with the different commune-ist and anarchist movements that have resisted liberalism since its inception. Even if the perspective of affirmative biopolitics can shed new light on the phenomenon and meaning of civil society, this exercise would hardly be worthwhile, from a politico-philosophical perspective, unless this book can also defend the claim that affirmative biopolitics and its commune-ist orientation is not only compatible with, but necessary for, the continued relevance, validity, and vitality of republican ideals.

This inner continuity between republicanism and commune-ism is already at work from the earliest critiques of bourgeois civil society found in Hegel and Marx, through the development of Marxist critical theory in Lukács, Benjamin, and Adorno, and up to Arendt's political thought. The inheritors of the Frankfurt School and of Arendt, principally Habermas and Honneth, gave a "communicative" turn to the theory of reification and to the theory of natality found in Benjamin, Adorno, and Arendt. In this way, arguably, they divorced republicanism from its inherent commune-ist orientation. This orientation, in fact, can only be maintained if one articulates a biopolitical critique of political economy and civil society premised on the priority of species life (*zoe*) over individual life (*bios*), and if one assigns to politics the task of reappropriating through the organization of communes that surplus of life which in liberal society is alienated from society and distributed individually. In this book, I show why the accounts of reification and natality in Lukács, Benjamin, Adorno, and Arendt never lose sight of this biopolitical basis of critique, whereas this is no longer the case since Habermas. The consequence of the "communicative" turn of contemporary critical theory is that it blinds itself to the inner affirmative biopolitical content of the early Frankfurt School, leaving the republican intuitions shared by contemporary critical theory unable to connect meaningfully with the Hegelian-Marxist project of a critique of political economy, thus divorcing them from the commune-ist orientation that was still inhabited by Arendt and by the first proponents of critical theory.

The key to the affirmative biopolitics proposed here lies in the ways it understands the connection of natality and normativity as a form of resistance to the normalization brought about by the government of life. This connection between natality and normativity grounds the claim that there exists an inner continuity between republican rule of law and commune-ist economic organization envisaged by the critics of civil society from Hegel and Marx through Arendt and Foucault. In the following chapters, I rely on two main ideas or paradigms in order to think what it means for natality to be the ground of normativity.

The first idea is that of tragic conflict as worked out in Hegel, in Nietzsche, and in Benjamin, as a way to twist free and overcome the contradictions of late modernity. In these interpretations Greek tragedy becomes a schema that makes visible the destructive nature of the forced separation between natality and political life, and the need for their reconjunction within a postliberal form of social life. When interpreted through the lens of an affirmative biopolitics, the normative conflict between laws said to be characteristic of Greek tragedy (whether these are the law of the family versus the law of the state in Hegel, or the Dionysian versus the Apollonian in Nietzsche) in reality figures the clash between the law of natality and the order of normality, just as the clash between family (*oikos*) and state in reality betrays a rejection of a political economy (*oiko-nomia*) based on the living labor and sexual reproduction of those who are excluded from political power. Thus, as employed in this book, the late modern theory of tragedy from Hegel to Nietzsche and Benjamin serves to twist free politics from the hegemony of government in the name of the law (of natality) and establish the rule of law (of common life, *zoe*) over the order of individualism prevalent in bourgeois civil society.

The second paradigm running through these chapters is the idea of eternal life. Foucault claimed that the negative biopolitics of normality constitutive of modern civil society was but the other side of a "thanatopolitics," or a politics of death. The development of biopolitics in Italian theory has offered a series of important contributions to our understanding of the mechanisms that turn both the liberal and the totalitarian governments of life into varieties of thanatopolitics. In this book, I propose that an affirmative biopolitics, if it is going to resist such thanatopolitics, must be conceived starting from the intuition that life (*zoe*) is eternal. As I develop its concept here, eternal life names that form of life that exhibits the internal connection between natality and normativity without the intermediation of normality and its government of life. Eternal life is thus a form of life where species life and the life of the mind are indistinguishable, where creativity emerges from the inseparability of body and spirit, thing and person, beyond all reification and individualism. Eternal life is the name for the higher identity of natality and normativity that undermines all spiritualism and personalism; it is therefore a radically materialistic and atheistic conception of eternal life. In this sense, eternal life names the opposite of the immortality of the individual soul in which Platonism, then Christianity, and, in a secular fashion, the bourgeois pursuit of happiness, has seen the meaning of salvation on earth. By way of contrast, I show that if there exists a hope of salvation, then it cannot be a hope for us, for the salvation of our *bio*-graphical lives, but only for other ourselves, the carriers of an altering or revolutionary species life. This atheistic conception of eternal life, in its hopelessness, is therefore consonant with the tragic understanding of individual life (*bios*) and its necessary going-under. But, just as Greek tragedy does not give death the last word, so too the atheistic conception of eternal life put forward in these pages teaches that there is no real opposite to life (*zoe*) itself.

PLAN OF THE BOOK AND CONTENT OF THE CHAPTERS

Foucault's claim, at the end of *The Birth of Biopolitics*, that "civil society" names the social reality constituted by the governmental technologies of liberalism and neoliberalism, more than offering a conclusion, in reality opens up a field of inquiry and leaves behind many conceptual puzzles and stumbling blocks. Perhaps the first of these puzzles is to understand how the biopolitical matrix of analysis fits together with the now classic philosophical critique of civil society found in Hegel and Marx, which has exerted an enormous and enduring influence on later attempts to develop a conceptually rigorous grasp of modern society, especially with regard to political economy and the system of law. The goal of the first part of the book, "Biopolitics of Economy," is, on one side, to present a biopolitical reading of Hegel's and Marx's critiques of civil society, and, on the other, to show how the main lines of critique established by Hegel and Marx help to place Foucault's genealogy of governmentality in its proper context.[4]

In his last published essay in French, "La vie: l'expérience et la science," dedicated to Georges Canguilhem's fundamental theme of the relation between life (or natality) and concept (or normativity), Foucault writes that the modern notion of life enters philosophy only with German Idealism.[5] This claim suggests the possibility that Hegel may have formulated the earliest philosophical response not only to the rise of political economy but also to liberal biopolitics in his philosophy of spirit. In Chapter 1, "The Tragedy of Civil Society and Republican Politics in Hegel," I argue that his early philosophy of spirit is oriented toward a critique of political economy in view of establishing the political rule of republican law over the liberal government of life in civil society. The key to this biopolitical interpretation of Hegelian "spirit" is taking seriously the claim he makes, from his early work *Natural Law* onward, that the relation between civil society and state, between individual and political freedoms, is structured by a sacrificial logic. I argue that Hegel makes an important contribution to an affirmative biopolitics in the way that he employs the teaching of Greek tragedies like *Oresteia* and *Antigone* to think the inner relation between species life (natality) and human freedom (normativity) beyond sacrifice.

Marx thought that the *homo oeconomicus* generated by civil society would ultimately conquer the *vir civis*, or the republican citizen, unless republicanism undertook a transformation into communism. Both orthodox Marxists and neoliberals have interpreted this claim to mean that the rise of *homo oeconomicus* renders republicanism irrelevant, as if the constituent power of a people were merely superstructural and the economic basis of society were a "despotic" and irresistible power. In Chapter 2, "Living Labor and Self-Generative Value in Marx," I argue that Marx develops his theory of value from a republican perspective and show its importance for the commune-ist orientation that he gives his critique of political economy.[6] The chapter takes up Negri's interpretation of the *Grundrisse* according to which Marx's concept of living labor contains the condition of possibility for a "surplus life" endowed with a constituent power that overwhelms the law(s) of value uncovered by Marx. With and against Negri, I argue for the need to offer a biopolitical reading also of Marx's theory of value, and not just of his theory of living labor because if one understands the theory of value as a theory of constituted power, one can better account for the reason why the neoliberal reformation of capitalism has operated through the simultaneous juridification and depoliticization of the economy. Second, a commune-ist reappropriation of surplus value is possible only when the surplus life generated by the juridification of the economy in neoliberal regimes rejects the normalization of its life and engages in the political creation of new legal relations, and not simply new relations of production, between producers and consumers. It is in this sense that commune-ist political organization is the name for a republic of the living.

A second conceptual puzzle left by Foucault's discourse on biopolitics concerns the meaning of the term "life," which contains an irreducible duality between life as *zoe* (as a biological species life) and life as *bios* (as an individual form of life). In the second part of this book, "Biopolitics of the Family," I discuss the distinction between *zoe* and *bios*, perhaps the most controversial theme in the current discussion on biopolitics. Chapter 3, "Reification and Redemption of Bare Life in Adorno and Agamben," defends the position that an affirmative biopolitics, at both a descriptive and prescriptive level, must grant precedence to the dimension of *zoe* ("bare life") over the dimension of *bios*. Additionally, it shows how Agamben's interpretation of Benjamin and Adorno reveals the analysis of reification in the early Frankfurt School as a contribution to the biopolitical understanding of civil society. By staging a comparison between Agamben's and Habermas's understanding of reification, this chapter indicates how critical theory can regain its original commune-ist orientation by adopting a biopolitical rather than recognition theoretic approach to reification.

Chapter 4, "Natality, Fertility, and Mimesis in Arendt's Theory of Freedom," argues that Arendt's category of natality is the fundamental pedestal on which to build an affirmative biopolitics. I recover Arendt's debt to Benjamin's conception of "bare life" (rather than to Heidegger's analytic of existence) when it comes to the category of natality. But this interpretation of natality also takes distance from Italian biopolitics to the extent that in Arendt natality becomes the foundation of a republican conception of freedom and thus as the element that holds together my basic claim in this book that an affirmative biopolitics must be compatible with republicanism and not have an antinomian structure.

Chapter 5, "The Heroism of Sexuality in Benjamin and Foucault," returns to the problem of natality in Greek tragedy but this time within the horizon of Nietzsche's Dionysian interpretation of tragedy. I argue that Benjamin's analysis of Goethe's *Elective Affinities* as a "tragedy" (*Trauerspiel*) of married life reveals how the bourgeois family and its conception of heterosexual marriage blocks the recognition of the normativity of natality. But just as in Greek tragedies political life is revitalized whenever the power of natality breaks through its containment in familiar and kinship structures, so it is starting from the deconstruction of the bourgeois household that a republican critique of civil society can take place. The chapter then pursues the deconstruction of married life in both Benjamin's later work on Baudelaire as well as in Foucault's later reflections on the *ethos* of modernity and alternative forms of sexual life.

A third problem left by Foucault concerns the relation between legality and biopolitics. Does Foucault understand the rule of law as part of the order of liberal government or can it offer a resource to resist this order? The general thesis defended in the third part of the book, "Biopolitics of Rights," is that liberal civil society is based on the real subsumption of law by order, of normativity by normality. Interestingly, the subsumption of law by order is already identified by Marx as an essential moment of capitalism. This is evident in his many references to the police and to security as requirements of the reproduction of surplus value (both in the *Economic and Philosophical Manuscripts* as well as in the *Grundrisse* and *Capital*). Marx further emphasizes the centrality of the legal form of the contract for capitalist society. Yet Marx never conducts an autonomous study on these normalizing conditions for capital accumulation, and he did not see the real dimensions of the juridification of the economy. Foucault, in *Discipline and Punish*, attempts to show that the calculation of labor time, and thus the entire bourgeois theory of value, would have been impossible had it not been for the knowledge/power of discipline. But, at this stage, he still opposes disciplinary power to a concept of law tied to sovereign power and has yet to develop a governmental perspective on the problem of law.

Foucault only acquires this perspective after reflecting upon liberalism and neoliberalism in his Courses on governmentality.

In his lectures on neoliberalism, Foucault identifies Hayek as the inventor of the crucial neoliberal strategy of the juridification of the economy, or what he calls the "economic rule of law." But Foucault actually spends very little time discussing Hayek, preferring to focus his attention on the German Ordo-liberal and the Chicago School variants of neoliberalism. The recent historiography of neoliberalism shows quite convincingly that both of these variants are heavily dependent on Hayek's pathbreaking innovations.[7] Chapter 6, "Free Markets and Republican Constitutions in Hayek and Foucault," proposes a comparison of Foucault's theses on governmentality with Hayek's economical and juridical thought. The chapter argues that Hayek's turn toward juridical thinking, as well as Foucault's critique of neoliberal governmentality, both depend on their different appropriations of the republican, constitutional idea of the rule of law. The thesis of the chapter is that Foucault adheres to a republican viewpoint whereas Hayek seeks to undermine it.

Chapter 7, "Biopolitical Cosmopolitanism: The Right to Have Rights in Arendt and Agamben," offers a critique of the antinomian approach to rights found in much recent literature on biopolitics, especially the one influenced by Italian theory. By way of contrast, this chapter argues that an internal and affirmative relationship between law and life is absolutely necessary if politics is to overcome the disciplinarian and normalizing forms it has been given in liberal civil society. Such an account of law can be found in the new structure that Arendt gives to human rights as the "right to have rights." According to my interpretation, Arendt defends a republican (as opposed to liberal and neoliberal) account of human rights in which the original "right to have rights" is a biopolitical right, a "right" to constituent power rooted in natality. This chapter brings to a close the argument of the book in favor of a productive encounter between biopolitics and republicanism. To date, the productivity of this encounter has gone undetected by both sides: republican theorists ignore the biopolitical substance of civil society, whereas theorists of biopolitics are trapped by an antinomian reconstruction of biopolitics.

The fourth and final part of the book, "Biopolitics of Eternal Life," addresses the last major problem bequeathed by Foucault's discovery of biopolitics, which concerns the biopolitical meaning of normativity and its relation to a theory of the subject. By "subject" I mean here the capacity or power or potentiality to create something radically new, to initiate a real beginning. In essays like "What Is Critique?" Foucault associates this idea of the subject to an "ontology of the present," by which he means an archaeological and a genealogical illumination of one's historical situation as a revolutionary now-time that makes a real, unforgettable difference in the becoming of human species life. In his last Courses on *The Government of Self and Others* Foucault associates this idea of the subject and of critique with the possibility of carrying out a "philosophical" life, what the ancients called *bios theoretikos*. The main thesis of this concluding part of the book is that an affirmative biopolitical account of such a subject must take the form of an account of its eternal life (*zoe aionos*).

As Foucault details in *Security, Territory, Population*, liberal governmentality owes its enormous force to its incubation within Christianity. Christian pastoral and monastic practices are based on the belief that, in order to achieve eternal life, one must exercise government over the life of the soul and ascetic discipline over the body. For an affirmative biopolitics to stand in thoroughgoing opposition to the Christian ideal of eternal life it needs to develop for itself a radically anti-Christian, strictly materialist conception of eternal life. In this concluding part of the book, I argue that such a conception of eternal life is articulated primarily in the work of Spinoza and Nietzsche.

The possibility of an affirmative biopolitics has to be considered against the backdrop of thanatopolitics: for biopolitics to undo a politics of death, it is necessary to consider the possibility of a form of life that is "beyond death." Chapter 8, "Bare Life and Philosophical Life in Aristotle, Spinoza, and Heidegger," presents an account of the relationship between natality and normativity, between species life and philosophical thought, that is alternative to the existentialist and gnostic conception of a philosophical life as an escape from animal life and as a being-toward-death. The latter conception of a philosophical life is found in Heidegger and in his distinction between animal life and human existence. In this chapter I contrast Spinoza's view of eternal life to the Heideggerian being-toward-death in order to shed light on the recent proposal by Deleuze and Agamben to understand the subject as a thinking life, that is, a thinking *zoe* that undoes the separation of reason from life and reunites bio-graphical with species life in a political-philosophical constellation that lies beyond the liberal governmentality of self and others.

The Foucaultian question of an "ontology of the present" is addressed in Chapter 9, "Eternal Recurrence and the Now of Revolution: Nietzsche and Messianic Marxism." The recent post-Marxist recovery of the "idea" of communism has shifted Foucault's perspective on the revolutionary nowtime onto a messianic horizon that was relatively foreign to Foucault.[8] This last chapter explores the first connection between communism and messianism that was established in the work of Marxist thinkers like Lukács, Bloch, Benjamin, and Adorno. I argue that this early messianic Marxism is dependent on Nietzsche's and Blanqui's cosmological doctrine of eternal recurrence. This doctrine is employed to refute the radical historicism of modernity and its illusion of living in a perpetual present where capitalist relations are eternalized and no revolutionary change is conceivable.

The interpretation of the doctrine of eternal recurrence in Nietzsche and Blanqui that I propose here is the basis for a materialist account of the eternal life of the subject of revolution, which in its structural im-personality is entirely opposed to the Christian ideal of eternal life in the Pauline construction of the resurrected Christ that is at work in the secularized approaches to eternal life found in Agamben and Badiou, Milbank and Taylor. Thus, the book ends with an argument for why the revolutionary "economy of time" that Marx opposes to the time-consciousness of capitalism is separated from both the Christian divine economy of salvation as well as from the liberal belief in perpetual progress not only by a "messianic horizon," but also by the "cosmic horizon" offered by the cosmology of eternal recurrence. Eternal recurrence and messianic interruption are but two sides of the same concept of eternal life.

Introduction 13

PART I

Biopolitics of the Economy

1

THE TRAGEDY OF CIVIL SOCIETY AND REPUBLICAN POLITICS IN HEGEL

THE PROBLEM OF CIVIL SOCIETY IN HEGEL

Liberal civil society is characterized by intrinsically expansive dynamics, whose unforeseen consequences have become familiar to everyone: staggering accumulation of private capital that widens the gap between rich and poor and forces sovereign states into crippling financial crises; quantum leaps in technological and industrial advances that cause a dramatic destruction of nature and of the environment; proliferation of subjective rights and extraparliamentary legislation that is accompanied by a terrifying increase in police controls over individuals both within and outside of their society; and last but certainly not least, the worldwide web of information that has sacrificed the ideal of a free education on the altar of the culture industry and the society of the spectacle. By curtailing the political freedom of peoples with respect to markets and to systems of subjective rights, neoliberal policies have effectively overwhelmed the capacity of republics to control the expansive dynamics intrinsic to liberal civil society.

Hegel was the first great philosopher in modernity to understand the limitlessness, or as he called it, the "bad" infinity intrinsic to these dynamics of civil society. Hegel clearly saw that "political economy" designated a new field of objects that seem to obey quasi-natural laws of their own, even though these objects are the result of purely social relations among individuals, that is, they are thoroughly social and historical products. He also saw that submitting the human capacity for political self-organization under the constraints of the laws of the market threatened the very existence of human freedom. Like Foucault in *The Birth of Biopolitics*, in his early works from *Natural Law* to the *Phenomenology of Spirit* Hegel set out to show that the "naturality" of civil society is modernity's fundamental myth. To believe that the free market and personal liberties are absolute realities is for Hegel equivalent to sacrificing human freedom. He concluded that if a political organization is to realize human freedom then it needs to be capable of putting an end to the sacrifices imposed by civil society.

It is in his early book *Natural Law* that Hegel speaks of the "tragedy of civil society [*Tragödie im Sittlichen*]" and links it to a reflection on the institution of sacrifice and its function in social organization. In this chapter I offer an interpretation of the expression "tragedy of civil society" along biopolitical lines. Both Agamben and Esposito thematize the sacrificial structure that turns biopolitics into a thanatopolitics. For Agamben, every legal order creates "sacred life," which it exposes to death as a condition for preserving the peace and security of the members of society. For Esposito, every social order sets up im-munities against the contagion of the *munus*, the fundamental sacrifice and gift that constitutes the bond of com-munity.[1] Hegel also criticizes modern civil society for being a sacrificial *dispositif*, but he seeks in the concept of Greek tragedy a way to overcome the sacrificial mechanism of the "bad" infinity of capital accumulation and of individual rights entitlements in a civil society that resists the more fundamental recognition of the radical equality and liberty of all. I argue that through this reflection on tragedy and sacrifice, Hegel opens the possibility of an affirmative biopolitics of civil society that exposes the imaginary character of the values assigned to the objects of civil society and reconceives of republican politics as a function of the power to sacrifice, in the sense of giving up, the belief in the sacredness of life that characterizes civil society.

Hegel saw the rise of commercial society and the emergence of the science of political economy, analyzed by Adam Smith, Steuart, and Ricardo, as the new Fate against which subjective freedom must necessarily perish: "These are physical needs and enjoyments which, put again on their own account in a totality, *obey in their infinite intertwining one single necessity* and the system of *universal mutual dependence* in relation to physical needs and work and the amassing [of wealth] for these needs. And this system, as a science, is the system of the so-called political economy" (Hegel 1975, 94, emphasis mine). Constant's famous diagnosis of their epoch as being one in which commerce, not conquest, is the primary means of satisfying individual desires was known to Hegel.[2] He understood that the free market required citizens to enjoy liberty *from* politics and freedom *from* managing public affairs, something unheard of in ancient republicanism. Nevertheless, Hegel stubbornly refused to give up on the way the ancients think about freedom: something about the ancient ideal contained a crucial teaching about how to confront the challenges that modern civil society poses for the maintenance of the freedom and equality of all individuals. Specifically, in order to understand the tragic nature of the Fate of political economy, and so raise oneself above it, Hegel returns to the Greek experience as it is figured in the tragedies of Aeschylus and Sophocles.[3] Hegel does not advocate embracing the positive freedom of Greek democracy as much as the political wisdom that emerges out of the downfall of the ancient *polis*.

Greek tragedy is chosen because it indicates the kind of self-sacrifice that is required to overcome the Fate of civil society and that is essential to the very idea of political freedom, or to the survival of a free state, in the age where modern individualism is all conquering. Indeed, the very last sentence of *Natural Law* restates the centrality of self-sacrifice: political life "confronts the negative as objective and fate, and by consciously conceding to the negative a power and a realm, *at the sacrifice of a part of itself*, it maintains its own [political] life purified of the negative" (Hegel 1975, 133). Greek tragedies (and comedies) indicate the political actions that need to be taken and the political institutions that need to be established in order to overcome the mythical institutions of the sacrifice and the festival, which, as Freud shows, at once celebrate and atone for a crime that is constitutive of sociality itself. In Esposito's terms, Hegel's readings of Greek tragedy and comedy reflect a nonmythical, politically productive way to overcome the immunitary barriers set up by civil society to the contagion of the *munus*, of the common.

Alongside the free market economy, the other foundation of liberal civil society is the legal system of individual or subjective rights. Hegel became convinced that the conception of public law advocated by Kant and Fichte, which coerces individuals into respecting one another's rights, was insufficient for repairing the "bad" infinity of capitalist expansion and, as one would say today, valuing people over profit. Kant and Fichte, in Hegel's eyes, did not understand the new order of things that political economy and negative liberty had brought about, particularly its fatal consequences for the republican ideal of politics.⁴ For Kant, "right and the authorization to use coercion therefore mean one and the same thing" (Kant 1996, 6,232). This liberal idea of right is unacceptable to Hegel, and he dedicates a great part of *Natural Law* to refuting it. Hegel rejects the idea that one's freedom ultimately depends on the coercion of someone else's freedom. For him, no one can be free unless the absence of coercion becomes a reality for all, in and through the state as the highest form of ethical life: "Coercion is nothing real, nothing in itself. . . . It is an inherent contradiction to construct an idea that the freedom of the individual, through the externality of coercion, is with absolute necessity adequate to the concept of universal freedom" (Hegel 1975, 89). But through what logic or mechanism could the state "subjugate" civil society and its negative conception of liberty, thereby showing the nothingness of coercion and the actuality of true freedom, without returning to the ancient ideal of positive freedom (Hegel 1975, 92–93)?

Hegel thought that the modern system of rights had the potential of leading to "a perfect police . . . [and to] the harshest despotism in the way in which Fichte wants to see every action and the whole existence of the individual as an individual supervised, known and regulated by the universal and the abstraction that are set up in opposition to him" (Hegel 1975, 124). The "police" state (by which Hegel means a state administered by the principles of eighteenth-century *Polizeiwissenschaft* discussed by Foucault under the rubric of "governmentality") follows directly upon a liberal civil society that is unable to overcome the identification of one's individual freedom with the coercion of someone else's freedom. Hegel's attempt to distinguish a political conception of the state from the "policed" conception of the state turns on giving a different solution to the problem of legal application and legal exception. As Benjamin, Agamben, and Foucault have shown in their different ways, the problem of the "police" enters into politics as a function of the paradox that there is no law to apply a law, or that the application of the law occurs in a state of exception to that law.⁵ In *Natural Law* Hegel turns to Plato's *Statesman* in order to seek a new solution to the problem of legal exception, since this Platonic dialogue is the first text where the problem was addressed as such. For Hegel the essence of law lies in the relation that it establishes among crime, punishment, and atonement. Just like in Freud and Foucault, Hegel believes that the categories of crime and punishment contain the key to the relation between civil society and state.

Many interpreters believe that Hegel's alternative to Kant and Fichte never overcomes decisionism, but rather seems to be a kind of "liberal authoritarianism," a defense of the free market and of individual civil rights backed by a strong, antidemocratic, and bellicose state.[6] In this chapter I present Hegel's critique of liberal law as republican in that it advocates the view that what makes a people free is its power to judge and punish the "crime" that is generated by modern civil society in its unlimited pursuit of individual interests. Only a free people constituted into a state can reveal the inner "nullity" of both political economy and civil law, thereby setting their spheres within their proper limits, making it possible to realize the absolute equality and freedom of each with all. Hegel never stops being a republican political thinker: his achievement consists in grasping the tragic yet affirmative structure of republican freedom. The claim is that if one understands the relation between the state and civil society within the framework provided by Greek tragedy, as Hegel himself suggests, then it is possible to consider (in a nonliberal way) the meaning of the limits that economics and law impose on the state and on political life in order to conceive of the individual in its particularity. At the same time, by following the thread of Greek tragedy, it is possible to consider (in a nonauthoritarian way) the meaning of the limits that the state and political life must impose on economics and law so that each individual's liberty and equality can be recognized by all.

THE TRAGEDY OF THE HEGELIAN STATE

Why are Aeschylus, Sophocles, and Plato not surpassed (*aufgehoben*) by the march of spirit through history? Why do they "persist" in modernity? The answer that has become the standard view on Hegel's understanding of the Greeks is that Greek tragedy and Plato are a sort of *ironic* announcement of what is to come in modernity: they represent the "owl of Minerva" that takes flight at the dusk of a civilization (Hegel 1967, 13). What comes after the Greek experience of political life is a Christian idea of human subjectivity, whose ironic precursors in Greece were Antigone (in a tragic form) and Socrates (in a comic form). Tragic freedom, in this account, is *ironic* freedom, primarily in the sense that what is "meant" by the tragedy, namely, the proposition that all individuals are equal, appears "said" in the opposite form: the destruction of the individual and its individuality at the hands of the representatives of the democratic *polis* (exemplified by the destiny of Antigone and Socrates). On this traditional account, Hegel's project consists of constructing a new *Sittlichkeit* (ethical substance) capable of offering objective or institutional recognition to the new subjectivity announced by Jesus and realized in Protestantism.[7] This would be a possible reading of the famous formula of the *Phenomenology of Spirit*: "Everything turns on grasping and expressing the True, not only as Substance, but equally as Subject" (Hegel 1977, 10). On this view, the main danger for Hegel's project is the persistence of irony, that is, of a sense of individuality or subjectivity that stubbornly refuses to submit to the new normative order of modernity.

Two sophisticated interpretations of Hegel's motif of "tragedy in ethical life," those offered at a sixty-year interval by Lukács and Menke, still remain tied to the above ironical understanding of tragedy in Hegel. Despite the vast and illuminating differences between these two interpretations (which deserve a fuller treatment than I can offer here), Lukács and Menke both believe that the *persistence* of Greek tragedy in Hegel's political thought is ultimately symptomatic of a *failure* on his part to understand the ultimate reality of modern civil society and the final purpose that orients it. For Lukács, the free market economy is the ultimate reality of civil society, which, left to work out its inner contradictions between proletariat and capitalist classes, will necessarily overcome both the bourgeois state and capitalism and lead to communism (Lukács 1975). For Menke, the ultimate reality of civil society is the system of rights, which, left to work out its inner contradictions between autonomy and authenticity, leads to a postpolitical, "aesthetic" condition of subjective freedom (Menke 1996). For both, Hegel clings to Greek tragedy because he does not get at the bottom of the tensions animating both modern economy and modern law.

Hegel has another way of thinking about the persistence of tragedy in modernity: he does not simply see it as the irony of ancient community and the prophetic announcement of modern individualism. In *Natural Law*, Hegel concludes his treatment of modern civil society by going back to Plato's class analysis in the *Republic*. Modern civil society, Hegel argues, is a "system of property and law which, owing to its fixation of individuality, consists not in anything absolute and eternal, but wholly in the finite; and the formal must constitute itself *in a class of its own*, and in that case must be able to expand in its whole length and breadth, really separate from and isolated from the class of the nobility" (Hegel 1975, 102, emphasis mine). This class is that of the bourgeoisie, characterized by a socially recognized right to possession and by the virtue of honesty.[8] For Hegel, the bourgeoisie is defined by its "political nullity" since "the members of this class [the *bourgeois*] are private individuals." The bourgeois is compensated for its lack of a political life by "the fruits of the system, i.e., peace and gain and perfect security in their enjoyment individually and as a whole" (Hegel 1975, 103). Now, just like in Plato's *Republic* where a class of guardians, who lack private property, are responsible for bringing about justice through the use of coercive means, so Hegel thinks that in modern civil society "the class of earners, like a specializing species amongst modern nations, has in our time gradually ceased to do military service, and courage has constituted itself in a purer manner into a special class exempted by those others from acquisition, a class to which both possession and property are at best accidental" (Hegel 1975, 100). Thus modern civil society is characterized by its own kind of irony since what appears as a society based on individualism in reality turns out to be a society structured by class consciousness. But what is this second class in civil society charged with maintaining the political life of its apolitical members?

When he has to render the character of this second class of civil society, Hegel chooses to cite from Plato's dialogue *Statesman*: "The art of kingship 'exterminates by death and punishes by exile and the greatest disgrace those who have no share of courage or temperance or of any other virtuous inclination, and by the necessity of an evil nature are violently carried away to godlessness, arrogance, and injustice' (*Statesman* 308–9)" (Hegel 1975, 100–101). The "art of kingship" refers to Plato's claim that only political wisdom (or knowledge of justice), and not the right to private property, gives the title to sovereignty. Since no formal system of legal rules can ever apply the idea of justice, because what is right in one situation changes in another, Plato argued that the true sovereign stands above the legal constitution (we would say today: it is endowed with constituent power) and may act "tyrannically" for the sake of reestablishing justice in a corrupt society. Hegel intimates that sovereignty in modern civil society should belong to a class of "guardians" of justice, composed by a new aristocracy of warriors and philosophers who have no private property and are characterized not by the virtue of honesty, but by the virtue of *Tapferkeit*, or courage in facing "the danger of violent death—a danger which means for the individual the absolute insecurity of all enjoyment, possession, and law" (Hegel 1975, 104). On hindsight, one is tempted to say that Hegel assigns sovereignty to that revolutionary class capable of establishing social justice beyond the limits imposed by the unequal distribution of private property that characterizes bourgeois society.

The crucial point in Hegel's recovery of Plato is making the bourgeoisie conscious of the fact that they are merely one class of society, and not society as a whole. The bourgeoisie's class consciousness has to be inculcated in them from outside and by another class of society: the only way beyond the "bad" infinity or universality of the bourgeoisie, therefore, is to pass through class consciousness or species awareness. Only class consciousness permits "the supersession of this confusion of principles" between honesty and courage: a confusion that results in the situation that those who earn most also believe themselves entitled to exercise sovereignty. And it is only such class consciousness that permits the "established and conscious separation" of the classes through which "each of them is done justice, and that alone which ought to be is brought into existence (i.e., the reality of ethical life as absolute indifference, and at the same time the reality of that indifference as real relation in persistent opposition) so that the second is overcome by the first and this compulsion itself is made identical and reconciled" (Hegel 1975, 104). In other words, class consciousness is the only form of self-consciousness that allows the state (that is, the "reality of ethical life") to "conquer" civil society as a "real relation persistent in opposition" in such a way that it eliminates the coercion or compulsion inherent in civil society. But what class consciousness means for Hegel is not a simple matter to determine and requires a closer look, in the *Phenomenology*, at the transition from self-consciousness to spirit, as well as at the tragic form in which political wisdom actually exists in history (the topic that Hegel calls "the cunning of reason").

Tellingly, in *Natural Law* it is not Plato who determines the sense in which "compulsion itself is made identical and reconciled." In order to illustrate what the reconciliation between civil society and the state means, Hegel turns from Plato's *Republic* to Aeschylus's *Oresteia* trilogy:

> This reconciliation lies precisely in *the knowledge of necessity*, and in the right which ethical life concedes to its inorganic nature, and to the subterranean powers by *making over and sacrificing to them one part of itself.*

> *For the force of the sacrifice lies in intuiting and objectifying the involvement with the inorganic.* This involvement is dissolved by being intuited; the inorganic is separated and, recognized for what it is, is itself taken up into indifference while *the living*, by placing into the inorganic what it knows to be a part of itself and surrendering it to death, has all at once recognized the right of the inorganic and cleansed itself of it. This is nothing but *the performance of the tragedy of ethical life which the Absolute eternally enacts with itself*, by eternally *giving birth* to itself into objectivity, submitting in this objective form to suffering and death, and rising from its ashes into glory. (Hegel 1975, 103–4, emphasis mine)[9]

This dense and obscure passage describes the "tragedy of ethical life." One is immediately struck by the biopolitical language employed by Hegel: political ("ethical") life depends on a sacrifice of a part of "the living" in favor of the "inorganic." Political life is also caught in a circle of "eternal" life that passes through natality and mortality. Couched in these biopolitical formulations, Hegel expresses, for the first time, the two definitions of freedom that characterize his mature thought: first, the idea that freedom consists of being by oneself in the other (which here is given as: "eternally giving birth to itself into objectivity, submitting in this objective form to suffering and death, and rising from its ashes into glory"), and, second, the idea that freedom is "knowledge of necessity."[10]

As this passage indicates, both ideas of freedom depend on the meaning that Greek tragedy gives to the institution of the sacrifice. Hegel's logic as the logic of social reality emerges here in his analysis of how Greek tragedy reveals the true relation between the foundation of a free political life and the institution of sacrifice.[11] Hegel's understanding of a "tragedy of ethical life" is premised on his political interpretation of Greek tragedy (an interpretation he works out by way of Hölderlin's interpretation of *Antigone* as a "republican" tragedy).[12] This understanding of tragedy is not merely symptomatic of the failure to realize either communism or authenticity in bourgeois civil society, as Lukács and Menke respectively argue. For Hegel, Greek tragedy and its ideal of freedom (as knowledge of necessity) are eminently political: they disclose the true structure of the state and the nature of the ethical, or *sittlich*, bond as something absolute.

But in order for tragedy to disclose the true structure of the state, the state can no longer be thought of in terms of the positive freedoms that are associated with the *polis*, since the limits of those freedoms are shown by the tragic dissolution of the *polis*. The key to tragic freedom, for Hegel, is to see that tragedy affirms the *dissolution* of (archaic, tribal) community as the *ground* of (political) society: the political is the resultant of the tragic dissolution of the ethical substance of the *polis*. Tragic dissolution or conflict is no longer *only* ironic, that is, community-dissolving, but *also* politically constituent of a new social bond. This bond, however, can no longer be the fraternal one of the *polis*, or what Butler calls "the homosociality of state desire" (Butler 2000, 37), because such fraternity or homosociality is the very object of tragic critique. Tragic freedom indicates that the affirmative, the political bond, can only arise from the internal negativity of the communal or ethical bond, as a negation (or "compulsion") of that other negation ("coercion" or "crime") that structures the communal bond.

My claim is that, for Hegel, the "crime," "coercion," or "negation" that structures the communal bond refers to the use of the sacrifice in establishing tribal community, or what Hegel calls "natural *Sittlichkeit*" (Hegel 1979, 102/ 417). To this extent, Hegel's reading of the *dispositif* of tragedy is entirely consonant with Girard's thesis about sacrifice as the institution that regulates communal violence and, in particular, the ever-present threat of the dissolution of social differences into a never-ending cycle of revenge (Girard 2005, chap. 1 passim). Hegel conceives of the tragic as the negation, as the critique of this tribal institution of sacrifice. This conception of tragedy is analogous to Girard's idea that tragedy represents the "sacrificial crisis," namely, the consciousness that there is no "pure" violence and that what appears to be the "beneficial" violence of the sacrifice, intended to keep the cycle of revenge at bay, in fact turns out to be far worse than the original ill, giving rise to a universal violence that is shared by all parties to the tragic conflict (Girard 2005, chap. 2 passim).

The return to the war of all against all due to the failure of the institution of sacrifice is conceived by Hegel as a return to a "state of nature" in which the communal or tribal bond is dissolved by the rise of individualism and its "crime." For Hegel, the actual political relation between individuals can only obtain in the form of a final judgment and punishment for the individual's "crime": this judgment and punishment is the real content of the tragic destiny that befalls the "tragic hero." The "tragedy" of civil society therefore contains a theory of political freedom whose structure is constituted by the reflexive sacrificing of the "sacrifice" that establishes the tribal bond as natural *Sittlichkeit*. My thesis is that the tragic sacrifice of a sacrifice, or self-sacrifice, expresses the meaning of politics for Hegel. In what follows I shall illustrate this reading by taking up Hegel's interpretations of the two tragedies, *Eumenides* and *Antigone*, in *Natural Law* and in the *Phenomenology of Spirit*, respectively. But, before doing so, it will be necessary to briefly explain what I mean by sacrifice, its role in social theory, and how sacrifice is figured in Greek tragedy.

In *Totem and Taboo*, Freud gives one of the most fecund hypotheses concerning the functioning of the institutions of sacrifice and festival, which are constitutive of natural sociality, or *Sittlichkeit*. Freud's text is a fundamental contribution to what Hegel interpreters like Pinkard and Pippin now call the "sociality of reason."[13] When Girard wrote his book on sacrifice, he acknowledged that Freud's theory of totemism had fallen into general disrepute. Yet he insisted that Freud's theory was still the most sophisticated attempt at working out the logic of sacrifice and, in all essential ways, was compatible with his own views (Girard 2005, chap. 8 passim). Freud's work was situated within the realm of "primitive" or "archaic" society, whose "natural" sociality was built around totemism. From the perspective of Greek tragedy, totemism corresponds to the tribal, pre-*polis* social arrangement of families, in which clans (*phratries*) constitute the community of families. Freud has this to say about these tribes:

> The members of a totem clam are brothers and sisters and are bound to help and protect one another. If a member of a clan is killed by someone outside it, the whole clan of the aggressor is responsible for the deed and the whole clan of the murdered man is at one in demanding satisfaction for the blood that has been shed. The totem bond is stronger than that of the family in our sense. The two do not coincide since the totem is as a rule inherited through the female line, and it is possible that paternal descent may originally have been left entirely out of account. (Freud 1950, 105)

It is important to realize, when reading Hegel's drafts written during his years in Jena of a *System of Ethical Life* and a *Philosophy of Spirit*, that his conceptions of the family, of labor, of tools, of language, of possession, and of its socially recognized right—everything he terms "natural *Sittlichkeit*"—refers to this tribal or totemic context, and not to a more developed historical stage. Hegel is speaking about the archaic or mythical content that Greek tragedy takes up and works upon. For instance, the natural or divine "law" to which Antigone refers in order to justify her "crime" against the state, just like the revenge exacted by Clytemnestra on her husband Agamemnon in the *Oresteia* trilogy, harkens back to the right to exact revenge on the part of the whole against whoever has injured a member of the totem clan, inherited through the line of the mother.[14]

In the essay on *Natural Law* and later in the *Phenomenology of Spirit*, Hegel's use of Greek tragedy to advance his critique of civil society depends on the presupposition that modern civil "society" is still characterized by a tribal or "natural" form of ethical life (much like Freud claims that "primitive" societies afford the best insight into the psyche of current-day children and neurotics, or like Marx's claim that capitalist society remains part of humankind's "prehistory"). In Freud's reconstruction, the totemic formation of the communal or tribal bond operates via a system of taboos that reflect "ambivalent" social-psychical structures. The taboo divides social reality into the profane and the sacred: it sacralizes, or sets apart, a person or a thing from what is common, rendering it "untouchable."[15] The taboo, in effect, creates primary sociality—or the original social bond between a people—by dividing them amongst themselves and making them unequal. In Hegel's reading of civil society, this "ambivalence" corresponds to the idea of a "reality" (Hegel 1975, 95) that is the result of *Entzweiung*, an objectifying division of spirit that characterizes the system of needs (where the person is objectified by becoming an instrument for the satisfaction of someone else's needs) and the system of rights (where the object as private property is personalized by becoming the content of personal rights). In his Jena writings, Hegel's theory of the family as natural *Sittlichkeit* examines the family structure within a tribal organization in order to demonstrate precisely this point: that the family establishes the common bond in and through inequality. This is why the crime through which the rights of individuals manifest themselves is the totemic battle of revenge.[16] Once the person is sacralized, he or she can be the simultaneous object of love and hate: he or she can be both the sign of the hated and the dead Father whose Law is loved and obeyed.

Freud's hypothesis is not only that taboos work by establishing something as sacred, but also that they serve as reminders of the *sacrificial meal* through which the band of brothers first killed—and then devoured—their Father (Freud 1950, 132–37). Devouring the sacrificed Father is the additional step that allows the brothers to internalize the Father's injunctions as their own and to set up the prohibitions against incest and murder that establish tribal or primary or natural sociality (Freud 1950, 141–43). The periodic transgression of the taboo is associated with the institution of the festival, in which all tribal hierarchies and divisions are brought down. By recreating the sacrificial meal (the eating of the Father), the festival reminds the tribe members of the reason for their sociality. The reason is that no one should behave like the Father once did if they want to continue living together. The structure of the festival brings this message home because, during the festival, everyone does what the Father did and, as a consequence, all sociality ceases to exist: the festival is enjoined only because it showcases the reason for overcoming "savagery" and returning to the peace and order of tribal society.

Hegel's reading of the social function of the tragic in Greek society recognizes a "reflexive" potential, what some would call a "learning-process," that is missing in Freud's attempt to understand the tragic within the social dynamics of tribal totemism. In Hegel's readings of the Greek tragedies, the tragic form is more than just a way for the Greek *polis* to represent the successful transition from tribal to political society. In Hegel, tragic form also operates a sort of reversal or a "return to the state of nature" by bringing the dimension of the tribal back into the *polis* in order to exorcise it, or, better, in order to exorcise what in the *polis* remains tribal (for instance, the fact that both Oedipus and Creon are kings is a totemic vestige within the *polis*). Analogously, Hegel sees in modern civil society a natural *Sittlichkeit* because it is a form of association based on the sacralization of its members with respect to one another, and, more crucially, with respect to the more universal (political) form of society. By sacralization, I mean the creation of a social bond through the exclusion of an individual who is both loved and hated: a sacrificial victim (Girard's theory of the *buc émissaire* and Esposito's theory of immunization refer to the same process of sacralization). According to this view, the juridical persona made possible by the system of individual rights and the commodity-form made possible by the system of political economy sacralize both individuals and things. They turn what is absolute and eternal into something finite and destined to die.

In Hegel's account, tragedy affirms that the dissolution of civil society, through the kind of individualism it has brought about, is the only possible grounds for a truly political bond. It is nowadays fairly accepted that the tragic conflict thematized by Greek tragedies is one that originates from a sacrifice that is also a meal, in the sense that the sacrificial victim is hunted and eaten like a savage animal.[17] Tragedy thematizes what is sacrilegious about the sacrifice itself. In the terms of a biopolitical analysis, one can say that the "sacrilege" performed through the sacrifice is the hunting and killing of *zoe* for the sake of establishing the sovereignty of *bios*. Thus, Agamemnon's sacrifice of Iphigenia and Clytemnestra's sacrifice of Agamemnon are examples of sacrifices that are also meals: they designate totemic sacrifices that express tribal sociality, but do not put an end to violence and social conflict. On the contrary, tragedies show how these "bad" sacrifices give rise to the kind of conflict that is constitutive of tribal or primary sociality, namely, what Hegel calls the conflict around "honor." Its outcome is inevitably a war between clans or families. These sacrifices, which set off the tragedy, are failed attempts at pacification.

Thus what moves the plot of the tragedy along is a moment of self-reflection: it becomes necessary to "sacrifice" the sacrilegious sacrificer. Clytemnestra sacrifices Agamemnon; Creon sacrifices Antigone, and so on. This double sacrifice has two consequences: on the one hand, it occasions the destruction of all natural sociality, the complete breakdown of the social and political order. When the son kills his mother, the father kills his daughter, or the wife kills her husband, no higher social order is conceivable. One gets the radical negativity of pure warfare as barbaric destruction or terror that, for Hegel, is always posterior to natural *Sittlichkeit* (Hegel 1979, 129/447, 142/ 460). This moment, when read diachronically, signals a break with ancient *Sittlichkeit* that corresponds to the kind of break with the ancient conception of the political that Hobbes artificially institutes via the *dispositif* of the "war of all against all," as has been remarked by Strauss and Foucault. This break is the condition of possibility for a purely contract-based, and therefore anticommunal, conception of civil association.

By contrast, the motif of a double sacrifice, of a sacrifice of the sacrifice, has another meaning that offers a solution to the tribal condition of ambivalence. The solution is *not* to base the political relation on the natural or totemic relation, that is, *not* to treat the state as a fraternity or a band of brothers. This is precisely the solution proposed in Hegel's reading of *Antigone*. In purely formal terms, the solution consists in "sacrificing" (in the sense of "giving up," of *Freigabe*, of *aufhebung*) the very institution of sacrifice.[18] The essence of the political bond in Hegel should therefore be conceived of as a sacrifice of the sacrificial *dispositif*, that is, it should be understood as a self-sacrifice on the part of *bios* that brings *zoe* out of its sacred/sacrificed state (what in Esposito corresponds to the moment of auto-immunity, like when the mother's body lowers her immunitary defenses so as not to reject the alien body of the fetus growing inside her). Politically speaking, this solution suggests that by "giving up" on the totemic structure of sociality that keeps the "state of nature" separate from the community, Hegel is asserting that the political must make place for a qualified "return to nature" within the political association. Politically, the state imposes the equality of all (the nonseparation of all) on the basis of the "natural" equality of all to kill each one, but not in the sense in which this "state of war" is found in Hobbes—where it refers to any individual's capacity to kill another individual—rather, in the sense that the state must undo the "security" enjoyed by the bourgeoisie, which it does in one of two ways: either by engaging in warfare with another nation-state or by punishing the "crime" committed by each one as a member of civil society.

THE COMEDY OF THE HEGELIAN STATE

How can the sacrificial meal itself be "sacrificed" or "given up" (*aufgehoben*)? I suggest that, in Hegel, this giving-up of sacrifice takes the form of what Marx later calls civil society's profanation of everything sacred. In his *Communist Manifesto*, Marx famously describes civil society as an enormous mechanism designed to bring down what is most holy: "all that is solid melts into air, all that is holy is profaned." Hegel's view of civil society in *Natural Law* shows a greater affinity with this intuition than previously acknowledged except that, for him, the profanation of civil society must be carried out by the state: it is a political task. Hegel's association of the structure of tragedy with the self-overcoming of civil society confirms that, for him, the tragic must be interpreted along the lines of a process that profanates the sacralization characteristic of civil society. The ultimate motif of "tragedy in *Sittlichkeit*" is nothing short of this: civil society is itself the sacrifice of the sacrifice. That is why, in Hegel, civil society necessarily culminates in the negativity of war and crime. The political, or the level of the state, is attained only when civil society profanates all that is sacred. This is because such profanity, such giving up of the divisions that turn the equal into the unequal, simply preludes the function of the state and of the political, namely, the ultimate assertion of the radical equality of all with all.

The profanation of the sacred, as it appears in the reflexive structure of the sacrifice of the sacrificial meal, entails a process of giving up taboos. According to Freud's hypothesis, the taboo is representative of the primordiality of the father-son relationship in the social structure. It therefore comes as no surprise that the tragedies chosen by Hegel problematize this relationship and put the *polis*-based meaning of "fraternity" in crisis by locating it at the root of all (legal) harm and wrong-doing in the *polis*. Tragic freedom thus necessitates that the political relation overcome the father-son dynamic: strictly speaking, tragic freedom requires a different biopolitical crossing of natality, normality, and normativity.

This alternative crossing can be seen in Antigone's "love" for the exiled brother (an enemy of the *polis*) and in the biopolitical understanding of normativity that justifies her disobedience to the man-made laws of the *polis*: "What law backs me when I say this? I will tell you: If my husband were dead, I might have had another, and child from another man, if I lost the first. But when father and mother both were hidden in death, no brother's life would bloom for me again. That is the law under which I gave you precedence, my dearest brother" (Sophocles 1991, 960–70). Here, Antigone refers to a "law" that does not regulate fertility or sexual reproduction under patriarchical social conditions but, instead, affirms a new political bond based on the "fact" of natality. Antigone believes that natality calls for a solidarity that clearly runs counter to the "fraternity" of the *polis* modeled after the father-son relationship.[19] And, in the end, it places this relationship in crisis. This can be seen in *Antigone* through the unravelling of Creon's relationship with Haemon, and in the suicide of the latter. The tragic insight that comes from blindness to the essence of the father-son, Oedipal relationship is that unless the *polis* opens itself up to the kind of "incestuous" and political *philia* of Antigone, that is, to another articulation of "fraternity" that is based neither on the *polis* nor on the clan of brothers, then the political life that happens in the *polis* will eventually perish.

An analogous process appears in the *Eumenides*, where the mapping of the father-son relationship onto the *polis* is criticized and revised as the only solution for breaking out of the cycle of revenge. The solution in

Aeschylus's drama is Athena's establishment of a people's court of justice.[20] Hegel points out the decisive fact that, here, the people's state is understood to be judge of the crime. By crime, Hegel means what lies at the end—and poses a limit to—civil society (G. Rose 1981, 66–69). The response to crime cannot, in this sense, be left up to the courts of justice within civil society: rather, this response (this punishment) must be the judgment of the state.

Athena's argument for establishing the state as the last court of judgment, that is, for making the people judges (an utterly republican conception), is based on another explicitly biopolitical argument that rejects the taboo that instituted the fraternal relationship of father and son. Like in Antigone, Athena's argument prioritizes *zoe* over *bios*: "It is my task to render final judgment here. This is a ballot for Orestes I shall cast. There is no mother anywhere who gave me birth, and, but for marriage, I am always for the male with all my heart and strongly on my father's side" (Aeschylus 1953, 735–40). The goddess in fact claims that she is a daughter who has no mother, only a father (Zeus), and she herself is not married to a man. Athena is born outside of the cycle of fertility, of Demeter, and of matriarchy. But despite these appearances to the contrary, she is not simply the goddess of patriarchy. Athena is born out of the head of Zeus "fully armoured" and embodies the virtues of warriors: one could even say that she is an Amazon of sorts.[21] Her military spirit is evidenced when, in her last bid to the Furies, she argues: "Let our wars range outward hard against the man who has fallen horribly in love with high renown. No true fighter I call the bird that fights at home" (865). In other words, Athena—a female goddess—becomes associated with two qualities of republican citizenship: the use of persuasion within the city and the virtue of the citizen warrior. These qualities are paramount to the struggle against monarchy ("the man who has fallen horribly in love with high renown").[22]

The crucial question, though, remains the logic behind her biopolitical argument, and why Athena thought that it could "persuade" the matriarchal Furies not to take out their anger over Orestes's matricide in the form of a civil war, thereby perpetuating the cycle of revenge. Athena's argument directly connects the singularity of natality (since she comes from no mother, she cannot be reproduced) with the virtues of republican citizenship. But why do the Furies, the divinities who protect the rights of mothers (of *Mutterrecht*, matriarchy), accept this argument and transform themselves into the Eumenides, or the protectors of the household?

In so doing, they deprive the family of its tribal, totemic context and bring it within political society, as the place of maternal and paternal affection toward children, of marriage, and of social recognition based on familial affection. This function of the family remains a constant theme in Hegel from the *First Philosophy of Spirit* through his mature *Philosophy of Right*. The reason seems to be that Athena's way of being born, without a mother, also deprives the father of his sons (sons to eat, as in Ouranos, and sons to be eaten by sons, as in Kronos, father of Zeus). Athena is a non-Oedipal manifestation of the biopolitical relationship between natality and normativity. In fact, it could even be hypothesized that the phrase cited above, "the man who has fallen horribly in love with high renown," refers to Oedipus Rex. For that reason, the Furies' logic of revenging the mother by killing the son no longer applies; it is set out of order. Without the sacrificial meal there is no need for the Furies, and the sacrificial mechanism is given up, or sacrificed. The Furies accept their own place as divinities of the household hearth (*Hestia*), to be found around the fireplace, which is no longer the location of the sacrificial holocaust, but rather the place of the everyday transmutation of the raw into the cooked, of nature into culture: the hearth fire that is worshipped by the state but is no longer a part of it.[23] The analysis of the tragic essence of civil society is thoroughly biopolitical; that is, it finds itself at the crossing of natality, normality, and normativity.

In the passage I cite above from his essay on *Natural Law* in which he explains the meaning of "tragedy in civil society," Hegel suggests that Aeschylus's *Eumenides* offers a way to understand the relationship between civil society and state through the profanation of the sacred. It is a solution that is both tragic and constitutive of a political, modern republican freedom. The solution rests on the idea of a mutual self-sacrifice on the part of civil society and the state. The state sacrifices its own classical (and Rousseauian) "republican" ideal of the political equality of the *citoyen* to the *bourgeois*, by allowing the existence of a civil society in which inequalities persist and multiply.[24] The state permits the worship of the entrepreneur (the "self-made man"), much like how the Athenians pacified the Furies by accepting them into the city as the divinities of the household, the Eumenides. Properly understood, civil society is nothing other than the self-sacrifice of the state, but only if by "self-sacrifice" one also means negation, or the "sacrifice" of the sacrificial *dispositif*, that is, the end of the sacred. Thus, by letting civil society exist, the state at once abolishes it as a principle of sacrality. The political, or the level of the state, is attained only when civil society is allowed to profanate "all that is sacred," for such profanity is a process of giving up all the divisions that turn the equal into the unequal. That is why the principle under which the modern republican state allows civil society to exist is the principle of equal opportunity. Such a principle is a prelude to the function of the state and of the political: the assertion of the radical equality of all with all.

In turn, the *bourgeois* must sacrifice his or her property and life (everything he or she considers "sacred," but which stands in the way of equality) for the citizen. For the *citoyen*, civil society sacrifices the "peace and stability" of the *bourgeois* by allowing for the necessity of wars conducted by republics against states that are not republics, and for accepting that the warrior class is a universal class (open to all races, classes, sexes, and genders). The key to this idea of a mutual self-sacrifice is to understand it as an act of profanation rather than sacralization: the sacrifice of the "purity" or "sacredness" of the values of the state and of civil society, respectively, is compensated for by the "profanation" of the opposite deities and values. This allows them to find their proper location, their proper center or *Hestia*, thereby taming their "bad" infinity.

But the political nature of this tragic structure of self-sacrifice would not be revelatory of the rational nature of the political if it did not lead to the profanation of the very "divinities" that stand behind civil society and the state. They are respectively, the "lower gods" and the "gods of light" in Aeschylus's drama. To compensate for the fact that the state has to give up the "purity" or "sacredness" of its republican values, the opposite deities and values of civil society must be profanated, and vice versa. This mutual profanation of everything sacred corresponds, in the practice of Greek tragedy, to the comedy that has always accompanied the performance of tragedy: the satyr-play, which is literally a satire of the "festival" institution of tribal, totemic *Sittlichkeit*. This comic dimension of the political is clearly expressed in Hegel's *Natural Law*: "The comedy so separates the two zones of the ethical that it allows each to proceed entirely on its own, so that in the one the conflicts and the finite are shadows without substance, while in the other the Absolute is an illusion. But the true and absolute relation is that the one really does illumine the other; each has a living bearing on the other, and each is the other's serious fate. The absolute relation, then, is set forth in tragedy" (Hegel 1975, 108). The state's first tragic self-sacrifice—with respect to its "ideal" of equality—is compensated for by turning the sacred and taboo deities of the feminine powers (represented by the Furies, the forces of productivity, and the labor force unleashed by bourgeois political economy) into profane deities that support the state through the progressive taxation of their profits and the establishment of a welfare society. As he shows in the *Phenomenology of Spirit*, labor-power represents the taming of "necessity" or fate into "needs" that can be socially satisfied at the price of the individualizing education of each, paid for by the redistribution of wealth through taxation. A progressive taxation scheme financing public systems of health, education, and social security is the "comic" reconciliation of class inequalities in civil society.

Civil society's tragic sacrifice of accepting a government whose essential task is to dole out punishment and war is compensated for by turning the sacred and taboo deities of the *polis* (the figures of the absolute sovereign, the king-judge, and the warrior-lord) into profane deities that protect civil society through warfare. It is "comic" that, in Hegel, the universal class in government is made up of gray and poorly paid civil servants. They are quite the opposite of the colorful and rapacious nobility of feudal societies, who feed off the people they protect. The monarch, for his part, is constitutional and his authoritative decision consists of nothing more than dotting the i's and crossing the t's: he has become a caricature of the absolute sovereign.

Thus, the political understanding of the tragic is not, as Freud suspects, a festival of the state whereby the people project the guilt they feel for their crime against the Father back onto the hero—a father representative (in this case, onto civil society)—in order to witness his punishment. Tragedy is not the "refined hypocrisy" (Freud 1950, 156) that ritualistically calls for the state to swallow up civil society, only to then replicate its laws. Instead, Hegel's political thought spells out the tragic solution of the "sacrifice" of the "sacrificial meal." It institutes a (self-)sacrifice that profanates its own sacredness and does so in a reciprocal fashion: profanation of the inferior *and* of the superior gods. Unlike in Freud, the political bond in Hegel becomes the result not simply of a communal crime, but of a crime against the communal crime.[25] The tragic hero is nothing short of that "reflective" criminal whose activity of profanation manages to "tame" or limit the "indefiniteness," or the "bad infinity" characteristic of the sacred.[26]

THE VALUE OF CRIME: THE PROBLEM
OF LEGAL APPLICATION AND HEGEL'S CRITIQUE OF KANT

This reciprocal sacrifice, however, does not simply restore the "equilibrium" between civil society and the state. For Hegel, the double profanating sacrifice (of sacrifice) *is* the way in which the state "subjugates" civil society: "The ethical whole must on the contrary preserve in this system [the economy] the awareness of its inner nullity" (Hegel 1975, 94). The tragedy completes the institution of the political, of the state, as a rule over individuals while also constituting their objective freedom. Hegel employs a metareflection on the relation between crime and punishment in order to illustrate the meaning of the political "subjugation" or "conquest" over the economy and formal systems of law. The argument is as follows: insofar as civil society is a process of profanating taboos, it generates "crime" rather than "sacrilege." The negative liberty established by the system of civil rights necessitates that individual particularity rise to the level of a crime. Thus, the general will (in which everyone is recognized by everyone else as equal) occurs in the moment of punishment, when the state punishes the crime of the singular individual in civil society. Hegel's theory of recognition culminates in a theory of punishment (Hegel 1987, 234–35).

The final part of *Natural Law* returns to the problematic relationship that political economy has with civil (or private) law and, in particular, to the Kantian identity between right and coercion. Hegel proposes to understand the political subjugation of civil society (which in its totality is understood as crime) as that which corresponds to the (good) infinity of the judgment (of the state). In the *Eumenides*, the reconciliation of the feminine powers of the matriarchical order with "woman as the eternal irony of the community" establishes the Athenian *demos*, or people, as judge of the individual crime in order to break the cycle of revenge. Similarly, in *Natural Law* Hegel argues that only the state, understood as the constitution of a people (*Volksgeist*), can judge the crimes of the bourgeoisie and dole out punishment. In this sense, "punishment is the restoration of freedom, and the criminal has remained, or rather been made, free, just as the punisher has acted rationally and freely. Punishment is thus something in itself truly infinite and absolute.... [I]t issues from freedom and, even as subjugator, remains in freedom" (Hegel 1975, 92). The courts of justice within civil society cannot properly adjudicate the "crime" that civil society inevitably generates, and, indeed, that civil society *is* whenever it pretends to exist independently of the political or refuses to acknowledge its own "political nullity." These courts deal only with the civil, property, and personal rights of the bourgeoisie, and not with the higher right of the citizen as an equal and free member of a people.[27]

The problem with the Kantian and Fichtean conceptions of right is that "this external justice (infinity reflected in the persistent finite, and for this reason formal infinity) that constitutes the principle of civil law has secured a special predominance over constitutional and international law" (Hegel 1975, 123). For Hegel, the proper response to civil society as a crime and the proper punishment for the bourgeoisie must be the sole province of the people, as constituted into a state (only this reversal can restore the rightful priority of constitutional or public law over civil or private law). Because punishment is the real purpose of the state, Hegel understands the unity of the three powers of the state in a way that gives priority to the executive over the judiciary (Hegel 1979, 174, 496). In contrast, in his *Doctrine of Right*, Kant assigns the synthetic moment in the *trias persona* of the state to the civil judges in civil courts. This means that, for Hegel, there can be no social (*sittliche*) justice if the judgment of the people over individuals and their crimes is mediated by the civil, bourgeois rights of these individuals.

In *The Birth of Biopolitics*, Foucault discusses the idea of civil society and the concept of the *homo oeconomicus* after treating Becker's neoliberal conception of crime and punishment, which applies the logic of market transactions to these quintessential powers of the state. In *Natural Law*, Hegel sums up the problem of liberal civil society in similar terms: in civil society, he argues, "punishment is understood as coercion [*Zwang*], it is posited merely as a specific determination and as something purely finite, carrying no rationality in itself.... The state as judicial power trades in specific wares, called crimes, for sale in exchange for other specific wares [punishments], and the legal code is the price list" (Hegel 1975, 92). Against this liberal conception of punishment, Hegel proposes that the true relation between crime and punishment is "that retribution [*Wiedervergeltung*] alone is rational in it; for through retribution the crime is overcome, conquered [*bezwungen*].... Thus the punishment is the restoration of freedom and the criminal has remained, or rather been made free, just as the punisher has acted rationally and free. In this, its determination, punishment is thus something in itself, truly infinite and absolute, revered and feared on its own account. It issues from freedom and, even as conquering [*selbst als bezwingend*] remains in freedom" (Hegel 1975, 94). Hegel therefore characterizes these two opposing conceptions of punishment as coercion and as conquest. Under the former conception, punishment is "payment" for the crime, and this presupposes that the criminal is a debtor.[28] The question then becomes how much the state is willing to pay in order to redeem the crime or debt. Becker, for instance, argues that it makes no economic sense for the state to indebt itself in order to redeem society from all crimes or debts.

Hegel rejects the idea of the criminal as a debtor because this conception of crime places the individual in the position of a slave who needs to be coerced into doing the right thing because he is unable to do it of his own volition. But if this were the case, it would be impossible to overcome revenge and move toward justice and right because both categories presuppose the concept of a free and equal person, not of a slave. The criminal, for Hegel, is not a slave but a limited citizen: a citizen whose identity with the whole remains hidden to him. Punishment dissolves this limitation and allows every individual to become a full citizen, or to attain what Rawls calls "full autonomy." That is why, for Hegel, punishment must remain an attribute of the political, and not of the civil sphere. The political sphere recognizes the absolute equality of all with all—which the crime knowingly rejects—and therefore affirms its truth. Hegel rejects the claim that one can understand what is peculiar to the right of the state if one starts from civil law. Hegel's theory of government reasserts the priority of the executive over the judiciary, whereas Kant's theory of government placed the judiciary over the executive. But the reason for this reversal lies in Hegel's understanding of the problem of legal application or rule-following.

In *Natural Law*, Hegel delivers his key argument through a critique of legal application drawn from Plato's *Statesman* 294:

> It is clear that the art of legislation belongs to the art of kingship. But the best thing is that the man who is wise and kingly, and not the laws, should rule.... Because the law could not completely prescribe with precision what would be most excellent and most just for everybody always.... But we see the law aiming at almost this uniformity, like an obstinate and ignorant man who lets nothing happen contrary to order and allows no one to question his order even if something new and

better, though against his order, turns up for some individual.... Thus it cannot be a good thing to apply a universally simple rule to what is never simple. (Hegel 1975, 96)

Here, Plato's critique of a formal, universal law once again meets up with the wisdom of Greek tragedy that expresses the horrible consequences that follow whenever a law fails to recognize the validity of another law outside of its jurisdiction. In fact, Hegel's critique of civil society unites Plato and the tragedians around the problem of jurisdiction: Who is authorized to say which law applies to which case or individual?

Hegel's point is that a universal but empty law—a law that formally applies to everyone—cannot be determined simply by being applied by civil judges: if one thinks that punishment ought to result from the application of the law, one does not understand that the existence of the crime is the consequence of the indeterminate nature of the formal, universal law. Crime is only "conquerable" at a higher, political level of constitution making, not at the juridical level of legal application. Hegel insists that "inherently absolute and specific law and duty" cannot possibly result "from the formal indifference, or the negative absolute, which has its place and is indeed implicit only in the fixed reality of this sphere [of civil society] ... perfect legislation is inherently impossible, just as true justice, corresponding to the determinacy of the law, is impossible *in concreto* (in the exercise of the power of jurisdiction)" (Hegel 1975, 96–97).

The problem of legal application is perhaps at the root of all of Hegel's political thought. One finds it expressed already in Hegel's fragments from 1799 to 1801 on the German constitution, *Deutschland ist kein Staat mehr* (Hegel 2004). There Hegel argues that only an act of the state's executive branch carries a particular judgment that is also universal because it treats everyone (no matter how wealthy or poor they may be) in exactly the same way.[29] In such an act, therefore, there is no external particularity to which a universal, but merely formal law must be applied—and applied by referring oneself to yet another rule (Hegel 2004, 195–96). The latter is what occurs in civil law and lies at the root of the power of the judiciary, but civil law is constituted so that the judge is not the collective people who make the law. The judge in civil law is not confronted by a people, but by two parties, each of whom claims that its rights have been violated. But where the people constitute themselves into what Hegel understands by the term "state," then such a people are simultaneously judge and legislator (as with the Athenian popular courts of the *Eumenides*), and there is no room for a problem of legal application.

Indeed, Hegel's entire point in his early constitutional writings is to show that Germany "has no state" precisely because of the hegemony of the judiciary power that defends the rights of the individual and not the universal right of the people (Hegel 2004, 201–2). In other words, where the right of the individual is stronger than the right of the state (that is, of the general will of the people), there violence becomes the sole basis of right. Conversely, where the right of the people is stronger than the rights of the individuals, it comes to be true that right is stronger than violence because the state has realized the "nullity of coercion" and thus the absolute freedom and equality of individuals (Hegel 1975, 88). Only when coercion is politically nullified, only when the state achieves the negation of domination, does it become true that "the essence of the ethical life of the individual is the real and therefore universal absolute ethical life" (Hegel 1975, 112).

SPIRIT AND THE IMPOSSIBLE SOVEREIGNTY OVER LIFE

When the other no longer needs to be coerced in order for me to be free, but, on the contrary, when the other's enjoyment of "perfect freedom and independence" enables my own perfect freedom, then and only then political substance has become what Hegel calls "spirit": "'I' that is 'We' and 'We' that is 'I'" (Hegel 1977, 177). Spirit is defined as the simultaneous identity-in-difference of the "I" of self-consciousness with the "We" of ethical substance. In the *Phenomenology of Spirit* the passage from self-consciousness to spirit, from life as self-preservation to political life, is illustrated by Hegel through the dialectic of lordship and bondage. Two of the most influential readings in the twentieth century of this section of the *Phenomenology*, those offered at a fifty-year interval by Kojève and Honneth, have emphasized the category of labor (Kojève) or the category of language (Honneth), while downplaying the category of life and its function in the transition from self-consciousness to spirit.[30] A recent trend in the Anglo-American reception of Hegel, linked to interpreters such as Brandom, Pinkard, McDowell, and Pippin, has returned to this famous section of the *Phenomenology of Spirit* in order to show how "spirit," or the intersubjective "truth" of self-consciousness, is constituted. Pippin's interpretation, in particular, takes the moment of life in the text more seriously, perhaps even privileging it over the moment of labor and the moment of language, thus providing a latent biopolitical reading of these sections of the *Phenomenology of Spirit*, which I shall exploit in my own attempt to show that the passage from self-consciousness to spirit is entirely structured along biopolitical lines. Just like with Hegel's reading of Greek tragedy, so too in the master-slave dialectic the claims of sovereignty over animal life (*zoe*) made by the self-consciousness of the master are ultimately undermined by the slave's attachment to *zoe*, which reveals the true nature of the social essence of self-consciousness and of its freedom.

The *Phenomenology of Spirit* takes up the Kantian thesis that all consciousness or perception (correlated to the appearance of an object) is ultimately self-consciousness because, in order for something to *appear* to the subject, the subject has to take up a *position* or have an *opinion* about that appearance of the object: I do not just *see* something, I also *think* that something (perception) *as* something (concept) (Pippin 2011, 9). Hegel advances the thesis that this opinion or judgment (this self-consciousness or apperception) that accompanies all perceptions is an expression of *desire*, or an *interest* in the perceived thing: "Self-consciousness is Desire in general" (Hegel 1977, 167). The self moves about the world oriented by its interests. At one level, this is true of all living things, whose highest interest seems to be that of persevering in life. Hegel is interested in capturing the moment of anthropogenesis, when "animal" interests become "human" ones, and life itself becomes, as Hobbes characterized it, an endless pursuit of desires and interests so that "self-consciousness achieves its satisfaction only in another self-consciousness" (Hegel 1977, 175). The reason that Hegel thematizes this transition from animal to human desire is precisely because he is as aware as Foucault that in the "social imaginary" of modern civil society, the *homo oeconomicus* is driven by its "interests" as the irreducible core of its being (Foucault 2004, 276–77), and that these interested pursuits "police" and "polish" the human being, thus making possible a "civilized" society.[31] This crossing between quasi-biological interests and normative behavior characteristic of modern civil society is the reason why Hegel calls it the "spiritual-animal kingdom," an expression that provides ample justification for a biopolitical analysis of civil society.

How does normativity (spirit) really emerge from biological life? On Pippin's account, animal desire is also a form of taking a position or having an opinion about the world, but human desire is separate from animal desire because the latter "is simply *subject to* one's desire and subject to the fixed requirements of one's species-life, subject to what Hegel refers to as life itself" (Pippin 2011, 66). The basic claim is that when self-consciousness takes the form of animal life (*zoe*), it is subject "to" life (desire), but when self-consciousness takes the form of a human life (*bios*), then it becomes subject "over" life: to master species-life becomes the inner truth of human self-consciousness or spirit. Pippin thus believes that the (self-)mastery encased in human desire (*bios*) requires transcending animal life (*zoe*), which is something that one does by being willing to risk or sacrifice one's biological life in a struggle for recognition with another human being, as occurs in the master-slave dialectic. But if what I have argued so far is correct, namely, that for Hegel the political condition of human beings entails a sacrifice of the sacrifice of *zoe*, then Pippin's way of reading these sections of the *Phenomenology of Spirit* is one-sided.

The belief that desire starts out as *subject to life* and must sacrifice this life (*zoe*) in order take its place as *the subject of life* (*bios*) assumes that animal life is merely a matter of self-preservation (a self-love closed to otherness) whereas human life (*bios*) alone is lived with the opinions, interests, and desires of others in mind. Hegel shows that this humanist assumption is false. When self-consciousness takes a position with respect to the object of consciousness, it divides itself between the "I" that judges the object and the "I" that is the object judged (Pippin 2011, 26). In the *Phenomenology of Spirit*, this distinction between self-consciousness as the having of an opinion and self-consciousness as being the object of an opinion is addressed in paragraph 167, just before Hegel introduces the category of life: "This antithesis of its appearance and its truth has, however, for its essence only the truth, viz., the unity of self-consciousness with itself; this unity must become essential to self-consciousness; i.e. self-consciousness is Desire in general.... In this sphere self-consciousness exhibits itself as the movement in which this antithesis is removed, and the identity of itself with itself becomes explicit for it" (Hegel 1977, 167). Self-consciousness is the desire or aspiration to achieve a unity between its truth and its appearance because the power to judge the world (which is the truth of self-consciousness) depends on what judgment the world has of the judging subject (that is, it depends on how the self appears to the world). The opinion that the world has of this self-consciousness depends on how it appears to others (both human and nonhuman life), or on how it is reflected in the opinion of these others. In other words, Hegel's point is that how one judges things in the world is dependent on how one desires to appear to and be judged by others. Hence, self-consciousness as desire is co-substantial with the desire for glory, or what Hobbes calls "vainglory" (that is, how one appears in the eyes of the other).[32] This desire for glory or ambition is what makes man a "wolf" to man.

When speaking about self-consciousness as desire, Hegel is reflecting not only on Hobbes but also on Rousseau's distinction between *amour de soi* and *amour propre*. Hegel is as aware, as Rousseau was, that the love of oneself (*amour de soi*) cannot be separated from the opinion one has of oneself; thus, the desire for self-preservation is linked to the desire to appear positively in the eyes of others (without this being the same as *amour propre* that occurs only with the institution of private property).[33] The "unity of self-consciousness with itself" is the unification of the truth and the appearance of self-consciousness, which can only take the form of an action—for action makes the truth of who one is visible—and action is the realm of honor or dishonor, glory or infamy. Thus the "truth" of my opinion about X depends on whether I am capable, whether I have the "right" to having truthful opinions, and this is a question that entails my political status before others, the appearance to others of the "truth" that I am. Self-consciousness is fallible because it is rooted in the power of opinion, and this power depends on others; the power of opinion is "political" and not the property of the self as autonomous or self-legislating. If opinion were merely the property of a self, then self-consciousness would never find its truth in spirit, that is, in the recognition granted by another living being. The transition from vainglory to real glory, or the process of testing the opinion one has of oneself, takes place through the struggle for recognition. The problem of recognition is already inscribed in self-consciousness as desire, but this is only because recognition is inscribed within the sphere of opinion, which logically presupposes the question of how one appears to others.

Just like for Hobbes, Spinoza, and Rousseau, so too for Hegel the necessity of appearing to others, of being the object of an opinion, is itself inscribed within animal life (*zoe*). Once the subject becomes preoccupied with the opinion it has of itself and understands itself as having a desire for the other's opinion, Hegel claims that the object "has, on its side, returned into itself... through this reflection into itself the object has become life ... *the object of immediate desire is a living thing*" (Hegel 1977, 168, emphasis mine). The love or desire of self is equivalent to the love for oneself as a living thing. But this does not mean that animals are characterized by "mere sentiment of oneself as living and as having to maintain life" (Pippin 2011, 31). On the contrary, Hegel says that desire always goes beyond itself (beyond itself as self-consciousness) and passes into life because the opinion self-consciousness has of itself depends on how it appears to others, that is, on its desire to appear "great" to them, and one will only appear great if it overpowers them. Desire seeks out other living things so as to overpower or be overpowered by them. In short, Hegel, like Hobbes and Spinoza before him and like Nietzsche and Freud after him, *directly* links animal life and the overcoming of another living being with the opinion or the appearance of itself in the world, as a living thing among other living things.[34]

Human desire is no more "political" or "spiritual" than animal desire: anyone who presupposes otherwise proves not to have a "scientific" approach to natural right. It is not for nothing that in *Natural Law*, whose subtitle claims to offer "the scientific way of treating natural law," Hegel cites Plato to the effect that "the absolute *life of the ethical* ... 'is an *immortal animal* whose soul and body are eternally born together'" (Hegel 1975, 109, emphasis mine). Later in the same text, Hegel emphasizes the identity of ethical life with *zoe*:

> *Like everything living*, ethical life is sheer identity of universal and particular, and for that reason is an individuality and a shape.... Just as *the totality of life* is fully present in the nature of the polyp as in that of the nightingale and the lion, so the world-spirit, in every one of its shapes, enjoys its weaker or more developed but always absolute self-feeling, and in every people, in every totality of laws and customs, it enjoys its being and itself. (Hegel 1975, 126–27, emphasis mine).

By hunting other animals the lion shows itself to be ferocious and deserving of its "rank" in the so-called "animal kingdom," just like, in totemic societies, it is by identifying with the totem animal and hunting animals of prey that human animals show themselves to be worthy of their "rank" and pursue honor (which is manifested socially by wearing the bones and pelts of the totemic animals and by sporting animal markings on one's skin, for example, tattoos). Above, I showed that in the Greek tragedy the dimension of the hunt is inseparable from that of the sacrifice, for both are essential to natural *Sittlichkeit*. But there is no doubt that in this treatment of animal desire and animal life, Hegel also has in the back of his mind Machiavelli's injunction in chapter 18 of *The Prince* to think of the political or ethical actor not only in terms of human ways to struggle (through laws) but also in terms of the cunning and strength linked to the fox and the lion (that is, to animal life). The truth of self-consciousness in Hegel is always already biopolitical.

These passages suggest that Hegel may not be the advocate of the claims of *bios* over *zoe* that Pippin makes him out to be. Pippin believes that human *bios* is only possible on the condition that "the subject can establish its independence from life [*zoe*]" (Pippin 2011, 32) because life as *zoe* forces self-consciousness to be part of its infinite flux without allowing self-consciousness to raise itself, as "me," over and above life's cycle (Hegel 1977, 171). The cycle of *zoe* does not let *bios*, and thus an individual bio-graphy, emerge (Pippin 2011, 20). However, nothing about Hegel's conception of life in the sections of the *Phenomenology of Spirit* (sections 169–73) dedicated to analyzing the phenomenon of animal life (*zoe*) suggests that he believes *bios* is or ought to be ever "independent" from *zoe* in the way Pippin postulates.

Hegel describes life (*zoe*) as "simple fluid substance of pure movement within itself." Life is "infinity as the supersession of all distinctions, the pure movement of axial rotation, its self-repose being an absolutely restless infinity; independence itself, in which the differences of the movement are resolved, the simple essence of Time which, in this equality with itself, has the stable shape of Space" (Hegel 1977, 169). This admittedly difficult and obscure definition, which Pippin does not discuss, is instead central to Heidegger's interpretation of Hegel's *Phenomenology of Spirit* given in the 1930s. Heidegger sees in Hegel's reference to Time having "the stable shape of Space" an indication of the fact that Hegel (like Aristotle) takes Time to be an affection of Being. Heidegger's view is the opposite, namely, that Being is Time.[35] This same passage becomes decisive for Kojève's interpretation, less than a decade later, except that Kojève departs from Heidegger and instead opposes Hegel's conception of life to the Aristotelian distinction between the individual who lives and dies in time and the species that is eternal. "For Aristotle there is a concept 'dog' only because there is an eternal real dog, namely, the species 'dog,' which is always in the present; for Hegel, by contrast, there is a concept 'dog' only because the real dog is a temporal entity—that is, an essentially finite or 'mortal' entity, an entity which is annihilated at every instant" (Kojève 1969, 141n32). Such a conception of life has always already left behind the framework of desire as a function of self-preservation because life as infinite substance grows and develops not through the preservation of its own individuals, but through the infinite and constant death of its elements. The selection of traits that make up any given "species" is achieved at the cost of an infinite amount of extinctions. A species-life emerges only in and through this self-metabolism of life.

Once the flux of animal life gives rise to an awareness of animal species, then it is possible for self-consciousness to rank the different species: this is a judgment (as classification) that takes a position with respect to life itself. How one judges or feels about the world begins to depend on whether one is a "higher" or a "lower" form of animal life (*zoe*), whether one's life is ascending (healthy) or descending (pathological) in power (to echo characterizations found in Nietzsche and Canguilhem). Health and power will depend on life's capacity to adapt to variation, to change the "meaning" of things. This is the basis on which self-consciousness can attain a conceptual or normative relation to life as *zoe*: one aspires to be as brave as a lion, as clever as a fox, and so on. Only at this stage of self-consciousness, which is expressed in the totemic structure of social status, can a struggle for "pure prestige" or for recognition take place.

On the backdrop of this universal flux of life there exists, for Hegel, an "other" life defined as that self-consciousness for which the lives of animals exist as such. Such a classifying form of biological life is a "human" form of life: "This other life, however, for which the genus as such exists, and which is the genus on its own account, viz. self-consciousness" (Hegel 1977, 173).[36] This "other life" of self-consciousness (viz. *bios*) "will undergo the unfolding which we have seen in the sphere of life" (viz. *zoe*) (Hegel 1977, 173). Thus, for Hegel, human biography cannot be achieved by abstracting self-consciousness from the cycle of *zoe*, as little as concepts can be made by abstracting from the process of natural selection of biological life. On the contrary, a human *bios* is attained in and through the return of self-consciousness to the cycle of life, the return to a "state of nature," which is now characterized by two fixed endpoints, those of natality and mortality, birth and death. These endpoints of human *bios* make sense only against the background awareness that life itself (*zoe*) is an eternal "fluid substance" that neither dies nor is born.

Once self-consciousness becomes aware of its own natality and mortality as basic conditions of its individual *bios*, then it also becomes aware that mere overpowering cannot fashion a *bios*: the belief that the external object can satisfy desire by being annihilated by desire is false. It is false because the object and the desire are reproduced again and again. The (self-)mastery of the lion, shown by its hunting prowess, is not yet the mastery of a self. Desire fails to annihilate the independently existing object. The only way for desire to succeed, and thus be truly satisfied, is if the object negates itself, that is, becomes another *living* self-consciousness, or the self-consciousness of a living thing. "Self-consciousness achieves its satisfaction only in another self-consciousness" (Hegel 1977, 175). At that point, the truth of desire is no longer found in love of self (*amour de soi*) but in the love that another living being feels for it.[37] The opinion I have of myself no longer depends on my overpowering another living being, but in the opinion that this other has of my power, and this opinion is a normative opinion, it is a form of right. Thus, spirit is a form of life in which right is mightier than might. Individual self-consciousness can aspire to raise itself above the cycle of life and "lead a life" (*bios*) only if it seeks to attain an immortal "glory" (*doxa*, opinion) in the eyes of all others: such is "political" glory, the glory sought by Oedipus Rex or Agamemnon or Creon. But this desire for immortal glory on the part of the individual self-consciousness is not the only outcome of the struggle of recognition. For desire is not only an attribute of the individual but also of the species, and recognition of this desire is afforded by those actions that eternalize the life of the species: these are the actions that fall under the category of "unwritten divine laws," exemplified by Antigone.

The struggle for recognition between one self-consciousness (the master) and another "living" self-consciousness (the slave) (Hegel 1977, 176) is therefore misconstrued if it is reduced to "a situation in which one refuses to submit, risks life, and the other submits, and this is something like the ground situation of all human social existence" (Pippin 2011, 63). The reason is that the two opposing self-consciousnesses desire different aspects of life: the master desires the continuation of mortal life (*bios*) in "immortal glory," whereas the slave desires the continuation of eternal life (*zoe*) within mortal, all-too-human life. Self-consciousness as desire realizes itself as the mastery (of a human *bios*) over life (an animal *zoe*). However, animal life (*zoe*) as that which wants to desire realizes itself as subjection to the needs of life. Through service and work for others, the living self-consciousness (*zoe*) finds a ground for true self-mastery in something other than the sacrifice of life, namely, in labor as a living relationship with objective nature (with the independence of the object). The labor and service of the slave undo the vanity contained in the belief that objective nature can be mastered by the human being. Thus, in Hegel the individual human being does not attain a *bios* in the form of a "transcendence" or "overcoming" of animal life. On the contrary, the human being can transform its *zoe* into a political life ("ethical substance") only when self-consciousness has entirely submerged itself into the current of its species-life, that is, into the social organization of productive capacities. This move calls for a "sacrifice" that negates the master's willingness to sacrifice animal life: this is the reflexive sacrifice of sacrifice thematized in Hegel's reading of Greek tragedy.

The master seeks "status" because "how I take myself to be is self-constituting; I am who I take myself to be" (Pippin 2011, 72). This is another way of saying that "self-conscious beings do not have natures, they have histories" (Pippin 2011, 68). The master's sense of self is a result of his genealogy: his status comes from the belief that he descends from a superior "race" or "breed" (*ghenos*) of animals. The master leads the life of his *ghenos*: his actions follow from the social roles (*bios*) he adopts for its life (*zoe*). To "lead a life" is to live it according to the (human-made) norms that define that role. But it also means much more. In effect, Pippin holds that the transition to *bios* is a matter of assigning self-consciousness the *sovereign* "authority" to decide on life-and-death matters, on whether the desires of *zoe* are a "good enough" reason to act (Pippin 2011, 73). In this scenario, *bios* is characterized by the authority to place *zoe* in a state of exception. Much like Agamben's thesis in *Homo Sacer*, for Pippin, normativity is biopolitical in the negative, thanatopolitical sense: it presupposes that norm-following action occurs thanks to placing animal desire or life in a state of exception where it is under someone's authority to decide whether it lives or dies. On this view, one becomes a normative subject when one decides that there are values for which it is worthwhile to sacrifice biological life (one's own and that of others). The sacrifice of life (*zoe*) reflects the commitment that the master's self-consciousness makes to a "We" who stands at war with a

"Them." The normative "commitment" that Pippin sees emerging in the struggle for recognition is nothing other than the "decision" to risk one's life in a struggle against the "enemy" through which Schmitt defines the essence of the political.[38] The decision about life and death is supposed to give "mere life" a "meaning" or "value" that it previously lacked; the subject has now something to live for (allowing the subject to "lead a life," or attain a *bios*) (Pippin 2011, 79).

This interpretation of Hegel's master-slave dialectic was already sketched out by Schmitt and reappears in Strauss, who applies it to Hobbes's "war of all against all," and to the transition toward a social contract that establishes a civil society only by subjecting all individuals to an absolute authority.[39] Since Pippin makes the struggle for recognition into a struggle for the recognition of someone's authority to make norms, it is not surprising that Hobbes's *auctoritas non veritas facit legem* reappears in Pippin's construal of the notion of normativity in Hegel: the struggle for recognition, "this desire to be desired (to be properly recognized)" (Pippin 2011, 77n25), begins and ends with authority, not with reason: "*All* having such an authority *amounts to its being acknowledged—under the right conditions and in the right way—to have such authority*" (Pippin 2011, 77). There is no "good reason" that grounds someone's authority; conversely, it is because of someone's "authority" that one accepts what he or she says as "reasonable" or "justified." From the standpoint of the master's self-consciousness, one is in "the right" because of who one is (because of one's status, *hexis* or *habitus*) and where one comes from (because of one's descent, *ghenos*). Pippin's interpretation is a biopolitical reading of Hegel's struggle for recognition carried out from the perspective of the master (or "norm-giving" self-consciousness). It belongs to a vision of sociality that revolves around recognition of social status and absolute obedience to the taboos that make such status possible.

But Hegel himself does not give the struggle for recognition such a negative, decisionist biopolitical interpretation corresponding to the master's self-consciousness. The self-consciousness of the slave, in fact, harbors a republican and affirmative biopolitics of recognition. Hegel indicates that one must also understand the struggle for recognition from the point of view that is opposed to that of "autonomous" self-consciousness, namely, from the point of view of life's (*zoe*) self-consciousness, which corresponds to the position of the slave. What is distinct about this standpoint is that it profanates taboos in the name of a conception of law as something divine and eternal (which is represented for Hegel by Antigone's standpoint) and carries with it an entirely different sense of *ghenos* and of genealogy (and thus also of political life).

From that side of life (*zoe*) that desires to become self-conscious, the struggle to get recognized by (the master's) self-consciousness entails the willingness to sacrifice the ability to overcome other life. And for life to stop overcoming is for life to guarantee its death and disappearance. But in the case of the slave, by submitting to self-consciousness (that is, to the master) life lives on in the form of subjection rather than in the form of overpowering. "In this experience [of the struggle for recognition] self-consciousness *learns that life is as essential* to it as pure self-consciousness... or consciousness in the form of thinghood" (Hegel 1977, 189, my emphasis). Whereas the master establishes his self-consciousness (*bios*) by sacrificing life (*zoe*), the slave saves her life (*zoe*) and establishes her self-consciousness (in the form of a new sociality to come, of which the slave is not aware) by sacrificing "pure self-consciousness" (the individual *bios*), that is, by subjecting herself and serving another.[40] The slave's *zoe* is different from animal life and from the master's "all-too-human" life. It is a function of self-sacrifice realized through labor. Since the saved life of the slave entails service and obedience, it negates vainglory, the idea of being superior to other living beings, and the notion of being self-sufficient. In so doing, the slave comes to realize that the reality of living is a social one, not an individual one: *living* self-consciousness is always already class consciousness. That is why Marx later correctly understands "living" labor not as a form of individual *bios* but as the ground of a new form of *zoe*: a communist form of life of human animals endowed with class consciousness of their common species-life.

Self-consciousness comes to the slave through the experience of a special kind of fear (which Kierkegaard later calls "anxiety"), "the fear of death, the absolute Lord" (Hegel 1977, 194) that allows the slave to "posit himself as a negative in the permanent order of things, and thereby becomes for himself, someone existing on his own account" (Hegel 1977, 196). This living self-consciousness finds its realization "precisely *in his labor wherein he seemed to have only an alienated existence that he acquires a mind of his own*.... Without the discipline or service and obedience fear remains at the formal stage, and does not extend to the known real world of existence. Without the formative activity, fear remains inward and mute, and consciousness does not become explicitly for itself" (Hegel 1977, 196, my emphasis). Such an experience of *absolute* fear or anxiety requires, as a condition of its possibility, that self-consciousness understand itself as *entirely, irremediably* given over to life (*zoe*), that is, to the infinite flux of life that dissolves all particularity. That is why Hegel describes the death-in-life of the slave as "this pure universal movement, the absolute melting-away of everything stable, is the simple, essential nature of self-consciousness, absolute negativity, pure being-for-self, which consequently is implicit in this consciousness" (Hegel 1977, 194): the terms are exactly those employed to describe the genus of biological life as pure flux and negativity. Unlike in Heidegger, for whom the experience of anxiety and being-toward-death arguably permits human existence or *Dasein* to transcend animal life, in Hegel, the fear of death can only advene to a self-consciousness that is all and only living. Anything short of that would not allow it to feel absolute fear.

Since the master's self-consciousness feels disdain for animal life (and is willing to hunt it down and sacrifice it), this form of self-consciousness cannot really possess the power of absolute negation, which is realized by the role of death in the cycle of life. For that reason, the master's self-consciousness never actualizes that power in a new form of metabolism with objective nature: this new metabolism is brought about by living labor, now understood very particularly as the species-life of human beings. Living labor is the result not of the sacrifice of life but of the self-sacrifice of the living, or the sacrifice of the sacrifice of life, which gives rise to a political life that is beyond the master-slave distinction and which finds its actuality in the ethical substance of the republican state. Since this self-sacrifice rejects the struggle for honor or prestige that divides human self-consciousness into masters and slaves, it also leaves behind the tribal or totemic organization of society, for an organization of society based on the radical equality of all living self-consciousnesses. This radical equality is implicit in the idea of *zoe* as infinite flux and eternal life, against which background alone every living individual is born and will die, and this fact is the seal of their ultimate equality.

The conclusion of Hegel's analysis of the master-slave dialectic is that the "We" of the ethical substance that is also an "I," and vice versa, is *never* realized by a social organization established between masters and slaves, and based on domination. Rather, it is realized only in a political society that overcomes this division (namely, in a republican society), and does so on the basis of equality between masters and slaves, that is, in a society in which labor becomes the infinite life or substance of value. Because living labor does not destroy external things but, instead, modifies them (engages in a metabolic relation with the objective world), living labor is for pure self-consciousness a form of self-limitation. And that is why, along with the sociality of labor, the other fundamental feature of spirit is the idea of divine law, which Hegel introduces at the end of his section dedicated to "Reason," that is, at the end of his critique of the Kantian notion that law or normativity is something that "I" give myself.

Hence, for Hegel the correct understanding of normativity is first expressed by Antigone:

> The law is equally an eternal law which is grounded not in the will of the particular individual but is valid in and for itself; it is the absolute pure will of all ... [Hegel 1977, 436].... Thus Sophocles's *Antigone* acknowledges them as unwritten and infallible laws of the gods.... Ethical disposition consists just in sticking steadfastly to what is right, and abstaining from all attempts to move or shake it, or derive it.... It is not, therefore, because I find something is not self-contradictory that it is right; on the contrary, it is right because it is what is right. That something is the property of another, this is fundamental; I have not to argue about it, or hunt around for or entertain thoughts, connections, aspects, of various kinds, I have to think neither of making laws nor of testing them.... As soon as I start to test them I have already begun to tread an unethical path. By acknowledging the absoluteness of the right, I am within ethical substance; and this substance is thus the essence of self-consciousness. (Hegel 1977, 437)

Hegel's fundamental thesis on the essence of normativity, namely, that what is right is first given to individual self-consciousness in the form of divine laws, and is not the result of "making laws nor of testing them," clearly stands at odds with Pippin's suggestion that for Hegel self-consciousness "gives" itself its norms and is thus always "beyond" them. For Pippin, self-consciousness can and must take a sovereign, decisionist stance with respect to its own rule-following behavior: "Consciousness is always in a position to alter norms for correct perception, inferring, law-making, or right action" (Pippin 2011, 25). On the contrary, Hegel's analysis of the emergence of divine law out of the idea of eternal *zoe* shows that Hegel locates the condition of possibility for authentic political association precisely in the self-sacrifice of a "sovereign" conception of self-consciousness. It is not Oedipus Rex, Oedipus the sovereign, who follows mere human reason against divine law, but the tragedy of Oedipus as it unfolds in Antigone, that provides the guiding thread to Hegel's republican politics.

THE MACHIAVELLIAN MOMENT IN HEGEL'S ANTIGONE

Beginning in his Jena writings all the way up to the *Philosophy of Right*, Hegel argues that the political conquest of civil society takes the form of the (good) infinity of war conducted by a people because it gives expression to their will not to hold on to private property at all costs, with its social differentiation between classes and, thus, reasserts the absolute freedom and equality of individuals in their political relation with one another.[41] Hegel's account of war and of the state has been given a decisionistic and authoritarian interpretation, mostly by interpreters who follow the reading of the struggle for recognition offered by Schmitt and Strauss in the early 1930s. Yet in his *The Young Hegel* written in the very same years, Lukács had opened up another possibility when he remarked that Hegel's conception of war manifests a "return to nature" that corresponds to Antigone's divine law. For Hegel Antigone's conception of divine law corresponds to the self-consciousness of living labor and is oriented toward a form of social organization without domination, rather than to the decisionism that characterizes the master's self-consciousness. My claim is that Hegel's idea of war fits together with a nondecisionistic idea of law (Antigone's law) under the rubric of the "cunning of reason." By this term Hegel refers to one of the last figures taken up by the unfolding of spirit or political life, namely, just like an entire people, acting as state, needs to punish the crime of civil society, so history itself passes judgment over the crimes of the state committed in its pursuit of its particular state interests through its external wars of conquest. History's punishment of the state is the "cunning of reason" that operates behind the backs of the historical actors.[42]

Hegel's understanding of political freedom through Greek tragedy, particularly in *Antigone*, culminates in his conception of the cunning of reason. Already in his early Jena fragments, Hegel links this cunning to the feminine: "The will becomes feminine through cunning [*durch die List ist der Willen zum Weiblichen geworden*]" (Hegel 1987, 206–7).

54 *Biopolitics of the Economy*

Cunning, which is here the equivalent to the Greek *métis* (the ethical character that Athena puts into evidence in the *Oresteia* when she outwits the Furies), is explained in terms of a tragic self-limitation or self-sacrifice of might: "The glory of cunning against might, to grasp blind might on one side so as to turn it against itself [*Ehre der List gegen die Macht, die blinde Macht an einer Seite anfassen, dass sie sich gegen sich selbst richtet*]" (Hegel 1987, 206–7). In the *Phenomenology of Spirit*, the figure of the cunning of reason appears in Hegel's discussion of the dissolution of Greek *Sittlichkeit*, in the context of his interpretation of the *Antigone*. Cunning is again associated with the feminine and, more specifically, with what Hegel calls "womankind—the everlasting irony of the community." This particular passage from the *Phenomenology* has given rise to innumerable interpretations, some of them pointing to Hegel's "well-known endorsement of sexual inequality," where he appears to "take up Creon's mantle" (Markell 2003, 114), or when "womankind" is "left behind for war, left behind for the homosociality of state desire" (Butler 2000, 37).[43] But these interpretations of the passage seem to have overlooked a reference to Machiavelli's political thought in Hegel's reading of *Antigone* that may help to clarify the connection he saw between Antigone's divine law, the priority of war, and historical justice.

Hegel argues that modern ethical substance can no longer be conceived as "substantial" in the way in which the Greek *polis* was so conceived because it excluded the claims of individualism. The modern state, as ethical substance, must recognize the principle of subjectivity in and through civil society. Civil society is the permanent self-dissolution of the modern state, and if the state wants to persist, it must find the way to assert itself within its own dissolution. This is the tragedy of civil society. In early modernity, the first thinker to be aware of the self-dissolving character of the modern state is Machiavelli.[44] For Machiavelli, there is no longer a "natural" foundation (that is, a foundation in the social organization of natural *Sittlichkeit* or totemic society) to authority and to the title to rule. The state is itself the result of the encounters that individual *virtù* (from *virtus*, or strength) has with *fortuna*, with chance. Rancière has recently explained the republican meaning of this formula: a society lives politically, or establishes itself as a republic, whenever, beside the "natural" titles to rule (such as wisdom, wealth, breeding, and so on), it makes room for another title—the title granted by chance—to those who have no qualification to rule because they want a state of no-rule, a state that demonstrates what Hegel calls the "inner nullity" of coercion and domination (Rancière 2009, chap. 1, passim).

Machiavelli's formulation of the encounter between *virtù* as strength and *fortuna* as chance receives its most famous (or infamous) formulation in chapter 25 of *The Prince*: "Fortuna is a woman: if one wants to master her, it is necessary to beat and hit her. . . . And given that she is a woman, she is the friend of youth, because they are less respectful, more savage, and command her with more audacity." This Machiavellian formulation—"Fortuna is a woman . . ."—reappears nearly literally in Hegel's *Phenomenology*, precisely in the passage that links his treatment of *Antigone* to the dissolution of the ethical substance of the Greek *polis*:

> Woman in this way turns to ridicule the earnest wisdom of mature age which, indifferent to purely private pleasures and enjoyments, only thinks of and cares for the universal. *She makes this wisdom an object of derision for raw and irresponsible youth and unworthy of their enthusiasm. In general, she maintains that it is the power of youth that really counts.* . . . The *brave youth in whom woman finds her pleasure*, the suppressed principle of corruption, now has his day and his worth is openly acknowledged. Now, it is *physical strength and what appears as a matter of luck, that decides on the existence of ethical life and spiritual necessity.* (Hegel 1977, 288–89, emphasis mine)

As can be seen from the emphasis in this passage, the determinants of strength (*virtù*) and luck (*fortuna*) represented in Machiavelli's formula for the dissolution of ethical substance reappear verbatim in Hegel's own analysis of this dissolution at the hands of Antigone. The idea of a cunning of reason is ultimately Hegel's attempt to synthesize Machiavelli's politics with a Sophoclean understanding of the tragedy of world history.

In the cited passage, Hegel locates the cause of this dissolution of (masculine) political substance and its (masculine) "wisdom of mature age" in the alliance between the "brave youth" and "womankind," which reappears in the form of war, despite the attempts made by the *polis* to repress it. The desire of the "brave youth" for "womankind" is far stronger and more violent than the homosocial desire for male fellow citizens and the patriotic love of the fatherland (indeed, Hegel implies that the male youth desires a woman who is older and more knowledgeable than himself): it is precisely a desire for "recognition" or a desire for the desire of the Other (of the male citizen). This Other desire of Antigone cannot be reconciled with Greek political substance, for it must break violently free of that political substance that relegated womankind into the household: "The community, however, can only maintain itself by suppressing *this* spirit of individualism, and, because it is an essential moment, all the same creates it, and, moreover, creates it by its repressive attitude towards it as a hostile principle.... War is the Spirit and form in which the essential moment of the ethical substance, the absolute freedom of the ethical self from every existential form, is present in its actual and authentic existence" (Hegel 1977, 288–89). Hegel's point is that the cunning of reason is operative in the feminine "spirit of individualism," not in the male spirit of natural *Sittlichkeit*, and that this spirit is carried forth by the "war" that womankind (Antigone) conducts against the male state (Creon). Whatever Hegel's own prejudices against women may have been, he was never foolish enough to think that the modern republican state, unlike the Greek state, was designed to "keep women at home." After all, it is precisely civil society's profanation of everything "sacred" that inevitably brings to ruin the patriarchical family as "pillar" or "foundation" of the state.[45]

This passage about womankind and the brave youth is part of Hegel's general argument that classical natural right does not recognize the "spirit of individualism" in a universal or political fashion and, instead, sees individualism as a "hostile principle." The male *polis* composed of masters denies universal or political recognition to the natural rights of individuals as these are represented by Antigone's other, divine law of natality. Because of this lack of recognition, Greek ethical substance proves to be a form of right or justice that ultimately depends solely on violence and might for its survival. This dependency on violence against the individual and, in particular, the violence of the masculine *polis* against individual women, is generally expressed in the state's finality of warfare as a means of conquering slave labor. Since the male *polis* is entirely oriented toward war and conquest, the older citizens require the "audacious youth" to use violence in order to save that very legal order of the *polis* that has repressed women's right to live politically. At this precise moment, the cunning of reason, which is womankind's desire, steps onto the historical stage and both attracts and distracts the desire of the male youth, thereby turning the youth against the elders, and against the *polis*. The crucial moment of conversion in Hegel's text is his assertion that "because the existence of ethical life rests on strength and luck, the decision is already made that its downfall has come.... This ruin of the ethical substance ... is thus determined by the fact that the ethical consciousness is directed on to the law in a way that is essentially immediate." Strength ("manly virtù") and luck ("fortuna") make up Greek ethical life only because the *polis* relies on these factors (namely, the violence of the band of brothers and the fortune of being born into the male sex) in order to establish its (false) universality. The existence and validity of the law of the *polis* is "decided" by the confluence of *virtù* and *fortuna* only because the false universality of its law has cut off the possibility of recognizing that other law of natality (which is thus always "naturalized" back into the family and in that way depoliticized), until the latter remerges in another, happy and erotic collision of strength and luck, *virtù* and *fortuna*, which is itself, of course, violent: it is the violence of the audacious youth that carries out a woman's war against the warlike male state. Antigone's war, in this sense, is a "return of the repressed" economy of desire found in matriarchy and in its warrior class of Amazons.[46]

The identity of the audacious youth who uses violence against the *polis* to reestablish the validity of Antigone's excluded and reified law remains a riddle in Hegel's text. Most interpreters identify the youth with Polyneices, but given Hegel's citation of the Machiavellian formula, it may very well be that the audacious youth in this context refers not only to Polyneices but also to Cesare Borgia, the hero of Machiavelli's *Prince* who embarks on the project to found a modern state by arming the people's desire for freedom. Hegel cites approvingly Cesare Borgia's example in the preparatory draft of *Deutschland ist kein Staat mehr* (Hegel 2004, 132–35). Such is indeed the structure of the cunning of reason: it turns might against itself, it sets up (popular) power against (sovereign) power, so that law will no longer be characterized by the anteriority of violence. It employs decisionism to establish an order of justice in which decisionism no longer has any place because it lets a people in arms, and not a monarch, be the last judge as to whether the situation is one of war or one of peace. The alliance between womankind and male youth characterizes the "retribution" of republican, popular justice against a *polis* guilty of having pushed justice back onto natural (sexual and gender) determinants, thereby reifying justice. Hegel's reading of *Antigone* is republican, but in the sense of the modern, revolutionary republicanism he learns from Machiavelli.

Unlike with Hölderlin's republican reading of *Antigone*, Hegel thus denies that the ultimate meaning of the tragedy lies with the "equal" recognition of both the divine and the civil rights: Creon cannot be shown equality. First of all, for Hegel, the irony of "womankind" clearly shows the political superiority of the maternal line—that is, of the desires associated with natality—over the Oedipal paternal line—that is, of the desires of the *polis* and its brotherhood. Second, Hegel radicalizes the republican reading in a Machiavellian sense by allowing the *polis*–dissolving feminine principle to take over the state in the form of a bold youth: not Jesus, but a new Theseus, Cesare Borgia, or Napoleon, a new political constellation of tragic "cunning" and "strength."[47] The audacious youth seems to be a first representation of the idea of the world historical political personality, an absolute Spirit on horseback who founds a state of equality through a warrior class that fights for freedom not only through laws but also through force (using the lion and the fox, as Machiavelli says).

The Sophoclean sense of this cunning of reason is that every state will meet its own justice (or punishment) at the hands of other *peoples at arms* (that is, other republics who are not yet constituted powers, but rather constituent powers). World history as a tribunal of justice means, for Hegel, a world history determined by the tragic but necessary quest of all modern republics to become empires and to find their downfall in this way. The tension between freedom and conquest is the main theme of Machiavelli's *Discourses on Livy*, and it animates also Montesquieu's *Spirit of the Laws*, from which it is received by Hegel's *Phenomenology of Spirit*. For Hegel, the republican tragedy of the state on the stage or world history was represented in his own time by the republican general Napoleon Bonaparte. Napoleon was the founder of a republican state that established the principles of a universal and free system of public education and a civil code, both of which perhaps best express the sense in which, for Hegel, political power is a matter of culture over violence. Yet Napoleon also represents the inevitable fall of the republic through its own empire building: a fall that comes at the hands of other (constituent) peoples at arms, wherever they happen to be born on the face of the earth and outside of the *nomos* traced on the earth by the already constituted states. In the following chapters it will be a question of reconstructing this other "natural law" emerging from the fact of natality.

2

LIVING LABOR AND SELF-GENERATIVE VALUE IN MARX

THE SOVEREIGNTY OF VALUE IN CIVIL SOCIETY

As members of civil society, we seek the best "value" for our money; we tend to behave as if we believe that anything that increases the overall "value" in society is somehow legitimate, whereas anything that decreases it is somehow illegitimate. Individual persons and companies that generate "value" are considered good, whereas individuals or institutions that waste "valuable" resources are considered bad. Even if it is granted that democratic legitimacy comes from the agreement between actors reached under open and fair conditions of communicative activity, we sense that no amount of talking, or exchanging of "good reasons," in itself generates any additional magnitude of value. This seems to be why no political or moral consideration that questions the value of "value" creation, no matter how much democratic legitimacy it may enjoy, can in the long run trump the reasons of the economy.

Marx was the first to formulate a theory as to why the form of normativity in civil society must be understood as the form of exchange-value. In the *Grundrisse*, he states this position clearly: the bourgeois values of freedom and equality, on which all political claims to legitimacy must be based in civil society, simply reflect or express the freedom and equality of individuals (both workers and owners) who exchange commodities between themselves. Yet, despite all the evidence that points toward value being the fundamental form of normativity in modern civil society, Marx's theory of value is no longer taken seriously; perhaps it never even had the opportunity to establish itself as a serious theory of the economy. Within the Marxist camp, in fact, his theory of value soon fell prey to reductionist versions of the theory that equates value to a supposedly "objective magnitude" of labor required to produce it. Neoclassical economics, for the most part, seems to have placed Marx's economic theory in the rubbish bin of history simply by denying the reality of value and replacing it by a psychology of valuation. Economics today is the science that explains the prices of commodities, not their value, and these prices ultimately reflect how much the buyers and sellers of the commodities "prefer" them over other commodities. In both cases, the peculiar features of value that make it irreducible to either labor or price were lost, much to the detriment of Marx's overall account of civil society.

This chapter casts another look at Marx's theory of value. It shows that Marx's concept of the "form of value" functions as a source of economic legitimacy, as a sort of immanent juridical or constitutional framework of the capitalist economy centred on the self-generation of value (the creation of more value, or a surplus of value, out of value). Additionally, it argues that Marx's account of value is helpful in reformulating the biopolitical kernel in his theory of surplus value. Antonio Negri is rightly credited with giving Marxist theory a biopolitical turn that has been instrumental in restoring a new degree of plausibility to Marx's critical project and in shaking the hegemony of neoliberal economic thinking. But Negri believes a biopolitical interpretation of surplus value, centered on the phenomenon of the exploitation of "living labor," overwhelms any account of value. This chapter, instead, tries to show that the imbrication of law and economics is essential to a biopolitical account of civil society and requires holding on to a theory of value and avoiding its reduction to a theory of labor. The chapter begins by discussing the connection between law and economy in some of Marx's early writings, showing his early use of biopolitical language in order to understand the dynamics of civil society. The chapter then discusses the account of surplus value in the *Grundrisse* and tries to identify what is biopolitical in Marx's mature account of capital.

Marx first developed his ideas about civil society by submitting the concluding sections on state and constitution in Hegel's *Philosophy of Right* to a careful critique, while for the most part side-stepping the sections on private law, morality, family, and civil society. Shortly thereafter Marx moved to Paris where he began studying the classical economists: Sismondi, Say, Ricardo, and Adam Smith. The Parisian *Economic-Philosophical*

Manuscripts (1844) was the result of this shift of attention from analyzing the form of the state to analyzing the form of private property; here Marx formulated his conviction that everything that can be said about civil society is contained in the exegesis of the idea of private property, and that the "critique of political economy" is tantamount to a critique of civil society, that is, of bourgeois society.

The concept that allowed him to offer such a vertiginous condensation of civil society into the form of the commodity is the Hegelian claim that objectification (*Entäusserung*) is the alienation (*Entfremdung*) and the reification (*Verdinglichung*) of "spirit." This is the strange phenomenon discovered by Hegel whereby the subject (thought) exists in and as object (matter), and conversely the object (matter) exists in and as subject (thought), all for the sake of finally coming to see the deeper unity of self and world, thought and matter. This way of understanding objectification continues to play a fundamental role in *Capital*, where it appears as the idea of the "fetishism" of commodities. Commodity fetishism obtains when products establish social relations between themselves that dominate the relations between producers, making it appear as if the latter follow "natural" laws of behavior, laws subsequently studied by the scientific discipline of "economics."

But it took Marx more than a decade after his time in Paris to produce a rough draft of the *Foundations of the Critique of Political Economy* (*Grundrisse*) in 1857–58, a work that seeks to uncover how exactly reification relates to the theory of (exchange-) value that makes political economy possible, or, more exactly, how reification finds its "expression" in the process of value's self-generation (capital), which is the movement whereby money (thought) becomes commodity (matter) only in order to change back to more money (thought). Another decade went by before he was able to offer a "presentation" (*Darstellung*) of the system of exchange-value as commodity fetishism that he considered both theoretically and practically satisfactory in the first part of *Capital*, published in 1867.[1] From this brief sketch of his development, it is clear that explaining reification was never the problem for Marx: it was explaining value that turned out to be the task of a lifetime. This task required radicalizing the biopolitical dimensions of natality and normativity already present in Hegel's understanding of civil society and seeing how they operate in the power of "living" labor and in the "fecundity" or self-generative power of capital, respectively.

Marx's journey toward a critique of political economy started from Hegel's political philosophy because he shared Hegel's insight into the "tragedy of civil society" and the subsequent need to subordinate, or subjugate, the "Fate" of political economy to the satisfaction of the needs of the human animal species. This remains Marx's paramount point of orientation throughout his research on political economy and his struggle for a communist form of social organization, so much so that his intellectual and political engagements are always marked by a characteristic tension between, on the one hand, subjugating the power of money and, on the other hand, paying the price for the free development of society's productive forces unleashed by capital's fecundity. But following his *Critique of Hegel's Philosophy of Right*, Marx rejects Hegel's belief that the state can achieve this subjugation of money as Fate by means of a "tragic" sacrifice of the *bourgeoisie* at the hands of the sublimated *citoyen* (the sovereign and the civil servants of the state). Marx, on the contrary, believes the state, the once mighty Leviathan, becomes first the prey, then the sacrificial meal, of civil society, and particularly of the economy.[2] What is it that the young Marx discovered through his critique of Hegel's constitutionalism that led him to write the Paris *Manuscripts*?

For Hegel (as later for Schmitt), the sovereign exists only insofar as he is the "representative" of a self-articulated people or *Sittlichkeit*: the will or decision of the sovereign is both the particular will of a person and the general will of the state. Therefore, the decision of the sovereign as to whether to wage war or keep peace, the decision on the enemy (to put it Schmittian terms), represents the difference-in-unity of the individual subject with the substance of society: it is the highest expression of the people's mind, or the *Volksgeist* as Hegel calls it. For Hegel (as for Schmitt), this sovereign decision ought to trump the interests of the bourgeois, revealing a higher normative claim (a higher set of values) than the economic value pursued in civil society (namely, the "wealth of nations").

Marx uncovers the fact that the sovereign's will is not representative of the general will of society, but rather of the will of an alienated society, of civil society. Where society wants to show its general will through democracy and universal suffrage, the political representative of civil society instead upholds a (constitutional) monarchy that locates the dynastic principle, namely, the institution of primogeniture, at the heart of the constitution:

> In the constitution guaranteed by *primogeniture, private property* is the guarantee of the political constitution. In primogeniture this guarantee appears to be provided by a *particular* form of private property. Primo-geniture is merely the particular form of the general relationship obtaining between *private property* and the *political state*. Primogeniture is the *political* meaning of private property, private property in its political significance, i.e., in its universal significance. Here then, the constitution is the *constitution of private property*. (Marx 1975, 177)

Marx fixes his attention on what can only be termed the biopolitical signature of the Hegelian sovereign, namely, the right to receive all power by virtue of being the first born. The way the sovereign attains, through birth, a right that nullifies the rights the rest of the people also have by birth, suggests that the sovereign merely represents the sovereignty of private property, which, in a strictly analogous way, encompasses all the fruits of society's living labor in order to distribute them to one private person, the owner.

The consequences of Marx's critique of the representational nature of sovereignty are far reaching. If the representativeness of the sovereign (unity of subject and object, particular thing and universal capacity) is only the inverted mirror image of private property or money, then the sovereignty of private property over society must reside in money's representative character. Marx did not have a name, as of yet, for what gives money its representative character: only in the *Grundrisse* does he understand it as the "form of value." The form of exchange-value is what accounts for the decisive characteristic of bourgeois commercial society: "The power which each individual exercises over the activity of others or over social wealth exists in him as the owner of exchange-values, of money. The individual carries his social power, as well as his bond with society, in his pocket" (Marx 1974, 157). The true unity in difference or concrete universality, the effective joining of democracy (the unfettered exercise of the bourgeois "rational choice") and sovereignty, is ultimately not represented by the Hegelian prince, but by money.

The corollary of this analysis is that no constitutional form of state is ever capable of subjugating civil society because it can never master the democratic and juridical structure of the "form of value." This point shows where the problem lies in contemporary forms of post-Marxism, perhaps best exemplified by the opposite tendencies found today in the work of

Laclau and of Honneth. In both these thinkers, the problem of class struggle and class consciousness has lost its footing in a theory of value. Instead of being politicized immanently, economic tensions and contradictions are "politicized" from outside the economy, with the infusion of non-Marxist theories of the political coming from Schmitt in the case of Laclau, and from Rawls in the case of Honneth. By way of contrast, what Marx's biopolitical analysis of Hegel's doctrine of sovereignty indicates is that "the concept of the political" cannot, on its own, offer a critique of political economy because it is ultimately dependent on the "concept of value" of civil society (that is, on the concept of the "economy" itself).

A second important consequence follows directly from Marx's interpretation of the Hegelian prince: just as monarchy depends on primogeniture (which alienates the fecundity of the family to the first born), so too does private property depend on the alienation of species-life (*zoe*) for the benefit of the life (*bios*) of the individual, who is thus considered the "owner" of her labor-power, of the forces of production. Here one has, in a germinal stage, the thesis that Marx formulates fully only after studying the economists in the *Economic-Philosophical Manuscripts*. Marx's thesis is that alienation concerns not just the individual but the species, so that bourgeois society is a "spiritual-animal kingdom" in the precise sense that instead of living for the sake of producing like a species, human beings in civil society "work like animals" (that is, in exploitative social relations of production) in order either to make "a living" in the form of wages (if one is a worker) or in order to make "a killing," that is, to generate profit (if one is an owner of the instruments of production). Production in civil society has thanatopolitical features insofar as capital gets to live and reproduce itself by "letting die" the human species-life.

Marx establishes his famous comparison between the human species and other animal species in order to exemplify an affirmative biopolitical conception of production and to oppose it to the thanatopolitical one found in civil society. The comparison follows from a passage in *The Parts of Animals* I, 1, 640a10–640b4, in which Aristotle makes a distinction between gregarious and political animals and places both bees and human beings in the second category:

The practical creation of an *objective world*, the *fashioning* of inorganic nature, is proof that man is a conscious species-being, i.e., a being which

> treats the species as its own essential being or itself as a species-being. It is true that animals also produce. They build nests and dwellings, like the bee, the beaver, the ant, etc. But they produce only their own immediate needs or those of their young; they produce one-sidedly, while man produces universally; they produce only when immediate physical need compels them to do so, while man produces universally.... Animals produce only according to the standards and needs of the species to which they belong, while man is capable of producing according to the standards of every species and of applying to each object its inherent standard; hence man also produces in accordance with the laws of beauty. (Marx 1975, 329)

The analogy between human and animal production that Marx draws here is neither intended to reduce political activity to productive activity, and thus turn the human being into an *animal laborans*, nor is it intended to identify production as the feature that permits "humanity" to transcend animality and nature. Marx's point, instead, is that the true political character of human life emerges once production is understood as a feature of the human species-being, of human animality, rather than as the activity of an individual that stands in need of external, instrumental coordination to link up with the productive forces of other individuals.

A closer reading of the above passage shows that for Marx human production is a *generalization* of the animal's creativity, not its *overcoming*. Whereas animals are unconsciously creative, the human species creates consciously. Marx is speaking about the species, and not the individual worker. His point is that no individual worker actually produces "consciously" in this species-being sense of production: only as a species or, better, as a class, does a worker's production really become "conscious" (later he would say: "planned"). All snakes, as a species, engage in similar activities—but they do so unconsciously. Only human beings, considered as a species, have the capacity to plan their species-activities, to consciously engage in them, so long as "consciousness" here refers to class consciousness and its concept is derived directly from an analysis of the peculiar animality of the human species.

When Marx says human beings do consciously what other animal species do unconsciously, he does not mean the human species creates *unlike any other* animal species, but that the human species can create

66   *Biopolitics of the Economy*

like every other animal species, like all animals, whereas each animal species only creates what is specific to its species. Human production is the universalization of animal production; human production in no way "separates" humans from animals. This is particularly the case in human artistic production. The human condition is marked by the human being's power to be both a universal and a particular, both a thought and a thing, both supersensuous and sensuous. In a nonreified form, the work of art (according to Marx) is the symbol of this deep identity between the sensuous and the supersensuous, between matter and thought. In a reified form, this power to be simultaneously thought and thing is represented by the "form of value," which in the famous phrase of the first edition of *Capital* (which Marx later erased) relates to all other products, "as if together with and besides lions, tigers, hares and all the other real animals . . . there also existed the Animal, the individual incarnation of the whole animal kingdom."[3] That value is self-generative (money makes more money in its passage through the form of the commodity) is the upside-down mirror image of the fact that only "man creates man" (that is, that human beings create their own sociality or animality) in its passage through conscious production, that is, in its self-consciousness as species-being or animal.

Social relations allow human beings to understand themselves not as a species that has transcended all animality, but as "the Animal." Capital is self-generative because it is nothing short of the reification of human species life (or *zoe*) in the form of an individual form of life (the *bios* of the wage worker), and this personalization of production ultimately leads to the bestialization of the worker. Conversely, a communist form of production occurs whenever the *bios* of the worker takes as its sole content the *zoe* of human creation; that is, when human production becomes conscious animal creation, or simply "class consciousness." This is what is meant by Marx's famous yet obscure claim in the *Economic-Philosophical Manuscripts* that, in communism, nature is humanized and humanity is naturalized: "Only here has his *natural* existence become his *human* existence and nature become man for him. *Society* is therefore the perfected unity in essence of man with nature, the true resurrection of nature, the realized naturalism of man and the realized humanism of nature" (Marx 1975, 349–50).

MARX'S SOCIAL ONTOLOGY OF VALUE, OR THE FORGOTTEN SIDE OF THE FRANKFURT SCHOOL

The idea that an authentic social existence would be "the true resurrection of nature" (of animality), and not its denial and repression, was a decisive theme in the early Frankfurt School's theory of reification.[4] Along with the economic or scientific basis of Marx's theory of value, these themes were later jettisoned by Habermas's turn to the paradigm of communicative action.[5] The connection that Marx tried to establish between the biopolitical problem of animality and the economic problem of value was lost from sight. But within the Frankfurt School there were some notable exceptions who did continue to pursue the theory of value, such as Sohn-Rethel and Adorno's student Backhaus. The latter has had a considerable influence on the current renewal of scholarship on Marx.[6]

By translating Marx's idea of reification into the terms of Weber's process of rationalization, Lukács could understand bourgeois economics as the "science" of reified (that is, formally rationalized) entities that are human-made yet appear to human beings as if they are independent of their will and intention, as if they obey purely "natural" laws of society. Backhaus argues that the economic category of value lies at the heart of the reification of social relations, and that for this reason it became the central object of preoccupation for Marx: "Value reification [*Wertgegenständlichkeit*] is for Marx social objectivity par excellence" (Backhaus 1980, 112).[7] Lukács thought that the reification of social labor would generate a form of class consciousness, that of the proletariat, which could see through the illusion of "second" nature and return to human producers their power over their labor and its products. The late Adorno gives up on this conceit: for him "the autonomy of the domain of economy" is impermeable to subjectivity, at least in the form of class consciousness.[8] Backhaus pursues an intermediary strategy between that of the early Lukács and that of the late Adorno; he wants to provide the missing step in Lukács's program, namely, a demonstration that the self-alienation or "objectivity" of social relations is expressed in and as the "form of value."

The form of exchange-value is "universal" in the sense that money is the absolute mediation, the power over all things in civil society, the radical dissolution of all particular commodities, and yet it is also "abstract" because such power is abstracted or separated from society as a whole and appears as one more commodity on the market (Backhaus 1997, 56). Backhaus's point is that only if one shows how economics as a theory of value represents the self-alienation of social labor is it then possible to reverse the process and reconnect the theory of value to its "subjective" sources, namely, Marx's theory of the extraction of surplus value through the exploitation of living labor. Unless one knows (the structure of) *what* is being produced in capitalism (namely, a surplus of *exchange-values*), one cannot understand (the structure of) *how* it is being produced (namely, by exploiting abstract social labor-power) and vice versa. As surplus value, capital is based on a conception of value that reflects the transition, circulation, and exchange between material embodiments of value, that is, from money to commodity and from commodity back to money. Unless one discovers how this "formal" aspect of value works, until one identifies the "secret" third thing allowing something to be both money and commodity, thereby allowing for the exchange of commodities, and furthermore allowing for the exchange of value from the product to the hands of he who has not produced the thing, then one cannot return to its "material" basis or to the theory of labor as Marx envisioned it.

The contribution of Backhaus consists in questioning the tendency in Marxist theory to reduce Marx's proper theory of *value* to a Marxist theory of *labor* (as a source of *surplus* value). Perhaps one of the highpoints in this tendency consists in the polemic between Böhm-Bawerk's critique of Marx (1896) and Hilferding's reply (1904). Böhm-Bawerk had questioned the claim that the magnitude of labor determines value on the argument that the same amount of labor in two distinct products would have to determine the same value (price), but that this was not the case because prices are (also) determined by the production costs incurred by the producers, which may vary, for a series of possible reasons, while the amount of labor remains the same. Furthermore he claimed that Marx's theory of prices in volume III of *Capital*, which in his opinion was neoclassical, contradicted his theory of value in volume I. This critique, and in particular the problem of deducing prices from values, has determined a great deal of the work done in Marxist economics since.

Hilferding's reply essentially built his case on the claim that for Marx labor is the source of value "because labor is the social bond uniting an atomized society, and not because labor is the matter most technically relevant" in the production of the commodity, as Böhm-Bawerk had mistakenly imputed to Marx (Böhm-Bawerk 1975, 134). Irrespective of the strengths and weaknesses of both arguments, Hilferding's reply in the end reinforced the belief common to bourgeois economists that Marx did not contribute to the science of economics but, at best, to the sociology of labor relations (or sociology of classes): in short, that Marxist theory of value is more a sociology than an economics.[9] In contrast, Backhaus proposes to consider Marx's critique of political economy as a theory of economics and not of sociology. On his view, Marx's theory offers an explanation of economic entities and not an explanation of social entities (that is, of social relations) except that, according to Marx's account, these economic entities have an inherently social, and not natural ontology (which, in turn, is the upside-down, alienated or reified expression of the social ontology of abstract social labor). The theory of value is the economic (not sociological) account of the "social" ontology of commodities.

But if Marxist economics, generally speaking, ignores the social ontology of value and skips over the problem of value in order to focus on the theory of labor as the creation of surplus-value (and on the problem of the transformation of values into prices), then neoclassical economics for the most part operates as if exchange-value had no social ontology whatsoever. Like Böhm-Bawerk had done, it centers its analysis on prices and on the psychological mechanisms of evaluation or valorization found in individual actors. The marginalist revolution subsumes the idea of labor as principle of value under the idea of the costs of production, just as it subsumes the idea of a subjective ordering of preferences under the curve of demand. The correct market price for the commodity (the so-called natural price), the correct correlation of value to price, corresponds to the equilibrium point between both curves, that is, the point at which they intersect. With this transformation of economic theory, the question of the "form" of value simply disappears. The generation of surplus value becomes a question of generating a margin or profit, as a function of maximizing subjective gains (utility) and minimizing objective costs (by increasing efficiency). Backhaus is probably right when he affirms that bourgeois economists, ever since John Stuart Mill, have avoided the "what is it?" question concerning the "facts" of their science, namely, exchange-values. This "fear" of value (parallel to the "fear" of the masses that Balibar and Rancière identify in liberal democratic theory) explains why, after Marshall and Walras, mainstream economic science disregards questions as to the "substance" of economics and instead offers purely "functional," that is, mathematically formalized analyses of economic relations among commodities, prices, and capital.

Prior to the marginalist revolution of Marshall and Walras, classical economics was divided between two schools of thought concerning the nature of value. The objectivist school, exemplified by Ricardo, understood the value of the commodity to be determined by (abstract) labor because labor time offers a measure of what it costs to produce the commodity, namely, the time it takes labor to produce it.[10] The objective foundation of value in labor time gives a size or magnitude to the exchange-value and, thus, offers grounds for the transformation of value into price. But on Ricardo's theory, according to Marx, it becomes impossible to see how wage-labor exploits the individual who is working. In other words, it becomes impossible to see how capital (the surplus of the exchange-value) originates if one assumes that the value of the product comes from the way in which the owner disposes of the worker's labor time, which was fairly exchanged for wages in accordance with a contract.[11] With Ricardo, one misses how labor is the material basis, not of the commodity as such (considered in its cost of production or magnitude), but of the commodity as carrier of capital or surplus value because it materializes the form of value. The point is that value is "eternal": if a commodity loses in value, it is because another one gains it; value never gets lost in circulation, but passes from money to commodity and back again.[12] But if the form of value were merely given by the expenditure of labor time, as Ricardo believes, then value would be a temporal phenomenon and not an "eternal" one. This is what Marx discovers in the *Grundrisse* through his critique of Proudhon's proposal to use time-chits as money.

According to the subjectivist theory of value, found in Say and Sismondi, value is not objective. Value is not something found congealed in the product, but is a thought that exists in the mind of the producer or consumer: it corresponds to the seller or buyer's belief that the product is "scarce," that it satisfies a need, and therefore, it has a certain utility. Here, it is the subjective perception (evaluation, valorization) of the commodity's content, and not the magnitude of labor contained in it, that assigns it its exchange-value. But following the subjectivist theory of value, if money is what allows me to buy a commodity at a certain price (that I am willing to pay), it is then hard to see why this money gives power equally to all individuals who have it; this seems to contradict the apparently subjective source of valorization, which is rooted in each individual's belief. By asking this question we come to understand that money represents a *social*—not an individual—power over all commodities. The commodity's utility is not a function of its utility to one individual, but rather to society as a whole. Thus, the labor that produces this use-value (qua universally exchangeable value) must be what Marx calls a "social average labor." Only by paying attention to the "form" of value, considered over and above the "original [bourgeois] economic problem of the content and the size of value," can one follow the dis-placement of labor (which is sensuous existence) to the realm of ideas or information (which is supersensuous existence) and arrive at an understanding of the paradoxical "sensuous-supersensuous" nature of capital (Backhaus 1992, 81; Backhaus 1980, 111). On this account, the problem of the form of value offers a bridge from Marx's early account of the alienation or objectification of species-life as creative social activity to Marx's mature account of capital.

IS VALUE "THE SAME SHIT AS MONEY"?: THE NORMATIVE STRUCTURE OF VALUE IN *GRUNDRISSE*

Negri's work is to be credited with offering the first and most sophisticated biopolitical reading of Marx. In an excursus of *Multitudes*, he returns to his earlier interpretation of the *Grundrisse*, explaining that the real subsumption of labor by capital demands an explicitly biopolitical analysis of capitalism. Real subsumption, which he analyzed in *Marx Beyond Marx*, moved labor further down the road of abstraction than Marx thought possible. This subsumption gave way to a transmutation of capitalism wherein surplus value is generated by an "immaterial" or "intellectual and affective" labor producing not only commodities but also "services" or "forms of life" through which they now receive their use-value (Hardt and Negri 2005, 140–53).[13] Additionally, the focus on immaterial labor leads Negri to further question the labor theory of value; when labor becomes immaterial, what is "work" and what is "not-work" tends to blur, just as the differences between the factory or enterprise and the household tend to dissipate, making it nearly impossible to maintain that an objective measure of labor time exists, and thus of value.[14]

In my opinion, this shift from "abstract" to "immaterial" labor does not constitute a radical break with Negri's earlier reading of the *Grundrisse* as much as a radicalization of his earlier insight that capital valorizes or "subjectivizes" itself beyond its wage-form and is met by an equal and opposite subjectification or self-valorization on the part of the workers that explodes the very idea of "class," giving way to a new subject called "multitude." For this reason, a return to Negri's earlier interpretation of the *Grundrisse* is useful in considering the question of biopolitics in Marx's mature critique of political economy. The interpretation of the *Grundrisse* Negri gives in *Marx Beyond Marx* is significant in the history of Western Marxism because it signaled a shift from the theory of value to the theory of the wage-form as the fundamental element in Marx's theory, which in turn makes Negri's biopolitical approach to Marx possible. Here I propose another reading of Marx's biopolitics that retains his account of value as primary with respect to the theory of wages. This account of value is based on the immanent juridical or normative structure of capital without which it is difficult to understand the biopolitics of capital, namely, the processes of subjectivation of both capital and living labor that were rightly thematized by Negri.

Negri reads the *Grundrisse* by privileging the "Chapter on Money" over and against both the methodological "Introduction," in which Marx posits the priority of production over distribution and circulation for economics, and the "Chapter on Capital," in which Marx develops his theory of surplus value. Unlike Backhaus, Negri wishes to reduce the theory of value to the theory of money. "Value is the same shit as money" (Negri 1991, 23) except that money has the advantage of revealing whose "shit" it is: "Money has the advantage of presenting me immediately the lurid face of the social relation of value. . . . Money has only one face, that of the boss" (Negri 1991, 23). By beginning with an analysis of money, Negri claims that Marx's *Grundrisse* aims directly at the heart of the matter, at who has what and how much they have. Thus, the only political question here is who has pocketed society's wealth, or who has the people in their back pocket.

Seen from this perspective, which seeks to directly politicize the economy and economic actors, Marx's theory of value appears as an unnecessary detour: "The theory of value, as a theory of categorical synthesis, is a legacy of the classics and of bourgeois mystification" (Negri 1991, 23). For Negri, revolution essentially means "liberation from the entire form of the circulation of value, of value tout court—which is nothing but the form of the calculation of exploitation" (Negri 1991, 26). On this view, Marx was right not to include a chapter on commodities in the *Grundrisse*, whereas the fact that *Capital* begins with a chapter on commodities simply means that "*Capital* seems almost to be a propadeautic for the *Grundrisse*" (Negri 1991, 25). Not surprisingly, the term "fetishism of commodities" makes no appearance in *Marx Beyond Marx*, which seems to be written with the intention of bypassing entirely both Lukács and the Frankfurt School.

Negri is correct to think that the gap between money and political resistance to capitalism is narrower than the gap between value and political resistance. It is for good reason that "Occupy Wall Street" has some (minor) symptomatic political effects, whereas "Occupy Main Street" would be a nonstarter. Still, it is far from evident that Marx thought a theory of money would be possible without a theory of value at its basis. After all, despite Negri's claim that "the relation of exploitation is the content of the monetary equivalent" (Negri 1991, 26), the *Grundrisse* says that money is not the "representative" of the exploitation of labor, but rather of exchange-value and the "social bond is expressed in exchange-value, by means of which alone each individual's own activity or his product becomes an activity and a product for him; he must produce a general product—exchange-value, or, the latter isolated for itself and individualized, money" (Marx 1974, 32). Indeed, the entire transition from the "Chapter on Money" to the "Chapter on Capital" requires understanding that money, as measure and medium of the exchange and the circulation of values or commodities, is inextricable from a chain of equivalences and presupposes the (formal) liberty and equality of those who exchange money for commodities and commodities for money. No matter how hard one stares at a dollar bill, it cannot explain why it tends invariably to land in some pockets and not in others. Likewise, it is not easy to convince workers that they should not organize and fight for better wages; that it is a waste of time to work harder for those promotions; that tax cuts really hurt their wallets, and so on. If money had exploitation written all over it, then Negri's claim that "value is money, is this shit, to which there is no alternative but destruction: the suppression of money" (Negri 1991, 29) would acquire the force of self-evident truth.

In reality, the free circulation of money tends to connote equality rather than exploitation. That is why the French socialists at the time of Marx were overwhelmingly convinced (as many of them are still today) that the problem lay with the uneven distribution of money and credit, with the insufficient flow of money in society; therefore, the reform of the banking system was the royal road to real equality and freedom in society. The socialist solution to poverty turned on finding a way to put more cash in poor people's pockets. Proudhon, ultimately, could have had a civilized conversation with Friedman and Becker about supply-side economics and human capital theory, as on Marx's reading, Proudhon and Saint-Simonian bankers like Darimon were in fact advocating what became possible only with neoliberalism's financialization of the economy, namely, the so-called democratization of credit.

Marx begins his analysis of money in the *Grundrisse* with Darimon's banking schemes and continues his polemic against Proudhon's socialist time-chit schemes intended to pay the "fair price" for labor done precisely to prove the far-from-evident point that "one form of wage labor may correct the abuses of another, but no form of wage can correct the abuse of wage labor itself" (Marx 1974, 123; Negri 1991, 28) insofar as wage labor itself assumes that labor is a use-value like any other, forgetting that labor is always already a use-value for (increasing the amount of) exchange-value. Within a system of production of exchange-values, the very idea of paying for labor means, always already, that labor—in this relation to capital—is an exchange-value, a commodity in possession of the worker, which is exactly how Adam Smith understands it. For that very reason, Marx claims that Proudhon is unable to determine where the difference lies between use-value and exchange-value; as a result, he is unable to have a theory of value.

Negri, of course, is at the antipodes of Proudhon; his worry is that Marx's theory of value runs the risk of confusing the radical opposition between use- and exchange-value. In so doing, this theory may open the door to the argument that when the worker works for capital, she is also working for herself, and that generating exchange-values is the best way to ultimately get more and better use-values (better cars, better education, and so on), and that this is what it means not to be poor anymore. This is why, for Negri, the most important chapter of *Capital* is not the unwritten chapter on "Class" (as it was for Lukács), but the unwritten chapter on "Wage Labor." For Negri, "producing for money is at the same time a moment of exploitation and a moment of socialization. Capitalist socialization exalts the sociality of money as exploitation, while communist socialization destroys money, affirming the immediate sociality of labor" (Negri 1991, 33). The point is that, for Negri, the sociality of commodities is only possible because of the representative function of money. Since Negri assumes that money is a direct reification of labor time, it follows that an immediate, direct, and not-representative sociality among workers will destroy money and, with it, capitalism: "Communism is the negation of measure, the affirmation of the most exasperated plurality—creativity" (Negri 1991, 33). Here one can clearly see the argument that will later permit Negri to turn toward the figures of the multitude and immaterial labor.

The problem with this interpretation of money is that, for Marx, the prior sociality of commodities is the presupposition that allows money to take the form of a general object and gives money the privilege of "representing" all commodities. Commodities do not establish social relations among themselves because of the representative character of money, but, conversely, it is because they are already socialized (they are endowed with quantities of "social power"), that they can "elect," so to speak, their "constitutional" monarch, money. Money is "constitutional" precisely because it has to obey the same rules as all other commodities, namely, their generalized exchangeability. Money is a king among commodities, but it is not their tyrant. It is this implicit "normativity" of money's representative function that Negri, at this stage of his thinking, overlooks and for this reason writes as though "the boss" were an absolute monarch whose head must be cut off.

Marx's early intuition that Hegel's constitutional monarch was the political reflection of the *imperium* of money in civil society serves Marx well in the *Grundrisse* as he sets out to understand the relation between exchange-values and money. The problem of representation is not merely a political problem, a feature of sovereignty, but has its roots in the economy itself. Indeed, the relation between exchange-values and their general form (money) is entirely dependent upon a theory of representation found at the heart of the production process: "The commodity is an exchange-value because it is the realization of a *specific* amount of labor time; money not only measures the amount of labor time which the commodity represents, *but also contains its general, conceptually adequate, exchangeable form*" (Marx 1974, 167, emphasis mine). In other words, a particular labor (time) accounts for the magnitude of value contained in the commodity, but it cannot account for this magnitude's general exchangeability or equivalence with the magnitude of value contained in another commodity produced by another particular labor.

Money can be exchanged for any commodity (and vice versa) not only because it measures the amount of labor time objectified in the commodity (its value), but also because it represents something about the commodity that the particular labor did not give it, namely, its exchangeability for all other commodities. I shall refer to this exchangeability as the "equal dignity" that any commodity has with respect to other commodities, irrespective of the magnitude of labor (value) embodied in them. If commodities did not have this "sociality" *added* to them, money would be impotent to mediate their universal exchange. This "added" or "surplus" sociality is the form taken by their surplus value, which is added to commodities not by the activity of the individual worker that falls under wage labor, but by the disposable time that this wage buys—when the worker is not working for her self-reproduction but for others, that is, when society's labor is working for and through her.

This added sociality that leads to their universal exchangeability is expressed by the normative form of value (by the status of "freedom and equality") with which all commodities are born, which is their "natural right," and which finds its sublimated reflection at the level of money in the fact that any exchange of money necessarily takes the form of a contract between formally equal and free individuals. The "law of value" in Marx is not understandable unless one also points out the "value of law," without which the economy would cease to be a *political* economy.[15] This "republican" approach to political economy, attentive to the immanent constitutionality of value, is what ultimately grounds Marx's belief that the form of production determines the political and cultural forms of a society: the rights of the *bourgeoisie* mirror the "natural rights" of commodities.

In the "Chapter on Money" in the *Grundrisse*, Marx had not yet developed, or at least had not employed, the concepts of "abstract social labor" and "socially necessary labor time" to explain the condition of possibility for commodities as exchange-values, as he does in Part 1 of *Capital*. In *Capital*, Marx says that what is "contained" in all commodities as a condition for their exchangeability, "this common 'something' [is not] a natural property of commodities" but instead is the fact that all are products of "human labor in the abstract" (Marx 1976, 45), "the common substance that manifests itself in the exchange-values of commodities, whenever they are exchanged is their value" (Marx 1976, 46), and "the total labor-power of society which is embodied in such total of the values of all commodities produced by that society" (Marx 1976, 46). However, my analysis of the *Grundrisse* thus far suggests that Marx constructs the category of abstract labor precisely in order to explain what I call the "equal dignity" of all exchange-values, which does not depend on their magnitude (and thus on the particular labor time expended in their production), just like the "dignity" of any member of civil society does not depend on how much money they happen to possess at any given time.

Although money stands above all commodities and is distinct from them, it nonetheless achieves this elevation in order to stand for or represent, not itself, but the equality (equal interchangeability) of all commodities *with each other* (their "general character").[16] Since this is a critical point of contention in twentieth-century Marxism, it is worth belaboring the significance of the representative character of money, which is, after all, the conclusion of the "Chapter on Money": money is at once measure (of exchange-value), medium (of exchange), and treasure (exit from production and circulation).[17] Money is the monarchic-constitutional representation of the democracy of exchange-values; if all commodities were not exchangeable for money, no particular commodity could have the self-certainty that it is the equal of (the sum) of any other commodity. Marx does not think that money "commands" over commodities in a tyrannical way, as Negri's analysis sometimes leads us to believe. Rather, properly understood, money runs after commodities like a politician runs after the votes of his constituency. How many votes a commodity represents corresponds to how much exchange-value it contains, that is, how much alienated social power has gone into it in the production process. But the fact that a commodity is the place where social power is transmuted into electoral votes, which then attracts money (that is, attracts the politician, who is here an analogon to the price), is only understandable through the theory of the form of value. That this theory of value, and not the labor process itself, is democratically structured can be seen in the fact that "money can't buy votes" at the social level: no matter how much money the politician throws at his electors, it will not change the value of the commodity (analogous to the number of votes that any elector has to give).

The above discussion of the representative and constitutional character of money is fundamental in order to understand Marx's critique of what can be called the *pathos*-formula of capitalism, namely, Benjamin Franklin's dictum that "time is money." One of Marx's achievements in the *Grundrisse* is precisely to explain why Adam Smith is partially wrong when he "says that labor (labor time) is the original money with which all commodities are purchased" (Marx 1974, 167), and thus why it is false that (labor) time is (convertible into) money. Money expresses the fact that all products belong in a community; it expresses the equality of commodities, their "equal dignity," insofar as all commodities are equally products of one common substance of social labor: "The quantity of labor time must not be expressed in its immediate, particular product but in a mediated, general product . . . of the labor time not in a particular commodity, but in all commodities at once, and hence in a particular commodity which represents all others" (Marx 1974, 168). This is the concept of "average social labor time" found later in *Capital*. This concept corresponds to the basic intuition in Marx that all productive activity takes place thanks to a social relation between producers that is represented (alienated) by money understood as the form of the social relation between commodities: "In exchange-value, the social connection between persons is transformed into a social relation between things; personal capacity into objective wealth" (Marx 1974, 157).

The mistake of the bourgeois theory of value as found in Ricardo and Adam Smith is the belief that a specific measure of labor time is contained in each particular product. Marx denies this:

> Labor time cannot be directly money (a demand which is the same as demanding that every commodity should simply be its own money) precisely because in fact labor time always exists only in the form of particular commodities (as an object): being a general object [that is, considered as average social labor time] it can exist only symbolically, and hence only as a particular commodity which plays the role of money. Labor time does not exist in the form of a general object of exchange . . . but it would have to exist in that form if it were directly to fulfil the demands placed on money. The objectification of the general, social character of labor . . . is precisely what makes the product of labor time into exchange-value; this is what gives commodity the attributes of money which, however, in turn imply the existence of an independent and external money-subject. (Marx 1974, 167)

This passage contains a decisive critique of Ricardo and Adam Smith: seen from the perspective of the eternity of value, labor time has no price, time is not money.[18] The theory of surplus value finds here its condition of possibility, for surplus value is possible only because time is not, as such, money. The key insight is found in the opposition that Marx sets up between the particular amount of labor time needed to produce a particular use-value, and the general, social labor time expressed in that commodity which makes it into an exchange-value by virtue of giving it its general form of value (universal exchangeability) represented by money which, in turn, is functional to the production of surplus value. Marx adds that Adam Smith failed to capture the fetishism of the commodity because he does not see "in" the commodity, but merely "alongside" it, the double nature of time as "particular" labor time needed to produce the particular product, and "labor time as general object" needed to produce the universal exchangeability of the commodity (Marx 1974, 169). This dualism of time, which is constitutive of the commodity qua exchange-value, is the condition of possibility for the surplus theory of value, which simply spells out the contradiction between the two times: the labor time that is not money (the "necessary" time of labor that serves to reproduce the life of the worker), and the labor time (as general object) that is the reproduction of money (that is., that is capital as self-generative money, money making money). This contradiction is then perceived by Marx, in his "Chapter on Capital," to be the contradiction between the time it takes to reproduce labor-power, the time of the life of the worker, and the "disposable time" in the hands of the capitalist, which is the time of money or capital.

The Spinozist vocabulary employed by Marx to set up the analogy between the eternity of value and the eternity of substance is helpful to illustrate the fallacy in the belief that particular (labor) time is money. Since money represents the substance of value, the belief that particular (labor) time measures value is equivalent to the false belief that one can measure an absolute and infinite substance by placing next to each other the finite modes that it eternally produces and destroys. It is only as an expression of an intensive, not extensive magnitude that a commodity (mode) relates directly to value (substance) but this relation cannot be measured by money; it is, to cite a recent credit card advertisement, "priceless." Conversely, any portion of social substance is always convertible or measureable in an extensive magnitude (a sum, a combination) of commodities, and it is money that makes the latter calculation possible. This is why the equality of labor time with value posited by Smith and Ricardo can receive a price and is convertible into money. Prices are always prices for commodities, not for the particular labor time expressed in them (since time is not money, time has no price). Social labor time does not match, one to one, with the finished product, but only with the total sum of them: this is why their exchangeability and interchangeability are essential in order to make money out of this character of social time, which is what allows for the creation of surplus value.

Marx observed that the price one pays for each product or commodity is never its actual value, but is always above or below the average social labor time that it takes to produce it. The explanation for this phenomenon is that the surplus social labor that goes into any commodity is objectified not in the commodity that is its product, but in the universal exchangeability of that commodity for a combination of other commodities (Marx 1976, 57n1). Thus it gets expressed in money because the surplus value is congealed not in the product of living labor, but in its equivalent form, as a combination or sum of other commodities: "Linen = coat is the basic equation" of capital (Marx 1976, 56). The difference between Adam Smith and Marx, in this respect, is that, for Adam Smith, time is only an extensive magnitude while, for Marx, time is also an intensive magnitude. Ultimately, Marx's point is simply that time, and not use-value, is the substance of real wealth. Once human beings become aware of this, capitalism becomes an impossibility.[19]

FROM VALUE'S SUBSTANCE TO THE SUBJECTIVITY OF VALUE: BIOPOLITICS OF CAPITAL

Whereas Marx's account of value is based on a concept of (social) substance and its eternity, his account of surplus value is based on a concept of subjectivity and its temporality. The *Grundrisse*, in this sense like Hegel's *Phenomenology of Spirit*, seeks to understand value (in Hegel it was spirit) not only as substance but also as subject. My claim is that the passage from substance to subjectivity is constituted biopolitically. In the preceding reading of Hegel, I showed how self-consciousness takes up two entirely different and opposed forms of life in the master and the slave according to whether the sense of life is understood as *bios* or as *zoe*. Likewise in Marx, the substance of value attains its truth in two forms of antagonistic subjectivity: on the one hand, as capital or "self-generative" value and, on the other hand, as class conscious living labor. The subjectivity of capital depends on reducing the species-life of human beings to the *bios* of the worker, whereas the subjectivity of living labor emerges only once the worker sheds the illusion of bourgeois individualism and legal personality in order to adopt a form of class or species consciousness. The crucial transition from substance to subjectivity occurs in a process Marx calls the "real subsumption" of labor under capital. Negri's analysis of the *Grundrisse* leads him to offer a biopolitical interpretation of Marx because he follows the guiding-thread of this process of real subsumption. The question is whether the meaning of real subsumption carries the biopolitical consequences that Negri points out.

The turning point in Marx's argument in the *Grundrisse* from an analysis of value to an analysis of surplus value depends on refuting Adam Smith's and Ricardo's assumption that living labor can be directly equated with value or money. If it could be, then it is conceivable that some form of wage labor could be a "fair" payment for the worker's services, and then there would be no creation of surplus value in production and, hence, no capitalism. Labor time is not identical with value because "labor time itself exists as such only subjectively, only in the form of activity . . . labor time as subject corresponds as little to the general labor time which determines exchange-values as the particular commodities and products correspond to it as object" (Marx 1974, 171). There exists a fundamental opposition between the temporality of the subjectivity of the worker, and the temporality ("the general, self-equivalent labor time") that gives the commodity its subjectivity or "fetishistic" character. Labor time is not just a quantitative magnitude of value. Its reality or ontology as living labor is that of qualitative difference, singularity, antagonism, and finally, contradiction.

Marx leaves little doubt as to the biopolitical character of living, subjective labor. He speaks of it as "this *complete denudation, purely subjective existence of labor . . . labor as absolute poverty*: poverty not as shortage but as total exclusion of objective wealth. . . . Labor not as an object, but as activity, not itself as value but as the living source of value. [Namely it is] general wealth (in contrast to capital which exists objectively, in reality)" (Marx 1974, 295–96). The terms used to describe the power or capacity of living labor resemble the vocabulary that Agamben uses to speak about bare life. Like in Agamben, bare life has a double biopolitical connotation: it is the "absolute poverty" of workers when compared to the "wealth" of objectified labor or capital; at the same time, it is "the living source of value" and thus equivalent to "general wealth."

Negri's interpretation of the *Grundrisse* focuses on this dualism of bare life: his idea is precisely that living labor can win its "autonomy" against wage labor and capital, can escape from the subsumption of capital, when it makes its "absolute poverty" (in relation to capital) into a form of life.[20] The "autonomy" of living labor with respect to wage labor is what Negri calls the process of the self-valorization of workers, which undermines the self-valorization of exchange-value in the form of capital: "The workers' opposition [to the forced nature of its exploitation], the proletariat struggle, tries continually to broaden the sphere of nonwork, that is, the sphere of their own needs, the value of necessary labor" (Negri 1991, 71).[21] Interpreting Marx's dictum that "the real not-capital is labor" (Marx 1974, 274), Negri concludes that living labor needs to be understood as "not-work" (by which he means not-wage labor). The subjectivity of the worker is affirmed only where she is active outside of the form of salary.

In his earlier interpretation of the *Grundrisse* Negri maintains that capital and living labor confront each other as two mutually antagonistic forces because the real subsumption of use-value by exchange-value (of laborpower by capital) is ultimately achieved by force: "Its [living labor's] relation with exchange-value, that is, with command, property, capital is immediately forced ... the foundation of the capital relation, the forced closure of radically distinct elements, is irrational, and also inhuman" (Negri 1991, 68). Because Negri thinks that living labor has a use-value that is "radically distinct" from the use given to it in the capitalist process of production when it is subsumed under exchange-value (and its pursuit of profit), exchange-value becomes entirely "ideological" and "superstructural" to capitalism (Negri 1991, 67). Only living labor and use-value are considered by Negri to be biopolitical, but not the relations of production determined by exchange-value and its self-reproductive dynamic. My interest in the *Grundrisse*, by way of contrast, lies in identifying how the real subsumption of living labor by capital, of use-value by exchange-value, is a process driven by a biopolitical process of normalization and not simply by force or command. My claim is that this normalization of living labor depends on the worker internalizing the inherent constitutional, normative structure of exchange-value.

These two different approaches to the role played by biopolitics in real subsumption can be illustrated through Marx's use of Adam Smith's distinction between "productive" labor and "unproductive" labor (Marx 1974, 273), that is, between labor that produces exchange-values and labor that does not. Negri rejects this distinction because it throws into question his claim that the use-value of living labor *as such* is counter to exchange-value (Negri 1991, 64). On my reading, Marx holds onto Adam Smith's distinction between productive and unproductive labor for another reason entirely; for Marx, if living labor is going to generate exchange-value, then it must always already be subsumed under the form (the normativity) of exchange-value. Living labor must be wage labor in order for it to multiply exchange-value. Since wage labor is itself based on exchange and on its juridical, contractual framework (on the "constitutional" monarchy that is money), Marx's point is that the juridical structure of exchange-value is not "ideological" or external to the creation of value in and through labor. Rather, this juridical structure is what converts living labor into wage labor, thereby *generating* exchange-value and, thus, capital. Otherwise, there would be no explanation for why living labor, which Marx defines as the "living, form-giving fire; it is the transitoriness of things, their temporality, as their formation by living time" (Marx 1974, 361), should ever give rise to the "eternal" substance of exchange-value.

The use-value of living labor "becomes a reality only when it has been solicited by capital" (Marx 1974, 267; Marx 1976, 277). Living labor is "actualized" or can be put to work only when it belongs to the worker as her private property and thus can be sold: "As soon as it has obtained motion from capital, this use-value exists as the worker's specific, productive activity; it his vitality itself" (Marx 1974, 268). Wages do not pay for the use of living labor as such; they pay for the reproduction of the worker, for her "livelihood," as something independent and separable from her work or product (that is, the commodity). By definition, such payment would be impossible if living labor had not already become the "property" of the worker, that which she uses to reproduce herself and from which she "makes a living." That is why Marx puts these words in the mouth of the worker in her fictional negotiation strategy with the capitalist: "Like a sensible, thrifty owner of property I will husband my sole wealth, my labor-power, and abstain from wasting it foolishly" (Marx 1976, 343). The real subsumption of living labor under exchange-value requires a "normalization" of living labor that makes labor-power the "property" of a worker, which she can exchange for her "livelihood." But if the capitalist only got out of living labor what he paid for it, that is, if he made the worker work for the time that corresponds to her wages, as objectified labor time, then he would get no profit in return (Marx 1974, 321). The surplus lies entirely in the exchange of objectified or "dead" labor (wages), which pays for the "livelihood" of the worker, for the use of the species-vitality of living labor found in the worker (what Marx calls "value-positing activity") (Marx 1974, 323), which creates more value (the owner's profit). Marx says that this exchange of dead labor for disposable living labor is not really an exchange "because the capitalist has paid the price of only half a working day [to keep the worker alive] but has obtained a whole day objectified in the product, thus has exchanged nothing for the second half of the work day. The only thing which can make him into a capitalist is not exchange, but rather a process through which he obtains objectified labor time, i.e. value, in excess of the equivalent... The second half of the labor day is forced labor, surplus labor" (Marx 1974, 324). Yet this "not-exchange" (Marx 1974, 321) that is the process of real subsumption of use-value under exchange-value contained in the wage is not merely "theft" on the part of the capitalist because capital does not simply "take" from the workers because it "gives" them work to begin with, and hence their "livelihood." The "not-exchange" refers to the switch between a situation in which living labor produces value to a situation in which the production of value is the source of livelihood of the worker.

In capitalist relations of production, it is exchange-value as capital that makes for living labor, in the sense that capital already posits the product that is to be made by the worker in exchange for the worker's livelihood: "The labor objectified in the exchange-value posits living labor as means of reproducing it, whereas, originally, exchange-value appeared merely as product of labor" (Marx 1974, 263). Without presupposing the form of value, living labor cannot, as such, make exchange-values, for "in no moment of the production process does capital cease to be capital or value to be value, and, as such, exchange-value" (Marx 1974, 311). Capital as a surplus of value never loses "its economic-form character [*Formbestimmung*] in general," namely, the form of (exchange-) value itself. If wages were merely exchanged for labor, as a medium between two use-values (for example, money to buy food for the worker, a product of labor for the owner), as

Living Labor and Self-Generative Value in Marx 85

Adam Smith and Ricardo hold, then wage labor could never acquire more exchange-value, that is, a surplus of value. But in the cycle of capitalist production, living labor, which produces use-values, is merely the medium that allows for one exchange-value to pass on to a higher exchange-value, to increase value: "In the exchange of capital for labor, value is not the measure for the exchange of two use-values [as in 'the exchange of money for labor or service, with the aim of direct consumption'] but is rather the content of the exchange itself" (Marx 1974, 469). It is only because, from the start, capital posits the object of production as being an infinitely exchangeable commodity that it requires not labor capacity as such (pure use-value—Marx says that labor capacity is the "fire" of things, what gives them use-value) but merely the objectified labor of the worker, the "output" of the worker as part of the process that makes the commodity.[22] The commodity determines the work that needs to be done, and this work in turn determines the worker and not vice versa: "Use-value for capital as such is only value itself. Circulating capital realizes itself as value for capital as such only when it is sold. . . . . Fixed capital, by contrast, realizes itself as value only as long as it remains in the capitalist's hand as a use-value, as long as it remains in the production process, which may be regarded as the inner organic movement of capital, its relation to itself, as opposed to animal movement, its presence for another" (Marx 1974, 680). Capital becomes an "organic movement," a paradoxical metabolic process that eats up living labor (here equivalent to what Marx calls "animal movement") as a mere use-value for exchange-value. In turn, value "generates" living labor in the form of the "livelihood" of the worker.

Capital is thus biopolitical in two ways: first, it must become the source of the worker's "livelihood" (*bios*); second, it must become "self-generative" or "subjectivity" in virtue of creating the kind of labor (creating "jobs") that makes possible the "organic" self-reproduction of value, as if capital were a living species. The power of living labor to give birth to the human species as *zoe* gets limited, controlled, fettered, and cut off in the form of wage labor, which does not serve the reproduction of the human species, but simply the reproduction of the worker (*bios*), on one side, and of capital as pseudo or surplus "life," on the other. Both wage labor and capital emerge from the fact that living labor—as the creation of use-values—comes under the control, under the normalizing power, of exchange-value. The passage in Marx from natality (living labor) to normativity (capital as self-reproduction of money) is made possible by a moment of normalization (found in exchange-value). This is the biopolitical nucleus of Marx's critique of political economy.

Two consequences follow from this analysis of real subsumption: first, the form of exchange-value remains the key to the production of surplus value. Marx's last definition of capital given in the *Grundrisse* is formulated entirely in terms of the complete subsumption of use-value by exchange-value: "Capital is now realized not only as value which reproduces itself and is hence perennial but also as value which posits value. Through the absorption of living labor time and through the movement of its own circulation it relates to itself as positing new value, as producer of value" (Marx 1974, 744). Capital is here described as a metabolic, living process through which value "absorbs" or subsumes living labor for the sake of generating its own "perennial" or "eternal" life. Surplus value is a surplus in the form of value because what capital is paying for, in order to be "self-sufficient" and thus reproduce itself, is not the species life of the worker, but merely her livelihood. In this sense, capital is not reproducing species life for all the time that capital needs it to reproduce itself as value.

When living labor becomes thus subsumed under exchange-value, it takes the form of "general industriousness as the general property of the new species." "This is why capital is productive, i.e., an essential relation for the development of the social productive forces": capitalist relations of production set all of society to work for itself. The new species created by capital is that of the "worker" who lives from her wages. Marx uses, appropriately enough, a biopolitical term: capitalism produces another form of life, the *bios* of the worker which, when compared with the *zoe* of the human species-life is indeed a form of bare life.

The second consequence of this analysis is that a fundamental contradiction emerges in the capitalist process of production, a biopolitical contradiction: capital needs the living labor of the species all the time, but it only reproduces living labor part of the time (qua bare life of the individual worker). Thus, by subsuming the living labor of the species as wage labor of the individual, capital is unable, out of its own resources, to maintain species-life for the entire time it requires it. The "new species" of the worker establishes for capital an unsurpassable barrier: "It [capital] ceases to exist as such only where the development of these productive forces themselves encounters its barrier in capital itself" (Marx 1974, 325). Industriousness comes along with the development of machinery in order to raise the productivity of labor that, in turn, results from scientific advances and an economy of knowledge that makes use of the increased disposable time in ways that stand in contradiction with the use made of it by capital.

FROM THE LAW OF SURPLUS VALUE TO THE NOMOS OF SURPLUS LIFE

The real subsumption of use-value by exchange-value turns the process of capital formation into an "organic" quasi-biological process where money reproduces money as if it were its own living species. According to the *Grundrisse* this living process of capital is ultimately contradictory, in the sense that it is incapable of sustaining the species-life of the workers and leads capitalism into necessary crises of overproduction of commodities and consequent destruction of productive capacities (this is the thanatopolitical side of capitalism). Since Foucault's work on biopolitics, the biologization of capitalism foreseen by Marx has received new interpretations in an effort to explain why capitalism got a new lease on life beyond the Marxist predictions of its inevitable demise. In particular, it is the relation between surplus value and what I called above "surplus life" that offers new perspectives to understand why the contradictions of capital that Marx identified may function differently in neoliberal capitalism.

The *Grundrisse* not only contains Marx's first systematic account of surplus value but also a systematic development of his ideas about the necessary crisis and demise of capitalist relations of production. This discourse about the crisis and contradiction of capitalism is articulated around the idea of living labor as both a limit (*Grenze*) and a barrier (*Schranke*) to capital. Marx argues that capital is continuously setting its own limits in order to go beyond them. Capital is created by surplus time and is the opposite of the necessary time required for the worker to reproduce her own life. In this sense, the worker's necessary time is opposed to capital's disposable time: it is a limit for capital. Capital overcomes this limit by multiplying it: it seeks to multiply workers and, thus, to increase necessary time (Marx 1974, 334–35). Marx says that capital "puts to work" its money in order to create new sources of labor to exploit; this is how money makes money (Marx 1974, 348).

More industriousness means the need for more workers (Marx 1974, 400–401), but it also means that there is less work to go around because of the use of more and better machines, and thus less necessary labor time and less possibility of worker exploitation. Marx distinguishes between "relative" surplus value, defined by the productivity of labor within its capital relation, and "absolute" surplus value, defined by the increase in working time. Relative surplus value is always a function of a decrease in necessary labor (Marx 1974, 339–40). The increase of surplus labor time is possible only by a decrease in necessary labor time (Marx 1974, 384). Thus, when the productivity of living labor increases, less of it is needed to generate the same value, which means that less disposable time for capital becomes available, hence, a reduction in the rate of increase in profits: "The value of capital does not grow in the same proportion as the productive force increases, but in the proportion in which the increase of the productive force, the multiplier of productive force, divides the fraction of the working day which expresses the part of the day belonging to the worker" (Marx 1974, 337). Since the increase in surplus labor time is not relative to a multiplier of productive forces but is relative to a surplus of the fraction of the living work day that represents necessary labor, in excess of the same fraction divided by the multiplier of the productive force, it follows that there is one true "barrier" for capital's self-reproduction, and this is necessary labor: the greater the rate of increase in productivity, the lesser the rate at which necessary labor time diminishes, and thus the lesser the rate at which profits increase.

In the *Grundrisse*, Marx formulates the claim that the rates of profit tend to diminish with greater productivity as a "law of capital": capital has the "tendency therefore to create as much labor as possible; just as it is equally its tendency to reduce necessary labor to a minimum" (Marx 1974, 399). The former is achieved by fomenting industriousness and rising population; the latter occurs through increases in productivity and lower wages: "Capital exists only in so far as necessary labor both exists and does not exist" (Marx 1974, 401). Capital is "the living contradiction" (Marx 1974, 421–22). The adjective here—"living"—is to be taken biopolitically: capital needs to reduce necessary labor time and thus make the *bios* of the worker more precarious; at the same time capital needs to multiply the working population as a source of living labor. Capital both seeks to impoverish life (of workers) and to multiply this bare life.[23]

In *Marx Beyond Marx* Negri gives the first biopolitical reading of Marx's theory of capitalism's inherent contradiction. He interprets the "law of capital," according to which there is a necessary decline of the rate of profit, as if it were a "law" that describes the resistance posed by living labor to its subsumption under exchange-value. "The more labor is objectified into capital and capital is increased . . . all the more living labor opposes this growth in an antagonistic fashion. The more capital posits itself as profit-creating power . . . then the more living labor estranges itself from capitalist growth in a social and compact form" (Negri 1991, 90). Negri thus replaces Lukács's theory of revolution by way of attaining class consciousness by a theory of resistance to wage labor where revolution passes through the self-valorization of workers. As such, for Negri, "The *Grundrisse* aims at a theory of subjectivity of the working class against the profitable theory of capitalist subjectivity" (Negri 1991, 97). The emphasis is placed on the worker "investing" in her life in terms of expanding her needs and pleasures: "Necessary labor can valorize itself autonomously, the world of needs can and must be expanded" (Negri 1991, 101). The creation of surplus capital is met, according to Negri, by an equal and opposite creation of forms of surplus life by living labor.

Negri's lectures on *Marx Beyond Marx* coincide in time and space with Foucault's *Courses* in which he was elaborating on biopolitics. In hindsight, it is difficult not to see an affinity between Negri's discourse of self-valorization on the part of living labor and Foucault's discourse on biopolitics as a creation of "surplus life." Foucault seems to have understood this "surplus" in two, opposite ways. First, life poses a resistance to its subsumption by the apparatuses of power/knowledge, which Foucault had previously shown was crucial to the generalized industriousness of civil society: "It is not that life has been totally integrated into techniques that govern and administer it; it constantly escapes them" (Foucault 1990, 143). Second, the idea of a "surplus life" is understood by Foucault as a result of what he calls governmentality or "police." The aim of the police is that of *"permanently increasing production of something new*, which is supposed to *foster the citizens' life* and the state's strength. The police govern not by the law, but by a specific, a permanent and a positive intervention in the behaviour of individuals" (Foucault 2000, 415, emphasis mine). In this general sense of the term, "police" activity can be understood in terms of those policies and techniques of control that sustain the species-life of human beings (for example, by looking after the increase and health of the population) and in that way dissipate the "living contradiction" of capital according to which the increase in surplus value necessarily pushes the lives of workers into bare life.

Recent interpretations of Foucault's concepts of governmentality and of police, for instance in the work of Lemke, understand their apparatuses as functional to the process of the real subsumption of living labor under exchange-value.[24] As Foucault illustrates in *The Birth of Biopolitics*, neoliberal governmentality further normalizes the *bios* of the worker in the direction of the ideal of an "entrepreneur" of one's own life. The normative structure of exchange-value does not limit itself at recognizing the "rights" of workers to own and negotiate the value of their labor-power, but in addition it endows them with new "rights" over their biological lives and expects them to be morally responsible for increasing their "quality of life."[25] The analysis of what Lemke calls "the political economy of life" in reality confirms that the "police" promotes the "value" of life very much under the logic of real subsumption, since the goal remains that of augmenting the *bios* of the worker as a use-value for exchange-value.[26]

What Negri calls the self-valorization of the worker, or the affirmation of the subjectivity of living labor, falls ambiguously between the sense of "surplus life" as resistance to power and the sense of "surplus life" as a further realization and radicalization of real subsumption under exchange-value. Thus, living labor manages to resist its subsumption under capital only as "the abstract collectivity of labor's subjective power (*potenza*)" (Negri 1991, 70). This "abstract collectivity" in which bare life becomes the true wealth of a society later receives the name of "multitude," and the new source of real wealth is identified by the name of "the common" in the *Empire, Multitude,* and *Commonwealth* trilogy. In *Marx Beyond Marx* Negri argues that only by withdrawing itself from exchange relations can living labor find itself in a "natural" collectivity or sociality. He writes, "The liberation of living labor exalts its creative power, the abolition of work is what gives it its life in every moment" (Negri 1991, 160).[27] An important change in Negri's views with respect to *Marx Beyond Marx* takes place with the later work written with Hardt, in the sense that Negri and Hardt seem to abandon the claim that severing use-value from exchange relations will give rise to more "natural" collective relations. Negri and Hardt now seem to uphold the position that subjective labor needs to construct its own collectivity, its own sociality, if it is going to resist capital and its governmentality. According to their model, it is the very process of real subsumption of living labor under exchange-value that leads to the collectivization of labor ("the common") by requiring living labor to produce not only commodities but actual forms of life, or sociality itself. This is what they mean by the claim that living labor becomes "immaterial" labor. But the turn toward an idea of immaterial labor also brings Negri and Hardt close to advocating a *Vitalpolitik* of living labor that matches the *Vitalpolitik* of neoliberal governmentality studied by Foucault. In fact, in their latest book, *Commonwealth*, Negri and Hardt go so far as to offer positive biopolitical proposals to capital, and they speak of the need "for a new expansion of productive forces and an unfettered production of the common—in order, in other words, to save capital—a politics of freedom, equality and democracy of the multitude is necessary" (Hardt and Negri 2009, 302). They now advocate a "reformist program for capital" whose purpose is "to provide the necessities for developing entrepreneurship of the common and the innovation of cooperative social networks" (Hardt and Negri 2009, 307).

Negri and Hardt's advocacy of a paradoxical "entrepreneurship" of living labor within "cooperative social networks" of exchange is indicative of their having returned to Marx's original point in the *Grundrisse* according to which bare life cannot become collective or social *prior* to being subsumed in capitalist relations of production, *prior* to use-value being entirely taken up by exchange-value. Indeed, it is hard to see how one could build these interconnections or networks of subjectivities without exchange and, thus, without exchange-value, since abstract living labor without networks would be impotent (it would lack what Negri calls *potenza*). The point is that only a generalization of exchange-value, as Marx already sees in the *Grundrisse*, gives rise to those networks of knowledge that ultimately brings down capital relations of production by providing an alternative model of coordinating and exchanging the use-value of living labor.

In the famous "Fragment on Machines" of the *Grundrisse*, Marx indicates how the subsumption of use-value in exchange-value that makes possible capital's self-reproduction tends toward the replacement of the worker as worker; it detaches value from material labor and makes it depend on the "immaterial labor" of knowledge creation. Capitalism needs knowledge because it enables higher productivity of labor and thus a decrease in necessary labor time, which amounts to more disposable time and profits. But as Marx shows science and technology also facilitates more free time from labor itself, and without disposable labor time there can be no capital increase. Thus, the more productive labor becomes by virtue of it being done by machines that embody more knowledge, the less living labor is needed, and the smaller the rate of profit, since profit is made only through variable capital, that is, through the exchange of wages for labor capacity. Since capital investment in knowledge production entails diminished necessary time, less workers become available for capital, thus increasing the rate of unemployment. If workers are not increased, then capital cannot continue to reproduce itself, and this increase in population requires state expenditure, leading to higher rates of inflation. The conflicting demands of keeping both the rates of unemployment and the rates of inflation as low as possible, which is the basic dilemma of macroeconomics in civil society, is an expression of their ultimate conceptual dependence on Marx's law of surplus value, that is, the law of decreasing rate of profit. Marx says that the latter is "in every respect the most important law of modern political economy" (Marx 1974, 748), and it leads to the suspension of capital because "the capital relation [is] a barrier for the development of the productive powers of labor" (Marx 1974, 749).

Thus, Marx's infamous "law of capital" can be understood as formulating the irreducibility of a thinking species-life (*zoe*) to the working life of the individual, to the *bios* of the worker. Thinking is not part of the use-value of the worker for exchange-value. Marx considers that the production of knowledge (science) is a form of production that is inherently social rather than individualistic: knowledge acquisition requires the establishment of a network of subjective nodes that bring together useful knowledge wherever it may reside, since it is the most widespread and best distributed thing there is. This is one of the senses of Marx's idea of a "general intellect." Scientific production is not part of the reproduction of the worker (= necessary time) because it is social production; thus, capital's investment in science does not give the expected return in heightened productivity. It does not diminish necessary time, and thus, the rate of profit is less.

One of the most interesting ways in which neoliberal theory and practice registers this shift toward a generalization of exchange (in the form of general intellect and immaterial labor) is found in Hayek's attempt to redescribe the social ontology of value in terms of the idea of a network

Living Labor and Self-Generative Value in Marx 93

of exchange, or *catallaxy*, and the juridical *nomos* such a network presupposes. According to both classical and marginalist economics, prices are determined by the interactions between people (producers and owners, sellers and buyers). Hayek suggests looking at the concept of equilibrium from the assumption that peoples' interactions with each other are a function of prices. The equilibrium that prices reflect is not a function of human intentional actions, but rather must be understood as a function of the way in which commodities behave with each other. Hayek, in other words, accentuates and universalizes the phenomenon that Marx identifies as the fetishism of commodities. Value is certainly not a quality of a substance, but it is also not a result of the subject's valorization. Rather, value is generated by the generalized exchangeability made possible by networks of communication in which subjects and things are embedded. Prices reflect neither something in the object nor something in the subject. Instead, they reflect the exchanges taking place in these networks that allow for the gathering and processing of dispersed information (plus transaction costs of computing or aggregating the information) so as to make possible both the object and the subject. According to this view, prices are the result of a *catallaxy* (a network of exchange, a "free market") when the latter is understood as a gigantic computation machine or neural network of information processing. On this model, competition becomes the *nomos*, the internal substantive normative order that permits the calculation and growth (the aggregation) of this network of information, information that is itself asymmetrically distributed along the nodes of a network. Hayek's concept of *catallaxy* thus overlaps with many of the insights found in Marx's reflections on the connection between science and economics, as well as the concepts of general intellect and immaterial labor that explain the meaning of his "law of capital." But Hayek exploits the inner normativity or governmentality of value in order to offer a new justification and explanation of capitalism.

But it is not only the normativity of value that is employed by neoliberalism in order to attempt to dissipate the effects of Marx's "law of value." The dimension of natality associated with species life comes under the dynamics of subsumption of living labor by capital according to some recent analysts of biocapitalism. In particular, Cooper has traced the creation of surplus value in neoliberalism as a function of the production of "life as surplus" through biotechnology. In the case of the bioeconomy, the extraction of surplus value from biological life requires that life be manipulated, controlled, and ultimately pushed beyond its "natural" limits so as to generate an excess or surplus of biological life. Examples range from microbial life that thrives in extreme conditions, to new immunitary devices, and from self-assembling artificial life forms to technologies of in-vitro fertilization and embryonic stem cell lines. What all these biotechnologies share is the idea that the "surplus" of life is found in life's dimension of natality, that is, in what Marx identified as the capacity of "man to create man," of *zoe* to begin itself repeatedly.[28] Here we have an attempt to subsume use-value under exchange-value not by way of normalization, as discussed above, but somehow and improbably through natality itself.

Marx claims in *The Economic-Philosophic Manuscripts* that the self-creation of the human species, the dimension of natality, makes the belief in God's Creation not simply false but nonsensical, and that is why communists were not atheists. These implications of natality make clear why the bioeconomy is not only a crucial concept for neoliberals (who as a norm are atheists) but also for neoconservatives (who are not). It is no accident that the twin concepts of the un-born and the born-again play a fundamental role in neoconservative thinking. Indeed, when natality is reified as a source for a surplus of biological life it presents itself in the form of the promise of an "after-life" in one's own lifetime. Cooper argues that neoconservatives, at least in the United States, do not wish to see this potential of natality realized because that would effectively render the belief in Creation (and Final Judgment) moot, not simply according to current scientific theory (which can always be denied, or children forced to learn creationist doctrine at school) but in the lived experience of everyone enjoying the fruits of such an after-life during their earthly lives (fruits which no religious belief can match). For this reason, Cooper argues that neoconservatives reassert "actual limits" on the speculative nature of the biological after-life: the promise of the after-life is realized, and limited to, the un-born, whose right to life becomes the decisive political issue. For Cooper, neoconservatism figures the "struggle to reimpose the property form in and over the uncertain future. This property form, as the right-to-life movement makes clear, is inextricably economic and sexual, productive and reproductive. It is ultimately a claim over the bodies of women" (Cooper 2008, 171). Cooper sees here a verification of Marx's theory of living labor as a barrier to capital formulated in the *Grundrisse*; the emancipatory

Living Labor and Self-Generative Value in Marx

force of the promise in a biological, immanent after-life tied to embryonic research finds a barrier in the religious fundamentalist regulation of reproductive forces and liberties modeled on a patriarchical and heterosexual *nomos* of the family and marriage, very much in the same way that Marx postulated that capitalist forms of production eventually become a barrier to the inherently emancipatory development of productive forces they make possible. The biopolitics of natality, the promise of the unborn and the faith in the possibility of rebirth in this life, are topics better dealt with through an analysis of the *nomos* of family and sexuality in civil society attempted in the chapters of the following section.

PART II

Biopolitics of the Family

3

REIFICATION AND REDEMPTION OF BARE LIFE IN ADORNO AND AGAMBEN

BARE LIFE AS THRESHOLD OF SOVEREIGN POWER

In *Homo Sacer* Agamben argues that the project of total domination over life, which comes into its own with totalitarian and biopolitical forms of power, depends on a logic of sovereignty that has run through Western civilization since its origins in Greece and Rome. According to this logic, every legal system, in order to enforce its norms, must capture the bare life of its addressees in a virtual state of exception to its own laws (Agamben 1998, 27). Bare life (*nuda vita*) is a concept that Agamben develops from Benjamin's expression *das blosse Leben* found in his early writings like "The Critique of Violence" and "Goethe's Elective Affinities." These writings put forward the thesis that fate manifests itself mythically as violence over bare life, and that such violence of fate is "identical to lawmaking violence" (Benjamin 1996, 248). The legitimate violence that legal systems employ to enforce their own legal ends appears to Benjamin as a manifestation (and no longer a means) of a more primordial, mythical power over natural life. Symbolic of this power over life is the Greek myth of Niobe, who was punished by the gods for taking pride in her powers of childbearing. To Benjamin, this myth signals that law carries out the dictates of fate, ignoring the happiness or the innocence of human beings (Benjaim 1996, 203). The mythical use of law in order to exert violence over the living is a form of biopower: "Mythic violence is bloody power over bare life for its own sake [*Blutgewalt über das blosse Leben um ihrer selbst*]" (Benjamin 1996, 250). This power over life is what establishes bare life as guilty even before it has committed any trespass. The question that motivates Benjamin's theoretical production concerns the redemption or emancipation of bare life from this mythical power. I argue that Agamben's political thought is a continuation of this project.

Benjamin famously and controversially opposes the mythical violence exerted by legal systems to a divine kind of violence, "just as in all spheres God opposes myth":

> The dissolution of legal violence stems (as cannot be shown in detail here) from the guilt of bare natural life [*die Verschuldung des blossen natürlichen Lebens*], which consigns the living, innocent and unhappy, to a retribution that 'expiates' the guilt of bare life—and also doubtless purifies the guilty, not of guilt, but of law. For with bare life, the rule of law over the living ceases [*Denn mit dem blossen Leben hört die Herrschaft des Rechts über den Lebendigen auf*].... Divine violence is pure power over life for the sake of the living [*reine Gewalt über alles Leben um des Lebendigen willen*]. (Benjamin 1996, 250)

Mythical and divine forms of violence are manifestations of "power over life": both are biopolitical forms of power. But whereas mythical violence pursues this power as an end in itself, and therefore seeks to maintain everything that lives in its context of guilt and needful of punishment, divine violence pursues power in order to "expiate" the guilt of bare life and thus put an end to the rule of law over the living. "For with bare life, the rule of law over the living ceases": this mysterious claim seems to withhold the possibility that power over bare life not only has a mythical and deadly character, but also contains the root of a "positive" or life-preserving power whose manifestation is the bloodless violence of divine, expiatory punishment.[1] Perhaps for this reason, in *Homo Sacer*, Agamben thematizes "bare life" in a section entitled "Threshold," which concludes the part of the book dedicated to sovereignty.

The purpose of this chapter is to understand how a bare life that is entirely subjected to sovereign power can nevertheless be the only form in which human subjectivity escapes from the captivity of the law and heralds "the irrevocable exodus from any sovereignty" in the form of a "nonstatist politics" (Agamben 2000a, 8–9).[2] If life is to be emancipated from the "willed" state of exception that lies at the base of the juridical order tied to the state, Agamben needs to show the reverse of what he claims to have demonstrated throughout *Homo Sacer*, namely, he needs to think "law in its nonrelation to life and life in its nonrelation to law" (Agamben 2005a, 88). Such an affirmative biopolitics beyond state and sovereignty, which is pursued by both Benjamin and Agamben in their theorizations of bare life, echoes Marx's fundamental vision of the abolition of private property and the legal-political edifice that is built on it as a condition for the final emancipation of living labor in a communist association of free producers.[3] My guiding hypothesis is that Agamben's affirmative account of bare life, as I reconstruct it through a reading of his texts prior and subsequent to *Homo Sacer*, reworks four central motifs found in Marx's historical materialism: the facticity of alienated existence (section 2); the fetishism of commodities (section 3); the profanity of bourgeois society (section 4); and the nihilism of revolution (section 5). Agamben offers an account of facticity, fetishism, profanation, and nihilism as features of a bare life understood as the threshold between a state of being dominated and a new condition of freedom.

Much of Agamben's corpus provides an innovative interpretation and synthesis of Benjamin's theory of bare life with Heidegger's analytic of existence. The second goal of this chapter is to argue that this mediation, between the two great cultural antagonists of German philosophy in the early twentieth century, is consistently oriented by the negative dialectics developed by Adorno. Agamben's conception of bare life becomes intelligible only if one starts from Adorno's ground-breaking insight that "only to a life that is perverted into thingly form [is] an escape from the overall context of nature promised." Adorno gives this form of bare life the name of Odradek, an animated spool of wood and metal found in a story by Kafka. Odradek's life-world symbolizes the utter profanity, the "Hell" in which things exist in capitalism: used up, forgotten, left for lost or without employment, they call in vain for our care. In Agamben's reading, Odradek's world is a place where nothing has its proper place and every object has lost all relation to functionality or instrumentality. Yet Odradek's world also projects an image of "Heaven." For utopia is found wherever things can be enjoyed (or used) without being used up (or consumed); wherever our dealing with things escape the confines of a rationalized and professionalized activity. Odradek's placelessness is also the ou-topia that is the redeemed condition of communism. The importance of Adorno in the development of Agamben's conception of bare life has, to date, remained unacknowledged. If correct, my hypothesis suggests a way of understanding Agamben's political thought as a particularly radical and consequent continuation of the project of critical theory as developed in the early Frankfurt School. In particular, Agamben's recasting of

Benjamin's and Adorno's discussions over historical materialism sheds light on their differences with respect to the role that theology has to play in conceiving of the possibility and meaning of revolutionary praxis.

HEIDEGGER, FACTICITY, AND THE DISINTEGRATION OF THE LIFE-WORLD

Marx defines the proletariat as "a class of laborers who live only so long as they find work, and who find work only so long as their labor increases capital" (Marx 1998, 58). The life of the proletariat, in this sense, is a bare life because they find work only so long as their living labor gets transformed into private property ("dead labor" as Marx calls it), a social power that mortifies their very lives. The existential condition of reified labor-power, starting with Lukács's *History and Class Consciousness*, has been described by the concept of facticity. It is no surprise, then, that in his effort to identify the features of the bare life of "sacred man" (*homo sacer*), which promise an escape from sovereign power over life, Agamben recurs to Heidegger's fundamental reworking of the concept of facticity.

Facticity describes that feature of human existence "for which what is at stake in its way of living is living itself" (Agamben 2000a, 4).[4] In unpacking this definition, Agamben relies on the distinction between two Greek terms for life: *bios*, understood as a "way of life," and *zoe*, understood as the "fact of living" itself. By means of this distinction, Agamben can map the problem of Heideggerian facticity onto the space of modern biopower explored by Foucault. If biopolitics means that "modern man is an animal whose politics [*bios*] places his existence as a living being [*zoe*] in question" (Foucault 1990, 143), then this is equivalent to the claim that, under the capitalist conditions of production and reproduction of human life, in the "world" of existential possibilities, the *bios* of individuals can no longer be separated from the fact of living, or from the *zoe* of these individuals. For the factitious existence of reified living labor, the human world becomes all too literally a "life-world," that is, a context of social interaction with others in which one's "world," or the possible social roles (*bios*) that one can adopt in order to obtain recognition, are disclosed by the facts of one's biological "life" (*zoe*).

In *The Open* Agamben offers a political reading of the Husserlian-Heideggerian turn to the life-world in order to show both how biopolitical forms of power constitute themselves in and through the disclosure of life-worlds, and what kind of reinterpretation of the life-world is needed in order to move toward an affirmative and emancipatory biopolitics beyond the biopower of totalitarian and late capitalist neoliberal regimes. In order to situate Agamben's treatment of the concept of the life-world, it is useful to compare it with Habermas's application of this concept since *Legitimation Crisis*.[5] In that early work, Habermas argues that if a social system can be described as entering into a "crisis," then this is possible only because there are two irreducible forms of socialization: one dependent on the social system, and one dependent on the life-world. In the latter, according to Habermas, meaning is not generated as a function of the autopoietic requirements of a social system, but rather stems from the communicative action oriented toward reaching an understanding (*Verständigung*) among those who share the life-world. Meaning cannot be generated except as a process of exchanging reasons that justify the making of speech acts that raise universal validity claims. The possibility of a crisis (economic, political, and cultural-motivational) reflects the noncorrespondence or contradiction between the (forced) exchange of signs in social systems and the (free and undistorted) exchange of reasons in the life-world. In order to maintain the claim that the life-world has priority over the social system for the individual, one must develop an account of the fundamental motivation to make free use of one's life (for example, in the noneconomical practice of redeeming validity claims) at the level of life's factical reproduction. Agamben's interpretation of the motifs of facticity and the life-world in Heidegger, and their application for a critique of political economy, can be said to move toward such an account. Furthermore, his deconstruction of the Heideggerian concept of the life-world carries out and radicalizes motifs that are found in the first generation of the Frankfurt School.

In *The Open* Agamben offers a new account of the life-world as a machinelike process whereby the species "Man" (*anthropos*) is produced by the joining of *zoe* (life) and *bios* (world) in the form of the exception (both an exclusion that includes and an inclusion that excludes), whose end result or rest is bare life. Agamben sees this "anthropological machine" at work in the ancient life-world of the *polis*, where animal *zoe* is "included" in human *bios* only in order to "exclude" it from the political life of citizens in the form of "slaves," "barbarians," and "women" whose exploitation makes political life possible. Conversely, in the age of totalitarian biopolitics, entire human ways of life, or *bios* (for instance, those of "Jews,"

"Gypsies," "homosexuals," "handicapped persons," "stateless peoples," and "savages"), are "excluded" from political and civil life only so that they can be "included" in it as bestial *zoe*: "pests," "vermin," and "lives not worthy of being lived" who are to be separated from the rest of humanity and eventually exterminated or left to die (Agamben 2004, 37).

The constitution of a life-world makes "Man" into a separate species because, from the start, it identifies human life as a form of animal life that has the additional capacity of being-political or being-rational. Agamben shows that these identificatory characteristics (politics, rationality) emerge once the "animal" is posited as something negative, as something particular, in order for the "human" as universal to be determined by way of the negation of the negation. But such a negation of the negation only manages to bring in the particular as something subsumed by the universal, thus eliminating *zoe* or animal life as the nonidentical. Agamben's critique of the life-world, therefore, tacitly recurs to Adorno's conception of identification: "The equating of the negation of the negation with positivity is the quintessence of identification [*Die Gleichsetzung der Negation der Negation mit Positivität ist die Quintessenz des Identifizierens*]" (Adorno 2003, 161). The identification of a "human" nature turns out to be completely inhuman or bestial.[6] The legal and the anthropological machines featured in *Homo Sacer* and in *The Open* operate according to what Adorno calls the "totalitarian" and "circular" logic of identification (Adorno 2003, 174). The particular (that is, the exclusive) and the universal (that is, the inclusive) are not allowed to engage in their "reciprocal critique" (Adorno 2003, 148), and this places life and world in the condition that Marcuse calls "one-dimensionality." The anthropological machine is Agamben's biopolitical version of the dialectic of enlightened humanism: in and through the humanistic (identificatory) distinction between Man and animal, it constitutes a monstrous continuum of dominated life in which animal life is personalized and human life is bestialized.

Agamben wants to run the anthropological machine backward. He seeks an Adornian "disintegration" of the life-world, where both terms, life/*zoe* and world/*bios*, are allowed to fall apart and escape identification. *Bios* is bracketed from *zoe*, world from life, in order to understand the particularity of animal life as the nonidentical with respect to the human life-world constituted by identifications. This newly understood *zoe* is not joined to *bios* by way of an exclusive inclusion, but rather is placed in a "nonrelation" to it: human worldliness is reinterpreted by Agamben as the outgrowth of the experience of being excluded or shut out, not from the *polis* or world (as happens in modern biopolitics), but from what includes the animal in its environment.

For Heidegger, animals relate to their environment because they are captivated (*benommen*) by certain things in it that function as triggers for their instincts. Unlike the animal, which is "absorbed" (*eingenommen*) by what surrounds it, Heidegger believes that the human being or *Dasein* creates distance from things for itself by establishing a "world-disclosure" or a horizon of linguistically mediated sense (*Sinn* as *Bedeutsamkeit*) (Agamben 2004, 54).[7] Agamben turns Heidegger on his head by defining human freedom as a function of its proximity to, rather than its distance from, animal life. To have a world now means "a grasping of the animal not-open," much like how Adorno calls for a grasping of the nonidentical in a rational identity (Adorno 2003, 150).[8] Such a noncaptivating enclosedness corresponds in Agamben to the nonidentical qua suffering body in Adorno and has its ultimate presupposition in Marx's idea of nature as the material that is always presupposed, and never exhausted, by human labor (Adorno 2003, 202–3).[9] In a disintegrated life-world, *zoe* would no longer provide the "content" for *bios*; rather, *bios* would become a "form-of-life": "a life that can never be separated from its form, a life [*bios*] in which it is never possible to isolate something such as bare life [*zoe*]" (Agamben 2000a, 3).[10] The idea of a form-of-life, "an existence over which power no longer seems to have any hold" (Agamben 1998, 153), depends on recovering Marx's understanding of human praxis as a "metabolism" with nature or the environment.

Like Heidegger, Agamben locates the point of emergence of human *bios* from animal *zoe* in the mood of "profound boredom." But, for Agamben, this mood signals that the properly human condition is one of being consciously "fascinated" by things without wanting to "do" anything with them or about them, analogous to the sense in which the animal finds itself contained by its environment. The inability to make use of things because of the fascination they exert on us becomes the emissary of a new metabolism between the human being and its environment, far removed from the dominating pretensions of *homo faber*. The experience of profound boredom, when human beings are excluded from the world of occupations and professions, the world of busy-ness, contains the threshold or passage through which human life is included in animal life: "Dasein is simply an animal that has learned to become bored; it has awakened *from* its own captivation *to* its own captivation. This awakening of the living being to its own being-captivated, this anxious and resolute opening to a not-open, is the human" (Agamben 2004, 70). Agamben's affirmative biopolitics is thus a call for the human being to appropriate "his own concealedness, his own animality, which neither remains hidden nor is made an object of mastery, but is thought as such, as pure abandonment" (Agamben 2004, 70). In this condition, "the [anthropological] machine is, so to speak, stopped . . . in the reciprocal suspension of the two terms, something for which we perhaps have no name and which is neither animal nor man settles in between nature and humanity and holds itself in the mastered relation, in the saved night" (Agamben 2004, 83).[11] Bare life appears to be saved when it becomes the object of a "profane illumination" that has given up all hope (at least, hope for us) of transcendence. This illumination sheds a light on things that does not dissipate the "night" or the unknowability in which nature remains immersed, but is nevertheless "strong enough" to emancipate the human being from the mythical power of unredeemed nature, both externally and internally.

ADORNO, FETISHISM, AND THE END OF USE-VALUE

The later Benjamin seeks profane illuminations amidst the "spiritual-animal kingdom" of modern political economy where, by rendering individuals captive to things that have lost their utility by becoming exchange-values, commodity fetishism anticipates the "reconciled" human condition. From the beginning, Agamben's readings of Benjamin follow the guiding thread offered by the phenomenon of commodity fetishism. The fetishism of commodities refers to a condition where things—the products, rather than the individuals, or producers—enjoy a properly social relationship. Under commodity fetishism, producers are isolated from one another, unaware of the social nature of their productive activity; what social life they do have is reduced to the bare life of consumers. Benjamin and Adorno think that commodity fetishism, if looked at dialectically, contains within it the resources to overturn the alienation of consumers and create a community of free producers. The key to this reversal is to understand that things are not destined to be simply the means through which human beings reproduce their lives. By establishing social relations among things, commodity fetishism shows that things have the potential to enjoy a life beyond that assigned by their use- and exchange-values, and that human emancipation from the domination of mythical nature passes through the redemption of nature from its mythical aspect. Recognizing this surplus of life in things establishes a relationship with nature other than that of domination and exploitation: just as facticity does, the phenomenon of fetishism provides another sense in which bare life functions as a threshold concept between domination and freedom.[12] Agamben's actualization of historical materialism is largely a reflection on the exchanges between Benjamin and Adorno with regard to the dialectical character of commodity fetishism.

In the first section of his exposé on the Arcades project, entitled "Paris, the Capital of the 19th Century," Benjamin presents the standpoint from which he intends to renew historical materialism:

> Corresponding to the form of the new means of production, which in the beginning is still ruled by the form of the old (Marx), are images in the collective consciousness in which the new is permeated with the old. These images are wish images; in them the collective seeks both to overcome and to transfigure the immaturity of the social product and the inadequacies in the social organization of production. . . . In the dream in which each epoch entertains images of its successor, the latter appears wedded to elements of primal history [*Urgeschichte*]—that is, to elements of a classless society. And the experiences of such a society—as stored in the unconscious of the collective—engender, through interpenetration with what is new, the utopia that has left its traces in a thousand configurations of life, from enduring edifices to passing fashions. (Benjamin 2002, 33–34)

Every society, according to Benjamin, dreams of the society that will succeed it. This dream, following Freud's fundamental thesis, formulates the fulfilment of a wish that society were otherwise than it is.[13] Such a wish-fulfillment is expressed as an image (analogous to Freud's rebus), characterized by the return of a "primal history" in which society has no class divisions; that is, the image contains elements of primitive communism. In the dreamwork of society's collective unconscious, these primitive elements of a classless society are fused with the recent elements of the new forms of production that seek to transform society into utopia and that correspond to nonprimitive communism, that is, to communism as understood by Marx, as the end of the long human prehistory and the beginning of a conscious praxis on the part of the human species. To wake up to this collective dream image is, for Benjamin, the only way to realize the collective unconscious wish for communism.

In a later passage of the same exposé, dedicated to the question of how Baudelaire's lyric poetry can render the industrialized landscape of the metropolis, Benjamin specifies his idea of dream image: "Such an image is afforded by the commodity per se: as fetish. Such an image is presented by the arcades, which are house no less than street. Such an image is the prostitute—seller and sold in one" (Benjamin 2002, 40).[14] The commodity understood as a fetish; the arcade insofar as it denies the difference between the private and the public, the interior and the street; the prostitute as owner (of the means of production), worker, and commodity all in one: in each case the "primitive" is joined with the "modern" so as to offer a "dialectical" image of historical progress. This image is a radical contraction and transformation of the past into the present, which brings the linear unfolding of historical time to a standstill and opens up a new place or space (literally: ou-topia) for things in which they are "saved": in this instance, communism as the "saved night" of nature.

In a now famous letter, Adorno writes Benjamin a long response to his text, which, in my opinion, contains the crucial discussion out of which Agamben's own interpretation of Benjamin emerges. Adorno contests the "undialectical" approach to utopia that he finds in Benjamin's idea of a dialectical image:

> You interpret the relationship between the oldest and the newest . . . in terms of a utopian reference to the 'classless society.' The archaic thereby becomes a complementary addition to the new, instead of actually being 'the newest' itself, and is therefore rendered undialectical. However, at the same time, and equally undialectically, the image of classlessness is projected back into mythology . . . instead of becoming properly transparent as the phantasmagoria of Hell. (Benjamin and Adorno 1999, 106)

For Adorno, Benjamin's idea of the image only relates the modern (the newest) to the archaic (the oldest) in a contingent manner; it does not take into account their common identity. Adorno reasons as follows: only if the modern is captured in all of its primitiveness will it stand in contradiction with its concept, and only the awareness of its self-contradiction can motivate the present to transcend itself and realize a "better" society. Conversely, Benjamin is also charged with not rendering the primitive, that is, the idea of a classless society, as sufficiently modern. Communism, according to Adorno, should arise as the phantasmagoric image of "Heaven" that is projected up from the "Hell" of the capitalist present. In Benjamin, instead, Adorno finds that the idea of communism remains tied to an archaic past, to the figure of the Golden Age, which, by definition, is an epoch that precedes history and for that reason is forever gone.

At stake in this criticism is the status of the commodity as dialectical image. Adorno is concerned that Benjamin negates the "Hell" of commodity fetishism in a manner that seeks to restore the primordial, "natural" use-value back to things, as depicted in the myth of the Golden Age. But, on his view, the importance of the capitalist mode of production is that it constitutes the commodity as

> an alien object in which use-value perishes, and on the other, it is an alien survivor that outlives its own immediacy. It is through commodities, and not directly in relation to human beings, that we receive the promise of immortality.... It seems to me that this is where the basic epistemological character of Kafka is to be identified, particularly in Odradek, as a commodity that has survived to no purpose. (Benjamin and Adorno 1999, 108)

The loss of the use-value of things is ultimately a gain, both for things and for individuals. A return to primitive communism rejects the positive aspects of the historical development of productive forces and means. Only this development furnishes the properly materialist ground on which to realize the promise that labor can be abolished without regression, in the form of an emancipation of productive forces in a rationally organized society.[15] Adorno thinks of communism as a state in which commodities "outlive" or "survive" their use-value, while not regressing back to the stage in which they were "merely" things. That is why he speaks of the need to "liberate things from the curse of their utility" (Benjamin and Adorno 1999, 107).[16]

Adorno baptizes this idea of a "saved" commodity with the name of Odradek, after the character found in Kafka's story "The Cares of a Family

Man" in *A Country Doctor*. Odradek is a star-shaped spool of thread with two wooden crossbar sticks coming out of it, which allow it to "stand upright as if on two legs." Odradek is "extraordinarily mobile and impossible to catch"; it lies about in attics, on staircases, in corridors; sometimes it moves out of the house to other homes, but always returns. At times it even answers very simple questions "like a child" (Kafka 1986, 129).[17] Odradek appears to be immortal because beings that lack purpose or end cannot die. And this very fact of the commodity's immortality is the "concern" (*Sorge*) of the "father of the house": Odradek might still be around for his children and his children's children, having "survived" the death of the father.

Odradek plays a small but significant role in Benjamin's interpretations of Kafka. Benjamin refers to him as "the most singular bastard which the prehistoric world has begotten with guilt.... Odradek is the form which things assume in oblivion. They are distorted. The 'cares of a family man,' which no one can identify, are distorted" (Benjamin 1999b, 811). Odradek stands for a human product that was "begotten with guilt." It is both a thing and a child: the object of an indistinguishably biological and economic production. The "father" of the house constantly tries to forget about it or remove it from consciousness, but this removal causes him anxiety. Adorno criticizes Benjamin's interpretation of Odradek as an object that springs forth from "the immemorial world and guilt." He proposes that Odradek be interpreted as "the other face of the world of things ... a sign of distortion—but precisely as such he is also a motif of transcendence, namely, of the ultimate limit and of the reconciliation of the organic and the inorganic, or of the overcoming of death: Odradek 'lives on.' Expressed in another way, it is only to a life that is perverted in thingly form that an escape from the overall context of nature is promised" (Benjamin and Adorno 1999, 69). Adorno thus reads Odradek as an allegory of commodity fetishism, applying Benjamin's own mystical interpretation of allegory to the commodity. Odradek is "a sign of distortion" because it stands for a reified human praxis. But Odradek is also "a motif of transcendence" because it figures the survival of things over their own inorganic nature, a bare life that is a function of their fetishism.

According to Adorno, Odradek, the creature, shows concern (*Sorge*) for the father of the house, for its creator: it desires the redemption of the father.

> If his [Odradek's] origin lies with the father of the house, does he not then precisely represent the anxious concern and danger for the latter, does he not anticipate precisely the overcoming of the creaturely state of guilt, and is not this concern—truly a case of Heidegger put right side up—the secret key, indeed the most indubitable promise of hope, precisely through the overcoming of the house itself. (Benjamin and Adorno 1999, 69)

By meeting the gaze of the father, Odradek undoes the father's alienation, which proceeds from his economy, from the law of his household (*oikos-nomia*).[18] Heidegger is turned "right side up," as Adorno puts it, because with Odradek the forgotten things show concern or care for *Dasein*, and not simply the reverse.[19] For Heidegger, *Dasein* projects into the future through its concern for its own being, and caring for things is part of this concern. But if things were to begin to care for human beings, or return their concern, then the continuum of history, which Adorno calls the "catastrophe," would be interrupted and we could finally grasp the utopia in which humankind "already" finds itself.

Agamben's historical materialism returns to Benjamin's and Adorno's idea of commodity fetishism as dialectical image. But in his interpretation of the dialectical image, Agamben clearly favors Adorno's conception over that of Benjamin. Furthermore, in his analysis of fetishism, Agamben adopts and radicalizes Adorno's inversion of Heideggerian care, the crucial category of factitious existence. Agamben's preference for Adorno's conception of dialectical image is already visible in his first major book, *Stanze*, which contains a chapter significantly entitled "In the World of Odradek." Although this chapter is a loose commentary on Benjamin's 1935 exposé, from his choice of title, it appears that Agamben's reading of Benjamin is filtered through the lens of Adorno. As I have shown, to read Odradek as a dialectical image of commodity fetishism is an Adornian development. When Agamben takes up Benjamin's question of the relation between Baudelaire's lyric poetry and advanced capitalism, it is once again Adorno's thesis that emerges:

> [Baudelaire] attempted to create a commodity . . . in which the process of fetishization would be pushed to such an extreme that it would annihilate the reality of the commodity as such. A commodity . . . whose value consists, thus, in its uselessness, and whose use consists in its own

unhandiness is no longer a commodity: the absolute commodification of the work of art is also the most radical abolition of the commodity. (Agamben 1979b, 51)

The strategy for overcoming commodity fetishism that Agamben wishes to attribute to Benjamin's reading of Baudelaire in fact shares much more with the theory of free exchange formulated by Adorno. The priority of exchange over use-value is the sine qua non of Adorno's negative dialectics. On the one hand, the exchange-value of things is the social reality of identification. On the other hand, there is no returning to original use-value, for this would amount to a "regression into past injustice" (Adorno 2003, 150), when matters were decided on the basis of violence and expropriation, and not through exchange. Only the "realization" of "the ideal of free and just exchange [*das Ideal freien und gerechten Tausch*]" can lead beyond capitalist exchange (Adorno 2003, 150).[20]

The attempt to read Heidegger's conception of the facticity of human existence together with Adorno's conception of the fetishism of commodities is one of the oldest and most constant motifs in Agamben's work. The inversion of Heideggerian care, in which Adorno identifies the key to "saving" the fetishized commodity, resurfaces in Agamben as follows: "[Care] wants the thing with all of its predicates, its being just so [*il suo essere tale qual è*]. It desires the 'what' only in as much as it is 'so'—this is its particular fetishism [*Esso desidera il quale solo in quanto è tale—questo è il suo particolare feticismo*]" (Agamben 1990, 4, translation mine). The hermeneutic care for things that lays them out (*auslegen*) "as" what they "are" is here rendered in terms of the peculiar fetishism that grasps the essence or in-itself of things in their self-exhibition of qualities.

Benjamin's 1935 exposé links the fetishism of commodities with a third kind of value, beyond their typical use- and exchange-values, which he calls "exhibition-value." Exhibition-value is what art gains in the age of its mechanical reproducibility at the price of losing its "aura," the experience of an unbridgeable "distance" with respect to things (Benjamin 1968, 222–23). Agamben retrieves the dialectical potential of the exhibition-value of things by identifying it as the correlate of a way of being that is entirely exposed to the self-exhibition of things. On this reading, the exhibition-value of things neither reduces the thing to the identification made possible by these qualities (that is, to the status of a use-object), nor does it reify *Dasein* itself. Because *Dasein* consists in being (*sein*) the openness or exposition (*Da*) of things as they exhibit themselves as they really are, in their just-being-so, *Dasein* remains faithful to the fundamental lack-of-essence, or emptiness-of-content, which corresponds to the nonreified, nonnaturalized conception of human existence.

Agamben's reading of Heidegger's analytic of care as a critique of reification is comparable to Lucien Goldmann's Lukácsian reading of Heidegger, except that Agamben aligns himself with Adorno's critique of Lukács's conception of reification as being caught within identity thinking.[21] Adorno's intuition is that the reification of the subject needs to be counteracted through the affirmation of the priority of the object: "As fragments of what was dominated, things grow hard; to love things is to redeem them [*Die Dinge verhärten sich als Bruchstücke dessen, was unterjocht ward; seine Errettung meint die Liebe zu den Dingen*]" (Adorno 2003, 191, translation mine). The love for things that is expressed in the fetishism of commodities is a necessary moment in overturning the "enmity against otherness" that defines identity-thinking and its assertion of the priority of the subject over the object (Adorno 2003, 191).

Agamben employs Adorno's insight in order to rethink the conditions of the Marxist demand for an authentically social mode of production, the commune of free producers. Fetishism becomes a point of inversion in the relation between object and subject that allows the subject to divest itself of its self-identity as an owner of the object in order to establish a commune with others. The division of labor in capitalist societies calls for individuals to be in one way or another, but never to be "just" so, to be their bare life: "a singularity without identity, a common and absolutely exposed singularity" (Agamben 1990, 44, translation mine). Agamben suggests that a dialectical understanding of the fetishism of the commodity indicates what is required for this coincidence of singularity and community to take place. The truth behind the fetishism of the commodity, whereby things relate to each other in a social manner, is that it provides an inverted image of the kind of impersonal and common relation individuals would have to attain with their own living labor in order to escape the alienation into which they are cast by virtue of "owning" (and then "selling") their labor-power. In "a community of free individuals, carrying on their work with the means of production in common" the labor-power of each would no longer be their private property; rather, it would be used consciously by the commune for the sake of the life of the individual rather than for the sake of its products.

> If instead we define the common . . . as a point of indifference between the proper and the improper—that is, as something that can never be grasped in terms of either expropriation or appropriation but that can be grasped, rather, only as use—the essential political problem then becomes: 'How does one use the common?' (Agamben 2000a, 117)

Such use-of-the-common corresponds to Adorno's formulation of communism as a "reconciled condition" in which what is other (*das Fremde*) "in the vouchsafed proximity remains the far and the distinct, beyond what is heterogeneous and what is one's own" (Adorno 2003, 192, translation mine). In this social condition, the individual would no longer have to appropriate for itself the ways of being disclosed by the world of commodities through acquiring a profession (which ultimately expropriates the individual of its bare life). On the contrary, the bare life or labor-power of the individual would be called upon by the commune or "community of free individuals" in order to be made use of "in accordance with a settled plan" (Marx 1978a, 327),[22] with the end of releasing this life from its laboring condition and into its singularity or "just" being so.

PAUL, PROFANATION, AND THE FREE USE OF THE COMMON

In his book on the "spirit" of modern capitalism, Max Weber shows that for anything to be put to a use in modern, rationalized capitalism, the productive activity in which such use is found requires a "vocation" that places the activity beyond the principle of utility (Weber 1958, 54). In modern capitalism, the rational calculus of utilities is only possible on the condition that things get done not because of the happiness this will bring, but because everyone conducts their life as a professional, because one arrives at one's activity by following a vocation. The professionalization of activity, insofar as it entails an ascetic conduct of life (the "Protestant ethic"), is as such redemptive, a sign of received grace: in capitalism, the categorical imperative takes the form of an injunction to "do one's job," come what may. In order to attain what Agamben calls a "free use of the common," it is necessary to emancipate praxis from its captivity under the category of the idea of vocation understood as profession. To do so, Agamben turns the idea of vocation from its Lutheran, worldly secular signification back to its originary, Pauline, messianic formulation.

Weber rests his interpretation of the Protestant ethic and its role in generating the "spirit" of capitalism, in large measure, on the claim that Luther creatively mistranslates Paul's eschatological idea of calling (*klesis*) into the mundane idea of profession (*Beruf*), understood as a way of conducting oneself through life (*Lebensführung*).[23] For Weber, Pauline *klesis* does not have the worldly connotation that Luther gives to the idea of calling: Paul's command that "every one should remain in the state in which he was called.... For he who was called in the Lord as a slave is a freeman of the Lord. Likewise he who was free when called is a slave of Christ" (I Cor. 7, 20–23) is eschatologically indifferent to worldly status. The idea is that there is no need to worry about one's standing in life since there is not much time left before this world comes to an end with the second coming of the Messiah. Agamben, instead, reads Paul's idea of vocation as a messianic injunction that refers to "a most intimate shift of every single mundane condition by virtue of its being 'called'" (Agamben 2000b, 28, translation mine). Here, Agamben identifies vocation with the messianic tension that "shifts" everything into its proper place, as thematized in Benjamin's and Adorno's discussions concerning Odradek. The world's coming-to-an-end is not an event that happens at some future point in linear time; rather, it is the arrest and interruption of the linear and homogeneous unfolding of time in which one conducts one's life professionally, without an end in mind.

Agamben claims that the "most rigorous definition of messianic life," that is, of this "shift" that saves the profane world, can be found in the following passage from the First Letter to the Corinthians:

> I mean, brethren, the appointed time has grown very short; from now on, let those who have wives live as though (*hos me*) they had none, and those who mourn as though (*hos me*) they were not mourning . . . and those who deal with the world as though (*hos me*) they had no dealings with it. (I Cor. 7, 29–32)

Agamben takes the expression "as though" to denote that place to which one is called by the vocation. Thus, vocation means to be called "towards nothing and to no place: that is why it can coincide with the factical condition in which each thing finds itself called. But, precisely because of this, the call completely revokes the condition. The messianic vocation is the revocation of all vocations" (Agamben 2000b, 30, translation mine). On this messianic reading, Paul's conception of the vocation is radically anti-Lutheran because it revokes the professional character of every worldly status and activity with which one is involved and commands that we turn over the things with which we busy ourselves to a free and common use. Thus, it is not surprising to find the motif of the Franciscan *usus facti* resurface in Agamben's reading of Paul's idea of use as *chresis* (Agamben 2000b, 32). Nor is one perplexed by his anachronistic association of Pauline *klesis* with the idea of social "class" and his linking of the messianic community (*ekklesia*, the community of messianic *klesesis*) to the idea of a class consciousness. To attain a class consciousness now means to remain in one's profession or calling while all the time revoking the use that these professions assign to things and, in so doing, bring the division of labor to an end (Agamben 2000b, 35).

But what can it mean, to revoke our professional ethos and give things back to their free use? Agamben addresses this question in his essay dedicated to the idea of profanation. He begins by returning to the origin of the idea of a fetish in archaic religious practices. The fetish is an object that has been removed from the common use given to it by men and translated into the space of the sacred by means of a sacrifice (Agamben 1979b, 58). If communism means the simultaneous "freedom" of things from their use-value and their return to a "free" and common use beyond use-value, then the separation or alienation entailed by the fetish and its sacred space needs to be profanated. Profanation becomes the model for revolutionary praxis. Marx thought that the profanation of capitalist production would itself dispel the "mystery" of commodity fetishism.[24] Yet neither Benjamin nor Agamben shares his optimism about the profanating force of capitalism. In a fragment entitled "Capitalism as Religion,"[25] Benjamin argues that capitalist enterprise is not only motivated by a secularized religious "spirit," as Weber describes it, but itself constitutes a religion. Unlike other religions, however, the cult of capitalism is not dedicated to the redemption from guilt as much as to its exacerbation. Capitalism as religion seeks to build up the debt of believers, and (following Nietzsche's original identification of the root of guilt in a state of indebtedness) it therefore accumulates their feelings of guilt (Agamben 2007a, 77). Debt accumulates because capitalism separates each thing from itself, in the form of the division between its use- and its exchange-value, so that no free use can be made of it. Capitalism sacralises things by withdrawing them from the sphere of free use and turning them into objects of consumption: what can only be used up is what can no longer be freely used. On this model, the production of commodities as the fetishism of things is the basic ritual of capitalism as religion. As Agamben points out, consumer capitalism paradoxically seems to hinder, rather than bring to fulfilment, a process of profanation (Agamben 2007a, 89).[26]

Agamben thus proposes to rethink profanation not simply as what negates the sacred or fetish character of things, but as what brings sacred things back into the order of the profane, back into a free use, while allowing them to remain immune from having use-value. A rest of the sacred is preserved in the profanation of things.[27] Agamben uses the term "playthings" to define those things that are brought back into common use, but maintain the rest of sacredness that puts them beyond utility and use-value. Therefore, the messianic revocation of professional conduct amounts to a profanation of the objects of a profession or vocation by playing with and through their fetish character (Agamben 2007a, 72–73).

Agamben gives two striking and intentionally profanatory illustrations of what this profanation of a profession or vocation entails. The first illustration recapitulates the motif of the disintegration of the life-world with his analysis of commodity fetishism. Agamben makes the following analogy: just as the plaything with which a cat pretends to hunt takes the place of a real mouse without being one (that is, because of its fetish character), so too this playful use of the fetish actually "frees" the mouse from being a biologically determined trigger or disinhibitor of the cat's (aggressive) instinct (Agamben 2007a, 83). Playing with fetishes is the only way for the human being to become open to its instinctual captivation, thereby escaping the "destiny" or "vicissitudes" posed by its instincts. The fetish plaything of the cat becomes exemplary of a "pure means," an object which no longer has a use, which is no longer a means to attain a pregiven end. Agamben thus reaffirms Adorno's and Horkheimer's critique of "instrumental rationality," but does so in a form that has been purified of the rationalistic, civilizational framework in which it was first formulated. At the same time, this "pure means" frees the mouse (the original trigger of the instinct) to "be" just what it is, and no longer to "be" only in function of the instinct of the cat, that is, to be the cat's prey. Agamben thus maintains Heidegger's motif of authentic existence, but cleansed of the humanistic framework in which it was first expressed.

The second illustration of the idea of communism beyond use-value found in the essay on profanation is given through a reading of pornography (Agamben 2007a, 87–91). Agamben argues that in the films of Chloé De Lysses one can witness the subversion of the exhibition-value of her body. Giving the body an exhibition-value is what the jargon of modeling refers to as "striking a pose." The porn actress in question, according to Agamben, is capable of striking poses that function as "pure means": her impassivity during the sexual act no longer communicates anything. There is neither the mimesis of pleasure nor the mimesis of a complicity with the viewer. Much like the cat playing with the fetish mouse, the poses of the actress play with the body in a way that no longer triggers the erotic "instinct" of the viewers, and thus frees their bodies from the captivation entailed by the instinct. Here the actress, one is led to surmise, reappropriates her alienated body in and through its most extreme fetishization: not by putting the body to a nonsexual or nonpornographic use, but by separating it from all predetermined purposes (this separation in and through profanation is the "rest" of sacredness that remains amidst the greatest profanity), and thus freeing it up for an altogether other use in common. On this reading, Chloé De Lysses's impassive poses signal a "new, collective use of sexuality" in which the body becomes a sacrificial altar of private property.

Agamben intends his interpretation of St. Paul's messianism as a clarification of Benjamin's messianic politics. In the *Theologico-Political Fragment*, Benjamin defines the messianic as a *restitutio in integrum*: a return of nature, both spatially and temporally, into a state of completion. Corresponding to the "spiritual *restitutio in integrum*" in which the flesh resurrects after death, Benjamin posits a "worldly restitution that leads to the eternity of a downfall [*die Ewigkeit eines Unterganges*].... For nature is messianic by reason of its eternal and total passing away" (Benjamin 2002, 305–6). The redemption of nature does not mean that nature has to be transcended into a sphere that is supernatural: nature reaches its completion in and through an "eternal" decline. The examples of profanation discussed above can also be read as figures of a redeemed nature. From this perspective, Benjamin defines revolutionary action as a striving "for such a passing away—even the passing away of those stages of mankind that are nature";

and that is why its "method must be called nihilism" (Benjamin 2002, 306). Agamben provides a Pauline and Heideggerian declension to Benjamin's politics of nihilism: the destruction of the world means the revocation of all of its ways of being, of all of its possibilities, into the facticity of the life that can make a free use of them. In the messianic condition things are not simply remembered (taken out of the oblivion that connotes guilt); rather, they are "in us and with us as forgotten, as lost—and only in this sense are they unforgotten" (Agamben 2000b, 38, translation mine). Agamben's Pauline rendition of Benjamin's idea of play is a "serious" interpretation of the recovery of forgotten things as a form of their "resurrection."

In *Negative Dialectics*, Adorno formulates the program for a recovery of the lostness of things (where being lost refers to their being subsumed as objects by identity-thinking) in terms of the desire for the nonidentical to be named or identified as what it is. For, in being identified, it is necessarily missed or forgotten (Adorno 2003, 152). It is not entirely by chance, therefore, that Adorno ends the second part of *Negative Dialectics* with a Pauline reference, namely, the claim that the historical materialist "agrees with theology where he is most materialistic. His longing would be for the resurrection of the flesh [*Mit der Theologie kommt er dort überein, wo er am materialistischesten ist. Seine Sehnsucht wäre die Auferstehung des Fleisches*]" (Adorno 2003, 207, translation mine). Agamben's interpretation of Paul contains assumptions that correspond to what Adorno demanded, in vain, of Benjamin: "a restoration of theology, or rather a radicalization of the dialectic down to the glowing core of theology" (Benjamin 1994, 498). But this interpretation does not decide the question of whether Benjamin himself employs Pauline theologemes in view of such a spiritualist interpretation of *restitutio in integro*.

KAFKA, THE MESSIANIC, AND REVOLUTIONARY PRAXIS

During the 1920s and 1930s, Benjamin and Scholem engaged in an epistolary dispute over the significance of Kafka's writings, in particular his parable *Before the Law*. Scholem and Benjamin disagreed on how to understand the antinomian elements of the idea of messianism in Judaism and, more particularly, how Kafka's text reflect such antinomianism in the epoch of the destruction of tradition and experience (for Judaism this corresponds to the epoch of the crisis of the *aggadah*).[28] Agamben illustrates the threshold that divides and joins the mythical from the messianic aspects of bare life by staging the opposition between Scholem and Benjamin with regard to Kafka.

Kafka's *Before the Law* tells the story of a "man from the country" who stations himself before the open gate of the Law and waits, to the point of death, for the doorkeeper to let him in.[29] On dying, the doorkeeper reveals to him that this entrance to the Law had been left open only for him, and that it would henceforth be closed again. For Agamben this parable shows how the law exercises its mythical violence over life, captivating bare life in its logic of the exception: "The open door destined only for him includes him in excluding him and excludes him in including him" (Agamben 1998, 50). The parable describes the process through which life, caught in the state of exception, becomes entirely determined and taken over by law. This process culminates in the bare lives of the "sacred men" found at both ends of the spectrum of sovereign power: in the totalitarian egocrat as "living law," whose every desire becomes law, and in the inmates of extermination camps, whose bodies incarnate the "laws" of racial superiority or class warfare without the intermediation by positive, statutory laws that address them as individuals endowed with rights.[30]

Agamben argues that bare life in the "willed" or "virtual" state of exception characteristic of sovereign power is "life under a law that is in force without signifying. . . . And it is exactly this kind of life that Kafka describes, in which law is all the more pervasive for its total lack of content" (Agamben 1998, 53). Agamben employs an expression that Scholem uses to describe the status of revealed law in Kafka's *Before the Law*. According to Scholem's reading, the parable depicts the addressees of the Law as having lost the keys to unlock its meaning: they study the commentary (*aggadah*) but remain locked out of the law (*halakah*), unable to apply or follow it. Consequently, for them, the Law appears as Nothingness: it "has validity but no significance."[31] Although the Law is devoid of all meaning for its students, Scholem nonetheless suggests that it continues to demand obedience and must be transmitted even though it cannot be applied, since the gate guarded by *aggadah* remains open.[32] Agamben thereby identifies Scholem's "mystical" formula of revealed law in the time of *galut* with the *Arcanum* of the sovereign power of positive legal systems in the time of totalitarianism (in the period of states of exception). For Agamben, the loss of significance of revealed law coincides with the gradual but inevitable expansion of the "virtual" state of exception in and through systems of positive law, all the way to the point at which the state of exception is no longer exceptional but has become the rule.

Agamben takes up Benjamin's reading of the parable to illustrate the possibility of a revolutionary reversal of the "willed" state of exception in an event that would bring about a "real state of exception," where it is not life that gets taken over by the law, but rather that all law becomes "indistinguishable from life" (Agamben 1998, 55).[33] Benjamin reads Kafka's parables as illustrations of this revolutionary turnabout of bare life in "the attempt to metamorphize life into writing [*dem Versuch der Verwandlung des Lebens ins Schrift*]" (Benjamin 1994, 453). On Agamben's interpretation, this metamorphosis corresponds to an "absolute intelligibility of a life wholly resolved into writing" (Agamben 1998, 55). In the messianic condition, bare life is lived out as if it were written out ahead of the one living it, as if it were developing from a singular law unto itself. On this view, living in the messianic kingdom is equivalent to living in a condition in which law shall only have content and no form, in which law shall only do justice to each singular event and thing and will therefore cease to be a law whose mythical form is that of universal validity and whose mythical content is the bare life of *homo sacer*. "Benjamin proposes a messianic nihilism that nullifies even the Nothing and lets no form of law remain in force beyond its own content" (Agamben 1998, 53). Revolutionary praxis, on this reading, entails doing everything necessary to provoke the rule of law into finally declaring a real state of exception: "The messianic task of the man from the country . . . might then be precisely that of making the virtual state of exception real, of compelling the doorkeeper to close the door of the Law (the door of Jerusalem). For the Messiah will be able to enter only after the door is closed, which is to say, after the Law's being in force without significance is at an end " (Agamben 1998, 57). It is as if Agamben takes literally Brecht's utterance, reported by Benjamin, that Kafka is "the only true Bolshevik writer" (Benjamin 1991d, 1155).

THE LIFE OF LITERATURE AS THRESHOLD OF SOVEREIGN POWER

By way of conclusion, I propose an alternative interpretation of Benjamin's understanding of Kafka for, in my opinion, Agamben's reading of Benjamin's politics of nihilism is ultimately incorrect. Benjamin's essays on Kafka conclude with a meditation on the "distortion" associated with the guilt of human prehistorical progress through economies of exploitation, and how the little hunchback who represents this distortion will "disappear with the coming of the Messiah, who (a great rabbi once said) will not wish to change the world by force but will merely make a slight adjustment in it" (Benjamin 1999b, 811). In both essays, the messianic is associated with the motif of looking back on one's life as a way not to be moved away from where one finds oneself; where one finds oneself is always illustrated by the life of the village. Benjamin's interpretation of the messianic therefore removes it from the question of the application of (revealed) Law that structures both Scholem's and Agamben's readings of Kafka. Instead, the wish for the coming of the Messiah is analogous to the beggar's wish in a Jewish joke reported by Benjamin: a beggar dreams of being a powerful king whose country happens to be invaded so he is forced to abandon his castle and kingdom in the middle of the night, wearing only his shirt, so as to "finally arrive safely right here at the bench in this corner" (Benjamin 1999b, 812). The joke brings together a momentous event, a great reversal of fortune, the consequence of which is but a slight change: the beggar is still in his place, but now he has a decent shirt, the true object of desire. "Seek for food and clothing first, then the Kingdom of God shall be added unto you" (Benjamin 1968, 254).

Benjamin's comic approach to the messianic brings together a Marxist and a Freudian motif. For in the joke, the messianic is related to the undoing of the fantasy of sovereignty, perhaps above all the fantasy associated with the Messiah as King. The Freudian motif expressed in the joke concerns the emotional ambivalence that structures the possibility of sovereignty, where the elevation to a position of power is also the degradation of the person of the sovereign. In *Totem and Taboo*, Freud cites Sancho Panza's misadventures wherein he is mistaken for a king as evidence that corroborates his conception of the sacred as ambivalence (Freud 1950, 50–51). (Not entirely by coincidence, as I show below, Sancho Panza plays a crucial role in Benjamin's reading of Kafka as well.) The messianic in Benjamin, therefore, is that moment in the literary space when beggar and sovereign coincide in order to express both the ambivalence of sovereignty and the real object of desire behind revolutionary motivations: not the conquest of state power but, as in Marx's vision of communism, the satisfaction of material needs in the absence of sovereign rule.

Benjamin points out that, in Kafka, the descriptions of the messianic reversal are always directed toward the past: the messianic is a redemption of nature from the forgetfulness that befalls it in the form of historical progress. The messianic reversal, therefore, returns to nature its eternity in and through history. Benjamin takes up a position he first formulates in the *Theological-Political Fragment*, according to which "the rhythm of this eternally transient world ... the rhythm of messianic nature is happiness. For nature is messianic by reason of its eternal and total passing" (Benjamin 2002, 305–6). Happiness is made up of precisely those events that could have happened to us but did not so happen during our transient, worldly existence.[34] To recapture what never was, it must be possible to relive our past life, to recapitulate it, so to speak, and in this way restore its completeness without denying its pastness: profane, worldly life is restored in its "eternal and total passing away" in and through the messianic interruption of historical becoming or progress.[35] Just as, upon glancing at old photo albums that recapitulate one's life, one is unable to avoid thinking of one's happiness in a past in which, qua actual worldly past, one never was happy (as surely as one was not actually happy when the photographs were taken), so too the messianic does not point to a future life of eternal fulfilment (as pictured in the traditional images of Paradise), but simply seeks to realize the happiness promised by the past of natural history; the past we never actually lived. In Benjamin, the difference between what is and what ought to be, the difference in whose knowledge theory becomes "critical," is radically immanent to historical becoming: it always consists in realizing a meeting or appointment with a past that never happened. The eternalization of transience that Benjamin calls messianic nature is the realization in the present of what was but never happened.[36]

Viewed from such a messianic perspective, history appears like "a tempest that blows from forgetting, and study is a cavalry attack against it. Thus, the beggar on the corner bench rides towards his past in order to catch himself in the figure of the fleeing king. This ride, which is long enough for a life, corresponds to life, which is too short for a ride" (Benjamin 1999b, 814).[37] Benjamin compares study to a journey back in time to retrieve forgotten or repressed things like Odradek. The ultimate goal of study is to allow one to live one's life justly or barely, in the sense of living it within its own limits because the "burden" of guilt would be "taken off the back" (Benjamin 1999b, 816), undoing the distortion represented by the hunched back. Absent such an undoing or redemption from guilt through the practice of study, life remains always already ahead of itself (just as Heidegger understands it in the existential analysis of *Dasein*), thus appearing "too short," never quite right, to those living it.

But what kind of study can provoke the closing of the gate of the Law and, in so doing, open the "little door" through which the Messiah comes? Benjamin answers by referring to another character in Kafka:

> Reversal is the direction of study which transforms existence into script. Its teacher is Bucephalus, "the new lawyer," who takes the road back without the powerful Alexander—which means, rid of the onrushing conqueror. "His flanks free and unhampered by the thighs of a rider, under a quiet lamp far from the din of Alexander's battles, he reads and turns the pages of our old books." ... Is it really the law which would thus be invoked against myth in the name of justice? No, as a legal scholar Bucephalus remains true to his origins, except that he does not seem to be practicing law.... The law which is studied but no longer practiced is the gate to justice. The gate to justice is study. Yet Kafka doesn't dare attach to this study the promises which tradition has attached to the study of the Torah. (Benjamin 1999b, 815)

These are the lines in Benjamin's essay on Kafka that provoked Scholem to defend the "theological aspect" in Kafka. Scholem charges him with going too far in his "elimination of theology, throwing the baby out with the bath water."[38] The charge appears to be justified because, in the above passage, Benjamin seems to be saying that the practice of studying "our old books" counts more than the content or doctrine of these books and, in particular, more than the content of the Torah, the revealed law. The students in Kafka's narratives, who Benjamin interprets as "assistants to those creatures for whom, in Kafka's words, there is 'an infinite amount of hope'" (Benjamin 1994, 453), "are pupils who have lost the Scripture [*Schrift*]" (Benjamin 1999b, 815), yet, for all that, "do not belong to the hetaeric world" of myth

124   *Biopolitics of the Family*

(Benjamin 1994, 453). Nevertheless, Benjamin is unwilling to acknowledge Scholem's point that only the existence of the Law anchors the messianic: "Kafka's messianic category is the 'reversal' or 'study'" (Benjamin 1994, 453). This poses the definitive question for Benjamin: In what sense is the study of "our old books" paradigmatic of the messianic reversal?

His answer is already intimated in the figure of Bucephalus. Alexander the Great's horse runs away from world history and retires to study ancient tomes (whether they belong to Athens or to Jerusalem seems unimportant). In so doing, he becomes the advocate, the "new lawyer," of everything that has been left behind by the storm of progress, but which weighs on human life in the form of a mythical guilt and punishment at the hands of those who "practice" the law, whether in the form of mythical violence or in the form of divine violence. Bucephalus, as an advocate who nevertheless does not practice law and an animal who nevertheless is engrossed in study, represents a figure of cultivated bare life that lies beyond the anthropological machine and its separation of animality from humanity, nature from culture, *zoe* from *bios*. Bucephalus is the answer given to the plea that someone "pray for the little hunchback too" (Benjamin 1999b, 812).

But it is in the relation between Sancho Panza and Don Quixote, as set out in one of Kafka's prose poems, that Benjamin sees the essential gesture of "reversal" that contains the messianic:

> Whether the pupils have lost it [the Scripture in the sense of the Torah] or whether they are unable to decipher it comes down to the same thing, because, without the key that belongs to it, the Scripture is not Scripture but life [*nicht Schrift ist sondern Leben*]. Life as it is lived in the village at the foot of the hill on which the castle is built. It is in the attempt to metamorphize life into writing [*dem Versuch der Verwandlung des Lebens ins Schrift*] that I perceive the meaning of 'reversal', which so many of Kafka's parables endeavour to bring about—I take 'The Next Village' and 'The Bucket Rider' as examples. Sancho Panza's existence is exemplary because it actually consists in rereading one's existence, however buffoonish and quixotic [*Sancho Pansas Dasein ist musterhaft, weil es eigentlich im Nachlesen des eignen wenn auch närrischen und donquichotesken besteht*]. (Benjamin 1994, 453)

Without the key to unlock the meaning of the Torah [*Schrift*], the Torah no longer exists as a "secret law" that remains valid despite its lack of application. Rather, for Benjamin, the Torah has become the (way of) life in the village at the base of the Castle. In Kafka's parables a messianic "reversal" is staged in which the life lived in the village gets "metamorphized" into writing [*Schrift*]. Here, Sancho Panza and the images of traveling backward in time (whether of the beggar in the Jewish joke, or in the stories about riders and horses in Kafka, which Benjamin lists in the above citation) indicates, contra Agamben's reading, that the writing at stake is neither that of a Torah that fulfills itself in its transgression (as in Sabbatian interpretations of the Messiah), nor the writing of a new law "that nullifies even the Nothing and lets no form of law remain in force beyond its own content," a law represented by the idea of a writing that is fully intelligible to itself. To the contrary, the writing into which the village life gets metamorphosed and reversed (as if traveling backward through one's life) is the writing of fiction. The "old books" that Bucephalus pores over as if they were legal codices are, in reality, novels and plays.

The reason why the study of fiction is the threshold through which justice enters into life is contained in the analogy that Benjamin draws between the Messiah's slight adjustment of everything and the shifting that Kafka narrates in his parable dedicated to Sancho Panza:

> Without ever boasting of it, Sancho Panza succeeded over the years, by supplying a lot of romances of chivalry and adventure for the evening and night hours, in so diverting from him his demon, whom he later called Don Quixote, that his demon thereupon performed the maddest exploits—which, however, lacking a preordained object, which Sancho Panza himself was supposed to have been, did no one any harm. A free man, Sancho Panza followed Don Quixote on his trips and thus enjoyed great and profitable entertainment to the end of his days.[39]

Sancho Panza studies novels in order to divert his demon, Don Quixote. In Benjamin, the demonic stands for "the guilt context of the living. It corresponds to the natural condition of the living" (Benjamin 1996, 204), that is, to the condition Marx calls "prehistory" or to their "natural" history. Sancho Panza's "cunning" (an important Hegelian category that Benjamin retains) consists in diverting his demon, who previously ruled over his natural life, into a fictional life that recapitulates his own in the form of a novel.[40] This diversion allows Sancho Panza to stay put in a natural life of his own, no longer blown forward by the wind of progress, no longer goaded toward the future by his demon. In the novel that recapitulates his life in reverse, Sancho Panza goes out to ride with Don Quixote much like, in his dream, the beggar goes out to meet the king. The "weak" messianic force that encounters, from the opposite direction, the profane force of world politics described in Benjamin's *Theological-Political Fragment* and in the second of his *Theses on the Philosophy of History*, in reality refers to the recapitulated life of the novel, which is always lived as if going backward, from the end to the beginning. Life is transformed into literature in order to both distract and fulfill, fictionally, the destructive instincts that otherwise prey on bare life itself: these instincts manifest themselves in the ambivalent attitude toward the sovereign (or Father) as an object of love (Eros) and hate (Thanatos). Therefore the politics of nihilism that Benjamin advocates, the destruction of history to clear a site from where life can be constructed consciously and in common, is played out in the space of literature, more precisely, in the activity of critique that "politicizes art" (Benjamin 1968, 242).

The messianic reversal in Benjamin is distinct from that indicated by Agamben because it is not a question of restoring the rest of the sacred in a profaned life by letting bare life unfold its own singular laws. The profanation that saves bare life in Benjamin is expressed in the profanity of a Sancho Panza, who novelizes or metamorphizes life so as to give the demon a task to fulfill, a mission to accomplish, but whose object is no longer Sancho Panza's bare life. The author of the literary life is thereby freed or saved from having to incur the guilt that accompanies the necessary failure to fulfill the assigned task, to live up to one's destiny. This failure is then staged by Don Quixote, who becomes an allegory of a divine justice that is at once poetic and comic, as befits the idea of a demon (the agent of Fate) that itself fails to live up to destiny. For Don Quixote, in the novel, nothing is where or how it should be so that, for Sancho Panza, in a life that is barely and playfully lived out in all of its profanity, everything may be just (as in *gerecht*) where and as it should be. The slight messianic shift in Benjamin does not consist in an objective revolutionary reversal of the course of world history that would accomplish the Law in and through its transgression. The only act of "divine violence" that can expiate the guilt of bare life consists in shifting the Law into the register of fiction so as to enable the slight but unbridgeable abyss that exists between life and literature (and which is one of the themes of Cervantes's masterpiece) to become the fulcrum on which to divert the mythical away from bare life and loosen the hold that violence has on life. The study of literature, understood as revolutionary praxis, can alone propitiate the secret appointment with the forgotten past in which rests mundane happiness, the materialist version of *restitutio in integro*.

Agamben has argued that the messianic content in Benjamin's *Theses on the Philosophy of History* is given by Paul's theology (Agamben 2000b, 129–31). Yet, in the first of these *Theses*, the dwarf called "theology," which leads historical materialism to victory, is hunchbacked. Theology is thus affected by the distortion of all things in history.[41] Maybe it is time to consider the possibility that Benjamin sends Paul's theology ahead to engage the ideological illusions of his time (from Zionism to Stalinism), much in the same way that Kafka's Sancho Panza sends his demon, Don Quixote, to fight the windmills: "Sancho Panza, a sedate fool and a clumsy assistant, sent his rider on ahead; Bucephalus outlived his. Whether it is a man or a horse is no longer so important, if only the burden is taken off the back" (Benjamin 1999b, 816).[42] Benjamin employs theology in order to take the weight of spiritualism off the back of materialism, thereby allowing it to become effectively historical, galloping unhampered backward into history, against the storm blowing from Paradise called progress.[43] This cavalry charge of an effectively historical kind of materialism seeks to rescue neither the Father of the economy nor the debts He bequeaths to his children's children. It seeks to recover the sense of free praxis which Marx once described, in profane terms Sancho Panza would not have minded, as "making it possible for me to do one thing today and another tomorrow, to hunt in the morning, fish in the afternoon, rear cattle in the evening, criticize after dinner, just as I have a mind, without ever becoming hunter, fisherman, shepherd or critic" (Marx 1978c, 160).

4

NATALITY, FERTILITY, AND MIMESIS IN ARENDT'S THEORY OF FREEDOM

THE GENESIS OF ARENDT'S CONCEPT OF NATALITY

Arendt calls natality, defined as the fact that each human life begins with birth, the "central category of political thought" (Arendt 1958, 9). "Because they are *initium*, newcomers and beginners by virtue of birth, men take initiative, are prompted into action" (Arendt 1958, 177). The human capacity to act freely is said to be "ontologically rooted" in this "fact of natality" (Arendt 1958, 177). There is something very puzzling about identifying the root of human freedom in the condition of natality. Why should birth, of all things, condition human beings to live freely? The puzzlement only increases if one considers that Arendt appears to argue, throughout her work, that action, and therefore politics, are not biologically conditioned.[1] For Arendt, it is labor, not political action, which reflects human beings' dependency on biological processes that are not under their control and that they experience as necessity.[2] But if Arendt's political thought is so "antibiological," then why does she root human freedom in birth? Unless one comes to terms with this paradox, the sense of Arendt's political thought will remain unclear. This chapter tries to resolve the puzzle by arguing that, through her concept of natality, Arendt seeks to reconnect the essence of human freedom with biological life so as to give politics a new aim. Politics should no longer depend on the reduction of life to the sphere of necessity, as has traditionally been the case in Western political thought (Arendt 2005, 40–92). Instead, politics should be thought of as the dimension of freedom of life (*zoe*) itself.

In most recent discussions of Arendt's political thought, the human condition of natality, along with the closely related human condition of plurality,[3] is invariably mentioned in the context of treating her concept of action. Yet natality as such is rarely discussed in any significant detail, as if the relation between natality and action were either too obscure, or on the contrary, simply self-evident (Beiner 1984; Benhabib 1996; Canovan 1994; Pitkin 1998; Villa 1996).[4] Arendt herself, after a certain moment, begins to repeatedly and obsessively gesture toward this relation, always drawing support from a particular citation from St. Augustine, in which the Christian author seems to indicate that the divine creation of Man was for the sake of the human capacity to begin.[5] But Arendt never submits natality, either in its relation to biological life or its relation to divine creation, to a sustained analysis. Along with Arendt's doctrine on "judging," natality is the other keystone of her philosophical edifice, of which there remains nothing more than a few, fragmentary textual allusions.[6]

In the current literature dedicated specifically to the concept of natality, there is no extended discussion as to when exactly, and in what precise context, Arendt began to employ this concept (Bowen-Moore 1989; Collin 1999; Collin 2000; Durst 2004; Markell 2006). A few scholars have pointed out that the term "natality," or something close to it, is found in Heidegger's *Sein und Zeit*.[7] Heidegger, in fact, argues that death is "only *one* end" enclosing human existence (*Dasein*); the "other 'end' is the 'beginning', the 'birth'" (Heidegger 1986, 373) such that human existence can also be characterized by its "Sein zum Anfang" (being-toward-beginning) and not only by its "Sein zum Tode" (being-toward-death). Heidegger concludes the only treatment of birth found in his work with the claim that

> factical Dasein exists natively [*das faktische Dasein existiert gebürtig*] and natively it dies also already in the sense of being-toward-death [*und gebürtig stirbt es auch schon im Sinne des Seins zum Tode*]. . . . In the unity of thrownness and fleeting, that is, anticipatory being-toward-death, birth and death existentially 'hang together' [*In der Einheit von Geworfenheit und flüchtigen, bzw. Vorlaufendem Sein zum Tode 'hängen' Geburt und Tod daseinsmässig 'zusammen'*]. As care Dasein *is* this 'in-between' [*Als Sorge ist das Dasein das 'Zwischen'*]." (Heidegger 1986, 374, translation mine)

Although, in the above passage, Heidegger does seem to bring together the ideas of birth and the in-between which turns out to be fundamental for Arendt's mature concept of freedom, there are nonetheless good reasons to doubt that Heidegger's text is the sole, immediate, or even decisive inspiration for Arendt's concept of natality. In the first place, the term "natality" does not actually appear in Heidegger's text, as either *Gebürtigkeit* (Schürmann's translation of natality) or as *Gebürtlichkeit* (standard German translation for Arendt's term natality). Heidegger uses only the adjective *gebürtig* (native), which he employs adverbially, and he does not assign to birth the capacity or faculty that Arendt does.[8] Indeed, when Arendt first begins to employ the term in her essays, she does so in English, and on the evidence drawn from her recently published *Denktagebuch* (her notebooks dating from 1950 onward, mostly written in German), she seems to translate it back from English into German as "Natalität" (Arendt 2002, 461).

Moreover, in *Sein und Zeit*, Heidegger offers no further analysis of his concept of "being-toward-beginning" (*Sein zum Anfang*), but instead quickly returns to asserting the priority of being-toward-death for the self-understanding of human existence. This priority that Heidegger assigns to death is precisely what Arendt is already contesting in her 1929 dissertation on Augustine's theory of love. Most interpreters have all too rashly considered this text to have been written under the influence of Heidegger, basing this illation on Arendt's well-known relationship to her university teacher, rather than on a serious study of the dissertation itself (Arendt 1996). In reality, the dissertation seems to demonstrate, if anything, that from the start, Arendt rejected the basic foundations of Heidegger's analytic of *Dasein*.

Augustine was not a surprising choice for a dissertation subject in the 1920s among students who had felt the impact of Jasper's and Heidegger's "philosophy of existence." Both had mediated the reception of Kierkegaard and Nietzsche, whose works were completely ignored in the field of philosophy in the early twentieth century, into the German university and German culture at large, and both quickly realized that Kierkegaard and Nietzsche exploded to smithereens the modern peace settlement between faith and reason and, on the way, buried for good the idea of a transcendental ground of human subjectivity. In this context, it seemed imperative to return to the Christian Father who discovered inwardness through his meditations on faith and temporality in order to rethink the bases of subjectivity.

But for the Jewish students of Jaspers and Heidegger, there was an even more pressing reason to return to Augustine. The reason is that Augustine represented the first, and most crucial, victory against gnosticism in the West. The importance of the struggle against gnosticism became evident first to Hans Jonas, a student of Heidegger, friend of Leo Strauss and Hannah Arendt, and later longtime colleague of Arendt's in the Philosophy Department of the New School for Social Research in New York. Jonas's dissertation was dedicated to Augustine's theory of the free will, and his habilitation on gnostic religion was first published in 1934 (Jonas 1958). A few years later, Voegelin would publicly connect National Socialism (as well as Hegelianism, Marxism, and Existentialism) to a renewal of gnosticism in the West. In the 1960s, Hans Blumenberg set out to defend the "project of modernity" from the accusation of gnosticism, identifying in the modern "self-assertion" of human beings against nature a new, non-Augustinian response to the ever-permanent threat of gnostic temptations, thus rejecting the call by Voegelin, Strauss, and others to return to Platonic wisdom as the only real solution to the evils of gnosticism.[9]

Gnosticism is characterized by the rejection of the "goodness" of Creation: it was a Manichean religion that withdrew all value and significance from the world, seeing in it the product of the principle of "Darkness" in its fight against the principle of "Light." For gnosticism, God was not the Creator of the world (Jonas 1958, 227). Gnosticism, therefore, set itself up as a direct competitor to Judaism and Christianity, all three of them rejecting pagan wisdom. Above all, the gnostic rejection of worldliness was premised on the radical separation of *psyche* (principle of biological life) and *pneuma* (the foreign spirit trapped in the world): life was the prison-house of spirit, and the freedom of the subject (salvation) consisted in effecting, as best one could, this separation of spirit from life (Jonas 1958, 269–71, 333).

There is no doubt that the development of both Arendt's and Jonas's thought can be understood, in part, as an attempt to refute gnosticism by reconnecting human freedom back to worldliness and to biological life, making their separation in principle impossible. This desideratum, the inseparability of spirit from life, became, after the concentration camps and the appearance of "Musselmänner," an imperative. Totalitarianism, after all, was a political system that bases itself on the logical application of disembodied ideas ("ideology" as Arendt defines it), whose result is nothing short of the creation of thoughtless, but living bodies: life that can be totally dominated is thoughtless life.[10] In this sense, totalitarianism effects a separation between life and thought that has some resemblance to gnostic beliefs.[11] Natality in Arendt is countertotalitarian to the extent that it is a category that thinks the rootedness of freedom and subjectivity to life.[12]

Likewise, Jonas's entire work after his early pathbreaking study of gnosticism is dedicated to develop a philosophical biology for which freedom and subjectivity inheres in life.[13] Furthermore, as both Jonas and Arendt quickly realized, Heidegger's existentialism was an attempt to uproot the human subject from worldliness (understood by Arendt in terms of the foundational role of plurality and human community for the existence of *Dasein*) as well as to prove *Dasein*'s transcendence with respect to animal life.[14] Despite his well-known, complicated existential relation to Catholicism, Heidegger's philosophy (which was premised on the methodological separation of philosophy from faith) (Heidegger 1978, 45–78) betrayed a gnostic influence, or so at least Jonas thought. In this sense, one could argue that Arendt's Augustine dissertation, *Der Liebesbegriff bei Augustin. Versuch einer philosophischen Interpretation*, is an attempt to "seduce" Heidegger's thinking away from its gnostic trajectory.

Arendt's dissertation investigates the possibility of grounding the Christian call to "love thy neighbor as thyself" in the "love of God." It sets out to demonstrate that two irreconcilable conceptions of love or *caritas* coexist in Augustine's corpus, both of which, ultimately, stand in tension with the possibility of establishing a meaningful "love of the neighbor" as the human other. The first idea of *caritas* is modeled on the notion of desire as appetite: here, the love of God is understood in terms of the desire to acquire an object that cannot possibly be "lost" because it shares nothing with the transience of worldly things. According to Arendt, this idea of *caritas* requires "self-forgetfulness and complete denial of human existence ... [and] makes the central Christian demand to love one's neighbor as oneself well nigh impossible" (Arendt 1996, 30).

The second account of love that Arendt finds in Augustine is based on the Creator-creature dualism. It is in discussing this second idea of *caritas* that Arendt explicitly detaches herself from and criticizes Heidegger's analytic of existence. In Arendt's reading of Augustine, the Creator-creature distinction is set within the context of the possibility of achieving a "happy life." This preoccupation was completely foreign to Heidegger. By contrast, it was central to the development of Walter Benjamin's thought, from his early programmatic texts on the philosophy of language through his late *Theses on history*.[15] For Arendt, the source of this idea of happiness is our memory: "The knowledge of the possible existence of the happy life [*beata vita*] is given in pure consciousness prior to all experience, and it guarantees our recognizing the happy life whenever we should encounter it" (Arendt 1996, 46). Memory here is concerned with "safeguarding" a past that was never a present, something that was never experienced; the past constituted by a "transcendent and transmundane... origin of human existence as such," which is radically opposed to a transcendence oriented toward "goals" and which takes the future as its fundamental, temporal horizon (Arendt 1996, 48). Heidegger's discussion of birth and death in *Sein und Zeit* occurs within his deduction of the "historicity" (*Geschichtlichkeit*) of human existence. In this context, Heidegger argues that "destiny" and the "future" are fundamental to the historicity of human existence. Arendt's own treatment of historicity, by contrast, is clearly oriented, already in the dissertation on Augustine, toward an idea of freedom that is inseparable from the recovery of, or return to such an "absolute past": "It is memory and not expectation (for instance, the expectation of death as in Heidegger's approach) that gives unity and wholeness to human existence" (Arendt 1996, 55–56). In her later political thought, the experience of origins is fundamental for the development of her theory of revolutionary legitimacy (Arendt 1977, 1990).

The concept of recollection that Arendt teases out of Augustine offers, according to her, the basis for a different conception of love—one that is not based on appetite. By remembering the origin, the human being is oriented toward "loving" God's love (for humanity), as manifest in Creation, and not simply oriented toward a "love of God" (where God is a possible object of desire). In this new conception of love, what is loved by human beings is the "original interconnectedness of either man and God or man and world" (Arendt 1996, 30). Arendt later terms this interconnectedness "natality," christening it through a famous quotation drawn from Augustine's *City of God*. But in her original dissertation, neither this citation nor natality is to be found. In fact, Arendt only inserts the pertinent citation from Augustine ex post facto, when, in the period from 1958 through 1964, she revises parts of her dissertation (especially the section dealing with Creation) with the intent to republish it in an English translation (Arendt 1996, 132).[16]

More problematic still for those interpreters who insist on a Heideggerian origin of natality, is that in Arendt's discussion of the second conception of love, she mounts a sharp critique of Heidegger:

That man in his desire to be happy depends upon a notion of happiness that he could never experience in his earthly life, and that such a notion, moreover, should be the sole determinant of his earthly conduct, can only signify that human existence as such depends on something outside the human condition as we know and experience it.... This 'outside the human condition' actually means before human existence. Therefore the Creator is both outside and before man. The Creator is in man only by virtue of man's memory. (Arendt 1996, 49)

[Dass der Mensch in seinem Begehren durch das *beatum esse velle* von einer *beata vita* abhängig ist, die er innerhalb seines irdischen Lebens nie hat erfahren können, und dass diese *beata vita* wiederum das allein Bestimmende seines irdischen Seins ist, besagt, dass er in seinem Sein abhängt von etwas *ausser ihm*: und das diese *beata vita errinert* wird, obgleich nicht aus dem innerweltlichen Erfahrungszusammenhang, ist dieses 'ausser-ihm' identisch mit einem 'vor-ihm'. Das 'ausser-' und 'vor-ihm', das, was vor ihm war, ist der *Creator*, der nur insofern in ihm ist (*in me*) als er sich in der *memoria* als Streben nach der *beata vita* kundgibt]. (Arendt 1929)

The English translation contains a reference to "human condition" that is not in the original German, but Arendt's point remains unchanged, namely, that human existence is dependent on an Other that remains radically "outside" and "before" the conditions of "earthly life."[17] "The creature in its createdness derives its sense of meaningfulness from a source that precedes its creation, that is, from the Maker who made it.... The very fact that man has not made himself but was created implies that the meaningfulness of human existence both lies outside itself and antedates it. Createdness (*creatum esse*) means that essence and existence are not the same.... Hence to 'return to God' is actually the only way in which a created thing can 'return to itself'" (Arendt 1996, 50). The implicit rejection of Heidegger's position (that human existence is defined as a function of assigning "meaning" to Being) and the position of German existentialism (that human existence is defined by the identity of essence and existence) could not be clearer.[18] What changes from 1929 to 1958, the year of the publication of *The Human Condition*, is that the relation of human existence to that which is outside it and gives it meaning ceases to be called the "fact" of Creation and instead becomes "the fact of natality," where the emphasis is on its connection with the phenomenon of life rather than on its connection with divine creation.

Natality, Fertility, and Mimesis in Arendt's Theory of Freedom

With the recent publication of her fragments from the 1950s entitled *Was ist Politik?*, as well as her work diaries (*Denktagebuch*) from the same years, one can reconstruct with some historical precision the genesis of the concept of natality in Arendt's thought. Prior to and including the first edition of *Origins of Totalitarianism*, Arendt had not employed this concept. After finishing that book, starting in 1950, her work diaries and fragmentary texts are focused on rethinking politics starting from the fundamental distinction between "men," who are always in the plural, and "Man," the single species. This was an attempt to overcome the "contradiction" that she had identified in Augustine's conception of "social life" (*vita socialis*) and the role of the love of the neighbor in her dissertation on Augustine. Arendt thought Augustine posited a "double origin" for the human being, who is conceived at one time as "isolated" from others and from the world because existing essentially in relation to the singularity of the Creator, and at another time as "determined and co-constituted in its essence by the fact of belonging to the *genus humanum* [generated by Adam] [Der Mensch *ist* ein anderer, ob er sich als isolierter versteht oder bedingt und wesensmässig mitkonstituiert durch die Tatsache, dem *genus humanum* zuzugehören]" (Arendt 1929). Her central working hypothesis is that the entire Western tradition of political thought has ignored the distinction between "men" and "Man," attempting to think politics from the identity of all human beings qua specimens of the same species, rather than from their "original differentiation." This avoidance of plurality is found both in the Aristotelian conception of Man as *zoon politikon*, which makes politics inherent in human nature, and in the Christian conception of Man as created in the image of the One God, which orients politics toward omnipotence. This climaxes in modern philosophies of history, where human plurality is fused into the idea of humanity as the subject of history (Arendt 2003, 9–11; Arendt 2005, 94–95). To this Western political tradition, Arendt's objection is simply that "*man* is apolitical. Politics arises *between men*, and so quite *outside* of *man*. There is therefore no political substance. Politics arises in what lies *between men* and is established as relationships" (Arendt 2005, 95).

But at this point, as one can see from Fragment 1 of *Was ist Politik?*, dated August 1950, the plurality of men is still considered "a human, earthly product, the product of human nature," in opposition to the "fact" that "God created man" (Arendt 2005, 93). "*Man*, as philosophy and theology know him, exists—or is realized—in politics only in the equal rights that those who are most different guarantee for each other. This voluntary guarantee of, and concession to, a claim of legal equality recognizes the plurality of men, who can thank themselves for their plurality and the creator of *man* for their existence" (Arendt 2005, 94). Plurality has not yet found its definitive ontological placement: it remains a human product, analogous to the sense in which human political organizations are human products. What human beings have in common are human rights, for these belong to every human being insofar as he or she is a member of the species "Man," itself a creation of God. Human rights, at this point of her thinking, are prepolitical for Arendt. There is no way to think about what men, in the plural, have "in common" *as* the "absolute differentiation" of every singular individual, *as* what makes each individual *irreducible* to a specimen, to a member of the species. "God's creation of the plurality of *men* is embodied in the absolute difference of all men from one another, which is greater than the relative difference among peoples, nations, or races. But in that case, there is in fact no role for politics. From the very start, politics organizes those who are absolutely different with a view to their *relative* equality and in contradistinction to their *relative* differences" (Arendt 2005, 96). Absolute difference is here not yet immediately political. Likewise, the dimension of the political, the *in-between* of a plurality of men, is still thought of as an object of human practice, as something that can be "made" in one sense or another (Arendt says "human, earthly product"). The *in-between* is not yet ontologically rooted in a "condition" about which human beings can ultimately do nothing about, a condition that limits, a priori, its manipulability.

The first breakthrough seems to be traceable to an entry in the *Denktagebuch* dated April 1951. Arendt comments on two passages found side by side in Augustine's *City of God*, where the creation of Man is distinguished from the creation of animals. The first passage concerns Augustine's idea that God "started . . . with one man, whom he created as the first man . . . instead of starting with many" whereas, in the case of animals, "he commanded many to come into existence at once" (Augustine 1984, XII, 22). The second passage is the famous citation: "to provide that beginning, a man was created, before whom no man ever existed" (Augustine 1984, XII, 21). Arendt then comments on these passages:

> with men came into the world the beginning. On this rests the sanctity (*die Heiligkeit*) of human spontaneity. Totalitarian extermination of men as men is the extermination of their spontaneity. This means at the same time the reversal of creation as creation, as to-have-made-a-beginning [*die Rückgängigmachung der Schöpfung als Schöpfung, als Einen-Anfang-gesetzt-Haben*]. Maybe here is the connection between the attempt to destroy men and the attempt to destroy nature. (Arendt 2002, 66)

What makes this commentary highly significant is the assertion that the Western political tradition resists acknowledging the plurality of human beings because of their animality, since, if one follows Augustine's text, only animals were created in the plural, rather than starting from one specimen ("the first man"). By contrast, the existence of spontaneity, again following Augustine, is due to God having created Man, not animals. Only if animal life is directly connected to the capacity to begin, as Arendt later connects them through the concept of natality, does it make sense to assume that "the attempt to destroy men" is fundamentally connected to the "attempt to destroy nature."

The concept of natality makes its official entrance only two years later, in 1953, the year she delivers her unpublished Geuss lectures on "Karl Marx and the Tradition of Political Thought" at Princeton University and publishes "Ideology and Terror," which later becomes the last chapter of the second, 1958 edition of *Origins of Totalitarianism*.[19] The manuscript on Marx contains no reference to natality or to Augustine, but, on the contrary, has much to say about the category of labor as indicative of the insurmountable animality of man. Natality and the Augustine citation first appear in "Ideology and Terror," where Arendt thematizes the connection among action, natality and createdness. "Beginning . . . is the supreme capacity of man; politically, it is identical with man's freedom. *Initium ut esset homo creatus est*—'that a beginning be made man was created' said Augustine. This beginning is guaranteed by each new birth; it is indeed every man" (Arendt 1973, 478–79).

The available textual evidence, then, seems to indicate that Arendt begins to use the concept of natality only after the 1951 publication of the first edition of her study on *The Origins of Totalitarianism*. That year, in a letter to Jaspers, she writes that the evil of totalitarianism is condensed in the belief that the individuals of the species "Man" are superfluous for the realization of the species (Arendt 1992, 166).[20] Soon thereafter she begins to theorize a new, countertotalitarian politics that takes the birth of these "superfluous" individuals, in their radical diversity from one other, as its fundamental principle.

ARENDT'S POLITICAL THOUGHT AS BIOPOLITICS

If the above conjectures as to the genesis of Arendt's concept of natality are correct and she did begin to make use of the concept of natality only after having formulated the main lines of her interpretation of totalitarianism, then this would indicate that through this concept Arendt not only wanted to formulate a countertotalitarian politics, but one that would be as much a politics of life as totalitarianism was a politics of death. On this hypothesis, it would be false to suppose that Arendt wanted to counter totalitarian politics by separating her conception of politics from all connection to biological life. Totalitarian politics, which are based on the extermination of "superfluous" individuals, and Arendtian politics, which are based on the revaluation of the birth and plurality of such individuals, would then both belong within the discursive matrix that Foucault later calls "biopolitics." By interpreting totalitarianism as a biopolitical phenomenon, one is in a position to better understand what Arendt was trying to achieve with her concept of natality.[21]

Foucault defines biopolitics as that transformation in the idea of politics that took place in early modernity, wherein politics came to be defined as a "power over life," as the domination over life achieved through the control of the life process itself. Foucault argues that until the baroque age, the preservation of biological life, much like the capacity to speak, had been considered merely a precondition, not the end, of a political way of life. For Aristotle, politics presupposes that man is a living being (*zoon*) who speaks (*logon echon*), but the end of politics is "living well" (*eu zen*) not "mere living" (*tou zen*): happiness (*eudaimonia*), not life itself (Aristotle 1988, 1252b: 30; Foucault 1990, 143). According to Foucault, totalitarianism is one potential outcome of the modern redirection of politics toward species life. This is because the other side of a power over life is the power to let die:

Natality, Fertility, and Mimesis in Arendt's Theory of Freedom 139 totalitarianism is one manifestation of the politics of death that is always an immanent potential of biopolitics (Foucault 1990, 138–39). The power to "disallow life to the point of death" (Foucault 1990, 138) becomes an index of the degree to which life has come under human control and domination. This Foucaultian intuition merely expresses theoretically what Primo Levi, among others, have experienced as the real "purpose" of totalitarian regimes, irrespective of their ideologies: the "resolution of others to annihilate us first as men in order to kill us more slowly afterwards" (Levi 1996, 51). The Lager is "a gigantic biological and social experiment" (Levi 1996, 87) in which human life is dehumanized in order to create as end-product the "Muselmänner, the drowned . . . an anonymous mass, continually renewed and always identical, of non-men who march and labor in silence, the divine spark dead within them, already too empty to really suffer. One hesitates to call them living: one hesitates to call their death death" (Levi 1996, 90). Agamben refers to this dehumanized human life as bare life and the bearer of such life as *homo sacer*: somebody who can be killed without committing either murder or sacrilege because she has been expelled from the precincts of human and divine law because her life is no longer recognized to be a human life (Agamben 1998; Agamben 1999). Arendt, of course, was familiar with bare life in this sense, having dedicated an entire chapter of *Origins of Totalitarianism* to discussing "the preparation of living corpses" (Arendt 1973, 451) in the concentration and extermination camps, whose sole result was to achieve "total domination" through the destruction of the "uniqueness" and the "individuality" of human beings (Arendt 1973, 455).

To briefly foreshadow my conclusion, Arendt's answer to the phenomenon of the systematic production of bare life in totalitarian regimes is to base a new politics on the phenomenon of natality. Natality is a biopolitical concept that counters the "thanatopolitical" concept of bare life; it is a response to the politics of death implicit in modern biopolitics that was realized, for the first time, in the totalitarian regimes of the twentieth century (Esposito 2008). This, however, was not the last time: after all, it was during the 1950s that Arendt became convinced that totalitarianism was a new, but "essential" form of government, whose possibility must therefore correspond to some "basic experience" of human beings and, hence, is inherently repeatable. The "basic experience" to which totalitarianism "responds" politically is that of "loneliness" (Arendt 1973, 474).

Arendt's political thought after 1950 indicates that the negative consequences of biopolitics should be met with an affirmative biopolitics. Esposito has identified this dualism of biopolitical discourse, that is, the fact that biopolitics is split into a "life-affirming" politics and a "life-denying" one (Esposito 2008). But his own attempts to understand the grounds and logic of this dualism in what he calls the "paradigm of immunization" seems insufficient to explain the variety of ways in which life always carries with it a double, antinomical function in biopolitical discourse. One can see traces of this antinomical self-doubling of life in, for example, Freud's later dualism of fundamental drives (Eros and Thanatos) (Freud 1961), Foucault's distinction between sexuality and pleasures (Foucault 1990), Agamben's idea that bare life is "sacred" only when it comes under the form of the law but, otherwise, has a redemptive function (Agamben 2004), and perhaps most importantly of all, in Benjamin's distinction between "mere life" and "that life which is identically present in earthly life, death, and afterlife" (Benjamin 1999, 249–52). In all of these cases, if biological life can become the object (or, better, the *target*) of political control and domination in thanatopolitics,[22] then biological life must also be capable of becoming the subject (or, perhaps better, the *line of flight*) of resistance to domination.[23]

ZOE AND *BIOS*: HUMANISM AND ANTIHUMANISM IN ARENDT'S BIOPOLITICS

In order to play this double biopolitical role, biological life must be reconceived as containing a caesura, or a discontinuity within itself. On one side of this caesura, life is the politically passive object of domination; on the other side, it is the politically active subject of a new freedom. "Subject" here means literally *sub-jectum*, or what is thrown-under as a condition for a new action. In Arendt, natality is the name for this sub-jectivity, for this being-thrown(-under) that allows for the emergence of a new self through its own actions and words.[24] In the following sections, I show that Arendt's concept of natality is one of the names of this caesura of life within life. This caesura facilitates the transition from life as an object of power to life as a subject of freedom. Natality is the having-become of biological life: it refers to what may be called the "natural history" of life. The having-become of life is its pastness, or thrownness. This natural-historical dimension of life, for Arendt, refers life back to an origin that lies outside of life, an origin that is called creation. At the same time, natality is constitutive of the sub-jectivity of biological life in two ways: first, because it is the freedom of biological life; second, because it is the human being's condition of selfhood that includes the history of its self-initiated actions.

To avoid any misunderstandings with respect to the interpretative hypothesis I outline, it is important not to confuse the caesura of life figured by natality with the neo-Aristotelian division of life into species life (*zoe*) and human life (*bios*), a division that also plays a role in Arendt's texts (Arendt 1977, 42; Arendt 1958, 96–97). Undoubtedly, one of the strongest claims found in *The Human Condition* is the identification, critique, and rejection of the historical reversal by which the *bios politikos*, the political life, undertakes the management of *zoe*, the biological life shared by all living species. Since this management (or *oikonomia*) of biological life has been linked to labor throughout the Western tradition, Arendt concludes that totalitarianism became possible once political action was made to serve the *animal laborans*, rather than the other way around. This reversal of the hierarchy between action and labor, in turn, was facilitated by the Christian transformation of life into the "ultimate good," a belief that modernity holds onto, despite its secularism (Arendt 1958, 313ff).[25] The real question, however, concerns the philosophical basis for Arendt's rejection of the management of biological life as a goal of politics.

Interpreters have taken the above claims as license to argue that Arendt's conception of politics is completely dependent upon a neo-Aristotelian separation between "humanized" life (*bios*) and animal life (*zoe*).[26] Arendt, at times, encourages this interpretation by saying that species or animal life knows no birth or death, whereas human life begins with birth and ends with death (Arendt 1958, 96). "The biological process in man . . . [is] endlessly repetitive" (Arendt 1958, 98), whereas human life in its linearity is an "interruption" of the natural "circle" of life. Actions and words, in turn, are the political events that "mark" the linearity of a human life such that its *bios* can become the subject matter of a "story" written by those who have witnessed the effects of these actions and words. For Arendt, humans have *bio-graphies* whereas species do not (Arendt 1958, 97–98). The implication is that without such a *bios politikos*, without the actions and words of the actor, retold by the spectators, there is no "self" (Cavarero 2000). Whereas *zoe* belongs to the individual qua member of a species, the *bios* of the individual is something that happens "outside" of the individual and does not belong exclusively to her, but to the *in-between* that Arendt calls the "world" or the "public space." To be "dead to the world," that is, to be alive but insignificant to those others who alone can judge the significance of our words and acts, is to live a life that "has ceased to be human life because it is no longer lived among men" (Arendt 1958, 176). Even Collin, whose reading of Arendt is one of the few attempts not to take the neo-Aristotelian dualism between *zoe* and *bios* for granted, in the end, posits the priority of *bios* over *zoe*: "Freedom is not freedom against the 'facticity' of birth, from which it should in some ways tear itself free, but freedom is birth. It is the biological which sets itself apart from the biographical, and not the other way round: life as *zoe* is constructed or constituted on life as *bios*" (Collin 1999, 106).

But reading the distinction between *bios* and *zoe* in Arendt's work in neo-Aristotelian fashion leads to considerable problems when it comes to giving a coherent account of her thought. First of all, this distinction leads one to posit a human "nature" that is "political." It suggests that "having" *logos* and being a "political" animal determine the nature of the animal "Man" in distinction to other animal species. But Arendt clearly rejects Aristotle's "naturalization" of politics in the sense of his ascribing the capacity for politics to human "nature" (Arendt 2005, 95). She argues that Aristotle, like the Western political tradition after him up to but not including Hobbes, misses the basic distinction between "Man" and "men," between human nature and the human condition of plurality. It is this plurality of human beings that first enables the in-between of politics and, therefore, the in-between cannot possibly be reduced to the *bios politikos* of Man, as Aristotle suggests.

The second problem with such a reading of the distinction between *zoe* and *bios* is that it does not correspond to anything in Augustine, from whom Arendt draws the idea of natality in the 1950s. Indeed, it is clear from the *Denktagebuch* that Augustine's own discussion of natality occasioned a problem for Arendt's basic starting point of human plurality. In his discussion of the reason for God's creation of Man, Augustine claims that God created human beings as "Adam," that is, as a singular "man," in contrast to the creation of animals, which is always plural. As Arendt asserts, in the

Jewish-Christian creation myth and the concept of the political: everything hangs on the difficulty to grasp the specific human plurality. Men in contrast to animals ('plura simul iussit existere') descend from One Man ('ex uno homine') and have through this origin 1. the guarantee of their similitude to God, because God is One, and 2. the guarantee that peoples need not degenerate into races (*Völker nicht zu Rassen entarten*) or simply degenerate. In the 'ex uno homine', in the fact, that plurality is *secondary*, lies the guarantee of 'humanity'. . . . (Plurality as animality [*das Tierische*]!) The state as 'civitas terrena' exists in order to take on our animality in the most humanly dignified way possible, in order to protect men in their being-animal, that is, in their plurality. (Arendt 2002, 70–71)

Given Augustine's starting point, it follows that when plurality is assumed to be a secondary feature of human beings, as the ideal of "humanity" seems to require, politics becomes identical to the domination of nature and animality in human beings. This is Arendt's closest point of contact with the position Adorno and Horkheimer presented only a few years earlier in their *Dialectic of Enlightenment*. They argue that the "rational" control of nature and instinct, understood as the attempt to escape the mythical, simply proves to be the mythical itself.

One way out of the dilemma would have been for Arendt to rethink the political starting from the emancipation of the animality of human beings, thereby returning the political to the plurality of the animal.[27] But Arendt does not take this route and instead opts for what could be called an intermediate path that "saves" Augustine from himself. By interpreting the creation of Adam as the creation of man and woman, Arendt reconfigures the origin as being of two-ness and not of the one-ness of a common progenitor of the species, thereby relating this two-ness to plurality by way of fertility and childbearing. While I analyze this conception in further detail below, what is important here is to emphasize Arendt's rejection, on political grounds, of the reduction of human plurality to Adam, to the common progenitor of the human race.[28] For if such a progenitor becomes the model for political association, then this association will never be one that begins from the plurality of human beings. That is why Arendt has no hesitation in praising Hobbes, and modern social contract theory in general, for rejecting the Adamic origin of men and replacing it with the state of nature, thus preparing the way for thinking about the political from the originary plurality of individuals who form the in-between by way of compacts (Arendt 2005, 95). Natality, then, is a concept that Arendt employs to deconstruct the "humanist" opposition between animality and humanity based on the neo-Aristotelian distinction between *zoe* and *bios*, but which nonetheless retains an internal reference to divine creation.

If, notwithstanding her own arguments, Arendt nevertheless lapses, or seems to lapse, into a positive usage of the neo-Aristotelian distinction between *bios* and *zoe* in order to distinguish a properly "human" life from an "inhuman" human life, this lapse is undoubtedly motivated by her rejection of the totalitarian selection and annihilation of parts of humanity in order to achieve complete control over biological life through the creation of a "superior" race and the resulting "bestialization" of human beings.[29] But such attempts to counter totalitarian biopolitics simply by effecting the separation of humanity from biological life (and, conversely, by ambiguously denying full "humanity" to those "peoples" who are too caught up in "nature") for the sake of distinguishing a purely "human," "highly unnatural" life, only lead Arendt into an unnecessarily harsh version of ideological humanism in her early work.[30] And, in the end, they do not correspond to the deepest tenets of her thought, which always emphasizes what is most "human" as a condition of the living, and not vice versa.

Arendt's ideological humanism culminates with the idea, voiced toward the end of *The Origins of Totalitarianism*, that without "a place in the world," without participation in the political life of some determinate community, human life lacks humanity and dignity.[31] I take this to be the "humanist" conclusion Arendt arrives at around 1949, with the first edition of *The Origins of Totalitarianism*. Paradoxically, this "humanist" conclusion is very critical of the doctrine of human rights proposed, at least implicitly, in the 1948 Universal Declaration of Human Rights of the United Nations, as a solution to the problems of genocide and stateless people in general. Arendt rejects it on the grounds that any doctrine of "human" rights not based on the idea of an "essence" or "nature" of Man is a fragile doctrine. And, in Arendt's view, everything at the end of the twentieth century conspires against holding on to the idea of a human "essence" or "nature."[32] Yet, in 1949, Arendt has nothing better to propose than a vague defense of some sort of national self-assertion of a people, clearly having in mind the events leading up to the foundation of the state of Israel, wherein its formation was the least inadequate response to the Shoah.[33] Later, Arendt becomes increasingly critical of the Zionist solution, and although she is never an outright defender of the absoluteness of human rights, she never repeats her critique of human rights with the harshness of its first formulation (Isaac 1996; Parekh 2004).

It seems, then, that the "humanist" conclusion to the first edition of *The Origins of Totalitarianism* should be interpreted as a moment of impasse in the development of Arendt's thought. This first edition ends on a tone of hopelessness when faced with the unheard of "novelty" of totalitarianism as a form of rule. For, on the one hand, Arendt maintains that "our political life rests on the assumption that we can produce equality through organization, because man can act in and change and build a common world, together with his equals and only with his equals" (Arendt 1973, 301). On the other hand, "the dark background of mere givenness, the background formed by our unchangeable and unique nature, breaks into the political scene as the alien which in its all too obvious difference reminds us of the limitations of human activity" (Arendt 1973, 301). Arendt concludes that the political sphere will inevitably tend "to destroy" the "alien" as a "frightening symbol of the fact of difference as such" (Arendt 1973, 301). But, should "a civilization succeed in eliminating or reducing to a minimum the dark background of difference, it will end in complete petrification and be punished, so to speak, for having forgotten that man is only the master, not the creator of the world" (Arendt 1973, 302). Clearly, at this point in the development of her thought, Arendt has not yet found a way to reconcile the natural "fact of givenness" and her belief in "the creator of the world" with a form of political organization that is not, tendentially, bound to exterminate the "alien."

The impasse of the first edition of *The Origins of Totalitarianism* explains why, even after its publication, Arendt thought she had not yet fully "understood" totalitarianism since she had not figured out whether anything could be "done" about it. This explains why some of her first important essays after *The Origins of Totalitarianism*, such as "Understanding and Politics" and "On the Nature of Totalitarianism" (Arendt 1994), are centered on the problem of "understanding" totalitarianism in relation to the need to renew the traditional doctrine of the "forms of government" inherited since Plato and Aristotle. But her thinking anew about human political organization would have been incomplete if she had not found, in the concept of natality, the way to reconcile life with politics.³⁴ It is highly significant, therefore, that Arendt comes to define understanding as "the specifically human way of *being alive*; for every single person needs to be reconciled to a world in which *he was born a stranger* and in which, to the extent of his distinct uniqueness, he always remains a stranger" (Arendt 1994, 308).

If hopelessness still lingers in *The Human Condition*, this is only because the book has been interpreted as if it were putting forward the "humanistic" thesis that without a life in a *polis*, the human individual can never reach his or her "full" humanity.³⁵ But the assertion that *The Human Condition* is simply defending the priority of the Greek *bios politikos* against the revaluation of the worker in modernity must be rejected. This cannot be the point of the book precisely because, in it, Arendt wants to think politics from the idea of natality. She expressly says that natality is not a category of Greek political thought; rather, it is the only source of hope against totalitarianism (Arendt 1958, 247).³⁶

Natality is the condition of the world and of the political, but it is a condition that does not depend on the previous existence of an organized political space. That is, natality is the concept through which it becomes possible to think the political independently of the Aristotelian claim that the political (or the *polis*) is "natural" to Man, while still being a function of life itself. The "naturalness" of the political was of decisive importance to the development of Western political thought, both in antiquity and in the late medieval recovery of Aristotle. But for Arendt, unlike her contemporaries Leo Strauss and Jacques Maritain, this political paradigm had nothing left to offer against the onslaught of totalitarian politics. It is also crucial that natality can function where the world has become a "desert," since totalitarian society mobilizes the lonely crowds as if "setting the desert itself in motion."³⁷ The reason natality can function even in "desert storms" is because natality stands for the primordial "nomadic" condition of human life.³⁸ Most readings of natality found in the secondary literature are problematic precisely because they presuppose that one is born "into" the world, as if this in-between were already given, as if it always already contained natality.³⁹ But the idea of being born into an "identity by birth" (Durst 2004, 787) goes profoundly against Arendt's sense that the world can always become a desert. It also goes against her equally crucial reading of Abraham (Arendt 1958, 243; Arendt 1990, 172), for whom the crossing of the

Natality, Fertility, and Mimesis in Arendt's Theory of Freedom 147

desert has nothing to do with the "family" one is born into. Rather, it has to do with the possibility of establishing a contract with and a promise to the other, as a basic political phenomena, which is unrelated to the family or to love.[40] Natality is the key category for the politics that is to come after the end of the nation-state, after all the illusions of the earth as a *Heimat* are laid to rest, after all attempts to think the political from a familial model have shown their barrenness, and, perhaps, even after the disintegration of all political form and organization as such.

In reality, Arendt's conception of natality does not presuppose the neo-Aristotelian dualism of *zoe* and *bios*, but instead thematizes its limits and ultimately overthrows its logic. Arendt repeatedly claims that natality is not only what "inserts" life into a pregiven world, but also that natality is what "daily renews" this world itself, which otherwise would perish along with the death of individuals (Arendt 1958, 246–47; Arendt 2003, 49). Properly understood, this claim means that natality is irreducible to the *bios politikos*: natality is essentially antecedent with respect to the common world. To understand its meaning, one must bring the concept of natality back to the level of *zoe* and ask what difference natality makes within and for biological life (*zoe*). In sum, if in Arendt there is an affirmative conception of biopolitics, then it depends on conceiving of natality as a politicization of *zoe*, and not as an always already "political" *bios*. This politicization of life goes against what Esposito calls "the cycle of *ghenos* (descent, race)," and what Forti has analyzed in the "biopolitics of the soul" characteristic of Nazism, that is, it goes against a biopolitics whose supreme goal is the fabrication of a "good" descent or race: a eugenic biopolitics. If something like a *bios politikos* or a *vita activa* can survive in the posttotalitarian age, it will not depend on keeping politics apart from life and labor, as Arendt has too often been misinterpreted as arguing. On the contrary, it will depend on knowing how to politicize life and labor, and only these,[41] so that they may avoid becoming the targets of domination or the media of a politics of death.[42]

NATALITY AS CONDITION OF FREEDOM

For Arendt, a human life is a free life. Natality is fundamental to her idea of politics because she believes that freedom is the only meaning (*Sinn*) of politics (Arendt 2003, 31ff) and natality is the "condition" of this political freedom. After 1950, the central questions of Arendt's political thought become: What is freedom? and Why does freedom need to be conditioned by natality? Her answer has two components. The first is that freedom must be worldly and not private. This requirement, in my opinion, comes from her presupposition, which is of Heideggerian origin, that there is no "private" meaning (*Sinn*) and that what gives meaning is simply the world as a totality of interlocking references.[43] But Arendt develops this insight, against Heidegger, through her theory of "common sense," her revaluation of opinion (*doxa*), and her theory of judgment (Arendt 1978, 1982, 2005). So one component of freedom must be that it exists *for and before others*; it takes place *in-between* individuals; in short, freedom must be "phenomenalizable." The requirement of phenomenality is so decisive for Arendt that it leads her to consider freedom of movement as the fundamental freedom: movement through an "open" space is the most basic phenomenalization of freedom.[44]

But if this explains why freedom could be seen as the *Sinn* of politics, it does not answer the question of what freedom is. The concept of freedom in Arendt has three essential features. The first is a Kantian feature: the idea that freedom is spontaneity. "Action is unique in that it sets in motion processes that in their automatism look very much like natural processes, and action also marks the start of something, begins something new, seizes the initiative, or, in Kantian terms, forges its own chain. The miracle of freedom is inherent in its ability to make a beginning" (Arendt 2005, 113). What needs to be emphasized about this definition is that the capacity to begin a new series of events has an "automatism" that is analogous to the one found in natural processes, but unlike it in the sense that freedom is the automatism of an interruption of natural processes. Thus, natality is not just an "interruption" of the natural process, but an "automatic" interruption of it.

The importance of the automatism of beginnings becomes apparent when it is related to Arendt's fundamental claim that totalitarianism makes singular individuals superfluous through the systematic, even bureaucratic application of laws of Nature or History intended to produce one Humanity or Mankind (that is, to turn the plurality of human being into the species "Man"). "The law of Nature or the law of History, if properly executed, is expected to produce mankind as its end product. . . . Terror . . . makes it possible for the force of nature or of history to race freely through mankind, unhindered by any spontaneous human action" (Arendt 1973, 461, 465). Natality is what stands in the way of achieving or finalizing the human species because, according to Arendt, natality only brings forth singulars, radically diverse individuals, and not the species "Man." In her view, if one may speak of a "human" species at all, it is only as a result of the "multiplication" of singulars, that is, only on the basis of the biological "fertility" of a life that has been previously singularized by natality. The treatment of natality in *The Human Condition* begins with the idea of plurality as "the fact that men, not Man, live on the earth" (Arendt 1958, 7), which Arendt glosses by referring to the passage in Genesis I: 27 where it is written that God created "them," male and female, and not just "him" (*Adam*). Creation gives singularity, and men come out of this plural singularity as the result of "multiplication," that is, of life on earth, and the "fertility" of this earthly life (Arendt 1958, 8). The crucial point for Arendt is that createdness, not fertility, is the root of singularity. Fertility is merely the cause of the multiplication of singulars. "The force of life is fertility. The living organism is not exhausted when it has provided for its own reproduction, and its 'surplus' lies in its potential multiplication" (Arendt 1958, 108). In this sense, Arendt modifies what she had said in Fragment 1 of *Was ist Politik?*: human beings owe their plurality not to themselves, but to the fertility of life on earth; they have God's creation to thank not for their species, but for their existence as singulars. Singularity in *The Human Condition* is specifically opposed to species-life: labor "assures the life of the species" but not the existence of the singular, "the constant influx of newcomers who are born into the world as strangers" (Arendt 1958, 9).

The natural fertility of biological life, as well as the natural surplus of labor, are never opposed to natality in Arendt because this fertility makes "automatic" the singularization of life achieved through natality. In order to counter the biopolitics of totalitarianism that seeks to generate the species Man by applying law directly to life, that is, by eugenically and genocidally regulating fertility and labor so as to make the singularization of life superfluous, Arendt sets it against natality as the automatic singularization of life. In *The Origins of Totalitarianism*, Arendt shows that singulars cannot be made superfluous without, at the same time, making positive law and legal rights superfluous to the application of Justice, that is, to the exceptionless application of the Laws of Nature and History, since positive law and legal rights are, for her, the only possible form of equality that singulars can give to and recognize in each other. In *The Human Condition*, she argues that freedom requires the automatism of life while remaining counternatural, where "natural" means subsumed under a lawlike process. Natality is the only category that satisfies both of these, apparently contradictory, conditions: belonging to life yet not subsumable under the rule or law (and, hence, "miraculous"). Being born is an "automatic" feature of human life on earth. This means that what is inserted into the world through birth must remain unlawlike and exceptional in two, related senses: natality must bring forth singular, completely unique individuals, and these singulars themselves must be beginners, that is, they must be the origins of spontaneous interruptions to lawlike behavior.

Ultimately, Kant is less important than Augustine for Arendt's conception of freedom for several reasons. The definition of freedom as spontaneity is valuable to her insofar as it makes clear that the spontaneous beginning is an "interruption" to a natural series of conditioned conditions, that is, freedom is not conditioned by anything natural. But this definition of Kant's is not valuable to Arendt insofar as it assumes that spontaneity is an unconditioned condition, and, furthermore, that this unconditioned cause is noumenal, that is, tied to an idea or fact of reason and therefore radically separated from the sphere of life. What Arendt needs, instead, is a counternatural yet living condition of human freedom. For her, freedom needs to be a conditioned condition, yet not be merely an object, a piece of nature, as all conditioned conditions are in Kant's ontology. Freedom needs to be a nonobjective, yet conditioned, condition for a couple of reasons. First, Arendt requires that freedom be existential and not merely noumenal. Freedom must be able to be experienced, lived, and not merely thought. Otherwise, freedom would cease to be "political," that is, it would have no "sense," no phenomenality.[45] Freedom acquires phenomenality in Kant only in the beautiful (the symbol of the moral), which is the object of judgment, not cognition. Hence, Arendt is led toward Kant's theory of judgment only because of her interest in the phenomenality of freedom. Second, Arendt requires that freedom have a living condition in order to counter the politically dubious understanding of freedom in Heidegger, which is associated with the experience of resoluteness before one's being-toward-death, an understanding of freedom that Arendt criticizes in her essays on Heidegger and existentialism in the 1950s.

The second essential feature of Arendt's conception of freedom is no longer Kantian because it deprives freedom of unconditionality by making it conditional on natality. I call this second feature of freedom Benjaminian. "With word and deed we insert ourselves into the human world, and this insertion is like a second birth, in which we confirm and take upon ourselves the naked fact of our original physical appearance. This insertion is not forced upon us by necessity. . . . Its impulse springs from the beginning which came into the world when we were born and to which we respond by beginning something new on our own initiative" (Arendt 1958, 176–77). If freedom were unconditioned it could not be phenomenalized, and that would mean that it could not be plural: at best, it would be the freedom of humanity, but never the freedom of human beings, of singulars. By making natality into a condition of action, freedom is no longer unconditioned, yet, in what is apparently a paradox, this finitude of freedom only reinforces and intensifies it. Action and natality, conditioned and condition, stand in what may be called a "mimetic" relation with respect to one another: action can only be the intensification of natality, and never its limitation, control, or domination.[46] Although natality is a condition of action, it is responsible for the uncontrollable character of action, which Arendt describes in terms of its "boundlessness" (Arendt 1958, 190). As the intensification of natality, action occasions new actions in others and thereby "confirms" the natality of others. "Since action acts upon beings who are capable of their own actions, reaction, apart from being a response, is always a new action that strikes out on its own and affects others" (Arendt 1958, 190). That is why action qua beginning is not only conditioned by natality but, in turn, conditions natality.[47]

The third and final essential feature of Arendt's conception of freedom is Augustinian. In *The Human Condition*, Arendt concludes her discussion of natality with the following claim: "With the creation of man, the principle of beginning came into the world itself . . . the principle of freedom was created when man was created but not before" (Arendt 1958, 177). Natality, the condition of human freedom, is itself conditioned by an act of divine creation. But does this mean that freedom comes to life from a sphere that lies outside of biological life itself? Does God function here as the ultimate guarantor of the separation of human *bios* from species *zoe*? Is Arendt's conclusion that human beings cannot and should not create Mankind because that would be equivalent to usurping God's prerogative?

All of these are possible readings of Arendt's constant reference to divine creation, which are usually ignored by the secondary literature, and which fit together with what I previously referred to as the "humanist" interpretation of her political thought. But another reading of divine creation is also possible in Arendt, one that fits better with what I have argued thus far, namely, that Arendt's conception of natality is not "humanist."

Arendt suggests that God creates the human species so that life might have a beginning (that is, a moment of natality) and be about beginning (insofar as individuals respond to their condition of natality and intensify this condition by acting; these actions or beginnings then become the subject matter of stories that transmit their significance to future generations). It is important to note that this formulation of the Augustinian moment of natality in *The Human Condition* is different from the one cited at the beginning of this chapter, from *The Origins of Totalitarianism*. In the version from *The Origins of Totalitarianism*, Arendt does not linger on the point of createdness, nor does she linger on the question of the human being. The later formulation, instead, gives rise to the question: What exactly is created about human beings? Is it their faculty to begin, their creativeness that is guaranteed by their creatureliness? Is it man's "humanity" that is created? Or is it man's biological life? The answer, for Arendt, is neither. Rather, the creation of human beings gives natural life its freedom and what can be called its "afterlife." Natality naturalizes history as much as it historicizes nature. The creation of human beings, then, is to be understood exclusively as a function of the emancipation or redemption of nature, an emancipation that nature cannot achieve in and of itself. Arendt here is extremely close to the central thesis put forward by Adorno and Horkheimer, which is itself derived from Benjamin:

> In the self-cognition of the spirit as nature in disunion with itself, as in prehistory, nature calls itself to account; no longer ... with the alias that signifies omnipotence, but as blind and lame. The decline, the forfeiture, of nature consists in the subjugation of nature without which spirit does not exist. Through the decision in which spirit acknowledges itself to be domination and retreats into nature, it abandons the claim to domination which makes it a vassal of nature. (Horkheimer 1972, 39–40)

The Augustinian sense of natality is always already inscribed within Arendt's Benjaminian critique of Heidegger. This critique sets the creatureliness of human beings, the radical immanence of the human being in nature, in opposition to the finite transcendence of *Dasein* (Benjamin 1985). The reference to divine creation in Arendt's concept of natality indicates that origin toward which natality tears life out of life (*zoe*) in order to throw it into the world, but not before singularizing it. Natality is the caesura of life that turns human beings into creatures, linking the "fallenness" of nature directly to creation and redemption. In their awareness of being creatures, individuals not only understand that they are ultimately strangers in the world, that is to say, that no national or ethnic identity (*nascio-*) can ever correspond to their natality, but also that they exist only as the subjectivity of life (*zoe*) itself. Natality, by giving birth to singulars, is the freedom of biological life. Political action, insofar as it intensifies the condition of natality, is to be understood exclusively in terms of the freeing of life, and in opposition to the totalitarian attempt to dominate biological life by dehumanizing it, that is, by eliminating its singularity. This is what Arendt means when she pointedly refers to action as "the redemption of life" (Arendt 1958, 236). Totalitarianism, therefore, has nothing to do with a return of "nature" or "barbarism" amidst civilization. Rather, contrary to what Adorno and Horkheimer argue, totalitarianism is itself antinatural. Its mythical quality is simply the confirmation that just as "myths already realize enlightenment, so enlightenment with every step becomes more deeply engulfed in mythology" (Horkheimer 1972, 11).

Arendt therefore rejects the totalitarian dehumanization of human life on the basis of neither a belief in human "nature" (of Aristotelian and Thomistic derivation) nor a belief in the Kantian ideal of "humanity" or human "dignity," but on the grounds that to deprive life (*zoe*) of the existence of singular human beings is to deprive life of its natality, of its chance to be free. Both the neo-Aristotelian and the neo-Kantian readings of Arendt have to be set aside. The legitimacy of politics in the posttotalitarian age derives from the possibility of emancipating life from its domination. The ultimate ground for this domination of life is the curiously anthropomorphic desire of human beings to become an "animal" species of their own by becoming "human and nothing but human" (Arendt 1973, 297).

The chance that human natality constitutes for nature is, according to Arendt, rooted in the divine creation of human beings by God, but it is not a chance that is under the control or providence of God. God completes His creation and withdraws His providence from life precisely at the threshold constituted by the possibility of a free life. And that is why Arendt can maintain both that it makes no sense to speak of natality without divine creation, and that God has nothing to do with politics (Arendt 2005, 95–96). It is with the same consistency that she claims, in a letter to Jaspers discussing the radical evil of our times, that "on the personal level, I make my way through life with a kind of . . . trust in God. . . . There's nothing much you can make of that, of course, except be happy. All traditional religion as such, whether Jewish or Christian, holds nothing whatsoever for me anymore. I don't think, either, that it can anywhere or in any way provide a basis for something so clearly political as laws" (Arendt and Jaspers 1992, 166).

There remains one fundamental question that Arendt, so far as I can determine, never addresses in her writings: What is the phenomenological evidence that the fact of being born, the condition of natality, reveals the human being's creatureliness, that is, his or her createdness, and therefore leads to "trusting" in the existence of a Creator? It seems that this last assumption on the part of Arendt is entirely a matter of "faith" and relates her biopolitics to an entirely different discourse, namely, a negative political theology.

5

THE HEROISM OF SEXUALITY IN BENJAMIN AND FOUCAULT

NATALITY AND THE GUILT CONTEXT OF LIFE

When political rationality is deployed on the terrain of the biological life of the human species in order to make this life healthier, more capable, and more "worthy of being lived," it also postulates that some life can be potentiated only at the expense of killing off other life. Foucault thus introduces the idea of biopolitics along with that of thanatopolitics (Foucault 1990, 137). Since Foucault, one of the urgent questions has been how biopolitics turns into a thanatopolitics, and under what conditions this turn can be prevented or transformed into an affirmative politics of life. In this chapter I offer a reading of Benjamin's project that leads from thanatopolitics to an affirmative biopolitics. For Benjamin, biological life becomes the object of a thanatopolitics when it is inscribed into a context that makes it appear guilty, in need of punishment and expiation, and therefore doomed to death. This context is associated with natality, with the kind of social relations within which human beings reproduce their species. Benjamin's effort to ransom life from guilt and sin turns on offering a conception of life as eternal.[1] But since the "guilt context" is determined by the phenomenon of natality, eternal life is not an other-worldly spiritual life: it refers to that form of life in which sexual life and sexual difference is redeemed from guilt. What makes this life eternal is its relation to the idea of a messianic salvation of the world. Materialist, sexual, and messianic politics are always intertwined in Benjamin, from his early texts through his last Parisian writings.

Foucault thought that biological life came under the sway of thanatopolitics through *dispositifs* of sexuality and race developed in Europe in the eighteenth and nineteenth centuries (Foucault 1990, 2003). In my interpretation of Benjamin's texts on Goethe and Baudelaire, I suggest that, for Benjamin, it is likewise the politicization of sexuality and race that determines the "guilt context" of life that fatally leads toward a thanatopolitics.[2] At the same time, in Goethe's and Baudelaire's attacks on the *dispositifs* of bourgeois marriage and family, Benjamin seeks to recover the traces of the messianic motif of an eternal life from among the ruins of modern life. By focusing on marriage and kinship as the crucibles in which the tension between modern and messianic life explodes, Benjamin takes up a powerful theme from nineteenth-century political philosophy, which was strikingly formulated in Marx's conception of communism in the *Economic and Philosophical Manuscripts* of 1844: the idea that the key to realizing the political potential of the human species is contained in the dialectic between the natural and social dimensions of sexual relations. Anticipating somewhat Bachofen's and Lewis Morgan's discoveries that human society began in a state of primitive communism characterized by "group marriages,"[3] Marx says the following:

> In the approach to woman as the spoil and handmaid of communal lust is expressed the infinite degradation in which human beings exist for themselves, for the secret of this approach has its unambiguous, decisive, plain and undisguised expression in the relation of *man* to *woman* and in the manner in which the *immediate* [unmittelbare] relationship of the species [*Gattungsverhältnis*] is conceived.... In this relationship, therefore, is sensuously manifested, reduced to an observable fact, the extent to which the human essence [*das menschliche Wesen*] has become natural to human beings [*dem Menschen*], and the extent to which nature has become the human essence of human beings [*menschlichen Wesen des Menschen*]. (Marx 1978, 82)

Like Foucault in the *History of Sexuality*, Marx here understands sexuality as the most social of biological processes and the most biological of social institutions; it is the point where the metabolism between nature and the human species is greatest. Indeed, this coincidence between natural and social life, between *zoe* and *bios*, is captured by Marx's expression of *Gattungswesen* (species-being). How sexual relationships are disposed in social relations reveals the extent to which *zoe* (nature) has been made into *bios* (humanized) and *bios* (humanity) has become natural or instinctual (*zoe*) in people.

Owing to Agamben's influential interpretation, much of the contemporary debate on thanatopolitics turns on Benjamin's essay "The Critique of Violence," in which the life that is fated to die is characterized by "the guilt of mere natural life, which consigns the living, innocent and unhappy, to a retribution that 'expiates' the guilt" (Benjamin 1996, 250). Benjamin associates the context of guilt with the biological capacity for procreation and the fertility of biological life, in short, with the problem of natality. In the "Critique of Violence," guilty life is symbolized by Niobe, whose childbearing prowess renders her culpable in the eyes of Hera (another wife and mother) and the other Olympic gods. In fact, the mythical violence of these gods only targets the children of Niobe. In order to move beyond thanatopolitics, it is therefore necessary to undo the knot that ties natality to guilt. To do precisely this, Benjamin attempts a thoroughgoing critique of marriage and kinship, of the structure of the bourgeois family, which is the third fundamental subsystem of society, after law and economy. When, in his later work, the problem of guilt gets translated, materialistically, into the problem of debt, his interest lies in the role played by sexual reproduction in the reproduction of capitalist relations of production.

In his essay dedicated to Goethe's *Elective Affinities*—which he interprets as a *Trauerspiel* of bourgeois marriage—Benjamin returns in greater detail to the problem of innocent life, its premature death, and unhappiness, even as he continues to define fate as "the nexus of guilt among the living." *Elective Affinities* tells the story of the unraveling of the marriage between two former lovers (Eduard and Charlotte) who had each married different people but who later find themselves free to marry one another. However, upon doing so, they encounter another pair (the captain, Eduard's childhood friend, and Ottilie, Charlotte's niece) and, shortly thereafter, Eduard's feelings for Ottilie and Charlotte's feelings for the captain prove stronger than their marriage, leading to the ruin of all four. Once again in this essay, Benjamin focuses on the guilt of mere life as symbolized by the fate of a child, here, the child born to Charlotte and Eduard, who is conceived the very night they each realize, secretly, that they are in love with someone else. The death of the child, caused by a distraction on the part of Ottilie, makes it impossible for the parents to remain with their respective partners for whom they felt such "elective affinity." Benjamin comments on this death as follows:

> It corresponds wholly to the order of fate that the child, who enters it as a newborn, does not expiate the ancient rift but, inheriting its guilt, must pass away. It is a question here not of ethical guilt ... but rather of the natural kind, which befalls human beings not by decision and action but by negligence and celebration.... With the disappearance of *supernatural* life [*übernatürlichen Lebens im Menschen*] in man, his natural life turns into guilt, even without committing an act contrary to ethics. For now it is in league with mere life [*Verband des blossen Lebens*], which manifests itself in man as guilt. (Benjamin 1996, 308, emphasis mine; Benjamin 1991a, 139)

The thesis contained within this passage is that, so long as natality is the result of "negligence and celebration" rather than "decision and action" (*Entschluss und Handlung*), birth places the living in the context of guilt.

Decision and action are highly politically charged concepts, and Benjamin does not employ them by chance: from the start, he argues that natality winds sexuality, kinship, and politics into a tight knot. But Benjamin also throws a theological element into this mix by connecting natality to the idea of a "supernatural life."[4] I am convinced that Arendt became aware of the political valence and potential of the concept of natality by reading these pages in Benjamin's Goethe essay. Both Arendt and Benjamin, who were distant cousins, were preoccupied with the biopolitical dimensions of the idea of social contract found in the Abrahamic traditions, where a contract is established between God and man in order to generate a (holy) family and a saintly race (*ghenos*), thereby establishing a new type of sovereignty over the earth: the Abrahamic covenant is at once sexual, political, and theological.[5] But how people become parents is not only a concern of Abraham's God.[6] In the nineteenth-century studies of kinship structures in so-called primitive societies, pioneered by Lewis Morgan and Bachofen, the question of how natality gets socially organized is the essential indicator of the "evolution" of the human species. As is well known, these studies on the prehistory of kinship were extremely influential for Engels (to say nothing of Freud), who used them to underpin their own evolutionary or progressive rhetoric of historical development from the realm of necessity (fate) to the realm of freedom (expiation of guilt or debt).

The Heroism of Sexuality in Benjamin and Foucault

Yet Marx, Freud, and Benjamin all reject the Abrahamic conceit that redemption from the context of guilt depends on one's genealogy (the story of one's "race," *ghenos*), on the establishment of a "holy" family tree. All of them reject the belief in "original sin" or the idea that bare life is guilty "by nature" because, as Benjamin says, "what counts for *this life, as for every human life*, is not the freedom of the tragic hero but rather redemption in *eternal life* [*Erlösung im ewigen Leben*]" (Benjamin 1996, 320; Benjamin 1991a, 154).[7] All of them reject the conceit of Abrahamic religions according to which an abyss lies between animal life and eternal life so that no human evolution can bridge them, only a miracle of divine love (whether this love be the grace one is granted for having faith in the death and resurrection of God as Christ or by maintaining the bloodline of priests related to the Cohen *ghenos*).[8] Indeed, Marx, Freud, and Benjamin all would have subscribed to Hermann Cohen's belief that the messianic conception of redemption can rest neither on an individual Savior nor on any variation of a "holy" family line because messianism always understands salvation in terms of the human species as a whole: it is not the individual soul but only the entire "species-being" of humanity, what Benjamin calls in these early essays "the living," that can and will be emancipated from fate, guilt, and death.

In all of his major works of literary criticism, the question Benjamin poses is in fact one and the same: What is the form of life (*bios*) in which species life (*zoe*) and eternal life (*zoe aionios*) coincide? He becomes convinced that all biographical and political life (*bios*) will destroy itself unless it is capable of uniting animal and eternal life. In other words, his main point of inquiry is how redemption occurs not in spite of nihilism and catastrophe, but in and through it. In the *Origin of German Baroque Drama*, animal and eternal life only coincide once human history has been completely naturalized, emptied of any transcendent significance, by the allegorical vision. Likewise, in his later work on Baudelaire and the Parisian Passages, Benjamin finds this coincidence in the nihilistic form of the doctrine of the eternal recurrence of the same, the doctrine that corresponds to the naturalization of social relations embodied by the fetishism of commodities.

Benjamin also consistently opposes this messianic redemption of biological life to the political salvation of *zoe* in the form of a political *bios* theorized in Greek tragedy and philosophy. Benjamin opposes the messiah to the tragic hero who founds political life. The hero of Greek tragedy and the Greek *polis* represents the struggle that the "natural" life of man engages in against the power of fate or necessity, in the absence of a supernatural or messianic life. In the Christian, baroque form of tragedy (the *Trauerspiel*), Benjamin uncovers a form of struggle against fate that is offered by the "supernatural" life of man. But the peculiarity of this modern tragic form, which Benjamin ascribes to its allegorical structure, is that the supernatural appears only when the natural life of man decays to its most creatural, most bestial level: "Only the life of the creature [*das Leben des Geschöpfes*], never that of the formed structure, partakes, unreservedly, of the intention of redemption" (Benjamin 1996, 324; Benjamin 1991a, 159). The opposition between the civilized hero of Greek tragedy and the bestial antihero of modern tragedy is fundamental for Benjamin's interpretation of modernity. The tension between classical and modern heroism remains the guiding thread of Benjamin's interpretations of Goethe's and of Baudelaire's lyric poetry as an allegory of redemption.

MARRIAGE AND ETERNAL LIFE IN THE "ELECTIVE AFFINITIES" ESSAY

Marriage was never considered a philosophical problem until Kierkegaard made it one. More precisely, he argued that marriage posed an insurmountable problem and scandal for philosophy because it is not a problem that can be solved logically or rationally, but only existentially, that is, only by each and every individual "living" through it. Marriage can only be a problem for what Kierkegaard calls a subject, namely, whoever lives in the awareness that who she becomes is entirely a matter of her decision: nature and society can determine what we have (this or that genetic endowment, this or that talent, this or that amount of money, and so on), but neither can make us *become* who we become. Thus, every social relation becomes entirely contingent for a subject: such subjects emerge only in modern civil society. If modern subjectivity is radically disengaged from others, then, and only then, the decision to marry, that is, the decision to engage oneself to another for eternity becomes a serious problem, at once philosophical and political. Why should one engage oneself in this way?

Either I engage myself, or I do not engage myself: I shall regret it in both cases. This last assertion is the standpoint of what Kierkegaard called the "aesthetic" view of life (Kierkegaard 1987, 147, 159). For the aesthetic view of life, only what is "interesting" makes life worth living; otherwise, life is boring. The problem is that only other persons make life interesting. So, it is "interesting" to seduce another person, to establish an "erotic" (not sexual) relation with them: from the aesthetic point of view, only "first" love is real love, or, one only loves once. Compared to this immediate experience of love, to be actually engaged with the other, to have to spend time with them, to actually have to have sex with them, is always boring; in general, it is an axiom of the aesthetic view of life that the more time spent with any one person, the less interesting they become. Hence from the aesthetic point of view, the experience of habit and repetition in marriage is equivalent to a death sentence. One must seduce the other person, but one cannot marry them. This, in a nutshell, is the dilemma exposed in the first part of Kierkegaard's first major work, entitled *Either/Or*.

It is in the second part of *Either/Or*, which is much longer and intentionally written to be far more boring, that Kiergaard sets out to validate the claims of marriage. Marriage introduces what he calls the "ethical" view of life. From the ethical standpoint, marriage actually "saves" or "redeems" life because it shows that one's engagement with another for eternity is not incompatible with one's self-assertion, with one's becoming who one becomes. To become someone is to live; to live is to decide oneself, to decide oneself is to marry: ergo, there is no incompatibility, but only harmony, between the commitment to oneself and the commitment to another (Kierkegaard 1987, 163–69, 206). This, at least, is what the second part of *Either/Or* argues through the character of Judge Wilhelm, a happily married man, who is trying to convince the seducer of the first part of *Either/Or* to abandon his erotic lifestyle and settle down. The judge wants to convince the seducer that marriage is the most interesting, the most "erotic" thing one can be involved in: far from being boring, it fills time with meaning (Kierkegaard 1987, 138–43).

Kierkegaard believes that apart from the aesthetic and the ethical views of life, there exists also what he calls the "religious" view of life (Kierkegaard 1987, 147). If the aesthetic view of life is all about "conquering" the other's love, and the ethical view of life is all about "possessing" the other's love, then the religious view of life is all about "renouncing" the other's love (Kierkegaard 1987, 36). In the religious, one sacrifices everything that is most precious to one: if one is aesthetically minded, then one sacrifices one's sense for beauty; if one is ethically minded, then one sacrifices one's sense for duty; and one does all this for no gain whatsoever, for nothing. The religious view of life is, for Kierkegaard, contained in the belief that despite having sacrificed everything that has any meaning for one, one will be given everything back: everything will return to one, or one's life will be eternally repeated. Only the religious view of life gives access to eternal life (Kierkegaard 1983, 212; Kierkegaard 1987, 341–54). The fundamental problem that animates all of Kierkegaard's thinking life consists in exploring the relation between the repetition of marriage and the religious sense of repetition.

In a later work entitled *Repetition* Kierkegaard poses the question: Can repetition exist in human life? For the aesthetic view of life, repetition has no meaning: only what is new or novel is of interest, and it will be of interest only in and for a moment—the rest of time is despair, one is bored to death. For the ethical view of life, repetition also has no meaning: the only thing that matters is one's life trajectory, one's history or biography. Once the decision is taken to become who one becomes, no particular moment of one's life will ever stand out again because every moment will be equally full with one's life (*bios*) (Kierkegaard 1987, 305–8). That is how Judge Wilhelm describes married life: if one gets married, one will never again be bored, but also nothing in particular will ever be exciting. In the aesthetic view of life, one lives only for that one special moment; in the ethical view of life, every moment is just a part of one special life. In the former, history is sacrificed to the moment; in the latter, the moment is sacrificed to history. The religious point of view is meant to develop a conception of repetition in which the moment and history are both transcended and reconciled. From this perspective, neither the moment nor one's life history are unique: every moment is eternally repeated, so it cannot be special or new or interesting, but that also means that every moment, because it recurs eternally, is like the end of one's history. Every moment is thus both a moment of fallenness and a moment of salvation.

In *Pursuits of Happiness*, Cavell engages Kierkegaard's dilemma and attempts to offer a "religious" approach to marriage by arguing that the essence of marriage consists in the "the will to remarriage," in the renewal of the vows in order to approximate "eternal" love in the form of perfecting it through repetition (Cavell 1999, 243–44). As Koch has shown, Cavell notices a coincidence with Benjamin's theory of marriage yet distances his own optimistic and pragmatic view of marriage's repetitiousness from that offered by Benjamin (Koch 2003). Benjamin's view is that "in truth marriage is never justified in law (that is, as an institution) but is justified solely as an expression of continuance in love, which by nature seeks this expression sooner in death than in life [*in Wahrheit die Ehe niemals im Recht die Rechtfertigung, das wäre als Institution, sondern einzig als ein Ausdruck für das Bestehen der Liebe, die ihn von Natur im Tode eher suchte als im Leben*]"(Benjamin 1996, 301; Benjamin 1991a, 130). Marriage can avoid being a mythical institution only if one can understand how it allows love to traverse and, perhaps, even subjugate the Scylla and Charibdes of *eros* and *thanatos*. Benjamin develops his justification of marriage most fully in his essay on Goethe's *Elective Affinities*.

It is interesting to note that Kierkegaard actually refers twice to Goethe's novel in the second part of *Either/Or*, both times in a negative or critical way (Kierkegaard 1987, 20, 119). Benjamin, for his part, both employs Kierkegaardian ideas to interpret what Goethe is saying about marriage and, at the same time, defends Goethe's standpoint against Kierkegaard's critiques. The difference between Goethe and Kierkegaard on marriage is that Goethe advanced a "pagan" conception of marriage whereas Kierkegaard defended a Christian conception of marriage. Goethe is interested in examining how pagan Eros brings Christian marriage into crisis; Kierkegaard wants to show that Christian love, as exemplified in heterosexual marriage, overcomes pagan Eros. Benjamin's own standpoint on marriage will bring also a third perspective into play, namely, that of Jewish messianism.

Benjamin finds the above-mentioned truth about marriage reflected in Kant's un-Romantic definition of marriage as a contract for the mutual and indefinite use of the other's body for the purposes of sexual commerce (Koch 2003, 112; Fenves 2005; Gasché 2005). Benjamin knows full well that this definition has been universally rejected by bourgeois society: famously, in his *Philosophy of Right*, Hegel considers the idea of a sexual contract to be vile because it is destructive of the primary *Sittlichkeit* of the nuclear family in which married couples are meant to find their truth by becoming parents to their offspring and offering them the first social recognition that will allow them to grow into independent individuals. Kant's definition, of course, explicitly disregards the finality of reproduction and parenting as a justification for the commitment to marry: marriage is not about the children that may result from it, but about who one decides to have sex with for the rest of one's life.

It is the disconnection between marriage (as a sexual contract) and reproduction that Benjamin sets out to redeem in his essay on the *Elective Affinities*: he thinks that this disconnection gives expression to the truth-content of human love. For in Kant's formula for marriage, according to Benjamin, the "natural component" of sex "does not obstruct the path to the logos of its [marriage's] *divine* component—fidelity. For what is proper to the truly divine is the Logos: the divine does not ground life without truth, nor does it ground the rite without theology" (Benjamin 1996, 326; Benjamin 1991a, 163). The "supernatural" dimension of human life, then, consists in fidelity to the same sex (or, to the sex of some one): to remain faithful to this one sex, after the sexual encounter, is the "truly divine" ground of "natural" or "bare" life. In what follows, and using a play on words, I refer to this conception as the homo-sexual (same-sex) conception of married life.[9]

Benjamin's view on fidelity to the sex of someone needs to be understood in the context of the danger posed by "haeterism," or universal prostitution, a theme that haunts his essays on Kafka and on Baudelaire and which he probably picked up from his reading of Bachofen via Ludwig Klages.[10] Haeterism is Bachofen's name for the prematriarchical period of human development, in which every woman was the sexual object of every man, and brothers could sleep with their sisters, fathers with their daughters, sons with their mothers: a sort of unrestricted orgy to which Marx gives the name of "primitive" communism. According to Bachofen's matriarchy hypothesis, after a period of armed rebellion against universal prostitution led by the Amazons, matriarchy as a stable social organization emerges when women institute marriage and simultaneously assume political power in order to put an end to their own "free" circulation as sexual objects between men. The first constitutional monarch was a woman. Her figure stands as the most prominent of the temptations that the two heroes of Western patriarchical civilization must resist: for the Greek Ulysses it is Circe, and for the Roman Aeneas it is Dido of Carthage. Kant's definition of marriage, properly understood, still harbors vestiges of this matriarchical impulse behind marriage.

Benjamin's discussion of Goethe's fascination with the tellurian (as opposed to the Olympian) gods and the link between these divinities of the Earth and the matriarchal cult of women's fertility are clear indications that, lurking behind Benjamin's analysis of the crisis of the bourgeois, patriarchal conception of marriage, there lies an engagement with Bachofen's *Mutterrecht* and its fundamental thesis that historical development needs to be understood in terms of (an ever-repeating) struggle between the different social organization of sexual difference, between matriarchy and patriarchy, Dionysus and Apollo. It is not by chance that Benjamin cites Bachofen in order to justify his claim that Ottilie, the tragic figure of *Elective Affinities* who represents human beauty, is merely the Apollinian veil that Goethe draws over the Dionysian reality that necessarily causes the dissolution of all bourgeois (patriarchical) conceptions of marriage: "The mourning and pain of the Dionysian, as the tears that are shed for the continual decline of all life, form gentle ecstasy; it is 'the life of the cicada, which, without food or drink, sings until it dies.' Thus Bernoulli on the one hundred and forty-first chapter of *Matriarchy*.... What else was the meaning of Goethe's meditations on Ottilie's departure from life?" (Benjamin 1996, 349; Benjamin 1991a, 192). I shall refer more to this Dionysian reality below.

It is significant for my argument that, in this precise context of the *Elective Affinities* essay, Benjamin introduces the concept of the "shock [*Erschütterung*]" that was to become so important in his understanding of Baudelaire's lyrical poetry. Here it is the "shock" of Ottilie's death, which is none other than "the going under of semblance [*Untergang des Scheins*]," the death of beauty (Benjamin 1991a, 193). The death of beauty and the decadence or wasting away of innocence, though, is precisely what allows for the "going over [*Übergang*]" from the beautiful to the sublime, which Benjamin understands, in Kantian fashion, as the irruption of the supersensuous idea of freedom into the natural world of causality (Benjamin 1996, 349–50; Benjamin 1991a, 193). The play between *Untergang* and *Übergang* is strictly Nietzschean: indeed, it comes out of *Thus Spoke Zarathustra*. Benjamin seems to suggest that Goethe's "allegorical" traversal of the tension between the Apollinian and Dionysian is superior to Nietzsche's own attempt because it is ultimately "moral" in the Kantian sense of preserving the idea of freedom as a touchstone of all value, rather than as the will to power. Such an antagonistic relation to Nietzsche's central concepts is characteristic of Benjamin.

Benjamin understands the sexual fidelity that marriage entails in political terms. He conceives of this fidelity by distinguishing between "decision" and "choice" (Benjamin 1996, 326; Benjamin 1991a, 189). This Kierkegaardian distinction appears, in the Danish philosopher's own work, precisely in the context of a meditation on the "haeterism" of the aesthetic sphere and the challenge posed by the "either/or" of marriage. However, in Benjamin, this distinction receives the additional connotation found in Schmitt's conception of the political, where the decision of the true "political" actor (analogous to the decision to marry and seal the sexual contract with another person) is opposed to the "unpolitical" electoral choice of the bourgeois for a parliamentary representative (analogous to the uncommitted election of a sexual partner). In Benjamin, sexuality escapes mythical punishment when it is exchanged under the divine seal of the decision, rather than through electoral and elective affinities. According to Benjamin, Ottilie never decides herself (there is no space for ethical decision in the aesthetic realm of beauty); thus, her death does not count as "holy absolution" but as "atonement" through sacrifice, atonement for the "natural" guilt she incurred because of her innocent infatuation.

Hence, Benjamin's essay adopts the Kierkegaardian language of the teleological suspension of the ethical when approximating the motif of eternal life: "Because true reconciliation with God is achieved by no one who does not thereby destroy everything- or as much as he possesses—in order only then, before God's reconciled countenance, to find it resurrected" (Benjamin 1996, 342; Benjamin 1991a, 184).[11] To explain the meaning of this nihilistic conception of reconciliation, Benjamin ends his essay with a disquisition on the difference between "true" love and "semblancelike love," which is composed of passion and affection (Benjamin 1996, 344; Benjamin 1991a, 186). Benjamin argues that passion and affection are both caught up with the "natural" sphere of myth, which is the erotic.

> Love becomes perfect only where, elevated above its nature, it is saved through God's intervention [*Gottes Walten*]. Thus, the dark conclusion of love, whose demon is Eros, is not a naked foundering but rather the true ransoming of the deepest imperfection which belongs to the nature of man himself. For it is this imperfection which denies to him the fulfillment of love. Therefore, into all loving that human nature alone determines, affection enters as the real work of *eros thanatos*—the admission that man [*der Mensch*] cannot love. Whereas in all redeemed true love, passion, like affection,

> remains secondary, the history of affection and the transition of the one into the other makes up the essence of Eros. (Benjamin 1996, 345; Benjamin 1991a, 187)

The natural life of human beings, according to this passage, is characterized by desire, by passion, and by the languid decay into affection. Affection is the death of passion because it reveals that natural, sexual desire (*eros*) was always doomed to death (*thanatos*): it signals the impossibility of an eternal love between two individuals except by the intervention of the divine (or messianic) in human sexual life.

What is eternal in human life, therefore, is not the natural dimension of sexual desire but its "ransoming" in the form of the "redeemed true love." It follows from this "supernatural" possibility of love that "every love grown within itself must become master of this world—in its natural exitus, the common (that is, strictly simultaneous) death, or in its supernatural duration [*übernatürliche Dauer*], marriage" (Benjamin 1996, 345; Benjamin 1991a, 187). In the essay on the *Elective Affinities*, the eternal life of sexuality manifests itself in two possible ways, both of which are thoroughly "nihilistic" when compared with the natural basis of desire: either it manifests in the decision of the lovers to commit simultaneous suicide, or in their decision to marry and thus divinely "seal" their sexual contract.[12] This nihilistic path is the only way out of the "double failure" that is the bourgeois pairing, dissolution, and recombination of the couples in Goethe's novel: "While the one couple, in isolation, dies away, marriage is denied to the survivors.... Since the author could not let true love reign in either of the couples (it would have exploded this world), in the characters of the novella he supplied his work inconspicuously but unmistakeably with its emblem" (Benjamin 1996, 345; Benjamin 1991a, 188). In both ways of overcoming *eros thanatos*, bare life becomes eternal life through a decision that is taken in an instant, and then interrupts the natural course of love, from passion to affection and to the eventual death of sexual desire. This decision remains inexpressible within the work of art because ethico-religious life decisions are entirely antiaesthetical. Whereas the life of passion, made possible by the veil of beauty, can be rendered by the symbolic dimension of the work of art, the decisive life that sees through the veil of beauty and into the Dionysian reality of *eros thanatos* can only be rendered allegorically—interrupting, as it were, the "play" of the work of art.

"Only the decision, not the choice, is inscribed in the book of life [*nur die Entscheidung, nicht die Wahl ist im Buche des Lebens verzeichnet*]" (Benjamin 1996, 346; Benjamin 1991a, 189). Benjamin here refers to the Jewish eschatological belief that, on the day of the Last Judgment that comes after the messianic age but before the return of human beings to the Garden of Eden (that is, the resurrection of the body), God will make a final tally of those who proved worthy of living in the Age to Come (that is, in the Garden of eternal life) by remaining faithful to the Law and to the Messiah, and those who did not. If fidelity to the same sex (or homo-sexuality) reestablishes the original conditions of humanity before the Fall of Adam, then h(a)etero-sexuality (the unconditional use of every other's body for sexual gratification) is merely the formula for the death of desire—*eros thanatos*—whose double genitive refers, for Benjamin, to the transformation of passion into affection that makes up the natural history of love. Benjamin's point is that, if there is "hope of redemption" for human sexuality, then such hope belongs to those lovers who have given up seeking happiness in the natural history of sex, in its shifting, back and forth, between passion and affection. Only these hopeless lovers see through the Apollinian veil of beauty and live in the Dionysian reality that is the death of desire: they are represented by suicidal lovers and by those lovers who remain faithful to their marriage vow in the absence of passion and despite the withering away of beauty.

The hope [*Elpis*] that Benjamin famously evokes at the end of his essay as being "the sole justification of the faith in immortality [*das einzige Recht des Unsterblichkeitglaubens*], which must never be kindled from one's own existence" (Benjamin 1996, 355; Benjamin 1991a, 200), is the hope of a sexual life that lies beyond death and is thus identical to eternal life. But where does the idea of such hope come from? When Benjamin is writing about the divinity of marriage and connecting it to the hope of immortality for those who otherwise have no hope (namely, those who have been defeated by the rise of patriarchy and monotheism, those defeated by the rise of "Western civilization"), he was in all likelihood thinking about the lyrical descriptions of life under matriarchy found in Bachofen, characterized by an "abandonment without reserve to the most luxurious life of the senses and *fidelity to that best Hope that reaches beyond the grave* . . . *no idea* of struggle, of self-discipline, *of sin and repentance* disturbs the harmony of *a life at once sensual and transcending sensuality*" (cited in Gossman 1983, 33, emphasis mine).[13]

In what is perhaps the most famous sentence of the essay, Benjamin refers to this hope in the following terms: "For in the symbol of the star, the hope that Goethe had conceived for the lovers had once appeared to him. That sentence which to speak with Hölderlin contains the caesura of the work and in which, while the embracing lovers seal their fate, everything pauses, reads: 'Hope shot across the sky above their heads like a falling star'" (Benjamin 1996, 355; Benjamin 1991a, 200). Here, the falling star represents the hope for an eternal life (an "éternité par les astres" to cite the title of Blanqui's treatise) that contrasts with the mythical understanding of the stars. The mythical understanding of heaven sees, in the stars, the prefiguration of the "superhuman" task of the pagan hero: "The presence of this task and of its evident symbolism distinguishes the superhuman from the human life. It characterizes Orpheus . . . no less than Hercules of the Twelve Tasks. . . . One of the most powerful sources of this symbolism flows from the astral myth: in the superhuman type of the Redeemer, the hero represents mankind through his work on the starry sky. The primal words of the Orphic poem apply to him: it is his daemon—the sunlike one; his *tyche*, the one that is as changeable as the moon; his fate, ineluctable like the astral *ananke*. Even Eros does not point beyond them—only Elpis does" (Benjamin 1996, 322; Benjamin 1991a, 158). For Benjamin, the hope of an eternal life is not represented by the fixed nature of the starry skies, which make manifest the Herculean task of redeeming mankind and the belief that only a superhuman hero can do so. Rather, the hope of an eternal life is represented by the phenomenon of "shooting" stars that burn brilliantly for a short while and then die out. The shooting star indicates the failing nature of modern heroism. As Benjamin says in reference to Baudelaire, the gas lights of the big city cover up the starry skies and no longer allow the individual to find his orientation or his heroic tasks.

But I think that, in Benjamin, there is another source for this hopeless hope in the eternity of sexual life that is related to the Kabbalah. Benjamin claims that fidelity to the sex of someone is the divine grounding of biological life in truth. But what does truth mean in this context? Given the explicit citations to Kabbalistic eschatology found in his essay on Goethe, it is likely that that the term "truth" here refers to the esoteric knowledge provided by the Tree of Life, which stands in opposition to the exoteric Tree of "knowledge of good and evil," whose fruit Adam ate in the Garden of Eden, which led to the fall of both sexes and established the "guilt context" in which sexual life developed on Earth. Benjamin's allegorical reading of Goethe's novel, in the end, is but a transcription of a common eschatological theme of Judaism according to which, after the messianic age and the final judgment, in the World to Come—"God still remains in whose presence *there is no secret and everything is life.* The human being appears to us as a corpse and *his life as love [als Liebe sein Leben]*, when they are in the presence of God" (Benjamin 1996, 353; Benjamin 1991a, 197).

When he was still living in Berlin, Benjamin discussed these eschatological dimensions of Judaism with Scholem, and it is easy to imagine why he would have been fascinated by the results of Scholem's studies of the esoteric doctrine of "redemption through sin" found in the messianic currents of Kabbalistic Judaism. According to this doctrine, the revelation of the Tree of "knowledge of good and evil" is not the first, true revelation of God (which corresponds to the Tree of Life). Rather, it is a second revelation, written by Moses, after he breaks the tablets of the first revelation (which were written by God Himself) in a bout of anger over the lack of fidelity shown by his chosen people. This duality of revelations is the basis for the Jewish conception that there are two ways to interpret the Torah: in accordance with the written or the oral teachings that correspond, respectively, to the "conventional" or moral reading of the Law, and to a reading of the Law from the perspective of Life, beyond good and evil. This opposition between morality and life easily resonates with Nietzschean postulates, and it is not surprising that Scholem was obsessed with Nietzsche in his youth.

According to Scholem, the Kabbalistic interpretation of these two revelations culminates in the heresy of Sabbatianism, which holds the belief that the first revealed truth would, after the coming of the Messiah, again allow everything that God is said by Moses to have prohibited through the commandments of the second revelation (Scholem 1971).[14] What the second, written revelation prohibits are all practices and beliefs that depend on the possibility of the human species attaining eternal life. If one reads Scholem's famous, programmatic essay entitled "Redemption Through Sin," written in 1935, it is striking that his representation of Lurianic Kabbalah and the Sabbatian heresy is completely Nietzschean: the word "nihilism"—in the Nietzschean sense of being "beyond good and evil"—is constantly used in association with "messianic"—in the Sabbatian sense of a Torah without commandments or where the commandments are no longer in force.[15] As it turns out, during the same years in which Scholem was presenting his nihilist version of Jewish messianism, Benjamin was feverishly at work on his book on Baudelaire in which Nietzsche appears as a key figure in the nihilism-messianism constellation due to his concern with the problem of eternal recurrence.

Therefore, it cannot be ruled out that, as Benjamin was writing his essay on Goethe's novel about bourgeois marriage and betrayal, he not only learned about the nihilistic figure of a "redemption through sin" from Scholem, but also about one of the most disturbing and piquant discoveries Scholem made in relation to the heresy of Sabbatianism, namely, putting "redemption through sin" into practice through the esoteric exchange of sexual partners between married, outwardly "orthodox" couples.[16] Apparently, these sexual transgressions were understood as being a practical way of realizing Tiqqun, that is, the belief in the cosmic restoration of the whole universe to its original condition prior to the shattering of the "vases" containing God's emanation. Benjamin's reference to "falling stars" can be seen as an indication of a cosmic rearrangement of the astral constellations that were formed after this shattering or Big Bang. In all likelihood, this is also the background for Benjamin's later obsession with the idea that redemption will take the form of a cosmic revolution as well as his interest in the motif of eternal recurrence, shared by Blanqui, Baudelaire, and Nietzsche.

The Sabbatian heretical understanding of marriage gives an esoteric connotation to Benjamin's exoteric defense of Kant's conception of marriage. In the esoteric version, marriage is an "eternal recurrence" because there is a "repetition" of the natural component of the marriage contract in the Kantian sense—namely, as the mutual use of body parts for the purpose of free sexual commerce—which is "eternal"—in the Kabbalistic sense of the term—namely, as occurring after the messianic age. Here, fidelity in the marriage does not exclude the experience of ever novel or renewed sexual encounters; indeed, it is the only way to access this "free" or "redeemed" nature of sexuality prior to the Adamic fall and prior to sexuality being marked by the difference between Adam and Eve. One could say that the homo-sexuality (fidelity to the same sex) of marriage (and the moment of decision) is the archway through which hetero-sexuality (relations with other sexes) returns, eternally purified of mythical haeterism (universal prostitution). This constellation, perhaps, is not unlike what

Marx was seeking in his attempt to distinguish primitive from advanced communism: in both cases the patriarchical family is abolished, yet, in advanced communism, there is no return to the universal prostitution of primitive communism because what satisfies human needs is not the object produced from the exploitation of the relations of production, but rather the production of a truly social or political mode of sexual relation itself. Marriage here is understood in a Nietzschean way, in the sense that the eternal repetition of the same would be the gateway to a transvaluation of values that is at once also affirmative of (an eternal) life. Perhaps it is not coincidental that, in his depiction of eternal recurrence in both *Thus Spoke Zarathustra* and *Gay Science*, Nietzsche employs the idea of the eternal return as a "nuptial ring" that "seals" one's fidelity to life on Earth. In the last section of the third part of the first published version of *Zarathustra* entitled "The Seven Seals; or, The Yes and Amen Song," Nietzsche expressly refers to the eternal recurrence in terms of a coincidence between marriage and sexual desire: "O, how should I not lust after eternity and after the nuptial ring of rings, the ring of recurrence? Never yet have I found the woman from whom I wanted children, unless it be this woman whom I love: for I love you, O eternity. For I love you, O eternity!" (Nietzsche 1995, 228–31).[17]

DIONYSIAN LIFE AS A WORK OF ART

That Benjamin's reading of Goethe is soaked in Nietzschean motifs—and not just Kabbalistic ones—is not surprising since he was intensely aware of Rosenzweig's attempt in *The Star of Redemption* to pursue a synthesis between the different forms of modern "heroism" represented by Goethe and by Nietzsche. Benjamin thought that Goethe's most peculiar trait, not unlike Zarathustra, was his demonic drive to experiment, to experience the full spectrum of life from Greek paganism to Christianity and beyond, seemingly capable of holding together the greatest oppositions. For that reason, Goethe did not hesitate to plunge into what was most mythical (or "Dionysian") about the force of life. At the same time, Benjamin suggests that through the instrument provided by allegory, Goethe shows the "death mask" of this mythical vitalism and thereby escapes not only myth as such but *especially* his own self-mythologization as a modern Hercules. The polemical object of Benjamin's essay on Goethe is Gundolf's biography of the German poet, which puts forward the thesis that Goethe's true masterpiece, his highest symbolic achievement, was his own life (*bios*) through which opposites were held together in a beautiful totality. Gundolf's biography is premised on the idea that biological life (*zoe*) can be "aestheticized," but such an aesthetization also entails submerging bare life in the pulsions of *eros thanatos*. From Benjamin's perspective, if Gundolf is right, then Goethe forsook the true eternity of life for the sake of literary immortality.

Gundolf's reading of Goethe—which emerged out of the George Circle—is an early representative of the modernist motif of "life as literature" and of the poet as the true political hero, a motif that provided grist to the ideological mill of Nazist and fascist regimes.[18] Nietzsche himself, thanks to his sister and other anti-Semitic acolytes, received a similar treatment at the hands of his fascist interpreters. Through his allegorical readings of modernist literature, in particular of Goethe and Baudelaire, Benjamin tried to destroy the very idea of "life as literature" by showing the abyss separating the literary production (the work of art) from the life of the author: "The life of a man, even that of a creative artist, is never that of the creator. It cannot be interpreted any more than the life of the hero, who gives form to himself. . . . For human life cannot be considered on the analogy of a work of art. Yet Gundolf's critical principle for dealing with sources bespeaks the fundamental determination to produce such disfigurement. . . . [T]his stance is solely explicable from the fact that the life itself is seen as a work" (Benjamin 1996, 324–25; Benjamin 1991a, 160; Gasché 2005, 938). Demolishing this idea remains Benjamin's chief motivation for giving an allegorical reading of Baudelaire, who was generally considered, after Goethe, to be the late modern exemplar of someone who attempts to turn his own life into a "work of art."

Benjamin wants to separate bare life from the work of art because he wants to redeem bare life from guilt and debt, thereby reasserting the broken link between life's "innocence" (understood as "beyond good and evil") and happiness. The aesthetization of bare life only serves to preserve the illusion that a guilty life can be livable. The path to true happiness, though, takes a different route: as Benjamin says in the *Theologico-Political Fragment*, happiness is what everything "earthly" strives for by "going under [*Untergang*]." For Benjamin, it is the pagan hero who embodies the idea of life as a work of art, and it is the task of this hero not to let life go under but to save it in the form of a *bios politikos*, a political life. The hero does this by sacrificing himself for the sake of his community: hence the unhappy life of the hero and the tragic sense of life that he transmits to his community. The message of the ancient hero is that without self-sacrifice and hard work (the "tasks" to be accomplished by the hero) there is no salvation. Benjamin's conception of eternal life and true happiness is opposed to this heroic intuition because, for him, happiness can only be found when one lets what is (merely) "natural" about biological life go under or waste away, and this requires undoing the tragic conception of the heroic task. In order to achieve this deconstruction of classical heroism, the illusion that life is a work of art must be destroyed. All of these objectives are maintained and radicalized in his later interpretation of Baudelaire.

Having said this, it is quite clear that Benjamin ultimately owes this antiheroic reading of tragedy to Nietzsche's *Birth of Tragedy*. The thesis that happiness on earth is encountered only on the way down comes directly from Nietzsche's treatment of the Dionysian in the context of a tragic world view. Following Bachofen's groundbreaking insights concerning the matriarchical cult of Dionysus, Nietzsche develops, in the *Birth of Tragedy*, an interpretation of the hero in tragic drama in which the deepest joy, the Dionysian meaning of happiness, the most profane of all joys, arises out of the experience of the downfall of the hero understood as an experience undertaken by the principle of individuation, an experience that demonstrates the entirely illusory character of the belief that everything that is, is unique (Nietzsche 1993, 28–32). At the time of writing *The Birth of Tragedy*, Nietzsche had not yet had the revelation of eternal recurrence, but he did have an intuition that true happiness consisted in the breakdown of the illusion of individuality, a breakdown that he did not want to equate with the world-denying visions of Nirvana in Hindu mysticism that had attracted Schopenhauer.

It is perhaps only a slight exaggeration to describe Benjamin's literary criticism as a drawn out *Auseinandersetzung* with the fifth chapter of the *Birth of Tragedy*, in which Nietzsche brings together, in an extremely dense and compact text, the allegorical, the lyrical, and the comical aspects of Dionysian tragedy. Nietzsche is trying to transform the heroic conception of life as a work of art in accordance with the Dionysian conception of art as the result of the antagonism between life forces. According to Nietzsche, the "Dionysiac artist" or lyrical poet produces a "copy of that primal

Oneness . . . as an allegorical dream-image. . . . A dream scene symbolizing the primal contradiction and primal suffering, as well as the primal delight in illusion" (Nietzsche 1993, 29). Lyrical poetry, therefore, reflects both a fundamental contradiction in life (for example, that eternal love can only be had by accepting the death of sexual desire, or that true communism can only be had by exacerbating the fetishism of commodities) and the phantasmagoria (the illusion) that makes this contradiction bearable. In any case, Nietzsche clearly states that the essence of lyric poetry lies in its allegorical rather than its symbolical structure: the symbolic is the phantasmagoric aspect of lyrical poetry, whereas the allegorical opens up the Dionysian underlying reality.

The allegorical nature of tragedy sheds light on the true nature of lyrical poetry, which is not the artistic expression of the subjective feelings of the poet, but rather the experience of the subjectivity—or life—found in every object:

> The lyric poet's images are nothing but the poet himself, and only different objectifications of himself, which is why, as the moving centre of that world, he is able to say 'I': this self is not that of the waking, empirically real man, however, but rather the sole, truly existing self that dwells at the basis of being, through whose depictions, he also sees *himself* as a nongenius, as his 'subject' . . . if it now appears that the lyric genius and the nongenius connected to him are one, and that the former is using the little word 'I' to refer to himself, this illusion will no longer have the power of seducing us, as it has certainly seduced those who have described the lyric poet as the subjective poet. (Nietzsche 1993, 30)

The "I" that speaks in everything depicted is "the artistic power of the whole of nature" (Nietzsche 1993, 18) and not the power of the empirical self of the poet. The crucial intuition, therefore, is that the "I" expressed in the lyrical poem is not the poet's subjectivity but the impersonal dissolution of empirical, isolated individualities in the "medium" of the allegorical dream-images dreamed by nature, through the poet. Nietzsche, like Goethe, understood art as a production of nature, of life forces, and not as a human product: "The Apolline, and its opposite, the Dionysiac" are "artistic powers which spring from nature itself, without the mediation of the human artist" (Nietzsche 1993, 18).

The lyrical poet captures how life (*zoe*) makes humanity into its work of art. Poetry reveals the normative development of the human species as a function of its expression of the creativity of biological life.[19] "Man is no longer an artist, he has become a work of art: the artistic power of the whole of nature reveals itself to the supreme gratification of the primordial Oneness amidst the paroxysm of intoxication" (Nietzsche 1993, 18). Hence, the lyrical poet's allegorical dream images are the form in which biological life "intoxicates" itself (that is, achieves the highest happiness and joy, *Rausch*). Benjamin takes up these Nietzschean intuitions in a Marxist context and says that the dream images of the lyrical poet are the "artistic projections" of social forces of production ("the true creator of that world") in which the contradictions and illusions of that social form of life are embodied by the poet's existence and physiognomy. In the case of Baudelaire, Benjamin identifies the experience of the crowd as an intoxicant or rush for the flaneur. The lyrical poetry occasioned by *flanerie* is thus composed of the dream images that, triggered by this intoxication, represent the dissolution of individualism in mass society. Hence the poet's existence or form of life (for instance, in the case of Baudelaire, *la Bohème*) is society's work of art; the poet is helpless to transform its life into a work of art.

Or, more exactly, this modernist conceit is destined to fail, and in its failure, the true social function of art emerges. In the lyrical poet, therefore, it must be possible to witness the Dionysian aspect of the artistic power of nature that takes the form of ecstasy, of joy, in which "pain is experienced as joy" and "the breakdown of the *principium individuationis* became an artistic phenomenon" (Nietzsche 1993, sect. 2). The "aesthetic phenomenon [in which] existence and the world are eternally justified" is not the hero's life (the artist's life as a work of art), but, on the contrary, the downfall of all heroism (which corresponds to art as a creation of society): the eternity of life is visible only if one assumes that "the whole comedy of art is not at all performed for us . . . we are images and artistic projections for the true creator of that world, and that our highest dignity lies in the meaning of works of art" (Nietzsche 1993, sect. 5). Eternal life requires not only an allegorical, but also an ironical, self-effacing conception of heroism.

This Nietzschean thesis, from Benjamin's point of view, carries both a mythical and a messianic interpretation: the mythical reading of this thesis is the humanist reading, according to which nature is eternally justified or redeemed by the meaning it receives from human art. This mythical position is captured by the symbolic idea of turning biological life (*zoe*) into social life (*bios*) through art; the work of art speaks of the subjectivity of the artist. As I have shown with regard to Benjamin's interpretation of Goethe, this standpoint needs to be rejected by emphasizing the greatest distance between life and a work of art. Here, the messianic perspective is an allegorical one: it turns social life (*bios*) into the artistic creation of biological life (*zoe*). It is the idea that art (*bios*) is a creation of life (*zoe*) and that social relations are the place of true human creativity. Conversely, where social relations are entirely deprived of creativity, where they are entirely commodified, art tends to appear as "separate" from society. One therefore gets the idea that the artist is a hero and that his life is a work of art (that is, he is a dandy). Hence, at the crossroads between the decadence (going under) of the heroic equation of life with the work of art and the transition (going over) into the postheroic and messianic possibility of placing biological creativity at the center of social relationships, there stands the figure of the dandy.

THE "MAN" OF THE MASSES: THE SEXUAL REPRODUCTION OF CAPITAL

The great difficulty facing anyone who wishes to make sense of Benjamin's studies on Baudelaire is that they form the torso of a possible book that was never completed.[20] For instance, Jennings argues that the essay "On Some Motifs in Baudelaire" should not be taken as Benjamin's most complete theoretical statement of his mature thought (Jennings 2003, 94). It is, rather, the middle section of the projected book, the essay "The Paris of the Second Empire in Baudelaire" rejected by Adorno for publication, which should be given pride of place because it best reflects Benjamin's "understanding of commodity fetishism" as having "a central role in his theory of experience" (Jennings 2003, 96). As the epistolary exchange of 1938 with Horkheimer clearly indicates, the third part of the projected Baudelaire book was to turn around the "idée fixe of the New and the Eternally Same" (Benjamin 1991c, 1074, translation mine). Benjamin explains that "the antinomy between the new and the eternally same . . . [is] an antinomy which brings out the illusion with which the fetish character of the commodity dissolves the true categories of history" (Benjamin 1991c, 1083, translation mine). Benjamin's transition to this third part of the book in which the eternal recurrence of the same would have been discussed as the essential formula for late capitalism is found in the last section of "The Paris of the Second Empire in Baudelaire" dedicated to the question of modernity. To be modern is to be "heroic" in the face of the eternal recurrence. The problem of modern heroism is connected to the problem of allegory, lyric poetry, tragedy, and irony that interlaces Nietzsche's theory of genre. On another level, the problem of modern heroism is connected to the questions of love, marriage, contract, and prostitution within Benjamin's theory of sexual politics with which I began this chapter. They are all themes that reappear in Benjamin's "The Paris of the Second Empire in Baudelaire," particularly in the section dedicated to "La Bohème." Lesbianism, the whore, the Apache, the specter of masculine impotence: these are the important figures or forces that circulate in the Passages, along with the dandy and the flaneur. To put it into a formula, what Benjamin first theorizes in relation to the crisis of bourgeois marriage, he then projects onto the crisis of bourgeois capitalism: what circulates here are not wives but commodities, or both in one, as in the figure of the prostitute. And one must never undervalue the striking fact that Marx always approximates the decadence of the bourgeoisie by saying that capitalism has made marriage the same as prostitution. At the same time, Marx assures us that communism does not mean the generalized exchange of women. In fact, the section on "La Bohème" is also the section in which Benjamin discusses Marx's appreciation for Blanqui.

It is remarkable that when Foucault wants to defend his conception of genealogy—a Nietzschean conception—against Habermas's "blackmail of the Enlightenment," he identifies genealogy with an *ethos* or posture toward the present, which he calls "the attitude of modernity," and which he proceeds to analyze by taking up Baudelaire's conception of "la modernité," just as Benjamin had done several decades before him. Foucault uses Baudelaire to give an approximation of what he calls an "ontology of the present," while Benjamin uses Baudelaire to construct a critique of progress that brings to light the (eternal) "now" of the revolution and its "heroism." As Benjamin says, "The true task of the modern hero is to bring about the New [*das Neue, das ins Werk zu setzen die wahre Aufgabe des modernen Heros ist*]" (Benjamin 1991c, 1151, translation mine). I think Benjamin tried to work out this affirmative sense of eternal life in the context of Baudelaire's conception of "modernity" and, in particular, in the conception of the modern hero, who, as Benjamin says in *Thesis XVI*, is "man enough to blast the continuum of history."

Modernity, or *la modernité*, is defined by Baudelaire as the task of "sorting out in fashion the poetical moment that it can contain within the historical, drawing out the eternal from the transitory [*dégager de la mode ce qu'elle peut contenir de poétique dans l'historique, de tirer l'étérnel du transitoire*]" (Baudelaire 1992, 354, translation mine). In other words, a modern life is a form of life that sets itself the task of capturing eternity not beyond the fleeting instant, but in it. For Benjamin, the question of modernity is the question of heroism in the face of the eternal recurrence of the same: "The hero is the true subject of modernity. This means that, in order to live modernity, one requires a heroic nature" (Benjamin 2006, 103). Foucault repeats Benjamin's formula: "Being modern . . . consists in recapturing something eternal that is not beyond the present instant, nor behind it, but within it. Modernity is distinct from fashion, which does no more than call into question the course of time; modernity is the attitude that makes it possible to grasp the 'heroic' aspect of the present moment. Modernity is not a phenomenon of sensitivity to the fleeting present; it is the will to 'heroize' the present" (Foucault 1997, 310).

One of the most difficult questions of literary theory that emerges from Nietzsche's overturning of the concept of the lyrical poet has to do with the relation between irony and allegory. They both share the goal of establishing a perpetual "now," of arresting time, by showing the eternity of the here and now. The difference between them is that the messianic is present in allegory and absent in irony. I would like to illustrate this difference by discussing how Foucault offers an ironical interpretation of modern heroism, while Benjamin offers an allegorical one.[21] Foucault speaks of this "heroization" of the present in the practices of the flaneur and the dandy, which he characterizes as "ironic" (Foucault 1997, 310–11). However, he interprets Baudelaire's categorization of his friend Guys, a "dandy" painter, as a "man of modernity" to be an indication that the ways of the dandy are somehow superior to the "spectator's posture" of the flaneur. One can say that Benjamin reverses this order of rank.

Benjamin's allegorical view of modern heroism represents modern man as a corpse and his (eternal) life as love. To begin with, Benjamin identifies the Dionysian reality of the modern experience of beauty, which Baudelaire abstractly refers to as the coincidence of eternity and fashion, in the experience portrayed by the famous poem of *Les Fleurs du Mal* dedicated to *La passante* (the passerby). Benjamin discusses at length the "shock" expressed in that poem, which results from the realization that our eternal love will never be enjoyed because he or she just passed in front of us on a crowded street, never to be captured again. The shock of the passerby is the very fact that beauty "goes under" (which is comparable to the shock of the death of Ottilie). As indicated above, in *Le Peintre de la vie moderne*, Baudelaire gives as an example of the modern hero his friend, the painter Constantin Guys. Referring to Poe's story "The Man of the Crowd," which tells of a convalescent who follows an unknown man in the crowd because he is irresistibly drawn by his physiognomy, Baudelaire claims that Guys has the character of "an artist who will always be, in a spiritual sense, a convalescent" (Baudelaire 1992, 350, translation mine). The experience of convalescence is compared with a return to childhood in which everything appears as novelty, thereby fighting the boredom (*ennui*, *acedia*) generated by a society that is entirely commodified, that is, in which there is only the production of what is ever-the-same. Baudelaire thinks of Guys as a flaneur, as someone who finds his happiness in an intoxicating experience of the dissolution of the self in the crowds of modern cities: "His passion and his profession is that of marrying the crowd [*épouser la foule*]. For the perfect flaneur, for the passionate observer, it is an immense joy [*une immense jouissance*] to choose one's home in numbers, in what is wavering, in movement, in what is fugitive and in the infinite" (Baudelaire 1992, 352, translation mine). Hence, the flaneur appears as the "man" of the masses, in the sense that he seeks this moment, this fugitive encounter with eternity, through the masses and through the uncanny experience of "marrying" the crowd itself.

For Benjamin, it is "flanerie . . . that makes of necessity virtue and thus reveals the structure that characterizes in all of its parts the conception of the hero in Baudelaire" (Benjamin 2006, 100). The flaneur, more than the dandy, reveals the structure of the modern hero. The reason for the importance of the flaneur, and the proximity of the lyrical poet to this figure, is due to the medium in which the flaneur develops: "The flaneur is someone abandoned in the crowd. He is thus in the same situation as the commodity. He is unaware of his special situation, but this does not diminish its effect on him; it permeates him blissfully, like a narcotic that can compensate him for many humiliations. The intoxication to which the flaneur surrenders is the intoxication of the commodity in a surging stream of customers" (Benjamin 2006, 85). In other words, the flaneur is in exactly the same position as the lyric poet whose imagery constitutes nature's intoxication, that is, the joy in the loss of individuality carried by the commodity and the crowd.

Benjamin's analysis in these pages seeks to radicalize the analysis of commodity fetishism proposed by Lukács and his call to understand class consciousness as the impersonal consciousness of the commodity itself. Benjamin advances Lukács's standpoint by arguing that it is the lyrical poet who gives an impersonal voice to the commodity as the creation of social forces: "If there were such a thing as a commodity-soul (a notion that Marx occasionally mentions in jest), it would be the most empathetic ever encountered in the realm of souls, for it would be bound to see every individual as a buyer in whose hand and house it wants to nestle. . . . Empathy is the nature of the intoxication to which the flaneur abandons himself in the crowd" (Benjamin 2006, 85). Indeed, Benjamin asserts that in Baudelaire's prose poem *Les foules* [The Crowds] "we hear the voice . . . of the fetish itself, which Baudelaire's sensitive disposition resonated with so powerfully: that empathy with inorganic things which was one of his sources of inspiration" (Benjamin 2006, 86). Elsewhere he says, "His experience of the crowd bore the traces of the 'heartache and the thousand natural shocks' which a pedestrian suffers in the bustle of a city and which keep his self-awareness all the more alert. (Basically, it is this very self-awareness that he lends to the strolling commodity)" (Benjamin 2006, 91). Benjamin proceeds to argue that crowds "intoxicate" the commodities and make them more charming to potential buyers, just like drug addicts display more charm when high. He refers to the "holy prostitution of the soul"—meaning the soul of the commodity—which, like a prostitute, gives itself entirely to the "poetry and charity" of the unknown passerby or consumer.

It is important to note that the empathy of the commodity is the paroxysm of its fetishism. The degree to which people have become commodities also corresponds to their desire to engage in flanerie amidst the crowds: "The more he proletarianizes himself, the more he will be gripped by the chilly breath of the commodity economy and the less he will feel like empathizing with commodities" (Benjamin 2006, 88). Lastly, Benjamin identifies the dangerous face of the crowd: "This (statistical) existence conceals the really monstrous thing about them: that the concentration of private persons as such is an accident resulting from their private concerns. But if these concentrations become evident—and totalitarian states see to this by making the concentration of their citizens permanent and obligatory for all their purposes—their hybrid character is clearly manifest, particularly to those who are involved. They rationalize the accident of the market economy which brings them together in this way as 'fate' in which the 'race' is reunited. In so doing they give free rein to both the herd instinct and to reflective action" (Benjamin 2006, 93). The crowd here is the vehicle for a transition from capitalist biopolitics based on the fetish of the commodity to fascist thanatopolitics in which the utmost alienation of species-life appears in the form of a struggle between "superior" and "inferior" or "degenerate" races.

At this point, Benjamin introduces a crucial comparison between Hugo and Baudelaire: for the former, as evidenced by the great success of *Les Misérables*, the crowds are the new lyrical subject, the modern hero; for the latter, the modern hero seeks a hiding place in the masses. The reader is thus left with the pressing question: Who is the real "man" of the crowds, in the sense of the revolutionary leader of the masses? In Baudelaire, more directly than in Goethe, the veil of beauty—namely, the crowds—reveal the underlining of death that exists behind modern *eros*. In fact, in order to illustrate his formula that "all beauty contains, like all possible phenomena, something eternal and something transitory " (Baudelaire 1992, 153, translation mine), in his *Salon de 1846*, chap. 18, "Of Heroism in Modern Life," Baudelaire discusses modern suicide as being nobler than ancient suicide and then refers to the modern attire of the bourgeoisie:

> Is it not the necessary attire of our age, suffering and bearing on its black and thin shoulders a perpetual mourning? Notice that the black suit and the frock coat [*redingote*] do not have only a political beauty, as the expression of universal equality, but also a poetic beauty, as the expression of the public soul; an immense formation of undertakers [*une immense défilade de croque-morts*]. . . . We are all celebrating some burial. (Baudelaire 1992, 154, translation mine)

For Benjamin, the connection between suicide and fashionable black suits is the following: the black suit indicates that the bourgeois is walking behind the corpse of the proletariat, that capitalist civil society is a gigantic "marche funèbre."[22]

The proletariat's "heroism" lies in the decision to commit suicide rather than to submit to the dehumanization of Taylorism, Fordism, and now post-Fordist modes of production:

> The resistance that modernity offers to the natural productive élan of the individual is out of all proportion to his strength. It is understandable if a person becomes exhausted and takes refuge in death. Modernity must stand under the sign of suicide, an act which seals a heroic will that makes no concessions to a mentality inimical toward this will. Such a suicide is not resignation but heroic passion. It is the achievement of modernity in the realm of the passions.... Someone like Baudelaire could very well have viewed suicide as the only heroic act still available to the *multitudes maladives* of the cities in reactionary times. (Benjamin 2006, 105)

Benjamin sees in fashion's predilection for black "the symbol of constant mourning... for what was and lack of hope for what is to come," and in this sense modern fashion is also a sign of "the closest link between modernity and antiquity" (Benjamin 2006, 111). It will be remembered that in the essay on the *Elective Affinities*, the eternity of life can only be demonstrated either by marriage or by the double and simultaneous suicide pact of the lovers. However, neither possibility seems open in a system where the commodity and the prostitute blend into one another, where late capitalism brings back the prematriarchical stage of haeterism. Compared with this heroism of the worker, the resistance posed by the flaneur to the advance of Taylorism, which consisted in walking up and down the passages at the pace dictated by their pet tortoises, is a heroism in the most ironic of senses (Benjamin 2006, 84).

Benjamin's point, in part, is that in modernity the role of the hero is open to more than one person, or, put otherwise, no real heroes exist anymore. "For the modern hero is no hero; he is a portrayer of heroes. Heroic modernity turns out to be a Trauerspiel in which the hero's part is available" (Benjamin 2006, 125). The distance that Baudelaire establishes between the hero and the masses, the singular and the universal, turns all heroism into parody. The modern hero is not a hero of the masses, but uses the masses as a veil through which to lead its aesthetic existence: looking for beauty, looking for ways to make life more beautiful or bearable (more like literature), rather than looking for ways to make life more creative or artistic (which requires giving up the illusion of beauty). In other words, if the flaneur is a modern hero because he makes virtue out of the necessity of mass society, the flaneur is not virile enough to blast history open; he is not the real "man" of the masses. One has to look elsewhere, and not in heterosexual male sexuality, for such a revolutionary hero.

Benjamin's link between the material conditions of production in late capitalism and the development (or lack thereof) of sexual relations within the family structure has been made even more pertinent today, in the age of neoliberalism. On the one hand, the freedom of capital to move industries from one country to another in search of the cheapest possible labor-power, and the consequent dehumanization of the conditions of production, have led to a resurgence of the problem of worker suicide, whether it takes the form of jumping off the roofs of industrial plants in China or attempting to cross oceans in overcrowded dinghies. Likewise, neoliberalism has created incentives both for the massive exodus of women into the workplace and, due to the theory of human capital, the massive entry of economic considerations into the world of the family, marriage, and child rearing.

Marx in fact dedicates a text to the suicide of workers, not cited by Benjamin, in which he draws attention to the suicide of working women (the proletarian of the proletariat) because of patriarchical family structures.[23] In this way, Marx brings together his sympathy for Bachofen's thesis regarding the superiority of matriarchy with the need for the dissolution of the bourgeois family structure. The entrance of women into the ranks of the proletariat, and what this means for the reproduction of sexual relations, is also remarked upon by Benjamin:

> The nineteenth century began openly and without reserve to include women in the process of commodity production. All the theoreticians were united in their opinion that her specific femininity was thereby endangered: masculine traits must necessarily manifest themselves in women after a while. Baudelaire affirms these traits; at the same time, however, he seeks to free them from the domination of the economy. Hence the purely sexual accent which he comes to give this developmental tendency in women. The paradigm of the lesbian woman represents the protest of 'modernity' against technological development. (Benjamin 2006, 144)

The Heroism of Sexuality in Benjamin and Foucault 185

Benjamin's references to the "masculinity" of the modern hero play with the allegorical significance assigned to Hercules in Roman times and then again in the Renaissance, namely, as a figure of the "hero" who was capable of "mastering" the unpredictable change of situations (*fortuna*) and, in general, of making "virtue out of necessity." The connection between *virtus* (virtue) and *vir* (man) has often been pointed out. Benjamin even remarks that Baudelaire's constant reference point for his theory of modernity is "Roman antiquity." I mentioned above that the black frock coat was the emblem of a society that was in constant mourning for the death of its productive forces and that had nothing left to hope for. There is, however, another element to the color black in fashion that Benjamin does not mention, but which is significant for his argument, namely, the introduction of black pants and suits as a key element of women's fashion by Coco Chanel: here, fashion returns to an antiquity that is no longer that of patriarchy, but that of the matriarchal woman-king and her Amazons. But Baudelaire's lyric poetry is where the reference to *virtù* and masculinity breaks down, on the one hand, into the ironical impotence of the flaneur who is unable to interrupts the train of history and, on the other hand, into the allegorical decoding of Baudelaire's true concept of "masculinity" : "The lesbian is the heroine of *la modernité*. In her, one of Baudelaire's erotic ideals—the woman who signifies hardness and virility—has combined with a historical ideal, that of greatness in the ancient world" (Benjamin 2006, 119). If there is a "subject" of the masses who can interrupt history, then she is ultimately not a "man" at all, but has to be found with those "creatures"—the lesbian, the androgyne, the whore, the *Lumpensammler* (ragpicker)—in whom Benjamin appears to have identified "the intention of redemption" (*Elective Affinities*).[24]

This new revolutionary subject must be endowed with an antipower of life strong enough to halt, from within, the sexual and political cycles of reproduction of capital. For this reason, Benjamin ends his reading of Baudelaire with a reference to an early feminist socialist manifesto by Claire Démar: "No more motherhood! No law of the blood. I say: no more motherhood. Once a woman has been freed from men who pay her the price of her body . . . she will owe her existence. . . . only to her own creativity. . . . So you will have to resolve to take a newborn child from the breast of its natural mother and place it in the hands of a social mother, a nurse employed by the state. . . . Only then and not earlier will men, women, and children be freedom from the law of blood, the law of mankind's self-exploitation" (Benjamin 2006, 120). The figure of the social mother is again matriarchical, and Démar's proclamation is noteworthy for how it explodes the "law of blood" or *ghenos* that lies at heart of thanatopolitics: at issue is the separation of marriage from relationships, from sex, and from reproduction. The cycle of the reproduction of capital is attacked by the return of male impotence and lesbianism, which opens up a different eternal recurrence, a different cycle for natality and normativity outside of the demands for the self-reproduction of capital, which finds one of its best expressions in Foucault's own meditation on Baudelaire.

GAY LIFE AND THE HEROISM OF MODERN LIFE

Foucault contrasts "the attitude of modernity [that] does not treat the passing moment as sacred in order to maintain or perpetuate it" with the attitude of the flaneur, "the idle, strolling spectator, [who] is satisfied to keep his eyes open, to pay attention and to build up a storehouse of memories" (here I suspect he means what Benjamin calls *Erlebnisse*) (Foucault 1997, 311). What makes Guys more than a flaneur is the irony with which he treats the realization of the impossibility of eternal love in the crowd, the fleeting nature of this eternity:

> Just when the whole world is falling asleep, he begins to work, and he transfigures that world. His transfiguration entails not an annulling of reality but a difficult interplay between the truth of what is real and the exercise of freedom; 'natural' things become 'more than natural,' beautiful things become 'more than beautiful,' and individual objects appear 'endowed with an impulsive life like the soul of [their creator].' For the attitude of modernity, the high value of the present is indissociable from a desperate eagerness to imagine it, to imagine it otherwise than it is, and to transform it not by destroying it but by grasping it in what it is. Baudelairean modernity is an exercise in which extreme attention to what is real is confronted with the practice of a liberty that simultaneously respects this reality and violates it. (Foucault 1997, 311)

There is an uncanny similarity between this work of transfiguration and the themes Benjamin selects in his essay "The Paris of the Second Empire in Baudelaire." The ironic transfiguration of reality is not a question of transcending another time or world but, instead, refers to the capacity to wake up in a dream or phantasmagoria of the present. The phantasmagoria that puts everyone else to sleep—or in which everyone else is daydreaming—is represented as a collective wish-fulfillment.[25] The "more than natural" aspect of nature that modern art seeks to reproduce is the allegorical, "*übernatürliche*" idea mentioned by Benjamin in his Goethe essay. What lies "beyond beauty"—again—for Benjamin is the sublime (an Idea that has no intuitive representation). And, finally, the reference to the "impulsive life" or "soul" of commodities and the problem of the poet's *Einfühlung* is, for Benjamin, the key to the overturning of commodity fetishism. But Foucault remains silent about these features of modernity, choosing to emphasize another side of the same problem.

Foucault believes that the dandy best incorporates the ironic "heroization of the present." For Foucault, the dandy exemplifies "a mode of relationship that must be established with oneself"—the dandy becomes a model of normativity, of ethics. According to Foucault's reading of Baudelaire, the dandy "makes of his body, his behavior, his feelings and passions, his very existence, a work of art. Modern man, for Baudelaire, is not the man who goes off to discover himself, his secrets and his hidden truth; he is the man who tries to invent himself. This modernity does not 'liberate man in his own being'; it compels him to face the task of producing himself" (Foucault 1997, 312). Does this mean that Foucault adopts the "life as literature" mythology, like Gundolf does with respect to Goethe, or is he making a different point?

One indication that Foucault is not after an "aestheticist" understanding of the practices of turning life into a work of art is expressed by his remark that "Baudelaire does not imagine that these have any place in society itself or in the body politic. They can only be produced in another, different place, which Baudelaire calls art" (Foucault 1997, 312). Foucault thereby implies that Baudelaire remains caught in the doctrine of "l'art pour l'art," whereas he propounds a more materialist understanding of the social function of artistic creativity. In another text, he makes explicit what the cited phrase "liberate man in his own being" alludes to and in what sense his own proposal of "facing the task of producing himself" should be understood. The reference seems to be to Sartre's conception of "self-creation," for in this discussion of Baudelaire's "modern man," Foucault adds:

> From the idea [of Sartrian derivation] that the self is not given to us, I think that there is only one practical consequence: we have to create ourselves as a work of art. In his analyses of Baudelaire, Flaubert, etc. it is interesting to see that Sartre refers the work of creation to a certain relation to oneself--the author to himself--which has the form of authenticity or of inauthenticity. I would like to say exactly the contrary: we should not have to refer the creative activity of somebody to the kind of relation he has to himself, but should relate the kind of relation one has to oneself to a creative activity. (Foucault 1997, 262)

I think it is possible to understand Foucault's remarks much more along Benjaminian and Nietzschean lines, in which artistic creation is to be located at the level of life as *zoe* rather than as *bios*: the question is how to eternalize *zoe* by making living into an artistic practice, rather than immortalizing *bios* by making one's life into something beautiful (that is, symbolic).

During the same period in which Foucault was reflecting on the modernist motif of life as literature, he gave a series of famous interviews concerning his activism on behalf of gay rights that illustrate how he understood the dandy's work of self-creation. The project was to create an alternative *mode de vie* or form of life based on the material occurrence of sex: Foucault designated this *mode de vie* as "gay" to distinguish it from the practice of "homosexual" sex. Thus, in "Friendship as a Way of Life," he writes that "the problem is not to discover in oneself the truth of one's sex, but rather to use one's sexuality henceforth to arrive at a multiplicity of relationships" (Foucault 1997, 135). What Foucault means by these "relationships" is made clear by his comparisons with institutions and practices linked to "heterosexual" sex, namely, marriage, courtship, and chivalry. Foucault argues that sexual relations between men did not have the advantage of starting from an institutional basis like marriage or the practice of chivalry because, within the social construction of modern homosexuality in Western Christendom, the sexual act comes before friendship or love. Foucault implies that the reverse is true for the social construction of heterosexuality. The *mode de vie* therefore has to do with setting up a mode of relating to the person with whom one has sex so as to make possible what Benjamin calls the "continuance of love," the divine seal of fidelity that allows for sexual life to be eternal life. The normative status of these relationships that conform to a *mode de vie* is clear from the fact that Foucault speaks about being "gay" as a "way of life [that] can yield a culture and an ethics" (Foucault 1997, 138).

In another interview he speaks of how "a whole new art of sexual practice develops which tries to explore all the internal possibilities of sexual conduct" (Foucault 1997, 151), and he indicates the "laboratories of sexual experimentation" in the S&M phenomenon. In a third interview he arrives at what seems to be a final formulation: a gay form of life would exercise, first of all, "a new right to relationships [*droit relationnel*] that permits all possible types of relations to exist and not be prevented, blocked, or annulled by impoverished relational institutions" (Foucault 1997, 158). Once again, Foucault is interested in the normativity that emerges out of the artistic creativity of *zoe* outside of a guilt context and is therefore capable of eternalizing sexual life. The concept of a "relational right" that runs parallel to marriage exemplifies the sort of "rights of life" that Foucault postulates at the end of the first volume of *History of Sexuality*.

What is most interesting is that this new freedom to reinvent relationships that emerge on the basis of sex (and possibly race) means, in the case of "gay culture," "a culture that invents ways of relating, types of existence, types of values, types of exchanges between individuals which are really new. . . . If that's possible, then *gay culture will not only be a choice of homosexuals for homosexuals—it would create relations that are, at certain points, transferable to heterosexuals*" (Foucault 1997, 160, emphasis mine). In other words, if this "relational right [*droit relationnel*]" were to achieve political recognition in a republic, the patriarchical understanding of the opposition between homosexuality and heterosexuality would fall aside, giving way to what has been theorized as "queer" forms of life. Lastly, and most remarkably, Foucault claims that "the relational right is the right to gain recognition in an institutional sense [*dans un champ institutionnel*] for the relations of one individual to another individual, which is not necessarily connected to the emergence of a group. It's very different. It's a question of imagining how the relation of two individuals can be validated by society and benefit from the same advantages as the relations—perfectly honorable—which are the only ones recognized: marriage and family" (Foucault 1997, 162). In these passages, it seems to me, Foucault has managed to reinscribe the physiognomy of the gay and lesbian struggle for equal rights within a context that Benjamin would not have hesitated to call *la Bohème*, and in which—not unlike Marx—a kind of new sexual communism is being theorized. But it is precisely a kind of sexual communism that avoids the "haeterism" that, according to Foucault, characterizes homosexual sex in civil society because it advocates a *new right* to establish socially recognized relations on the basis of fidelity to the same sex (be this a homo-, hetero-, bi-, trans-, sex). This new right is exemplary of a republic of "the living" that lies beyond the guilt context and its thanatopolitics, and in which these new forms of "homosexual marriage" can—when translated back into the terms of bourgeois "heterosexual marriage"—prevent its inevitable slide into the mythical form of *eros thanatos*.

Ultimately, what is at stake in these transfigurations of married life is the interruption of the mythical violence exerted on children, which, as Benjamin shows, owes its origin to the guilt context associated with the separation and fixation on sexual difference. Foucault's meditation on the right to "homosexual marriage" and its incorporation into heterosexual relationships is not as far as it might seem from Benjamin's reading of Kantian marriage as the free sexual use of another's body on the basis of fidelity. As in Benjamin's thought, sexuality and eternal life come together in Foucault's conception of gay life. Indeed, Foucault's *plaidoyer* for a new right to relationships appears close in many ways to the logic that, according to Bachofen, locates the origin of marriage in matriarchy—before marriage became a patriarchal institution characterized by the domination of women by men. In both cases, unless the *dispositifs* of sexuality undergo one of these lines of flight, they will inevitably remain bogged down on "the Via Dolorosa of male sexuality," namely, impotence. Bringing together natality, normality, and normativity in one formula, Benjamin hypothesizes the true "social reasons for impotence: the imagination of the bourgeois class ceases to be occupied with the future of the productive forces it has unleashed. . . . In order to concern itself further with this future, the bourgeois class in fact would first have had to renounce the idea of private income" (Benjamin 2006, 141).

PART III

Biopolitics of Rights

6

FREE MARKETS AND REPUBLICAN CONSTITUTIONS IN HAYEK AND FOUCAULT

NEOLIBERALISM AS A FRAMEWORK OF BIOPOLITICS

The renewal of post-Marxist thought in the last decade—led by thinkers such as Negri and Agamben—was made possible in part by the reception of Foucault's posthumously published lectures on governmentality at the Collège de France. Up until that point, Foucault's thought had fallen out of favor with the Marxist and post-Marxist Left, mainly because of his rejection of the Freudo-Marxist "repressive hypothesis" in *The History of Sexuality, Volume One*. His genealogy of governmentality quickly revealed itself as a genealogy of liberalism and neoliberalism, two regimes that, to a degree, seek to substitute the ideal of government for the reality of sovereignty. The main reason for this positive reception by the Left is that the focus on governmentality offered a way to revitalize Marx's project of a "critique of political economy" and its critique of liberalism.[1] Governmentality, in the most general terms, refers to a form of nonrepressive power that allows for the "conduct" of human conduct in such a way that he or she who is so conducted understands himself or herself to be acting in "freedom" and "security," that is, acting in accordance to the quintessential liberal values.[2] Governmentality thus promises to give a new content to what is "political" about "political economy," namely, it promises an explanation of the conduct of the economic subject or *homo oeconomicus*.

In his lectures on *Security, Territory, Population* and in *The Birth of Biopolitics* Foucault indicated that the concept of governmentality is closely related to the idea of biopolitics, that is, a form of power whose effects target the species-life (*zoe*) of human beings, which Foucault identified (in part) with the emergence of the idea of "population" and the rise of statistics as a crucial instrument in liberal governmentality. But the relation between biopolitics, governmentality and political economy remained tantalizingly sketchy in Foucault's lectures. As a recent critic points out, the emphasis on Foucault's formula of the "conduct of conduct" tends to focus attention on the economic actor, paradigmatically on the figure of the entrepreneur, leaving to one side the functioning of other economic entities, such as labor, value, commodities, and the free market.[3] The point can be also phrased as follows: when "political economy" is interpreted through the perspective of biopolitics, all too often what emerges is a focus on *bios* rather than on *zoe*, on the (cultural) "forms of life" that liberalism and neoliberalism select for survival or disappearance, rather than on the (biological) living substrate of the economy that is targeted by biopower and governmentality.

Aside from the economy, there is another component of "political economy" that has received less analysis than it should in the reception of Foucault's concept of governmentality, namely, the dimension of jurisprudence and in particular the idea of the "rule of law." Interpreters have emphasized that the "conduct of conduct" takes place according to what Foucault called "norms" as opposed to "laws," where the latter are understood, in a legal positivist sense, as being the commands of a sovereign.[4] Although this is correct to a degree, in my opinion the strict opposition between norm and law (as sovereign command) carries with it the risk of missing the real legal structure of liberal and neoliberal governmentality, which is neither reducible to the idea of law as sovereign command nor to the idea of a statistical norm. In this chapter, I shall put forward the hypothesis that the fundamental conception of law at work in Foucault's concept of governmentality recovers, on one side, the archaic Greek idea of *nomos*, as a normative ordering of social life in which theological and philosophical doctrines, disciplinary practices, and political rule are all tightly interwoven. On the other side, liberal governmentality recovers the archaic idea of *nomos* in the form given to it by early modern republican doctrine on political constitutions. Thus, on my hypothesis, the jurisprudence of liberal and neoliberal governmentality operates a creative misappropriation of the archaic and the republican ideas of *nomos* as constitution.

The ancients opposed the idea of substantive normative order called *nomos* to an abstract body of written, positive "legislation" as much as to a philosophical conception of "justice" or "morality." The difference between a substantive normative order and a legal-moral code (a difference that plays an important role in Foucault's thinking from the beginning) is indicated by the subject matter of "security, territory, population" on which Foucault centers his treatment of governmentality. Indeed, these three terms spell out the contents of the archaic conception of *nomos*, which refers to the way in which a group or population (Nietzsche will say a "herd") is collected by another group ("shepherds") through a spatial division of territory (a grid), designed to provide "security" or "salvation" to the grouping and thereby governing complexity. In the fourth chapter of *The Nomos of the Earth*, Schmitt drew attention to this archaic idea of *nomos*, showing how its pastoral metaphors are organized around the economic finality of justifying "an original distribution of land" (Schmitt 2003, 68ff). But in Schmitt the problem of "security" as Foucault understands it, namely, as a spatial network of power relations intended to use contingency rather than protect against it, is missing.[5] The pastoral metaphor that is fairly unavoidable in the grammar of *nomos* is precisely what supports my claim that Foucault's account of governmentality draws upon what the ancients called *nomos*.

Is there a way to link up governmentality both to the biological roots of the economic ontology and to the jurisprudential (nomo-thetic) roots of political economy? In this chapter I present a hypothesis as to how biopolitics and governmentality connect in Foucault's late thought such that it carries explanatory force to make sense of the imbrications of economics and law in liberalism and in neoliberalism. To do so, I shall apply my hypothesis about Foucault's legal and biological understanding of governmentality to the work of Hayek, who has recently been identified as a major force in the construction of the neoliberal hegemony since the end of the Cold War.[6] The reason why I choose Hayek is precisely because I take his innovation in economic theory to consist in the introduction of the concept of *nomos* such that the constitutional and the biological dimensions of political economy are essentially and immediately related to each other.

One of the manifestations of the current hegemony of neoliberal discourse is found in the widespread use of the concept of "governance," perhaps neoliberalism's most successful theoretical product in the social sciences and in public policy. Governance is provided by what Talcott Parsons called a "normative order." As the term is employed currently, the expression "normative order" is ambiguous because it can have two meanings. First, it can refer to the social order that follows from individuals and corporations (legal persons) acting in accordance with certain legal norms and moral valuations. Here the norms generate the social order. It is in this sense that some theorists believe the sheer existence of frameworks for transnational agreements and legal regimes will bring about a transnational social order and, along with it, human beings with transnational political consciousness and new cosmopolitan ideas about their duties and rights.[7] I shall call this view of things a "juridification" of the political world.[8]

In a second sense, the expression "normative order" can also refer to the intrinsic normative intention that characterizes a given social order: here it is the order that generates the norms, and not the norms that generate the order.[9] I shall call this phenomenon the "biologization" of the political world because the claim that norms can be derived from order, or value from fact, is ultimately a claim that originates in a modern understanding of biological life.[10] What is important for the purpose of this chapter is the fact that the insight behind this claim—before the term of autopoiesis was coined by Maturana and Varela and applied to social systems by Luhmann—was elegantly captured by Canguilhem, the French philosopher of science and one of Foucault's teachers. Canguilhem argued that the phenomenon of life had to be understood within the binary "normal-pathological" because every living thing is an ensemble of parts that functions according to its own internal norms. Canguilhem also showed that every living thing is itself "normative" because it is capable of creating new norms for itself, upon which its state of health depends.[11]

As it turns out, both meanings of the expression "normative order"—what I have called the juridical and the biological construction of the expression—are found in Hayek's neoliberal theory of law. In fact, they constitute its very heart. Hayek's discovery is that "spontaneous" social (normative) orders like the free market depend on certain legal rules: the coordination of expectations of individuals having very different knowledge is only possible thanks to the assumption that they all are following "abstract" rules of law (which are, nevertheless, not commands of a sovereign authority). Likewise, the biological understanding of normative order is also found in Hayek. I do not refer here merely to his evolutionary conception of the growth of knowledge,[12] but more precisely to his claim that only spontaneous social orders generate their own kind of normative subjectivity: a free market works because of competition, but competition is not premised on conditions of perfect equilibrium (knowledge) between sellers and buyers, but, conversely, if an equilibrium will be reached this is only because of the "unpredictable" factor of the "freedom," "creativity," and "responsibility" of the economic actors, not in spite of these normative characteristics.[13] And this freedom and responsibility is itself normative in that it generates new norms: the name for such a normative individual, the free subject of economics, is the entrepreneur. The entrepreneur's conduct is normative because he or she is routinely placed in the situation of having to decide where to invest his or her energies and capital and where not to, what to select, strengthen, and help live, and what to ignore, cast aside, and let die.

Although it can be argued, as I have done earlier in this study, that Hegel's and Marx's analyses of civil society anticipated the simultaneous juridification and biologization of the political world in late modernity, Foucault is the first to recognize this as the salient feature of neoliberalism. Hence, his pathbreaking hypothesis that neoliberalism ought to be understood as offering the "general framework" for biopolitics (Foucault 2010, 22n). Foucault claims that neoliberalism introduces a new form of individuation that requires everyone to become an entrepreneur in their own biological lives (Foucault 2010, 144–50, 172–77). At the same time, he claims that with neoliberal biopolitics:

> We have entered a phase of juridical regression.... We should not be deceived by all the Constitutions framed throughout the world since the French Revolution.... A whole, continual and clamorous legislative activity: these were the forms that made an essentially normalizing power acceptable. (Foucault 1990, 144)

On the one hand, Foucault notices that neoliberal governmentality leads to an unparalleled expansion in new legalities and normative orders, most of which go beyond the scope of the sovereign state: this is what we have come to know as the rise of a "civil" and now a "world" society. At the same time, paradoxically, Foucault believes that neoliberalism is an age of "juridical regression." In this chapter I shall argue that this "regression" is due to the fact that the dependency of order on law in neoliberalism masks another reality, namely, that the republican conception of a constitution has been hijacked by political economy in order to depoliticize civil society. Additionally, I show that Foucault holds on to this republican conception of law in order to criticize biopolitical governmentality. My analysis of Hayek is intended to show in what way the neoliberal juridification of politics is a condition of possibility of political economy by allowing for the control over the biological substrate of economic ontology, thus showing how the idea of neoliberal *nomos* not only fashions a crucial link between biopolitics and political economy, but also shows the illusory character of the neoliberal belief that spontaneous social orders like the free market are most conducive to the "natural" liberty of human beings.

FOUCAULT AND THE ANTINOMY OF LAW AND ORDER

There is a commonly held opinion that Foucault wrote about power but neglected law.[14] I think this is misleading. In one of his late essays, Foucault claims that modern political rationality, that is, modern governmentality, is caught within "the *antinomy of law and order*. Law, by definition, always refers to a juridical system, while order refers to an administrative system, or to a state's specific order" (Foucault 2000, 417). This claim, which takes for granted a principled separation between law and state, may sound surprising because Foucault is famous for having advanced an "analytics of power that no longer takes law as a model and a code" (Foucault 1990, 90). In the *History of Sexuality*, Foucault asserts that instead of the representation of "power-as-law," modernity is witness to the emergence of a new kind of power, or the "power over life" (Foucault 1990, 139), whose two forms are disciplinary power and biopower. This new representation of power works through "norms" instead of "laws": norms both generate an order and are the outgrowth of order (Foucault 1990, 144).[15] And yet the very fact that Foucault speaks of an "antinomy of law and order" suggests that, for him, power-as-law is not a model that can simply be surpassed by the new technologies of disciplinary or biopower.[16]

If one takes seriously the "antinomy" between law and order, three theses with respect to Foucault's view of law suggest themselves. First, neoliberalism as a rationalization of biopower functions by integrating the sphere of law into the sphere of order. Neoliberalism is a form of political rationality that attempts what Foucault calls "the reconciliation between law and order" (Foucault 2000, 417). A neoliberal order is impossible without a juridical foundation, but, at the same time, the neoliberal conception of law is deeply corrosive to the rule of law in its republican sense by turning the constitutional sense of law into an epiphenomenon of normative orders (in the dual sense of the term discussed above) and their normalizing effects. This is the basis for Foucault's negative or critical view of "civil society" as it has emerged in liberalism and neoliberalism.

My second thesis is that Foucault rejects all attempts at reconciling law with order: this project, he says, "has been the dream [of liberals], [and] must remain a dream. It is impossible to reconcile law and order because when you try to do so it is only in the form of an integration of law into the state's order" (Foucault 2000, 417). Foucault here appears as an advocate for the autonomy of law with respect to the (sovereign) state, a position that is often associated with republican (even Kantian) constitutionalism. In fact, there is an internal link between Foucault's work on liberal governmentality and his return to the Kantian idea of critique as a response to this governmentality. Here, Foucault turns to the autonomy of law in order to defend a positive conception of "civil society." But this conception is contrary to neoliberalism. The neoliberal rationalization of politics, by contrast, oversteps the limits imposed by the antinomy of law and order, and this is what makes neoliberal rationalization profoundly irrational. Foucault's critique of neoliberalism thus follows a Kantian structure: to engage in a critique of a form of rationality means to reveal its antinomies. Irrationality is not determined by the presence of antinomy, but rather by the ignorance of its inevitability.

My third thesis is that Foucault never entirely does away with the representation of power-as-law because there is no alternative understanding of legitimacy.[17] Biopower, as he says, is only "acceptable," that is, legitimate, because it claims to have a juridical framework. Within his genealogies of liberal governmentality, Foucault always tries to develop an alternative conception of power-as-law, one that subverts modern biopower in an effort to reestablish the antinomy of law and order as the unsurpassable horizon of all government. Some commentators have claimed that Foucault lacks a legal philosophy of his own.[18] Others have argued that if biopower still depends on the law for its acceptability, then maybe biopower is only the last mask adopted by sovereign power, and does not constitute a real break with sovereignty.[19] Still others have seen, in his later writings on liberal governmentality, a rapprochement to liberal ideals and an advocacy for new rights of individuals in the age of biopower, or what is now called "biological citizenship."[20]

In my opinion, none of these readings quite hit the mark: for the late Foucault, the law is not originally an expression of sovereign power, but belongs to an ideal of self-mastery, that is, to an ideal of political independence. In the Western tradition, such an ideal is linked to the republican conception of freedom, whereby an individual counts as free if endowed (by nature) with a *sui iuris* status, that is, if they are "capable" of (making) law because they are capable of judgment or capable of forming their own opinion on matters of concern to all. In his last courses dedicated to *The Government of Self and Others* at the Collège de France, Foucault became interested in the genealogy of this connection between self-mastery, the capacity for (making) law, and the freedom of opinion formation, or what the Greeks called *parrhesia* (free or frank speech). Foucault's genealogy of the capacity for law (the *sui iuris* status) opens up another possible reading of his growing appreciation for the discourse of rights and his support for Solidarity and other movements of dissidence in Eastern Europe, namely, it suggests a sophisticated attempt at saving the discourse of republicanism against liberalism and neoliberalism. For him, only a republican conception of law and power remains true to the antinomy between law and order, and therefore resists the reduction of politics (*Politik*) to a matter of governmentality or police (*Polizei*).[21] To sum up my position: Foucault understands that only a conception of the law that is independent with respect to technologies of power can reestablish the antinomy between law and order as the unsurpassable horizon of any and all forms of governmentality. In this sense, the return to the law offers Foucault a surprising source of resistance to the subjectivations of biopower (Foucault 2000, 331).

In order for there to be an antinomy between law and order, one would expect them to have distinct origins. This is in fact what one finds in Foucault's genealogy of modern governmentality. In the *History of Sexuality*, he offers one of his most complete characterizations of power-as-law. It is a form of power that resides in "the function of the legislator" and only says "no" (Foucault 1990, 83); this power can be either obeyed or disobeyed by a subject, who remains free to choose whether to follow the law. The origins of this juridical representation of power are said to be found in medieval times, when law became the crucial instrument in the development of sovereignty and of the state. Power-as-law emerges with the formation of the new monarchies who looked for "a principle of right that transcended all the heterogeneous claims, manifesting the triple distinction of forming a unitary regime, of identifying its will with the law, and of acting through mechanisms of interdiction and sanction" (Foucault 1990, 87). In this text from 1976, which recapitulates the conception of law found throughout his early work, Foucault claims that later condemnations of monarchy employ the very same juridical thinking that accompanied the development of monarchy. "The representation of power has remained under the spell of monarchy. In political thought and analysis, we still have not cut off the head of the king" (Foucault 1990, 88; Foucault 2003).

In opposition to this "juridical monarchy," Foucault proposes two new technologies of power. He calls these the governmentality of discipline and the governmentality of security (Foucault 2000, 298–325). In these forms of governmentality, power does not take the form of the law, but that of the norm. Foucault's conception of the norm derives from Canguilhem's work on the polarity of health and sickness in living systems.[22] Canguilhem distinguishes between two kinds of normativity: biological and social normativity (Canguilhem 1994, 351–84). Whereas normativity in a living system is an internal regulation of the parts of an organism that is "lived without problems" (Legrand 2007, 87), social normativity imposes arbitrary social norms on living individuals as a result of a normative intention and a normalizing decision (Canguilhem 1994, 370ff; Legrand 2007, 83). Here, the meaning of "norm" is the same as the Latin *norma*: a straight angle that is employed to "straighten" something. It is this sense of social normativity that serves as the basis for Foucault's famous studies on disciplinary power and its normalizing effects.

Canguilhem's theory of normative order takes as its starting point the radical difference between biological and sociological normativity. For Canguilhem, a living individual is normal, but never normalized. At the same time, Canguilhem is interested in a feature of sociological normativity that makes society more than a machine. According to his famous formula, "a society is both machine and organism" (Canguilhem 1994, 376). What this means is that when a society tries to organize itself, to plan its operations and become a functionally differentiated system of subsystems (to speak à la Luhmann), it is at once becoming more machinelike and transcending its machinic existence. This is because its technological self-organization is nothing short of an attempt to regulate itself in order to satisfy its own needs in a way that is analogous to a living being:

> We must see above all in planning endeavors the attempts to constitute organs through which a society could estimate, foresee and assume its needs instead of being reduced to recording and stating them in terms of accounts and balance sheets. So that what is denounced, under the name of rationalization—the bogey complacently waved by the champions of liberalism, the economic variety of the cult of nature—as a mechanization of social life perhaps expresses, on the contrary, the need, obscurely felt by society, to become the organic subject of needs recognized as such. (Canguilhem 1994, 374)

Foucault's theory of biopower—as opposed to his theory of disciplinary power—is based on Canguilhem's understanding of society's attempts to mimic the biological normativity of the individuals who compose it: "Social regulation tends toward organic regulation and mimics it without ceasing for all that to be composed mechanically" (Canguilhem 1994, 377). Just as Canguilhem argues that the living individual will always "enliven" social norms by appropriating them creatively,[23] so Foucault argues that in neoliberalism biopower manifests itself in the form of the subjectivity of the entrepreneur, who is always "innovating" and taking risks on the basis of the stability of expectations guaranteed by social normalization.[24]

Foucault was able to apply Canguilhem's comparison of biological and social normativity to the case of neoliberalism because of the mediation offered by Hayek's conception of spontaneous social orders, which, in one respect, is very close to Canguilhem's understanding of social normative order, and this despite Canguilhem's belief that his notion of social normativity is not compatible with liberalism's critique of social planning. The apparent opposition between Canguilhem and Hayek may be due to confusion with how the terms "organization" and "planning" are used in the different traditions within which Canguilhem and Hayek are working. Hayek polemicizes against the "planning" of society because it renders all social order a matter of "organization," thereby reducing individuals to nothing more than "cogs in the wheel" of the great machine of society. For Hayek, social organization does not take into account the creative potential of all individuals and fails to see that the best way to coordinate this creativity is to empower it through spontaneous orders of exchange or commerce. Only the latter orders make society more like a "living" thing, what Hayek calls a

"Great Society."[25] In both Canguilhem and Hayek, therefore, "civil society" pursues more freedom in order to become more "alive," and vice versa.

Having said this, I do not mean to belittle the fact that Canguilhem's thesis on social normativity also contains an affirmative biopolitical meaning, which he explicitly and rightly contrasts with the (neo)liberal attack on state regulatory activity. Canguilhem suggests that the attempt to plan economic production, far from being a rigid, machinelike barrier to entrepreneurial, creative activity, as neoliberals maintain, in reality indicates the attempt of the state to overcome itself as a machine in order to become a political "body" that is more "living," that is characterized by what I call a "surplus" of life. Such a political body would be one in which norms cease to function like disciplinary controls in order to become what Agamben calls "form-of-life," a coincidence of individual *bios* with social *zoe*. This suggestion of a deeper and more fundamental coincidence between planning and (surplus) life, opens the possibility of an affirmative, post-Marxist conception of biopolitics that is opposed to the neoliberal appropriation of biological normativity that resolutely tends toward decreasing the capacity of political (state) planning of the economy. Foucault adopts not only the negative conception of biopower to understand neoliberal governmentality, but also this affirmative, nonliberal biopolitics.

An important element of what I am calling Canguilhem's affirmative biopolitics is his idea that social regulation never manages to be exactly like biological self-regulation because the invention of social norms is always a response to crises and social conflicts among the parts of society and one doesn't find class struggle in the amoeba (at least, not in the same sense). I tend to interpret Canguilhem's point to mean that the fact of social or class conflict is responsible for a heightened normative creativity in political bodies, which finds its expression in the constitution as norm. As with everything in Canguilhem's conceptual tool box, this thesis finds a double and dissonant echo in Foucault's work. On the one hand, in the lecture course *"Society Must Be Defended"* Foucault seems to uphold the thesis that modern social conflict is part of the development of biopower as modern racism, since he postulates a "racial" origin to the idea of class struggle. By contrast, in these same lectures Foucault shows how the belief that sovereign power, far from bringing social peace, reflects an ongoing war (that is, his famous thesis of "politics as war") played a decisive role in the republican and protocommunist critiques of the conception of law as sovereign command that was advanced by absolutist theories of the state (for instance, in Hobbes). This critique of law as sovereign command inaugurates an entirely different conception of law upheld in the modern revolutionary republican tradition linked to the constituent power of the people. In the last section of this chapter, I discuss this republican aspect to Foucault's theory of affirmative biopolitical counterconducts and resistance to neoliberal biopower.

Building upon Canguilhem's insights on biological normativity, Foucault defines a norm as a mode of social regulation that transforms society from a machine to a (quasi)-living organism: it seeks "an ordered maximization of collective and individual forces" (Foucault 1990, 24–25). Such norms, as the regulations of governmentality, correspond to the biologization of law: to a modeling of law onto the internal normativity of life, which gives rise to the phenomenon of a "civil society" that appears "self-regulated," and thus endowed with a "nature" of its own. More specifically, whereas a law forbids certain *acts* but leaves the subject untouched, Foucault claims that a norm *generates an individuality*. Foucault gives the example of modern sexual regulations that transform someone who commits an act of sodomy into "a personage . . . a type of life, a life form, and a morphology, with an indiscreet anatomy and possibly a mysterious physiology . . . the homosexual was now a species" (Foucault 1990, 43). In other words, normalizing technologies of biopower produce subjectivities; they are a "mode of specification of individuals." Norms transform each individual into a specimen, while groups of human beings become subspecies ("populations") in and through this individualization.[26] This is the key to how biopower performs the task of coordinating the individual and the community: it governs the "conduct" of "populations."

Modern political rationality is a question of normalization, and normalization means the generation and government of the "conduct" of populations (or subspecies), which, at one and the same time, maximize individual forces and collective forces and integrate the individual into the life of the collective (or group). In this sense, biopower refers to the set of norms that establish the "conduct of conduct," in Foucault's famous phrase (Foucault 2001, IV, 237). Foucault's concept of biopower can be understood as a logical extension of Max Weber's assertion in *The Protestant Ethic and the Spirit of Capitalism* that rationalization consists of an "autonomous" *Lebensführung* [life conduct], following the secularization of the idea of vocation.[27] Foucault is here offering biopower as an explanation for how individual actions can be coordinated into a social normative order, thereby allowing for stable expectations and intentions.

Now, according to Hayek, the problem of coordination (or equilibrium) is the central problem of economics. For both Foucault and Hayek, then, the most rational social order is achievable only when individual conduct follows (as closely as possible) the self-regulation according to which life is lived: in a play on words, the shift from Weber to Foucault and Hayek is a shift from a "Lebens-*führung*" (understood as the conduct qua "ethic" of an individual life, a *bios*) to a "*Lebens*-führung" (understood as the conduct qua "government" of a species-life, a population endowed with *zoe*). Whereas in Weber, the individual is charged with giving a form to its life (*bios*), in Foucault and Hayek it is life itself (*zoe*) that provides the norms that constitute individuality or subjectivity. The difference is that Hayek embraces this rationalization, while Foucault criticizes it. In other words, Foucault's theory of biopower offers a new basis for the critique of political economy, and it is the only one—as I show below—that situates itself at the level of the ontology of the economic because it treats the fundamental economic "problem" of the coordination of expectations and its "solution" provided by the free or competitive market.

In the genealogy of governmentality that Foucault develops after *The History of Sexuality*, he traces the opposition between law and order back to a much earlier stage than the rise of sovereign power and of a "juridical monarchy." The form of biopower that establishes "conducts" for individuals such that they can "naturally" coordinate themselves and so achieve a stable social order or a true "civil society" has its origin in what Foucault calls the ideal of pastoral power, or a form of power and normalization he associates with the Jewish and Christian traditions of theocracy and divine providence where God is to men like the shepherd is to his flock. Against this idea of pastoral power, Foucault sets the idea of "political power." By "political power" Foucault does not mean what he called "sovereign power" in his previous works. On the contrary, Foucault understands political power as the power that makes law into the sole legitimate basis for the constitution of social order. Political power is the power that generates and is generated by what today we call a "constitution." There is no doubt that this "political" or "constitutional" conception of power originates in the democratic and republican traditions of Greece and Rome and is later recovered in the West through the efforts of Marsilius of Padua, Machiavelli, Spinoza, and Harrington, to name but the most important figures.[28]

Whereas pastoral power is a form of power that "governs men," Foucault says that political power is not at all about governing men. Rather, it is fundamentally about making law (or giving oneself a constitution) so that no individual will be ruled (Foucault 2009, 115–21). Without citing him, Foucault is alluding to Cicero's famous saying that one subjects oneself to the law so as not to have to obey another person, that is, so as not to have masters (and in that way confirm one's natural status as *sui iuris*). By way of contrast, the pastoral "idea of governing people is certainly not a Greek idea, and nor do I think it is a Roman idea" (Foucault 2009, 122). Foucault draws an absolute opposition between political and pastoral power: "The pastor is not fundamentally a man of the law" (Foucault 2009, 173ff). "The Greek citizen . . . is only prepared to be directed by two things: by the law and by persuasion. . . . The general category of obedience does not exist in the Greeks" (Foucault 2009, 173). Conversely, pastoral power is essentially the establishment of a relation of "complete subordination" between two persons (Foucault 2009, 175). Complete subordination or dependence is antithetical to the law because it means establishing a "relationship of submission of one individual to another individual": "Christian obedience is not obedience to a law . . . but subordination to someone because he is someone" (Foucault 2009, 175). Christian pastoral power appears to be the exact opposite of the republican principle that (constitutional) laws make for freedom.[29] Laws and opinions (persuasion) are the basis of political power, whereas the government of conducts is the basis of pastoral power.

The law, in the Greco-Roman republican tradition, has an internal reference to the value of independence, or what Foucault calls "mastery of self [*maitrise de soi sur soi*]," whereas the order that is generated by norms has an internal reference to the value of dependence (Foucault 2009, 184). Self-mastery, in turn, has an internal relation to the freedom to form an opinion about public or political matters. Foucault's last Courses were dedicated to the task of explaining what kind of alternative "technology of self" or *ethos* is required in order to exercise this freedom of opinion (or *parrhesia*) and achieve this mastery of self, which is in turn the sole condition for being ruled by laws and not by men, that is, the sole condition of the republican ideal of political freedom. He sought answers in the parrhesiastic practices of Greek democracy and Greek (Socratic) philosophy because "when one submits oneself to a philosophy professor, in Greece, it is in order to succeed in becoming master of oneself at a certain moment, that is to say to reverse this relationship of obedience and to become one's own master" (Foucault 2009, 177). "The Socratic injunction 'take care of yourself' [means] 'make freedom your foundation through the mastery of yourself'" (Foucault 1997, 301). Thus, the fundamental opposition in Foucault's late thought is between a politico-philosophical "care of self" and an ideal of divine providence or government, where one "lets" one's needs be "taken care of" by a normative order that transcends the individual and on which the individual must depend. The key task thus becomes that of tracing these two forms of "care of self" in the republican and in the liberal conceptions of the "rule of law," respectively. When Foucault speaks of "becoming one's own master" he is clearly referring to the republican tradition where the expression means becoming *sui iuris*, or capable of living under laws because one has the power to give laws, that is, the power that comes with being a citizen. Foucault's critique of governmentality is oriented by a republican and not by a liberal political ideal.

THE PROBLEM OF COORDINATION AND HAYEK'S RECONCILIATION OF LAW AND ORDER

Understood from within the above opposition between Greco-Roman political power and Christian pastoral power, the reconciliation between law and order that defines neoliberal governmentality according to Foucault is nothing short of an attempt to develop a concept of law that appropriates the republican status of being *sui iuris* and places it at the service of the capitalist political economy. The juridification of politics in neoliberalism is intended to legally regulate (to conduct) the conduct of every individual into a new situation of dependence and insecurity with respect to a spontaneous social order that no individual can master or even comprehend, and that, as if it were a secularized version of divine providence, provides for all the needs of the individual only insofar as it remains uncontrolled and incalculable to each individual or groups of individuals. This conception of a spontaneous order that grows and acts behind the backs of individuals, an order that cannot be mastered and yet on which everyone is absolutely dependent, is called by Hayek a *catallaxy* or "free market."

If the neoliberal conception of the "free market" is indeed a form of pastoral power, then this opens up the question of whether the coordination made possible by this order is based on a secularized form of divine providence. The relation between the conceptions of divine providence and the modern normative orders of civil society is a complex problem in the history of ideas which remains far from being resolved. The providential structure of civil society has been strongly advocated by (Agamben 2007) who argues that in Scholasticism divine providence is a synonym for the solution to the problem of coordination via secondary causes, and leads to an idea of a self-regulating "nature of things" which is, on his hypothesis, picked up again in modern political economy. That this thesis is a plausible extension of the theory of secularization may find support in the return of the Austrian School of economics to Scholastic theories of the just price.[30] But in my opinion, Hayek cannot be easily made to fit onto Agamben's hypothesis since for Hayek the problem of coordination tends to be resolved by the double appeal to a theory of law (*nomos*) and a theory of evolutionary biology and cybernetics, none of which are reducible to secularized versions of theological conceptions of natural order. Foucault himself seems to be of the opinion that what makes market mechanisms nontransparent, and so uncontrollable, is not their providential structure, but to the contrary the reliance on the notion of the circulation of events, on the adoption of chance and of the aleatory as a new principle of order (Foucault 2009, chap. 2 passim). In turn, this notion of chance or radical contingency is internally linked to the rise of a conception of the individual as a person endowed with the capacity to "choose" and with an "interest," both of which are "rational" rule-following behavior (in a Humean sense of the term) but neither of which is "reasonable" (to use Rawls's distinction) (Foucault 2010, chap. 11 passim).

In *The Birth of Biopolitics* Foucault refers to Hayek's thought as the clearest illustration of what he calls the "neoliberal project: to introduce the principles of rule of law into the economic order" (Foucault 2010, chap. 7 passim). As Foucault argues, in the Hayekian and German Ordo-liberal versions of neoliberalism, what makes possible the coordination achieved by the free market is that the "natural order" of the market has become radically impregnated and molded by a "certain legal order" whereby it is impossible to separate abstractly the economic from the legal dimensions of the relations of production. Foucault terms this crucial innovation in neoliberalism the constitution of an "economic rule of law [*État de droit économique*]."

If this is the case, then Hayek's neoliberal discourse depends on a rhetorical feat consisting in presenting its pastoral ideal of a normative order through the republican vocabulary of law found in the Greek and Roman traditions. Jurisprudence, not theology, is the "science" that Hayek employed in order to break from any "historicist," that is, providentialist conception of political economy and of the phenomenon of equilibrium.[31] It is indicative that neoliberalism can be traced back to the polemics of the Austrian School of economics against planned economies from the early 1930s through the 1950s. Von Mises and Hayek likened the ideal of a planned economy to organizing society around what one mind knows about all other minds, rather than around the knowledge that is spread throughout society and its individual members. Such a planned economy would require belief in the existence of a divine mind that foresees all accidents and variations and can plan accordingly; it also requires belief in a group of human philosophers who can see into the divine mind and impute true "class consciousness" to the rest of the ordinary mortals. Thus, during those years, the critique of providentialism and anti-Platonism were mixed together with anti-Marxism. Rhetorically, neoliberal thinkers juxtaposed this (supposed) Platonic-Marxist reliance on (secularized versions of) divine providence with the "evolutionary" cunning of a spontaneous order based on the unconscious interaction between many minds, and the selection of the best ideas through the mechanism of competition.[32]

One of the clearest examples of this audacious attempt at hijacking the republican tradition is found in Hayek's use of *nomos* in his last main work, *Law, Legislation and Liberty*, written during the 1970s. Hayek argues that the Greek word *nomos* should not be translated as *lex* (this is how Cicero translated it), but as *ius* (the equivalent of *Recht* in the sense of a "normative order" as I have explained it above). In this way, the ancient ideal of the "rule of law" (*nomos basileus*) is linked with what Hayek calls "judge-made law" and is explicitly opposed to legislation made through political procedures, such as parliamentary legislation, which is in turn based on a conception of the separation of powers and, ultimately, on republican constitutionalism.[33] Neoliberalism is that discourse of governmentality which places political power, that is, the power to make law, at the mercy of "political economy." The meaning of "political" in the neoliberal understanding of "political economy" can be pinpointed more precisely: it refers to the rhetorical transformation of republican laws into liberal norms, and the consequent rise of *judge-made laws* over *citizen-made laws* as basis for the constitution of a social order.

It is striking to see the degree to which Hayek's thought conforms to the Foucaultian sense of the distinction between law and order. Hayek's innovation—partially drawn from the work of Michael Oakeshott on rule following—consists in distinguishing between two fundamental ways of understanding the regularity of the expectations and intentions that characterize a normative social order: on one side, there is what he calls *nomothetic* regularity, which is achieved by the deliberate creation of laws. On the other side, there is *spontaneous* order, which is not created by design and which lacks all external purpose (Hayek 1984, 366ff). *Catallaxy*, or spontaneous regulation, is a term taken from the Greek verb *katallattein* "which, significantly, means not only 'to barter' and 'to exchange' but also 'to admit into the community' and 'to turn from enemy into friend'" (Hayek 1984, 367). The order of free markets and the "world wide web," or Internet, are examples of *catallaxy*. The meaning of the Greek term already indicates Hayek's strategic goal, namely, to find a way in which the freedom of exchange and circulation of opinions and persons become a new "constitutional" principle, since it is in relation to constitutional law that ultimate issues of inclusion and exclusion in political life, of friendship and enmity, are decided. Not surprisingly, in this essay, as throughout *Law, Legislation and Liberty,* Hayek explicitly takes issue with Schmitt's construal of constitutional law, at the same time adopting and undermining Schmitt's introduction of *nomos*.

During his early work in economics, Hayek believed that the central problem of economics lay in explaining the coordination between rational actors, each of whom had the capacity to make his own plans of action in order to maximize gains and minimize losses.[34] Hayek argued that neoclassical economics assumes that a point of equilibrium always exists, but it does not ask the *quaestio juris* with regard to equilibrium. Marginalist theory thus presupposes a theory of competition and a theory of price, without explaining their conditions of possibility. While still doing "normal science" within the field of economics, during the 1920s and early 1930s, Hayek saw that the classical theory of market equilibrium between sellers and buyers rested on the assumption that all actors shared the same knowledge of the objective situation. According to his biographer Caldwell, it was during the early 1930s that Hayek came to question this assumption, after becoming convinced that the knowledge of any given actor is subjective or perspectival, and thus variable and error-prone.

The fallibility of the knowledge of economic actors forces Hayek to abandon the search for purely "economic" explanations for market equilibrium and, instead, shift his attention to the legal-political conditions of equilibrium. It is at this stage in his development that Hayek discovers the legal conception of *nomos* as an essential moment in free-market economics. Basically, Hayek transforms economics into the study of normative or nomothetic orders. "The central concept of liberalism is that under the enforcement of universal rules of just conduct, protecting a recognizable private domain of individuals, a spontaneous order of human activities of much greater complexity will form itself than could ever be produced by deliberate arrangement" (Hayek 1984, 365).[35] Neoliberalism is impossible without this creative reappropriation of the idea of *nomos* or substantive "normative order" first introduced into the vocabulary of twentieth-century jurisprudence by Schmitt.

In Hayek's mature account, the opposite of a spontaneous social order, represented by the free market, is not the juridical law or *nomos*, but rather the idea of a political "organization," that is, the idea of man-made laws designed to bring individuals together by giving them a common purpose. Hayek's central premise is that the spontaneous order of the free market is *only* compatible with a restricted conception of juridical law understood as *nomocratic* and which is opposed to a *telocratic* conception of the law as the organization or constitution of a community (Hayek 1984, 366ff). Nomocratic rules are what Hayek calls judge-made law, and he sets them in opposition to "legislation" or sovereign- and parliament-made laws. While the former are rules of individual conduct that indicate what ought not to be done, the latter are rules of organization that say positively what must be done, that is, they prescribe a form of life in common. In Hayek's rhetoric, judge-made laws never command anyone to do anything, they merely demarcate areas of noninterference: they establish what belongs to each, but they do not state what everyone has in common. For Hayek, only the action of an individual can be just or unjust, depending on whether the act is in accordance with the judge-made law. But since the way in which a free market distributes goods or utilities does not follow anyone's intention or any hierarchy of ends, there is no sense in saying that the market is either just or unjust. The preoccupation with distributive justice, and thus the desire to interfere politically (not, obviously, juridically) in the workings of the free market, is for Hayek placed exclusively on the shoulders of a telocratic conception of the law as an organization of the state, that is, on public law understood as a political constitution: a "progressive permeation of private law by public law in the course of the last eighty or hundred years, which means a progressive replacement of rules of conduct by rules of organization, is one of the main ways in which the destruction of the liberal order has been effected.... This tendency has been most explicitly seen and supported by Adolf Hitler's 'crown jurist' Carl Schmitt who consistently advocated the replacement of the 'normative' thinking of liberal law by a conception of law which regards as its purpose the 'concrete order formation' [*konkretes Ordnungsdenken*]" (Hayek 1984, 372–73). Hayek blames those rules that organize citizens into a state, what the republican tradition has called the idea of a political constitution, for what he takes to be the irrational demand that the outcomes of the market be judged according to the principles of distributive justice. To add insult to injury, Hayek attempts to smear this republican, constitutional understanding of law by identifying it with Schmitt's understanding of *nomos*, thus in one swift move erasing the debt his own neoliberal idea of *nomos* owes to Schmitt and placing it upon the shoulders of republicanism.

If this interpretation of Hayek is correct, then the reconciliation of law with the spontaneous order of the market characteristic of neoliberalism is only achievable because Hayek offers a truncated conception of law, which denies any constitutional (that is, political) implications in the system of law and makes public right subservient to private law. One can say that Hayek reverses the Kantian order between "conclusive right" and "provisional right": for Kant, all private right was merely provisional until public right was based on a true republican constitution, according to which what was provisionally distributed in the form of private property to natural individuals prior to the state could now be conclusively redistributed to citizens in a republic and in a federal organization of republics.[36] For Hayek, by contrast, all "conclusive right" or constitutional law is but a means to establishing private property as a "provisional" and ever-changing right of consumers and entrepreneurs. The juridical framework of neoliberalism requires that the law be understood explicitly in antirepublican terms (while still employing the rhetoric of republicanism): in neoliberalism, the law is no longer intended to organize citizens, or law-giving subjects, into a free people (*civitas*). Instead, the law favors negative liberty ("free choice" and the "pursuit" of self "interest"), which, in turn, compels subjects to conduct themselves with respect to each other by following those legal norms that structure the spontaneous order of the free market (*societas*). This neoliberal conception of law refuses to see citizens as equal members of a people, in accordance with a constitution. Instead, it sees them as nothing more than specimens of a population who are subject to a normative order: a normative order on which they are entirely dependent.

POLICING THE ECONOMY: THE MEANING OF *NOMOS* IN NEOLIBERALISM

Foucault asserts that in neoliberal governmentality "the law operates more and more as a norm, and that the juridical institution is increasingly incorporated into a continuum of apparatuses whose functions are for the most part regulatory" (Foucault 1990, 144). By losing its political or constitutional significance, the so-called judge-made law of neoliberalism becomes part of national and transnational *administrative* orders: the law falls under the norms of what Foucault calls, after von Justi, *Polizeiwissenschaft* (the science of policy). There is an internal relation between judge-made law and policing activity that even Hegel was aware of. What Foucault shows is that the private space that liberal and neoliberal systems of law defend from state or political intervention is not a normative vacuum (it is neither, in Hegel's terms, the place of the bourgeoisie's "political nullity," nor, in Agamben's terms, the place of pure violence), but rather becomes the space for "security," provided by the normalizing activity of the police.[37] By police, Foucault means all *dispositifs* (or social arrangements) that provide "security" in order to maintain the free circulation of things, persons, and information essential to the existence of a *catallaxy*, as well as "insurance" for the unpredictable outcomes that may result from transactions on the free market.[38] Neoliberal government, whose fundamental goal is the institution of competitive and transparent free-market mechanisms that use legal norms to regulate the conduct of individuals, exercises biopower by "insuring the lives" of individuals through a series of controls that operate on (civil) society and assign the task to each individual to produce a "surplus" of biological life. Citing Foucault:

> The aim of the police is the permanently increasing production of something new, which is supposed to augment the citizens' life and the state's strength. The police govern not by the law, but by a specific, a permanent and a positive intervention in the behaviour of individuals. (Foucault 2000, 415)

In this sense, it is not an exaggeration to conceive of the police, in neoliberalism, as a name for all *dispositifs* that provide for "life insurance," in the widest sense of the term.

Insurance is needed because the negative liberties that are the outcome of the limits imposed by the liberal system of law and by the system of political economy on the sovereignty of the state, do not, as such, turn private space into a space of security. The laws of the state are, of course, intended to prevent individuals from "harming" each other. However, in liberalism, one does not legislate in order to "secure" the lives or the happiness of individuals. This is evident in Mill, whose "harm principle," which is the sole criterion of state law making, should not outlaw all kinds of experimentation, and therefore all kinds of insecurity, with regard to one's form of life, irrespective of whether the results turn out to be harmful or beneficial for the individual herself. As Hayek puts it:

> Not all expectations can be protected by general rules, but even that the chance of as many expectations as possible being fulfilled will be most enhanced if some expectations are systematically disappointed. This means also that it is not possible or desirable to prevent all actions which will harm others but only certain kinds of actions. (Hayek 1982, 102)

In civil society, it is the biological life of the individual that is exposed to a new field of "insecurity," generated by the very unpredictability and spontaneity that characterizes spontaneous orders.[39] It is not only a matter of the obvious insecurity into which workers are cast,[40] but also that, on the side of capital, the hegemony of financial capital and the so-called democratization of credit has led to the use of financial instruments, such as derivatives, that are intended to generalize the risk of an investment as a form of "insuring" a return. Not to speak of theories, such as those of

Minsky, that postulate financial instability as a prerequisite of investment strategies. In general, the radical lack of assurance that investments will turn a profit is demanded by the neoliberal idea of "competition," which is said to characterize the form or *eidos* of a free market economy.[41] Since the rules of just conduct that have been designed to protect the individual have in fact been found to expose her to further harm, insurance and the underwriting of risk have become fundamental to neoliberal normativity. In the absence of social justice, neoliberalism offers models that seek to approximate insurance coverage for all which reflects the universal exposure to risk.

Neoliberalism for Foucault names a kind of discourse that attempts to "insure" the biological or species life of the individual against the "risks" to which it has been exposed in civil society, that is, amidst a society that no longer needs to fear the sovereign power of the state. The norms of police power or biopower effectively "insure" each individual's biological life against the risks congenital to civil society. The police generate a "surplus-value," not of capital but of biological life itself. As Foucault says, the interventions of the police are intended to "supply [men] with *a little extra life*—and by so doing supply the state with a *little extra strength*. This is done by controlling communication, that is, the common activities of individuals (work, production, exchange, accommodation)" (Foucault 2000, 319, emphasis mine). On this hypothesis, only when the biological life of the individual is placed under total observation and control (in my terms: is "insured") does the negative liberty that the self-limitation of sovereignty grants its subjects no longer become a source of insecurity, which is activity inhibiting, but it invites the individual to become enterprising, to live in a "free and responsible" way that unleashes what political economists call the "competition" that lies at the heart of all production of surplus value in late capitalism. That is also why Foucault can say that the panopticon is not only the model for disciplinary power but also "the very formula" for liberal biopolitics (Foucault 2010, 67) . Thus, if the legal intervention into political economy discussed above accounts for the "juridification" of the neoliberal normative order, then the generation of security and "life insurance" accounts for the "biologization" of the neoliberal normative order. Both together make possible the "spontaneous" coordination of conducts characteristic of capitalist political economy.

LAW AS RESISTANCE: PEOPLE VERSUS POPULATION IN FOUCAULT

The idea of "surplus life" as the true product of neoliberal governmentality brings me back to the overdetermined character of the biological model of normative order in Canguilhem with which this chapter began. Implicit in Canguilhem's suggestion that the planning of political economy could be understood as the attempt by the state to make itself less like a machine and more like a living organism, is the idea that surplus life need not be only the result of the deregulation of the economy and increased policing of society, as advocated by neoliberalism, but can also be attained by an increase in the political capacity for self-organization (or, political constitution) of a people and a citizenry. After all, it is a leitmotif of republican thought that a political constitution endows the political body with an organization that permits every part of the people to engage in a permanent rebirth of itself in and through its political action, and this permanent rebirth of itself is the content of its political "life." Something of this intuition is also found in Foucault's attempt to open up the possibility of an affirmative biopolitics that takes advantage of the normativity of living beings in order to resist social normalization and reach a more creative relation to norms, a normative creativity that is at the antipodes of the normativity of the entrepreneur. On this hypothesis, political resistance would take the form of a communal reappropriation of what I have been calling "surplus life," which is expropriated from the political and economical life of the people by the neoliberal *nomos* and partitioned off into the various policed subpopulations. Generally speaking, this is opening that was taken up by the thinkers associated with the Italian reception of Foucault, mainly Agamben, Negri, and Esposito. In what follows, I merely indicate why Foucault's opening for the possibility of an affirmative biopolitics was inscribed within a revolutionary tradition of republican thought.

The (illusory) reconciliation of law and order in neoliberalism is made possible in two ways. First, the neoliberal *nomos* severs the law from its roots in a conception of the political self-organization of a people (that is, the republican idea of constitutionalism) and turns it into "judge-made law" (this neoliberal colonization of republican constitutionalism even reaches the constitutional courts, from where it cascades back into the entire legal system). Second, the neoliberal *nomos* makes legislation into a function of the policing of conduct and the generation of security in the form of "life insurance." The explosion of constitution making and other legislative activity in neoliberal regimes is due to the fact that only within a *nomos* does the "essentially normalizing power" of the police become "acceptable."[42] But if power-as-law remains the standard for the legitimacy or rational acceptability of power in neoliberalism, then the neoliberal reconciliation of the antinomy between law and order inevitably generates an antinomy of its own: the more the law is employed in its policing function, the less it can be employed in its political function, that is, as a means for the self-organization of the freedom of a people. In this way, every surplus of security is necessarily accompanied by a deficit in political legitimacy.

The "surplus of life" on which entrepreneurial conduct relies is paid at the price of an increasing deficit in legitimacy, for the legal system and for the legislative powers of the state. Recently, neoliberalism has attempted to ameliorate this contradiction by projecting the conduct of the entrepreneur outside the sphere of civil society and into the public sphere of the state: hence the global phenomenon of successful entrepreneurs becoming prime ministers and presidents, promising to run the country as they have run their companies. But this attempt will necessarily backfire; turning the entrepreneur into a model for the lawmaker can only accelerate the process of turning the state into a private company, thus compromising its ability to generate the very acceptability needed by those normalizing police practices. The lack of "representativeness" on the part of legislators is merely a symptom of the fact that the "laws" they claim to make have long ceased to be laws in a republican sense of the term. Thus their demand that the people grant them its support can only be met with attempts, on the part of the people, to take back their legislative power and become, in a direct manner, what republicanism always said they were, namely, the constituent power of society. The rising popularity of "direct democracy" initiatives in civil society is a symptomatic response, but in no way a solution, to the antinomy generated by neoliberal jurisprudence.

It is this sort of antinomy that led Foucault, in the last years of his life, to return to a republican logic of political rationality in which the sovereignty of the state is limited by a system of law that recognizes an "innate right" to civil and political rights. In the republican understanding of natural right, the innate right *to have rights* is the right to belong as a member of a constituent people that governs itself according to its own laws. The "innate right" to be a member of a people is *the only right that cannot be adjudicated by a judge-made law*. That is why Foucault insists on maintaining the "old" category of a people: "The people are generally speaking those who resist the regulation of the population, who try to elude the apparatus by which the population exists, is preserved, subsists, and subsists at an optimal level. This people/population opposition is very important" (Foucault 2009, 44). Foucault calls this republican understanding of rights "revolutionary" and opposes it to the liberal understanding of rights.

In the republican model of rights, the legitimacy of the state is a consequence of the government's self-imposed limitations before a new "field" of objects (in this case, rights), whose "nature" the state does not command. The question becomes: what is this "nature" of the innate right to have rights? Toward the end of *History of Sexuality, Volume 1* Foucault says that when biological life becomes an issue of politics, as it does in liberal governmentality, then political struggles and resistances to normalizing power become a fight for a whole series of new "rights", such as "the right to life, to one's body, to health, to happiness, to the satisfaction of needs. . . . [T]he right to rediscover what one is and all that one can be" (Foucault 1990, 145). I do not think that Foucault thereby meant to criticize these struggles for new rights: they are the "political response" to the return of pastoral power in neoliberalism.[43] What Foucault attempts to provide, in his last years, is a new account of a subject who can bear these new biopolitical rights. This search leads him from the Kantian question of critique (of "how to be governed less") back to the Greco-Roman understanding of self-mastery as a technique for reappropriating one's surplus life. But it is also a question of rooting the "innate right" to have rights in the features of biological life that are shared by all human beings as members of a living species and that exploit the powers of life to resist the normalization of social norms. The innate right to be part of a "people" cannot rely on the prior construction of a public space of mutual recognition that is structured by civil and political rights, for a people precedes such a space. Therefore, theorizing the biopolitical roots of the innate right to have rights—the right to form a people—is necessary in moving us beyond a territorial, or spatial, conception of a people. To develop an affirmative biopolitics of autonomous peoples, it becomes necessary to engage critically with the idea of a "*nomos* of the earth." The task of reconstructing a republicanism suited to the age of post-Foucauldian biopower is addressed in the next chapter.

7

BIOPOLITICAL COSMOPOLITANISM
The Right to Have Rights in Arendt and Agamben

THE BIOPOLITICAL MATRIX OF HUMAN RIGHTS

The general hypothesis of biopolitics is that the activity of government in modernity is no longer just articulated through law, with citizens as its agents. Instead, it has become exercised through disciplines and norms and it takes the living individual or population as its subject. If this is the case, then it is likely that the meaning of liberal rights also undergoes a similar transformation in the passage from "reason of state" to "neoliberal governmentality." The recent historiography of "universal human rights" has shown that their meaning, institutional reality, and political force have changed over time: from the first period of the revolutionary declarations of the "Rights of Man," through the age of imperialism and colonialism, into the interwar period, with the emergence of a posttotalitarian Declaration of "universal human rights" in 1948, and, finally, to their post-Cold War implementation, where they have become essential components of a neoliberal normative order, functioning as quasi-constitutional principles of a "global" civil society.[1]

Since the 1970s, the subject of universal human rights has become a new kind of biopolitical actor, who is neither the "Man" of Enlightenment universalist political doctrines nor the "Citizen" of a nation-state. The implementation of universal human rights "politicized" the bare life of those hundreds of millions of people who live at or below the margins of subsistence, who have no state to direct their claims to or protect them but can claim the "basic rights" of "subsistence and security" as well as "participation and liberty of movement," prior to and outside of the "full" rights of citizenship in liberal democracies, yet backed by international coercive force.[2] Simultaneously, the same implementation of universal human rights "biologized" the political life of citizens by bringing matters concerning the "quality of life" (addressed by the economic and social rights that feature centrally in the Universal Declaration of Human Rights) into the sphere of state and international legislation. Hannah Arendt identified these quasi-political actors who embody this politicized bare life and biologized political life with the refugees who by being "driven from country to country represent the vanguard of their peoples" (Agamben 2000a, 16–17). It is for this "vanguard" that Arendt coined her famous formula for human rights *after* "the end of the Rights of Man": the refugee is she who shows the existence of a "right to have rights (and that means to live in a framework where one is judged by one's actions and opinions) and a right to belong to some organized community" (Arendt 1973, 297).

In this chapter I shall argue the following points: first, that the "right to have rights" is a formula for human rights caught in a biopolitical predicament. Every interpretation of this formula that does not take biopolitics seriously will fail to understand it. Within contemporary biopolitical discourse, this thesis will come as no surprise; this is because such discourse overwhelmingly rejects the current implementation of universal human rights on the grounds that these rights are but the medium of global police action. My second point is to call into question this critique of human rights. I shall argue, instead, that Arendt's formula of a "right to have rights," when correctly interpreted, defends the possibility of an affirmative biopolitics of rights that is both republican and cosmopolitan. The key to this reinterpretation lies in the way in which Arendt connects natality with normativity in the idea of a "right to have rights" and, conversely, separates the juris-generative power of natality from the normalizing power of nationality that, in the case of the refugee, is evidenced by the instrument of "naturalization."

Human rights are caught in a biopolitical predicament because, in the age of neoliberalism, the traditional idea of personal "dignity," which was originally the referent of a human right, becomes overdetermined by the idea of the "sacredness" of the biological life of both the individual and the species. The category of "sacredness" has come to indicate the biopolitical structure of civil society: when life (*zoe*) is not only an object of political regulation and juridical legislation, but is also invested with normative power, as occurs in the form of "universal human rights" (when "life itself" becomes endowed with a function of legitimation),[3] then biological life becomes "sacred."[4]

Sacredness, in civil society, designates a fundamental ambivalence: on the one hand, it refers to the fact of being endowed with a peculiar "value" or "dignity" that is not itself an exchange-value and, therefore, is "inviolable." As it is put by the First Article of the Basic Law of the German Federal Republic (the exemplar of a modern constitution in which human rights appear explicitly in the first section on basic rights): "Human dignity shall be inviolable. To respect and protect it shall be the duty of all state authority [*Die Würde des Menschen ist unantastbar. Sie zu achten und zu schützen ist Verpflichtung aller staatlichen Gewalt*]."[5] This article has the peculiarity of treating "human dignity" as something that is at once living and beyond life. It is "living" because it requires "respect and protection" by the legitimate, state monopolized used of violence (*Gewalt*): it is the task of the policing (*Polizei*) function of civil society to preserve human dignity from violation. But human dignity is also "beyond" bare life in the sense that it cannot be "violated" because it literally cannot be "touched" or "manipulated" (which is, of course, not the case with bare life). The German term *unantastbar* connotes the archaic sense of taboo: that which is "untouchable" and "unexchangable" because it is sacrosanct.[6] The formulation of human dignity in the First Article, therefore, already gives expression to a slippage from the traditional referent of rights—the category of the "dignity" of the person—to the new referent of "human" rights—the category of the sacredness of (surplus) life, which occurs in the discourses on human rights in the age of neoliberalism.[7]

As Agamben has argued, the "sacredness" of life in civil society (which makes life something inviolable and, thus, something more-than-life or surplus-life) places life in a zone of "indistinction" between life and death, where some life is "let live" only by "letting die" or bringing life to a "terminal" stage, without committing either crime or sacrilege. The paradox is that in the age of Universal Human Rights, life (not only human life, but all life) has never appeared as "precarious," has never been as vulnerable to thanatopolitics (Butler 2004). Or, as Foucault puts it: never more than in our age does the "security" of life call for massacres of life. This paradox has not only been pointed out by Arendt and Foucault, by Esposito and Butler; it is also the central finding of post-Rawlsian analyses of world hunger and poverty, as is found in the work of Pogge, Nussbaum, Sen, and others.

But, assuming for a moment that such a slippage from dignity to sacredness exists, does this mean that the contemporary discourse of human rights is inevitably antinomian and aporetic or, worse, that human rights are simply the vehicle in modern society for the expansion of the police and of thanatopolitics?[8] Is the "politics of human rights" forever caught in the logic of the police? Or, conversely, must the project of overcoming the thanatopolitics of the neoliberal world order require going beyond the scope of a "politics of human rights?" The approach to the question of human rights and biopolitics found in Agamben, Negri, and Esposito—in an attempt to counter the neoliberal, biopolitical articulation of human rights—sometimes lets itself be understood as if they were claiming that the politics and governance of a global system of universal human rights would be nothing but the ideological cover for the universal expansion of the "state of exception" that, under neoliberalism, has become the "normal" condition of political life.[9] This happens whenever their understanding of biopolitics depends on positing a fundamental antinomy between law and life, such that life can come under the force of law only if law places it in a state of exception that permits the unleashing of mythical violence on bare life. In this chapter, I offer a critique of this antinomian way of conceiving of the relation between life and rights in order to argue that there is an affirmative biopolitical understanding of human rights. I argue that it is possible to think a positive relation between rights and life, which is nonetheless not a "liberal" or "neoliberal" way of thinking these terms but a republican one, as is indicated by the late Foucault's attempt to give a different, nonliberal reading of human rights. One finds a similar strategy in the attempts by Rancière and Balibar to move beyond the opposition between human rights and the rights of citizens in their efforts to rethink the tradition of revolutionary republicanism in a cosmopolitan dimension.[10] But neither Foucault nor Rancière nor Balibar, properly speaking, thematizes the affirmative, biopolitical and republican core of human rights, because each disregards the connection between natality and normativity that is characteristic of a republican conception of human rights.

MAKING ROOM FOR REPUBLICANISM IN
THE COSMOPOLITAN CONCEPTION OF HUMAN RIGHTS

Arendt's critique of the "Rights of Man" in the ninth chapter of *Origins of Totalitarianism* may well turn out to be her most influential piece of writing, judging by the importance it has accrued in the recent attempts to formulate a conception of human rights that is free from the burden of state sovereignty while remaining, at least in one sense of the phrase, "political, rather than metaphysical."[11] The sense in which the right to have rights is "political" is perplexing because it requires thinking beyond the typical opposition between cosmopolitanism and republicanism. Thus, on the one hand, for there to be a new basis for universal human rights, it would have to be one that is not conjoined to state sovereignty or nationality. Arendt's proposal to rethink human rights in the context of the problem of "stateless people" was a clear indication that whatever new theory of human rights was to take the place of the old Declarations, this theory could no longer posit "the Rights of Man" for these were "quickly and inextricably blended with question of national emancipation; only the emancipated sovereignty of the people, of one's own people, seemed to be able to insure them" (Arendt 1973, 291). As Arendt says, no one in the nineteenth century up to World War II took human rights seriously because "civil rights—that is the varying rights of citizens in different countries—were supposed to embody and spell out in the form of tangible laws the eternal Rights of Man, which by themselves were supposed to be independent of citizenship and nationality" (Arendt 1973, 293). Yet, despite the fact that human rights cannot be reduced to rights of citizens, these rights must nevertheless be "political" in a demanding, republican sense of the word: people who are deprived of human rights "are deprived, not of the right to freedom, but of the right to action; not the right to think whatever they please, but of the right to opinion" (Arendt 1973, 296). The deprivation "of a place in the world which makes opinions significant and actions effective" turns out to be, in Arendt's judgment, "much more fundamental than freedom or justice, which are rights of citizens" (Arendt 1973, 296). Paradoxically, for Arendt human rights partake of the "fundamental" meaning of (republican) politics more so than "rights of citizens," and this, not despite, but in virtue of their cosmopolitan meaning. How can this be?

Some interpreters like Balibar have sought to resolve the above perplexity by arguing that the right to have rights really means a "right to politics."[12] Illustrating this interpretation, Ingram has argued, "the right to politics is a right to autonomous political action.... A rights claim can potentially be made by anyone, anywhere, anytime. Human rights have thus become a central site of the emancipatory logic of modern politics, an expression of how the principle of equal freedom cannot be contained with existing institutions or conceptions of rights but rather invites its extension to new domains, settings, and scales" (Ingram 2008, 411). In this way, Ingram argues that Arendt provides a "democratic but nonstatist politics of rights" (Ingram 2008, 411). But does the constituent power that Ingram argues is implicit in the right to have rights belong to bare life as such? For Ingram, this is not possible because, basing his view on Balibar's concept of *égaliberté*, the original "right" to have civil and political rights must be understood in terms of "equal freedom." Now, for Arendt, the principle of equal freedom is indeed the fundamental principle of all *constructed* or *constituted* political spaces, but it is not the principle that gives all human beings their "right" to live in an isonomic space. By subsuming the "right to have rights" under the principle of equality, Ingram ends up subsuming the right to have rights under a "positivist" understanding of "politics" as the activity of contestation, deliberation, and even constitution making within an already constituted political space. Ingram is, of course, correct to claim that no "politics" (within an already constituted political space) is possible without such a contestatory activity. But refugees do not live, ex hypothesi, in such a space, so that if one speaks of their "right" to civil and political rights, then one cannot assume that they engage in such a contestatory "politics" without *petitio principi*. This is to lose sight of the distinction between politics and right. Arendt does not give into this temptation because her republicanism makes it absolutely clear and imperative that politics and law not be confused (Vatter 2007, 2005). She is also clear about the fact that the "right to have rights" must be associated with the dimension of law: "Human dignity needs a new guarantee which can be found only in a new political principle, in *a new law on earth*" (Arendt 1973, ix, emphasis mine). Thus, the right to have rights is not only grounded in a "new law on earth" (and not simply on a new conception of politics), but must also be guaranteed by something that is *not constructible*, on a *radical givenness*, which Arendt calls natality. Thus, the problem with construing the right to have rights as a right to politics is the failure to link natality to right (to the form of law and to its corresponding constituent power) from the very start. If right is subsumed under "politics," equality, and the constructible space of a given community (the *polis*), then one loses sight of the *generating normative power* or the *juris-generative* power of natality itself.

However, to say that Arendt's "new law on earth" or cosmopolitan "law of humanity" is nonstatist does not mean that one should think this law as standing in opposition to the idea of a "law of peoples." Arendt, like Rawls after her, distinguishes peoples from states, and she does not separate human rights from the idea of a law of peoples for she defends "the great principle upon which national organizations of peoples are built, the principle of equality and solidarity of all peoples guaranteed by the idea of mankind" (Arendt 1973, 161). This makes the challenge evident in the idea of a right to have rights: natality cannot be an antirepublican principle, or a principle of humanity that excludes humanity's division into "peoples." This cannot be the case because the crime against humanity committed by totalitarian regimes consists precisely in excluding from the earth—in giving no space on earth to—a people, a part of humanity, and not just a collection of individuals, no matter how many they are. Totalitarian regimes constitute an "attack upon human diversity as such, that is, upon a characteristic of *the human status* without which the very words 'mankind' or 'humanity' would be devoid of meaning" (Arendt 2006, 268–69, emphasis mine). Arendt's coinage of the term "human status" is unique, because "status" is typically a political term that refers to citizenship qua membership in a people. Arendt's term suggests that the "humanity" at stake in human rights refers to a paradoxical citizenship status within a people without being citizen of a particular nation or state. One has to understand how natality and plurality make this cosmopolitan-qua-republican human citizenship possible.

With regard to the right to have rights as being "not metaphysical," one encounters a similar perplexity to the sense in which this right was meant to be "political." On the one hand, if by "not metaphysical" one simply intends a "pragmatic" (sometimes called a "minimalist") construal of human rights, then such a construal fails to connect the dimensions of republicanism with cosmopolitanism, and as Benhabib has pointed out, the exclusion of a "metaphysical" foundation for human rights ends up evading the "robust" universalistic political requirements of human rights. By contrast, Benhabib and other critics of the minimalist approach to human rights are unwilling to further engage the "metaphysical" dimension of human rights because they fear falling into a "naturalistic fallacy," into the idea that human rights are "essential" attributes of "human nature." They believe that Arendt was correct to argue that "human nature" is neither knowable nor pertinent, since human rights refer to the character of the relation among human beings, and not to their "nature."[13] This would seem to mean that a right to have rights can only receive a "constructivist" meaning: it refers to a right that enables equal participation with others in a "procedure" to determine what positive rights are to be recognized and how they are to be implemented.

Yet Arendt's discourse on the right to have rights is more complicated with regard to the question of human "nature" because she grounds the condition for action in natality, and not just in plurality. The idea of natality makes it unavoidable to engage the "metaphysical" dimension of the foundation of human rights and the problem of "nature." If human rights after the "end" of the Rights of Man are to be given a new, cosmopolitan meaning, they must be able to account for the fact that

> the more at home men feel within the human artifice—the more they will resent everything they have not produced, everything that is merely and mysteriously given them.... The dark background of mere givenness, the background formed by our unchangeable and unique nature, breaks into the political scene as the alien which in its all too obvious difference reminds us of the limitations of human activity—which are identical to the limitations of human equality. (Arendt 1973, 301)

Any account of human rights that has nothing to say about the relation between the idea of right and this alienness of *zoe* or "mere existence" for political *bios* is useless. Natality has a fundamental role to play in connecting normativity to *zoe*. In this sense alone, Hamacher is correct when he says that "this mere existence is the only source of law for the right to have rights" (Hamacher 2004, 354). But he is wrong to believe that what follows from this "law" of natality is that "this world [oriented around the "universality" of the singular, bare life] could not be a legal one or a world of rights: it would have to be a world in which this each-time singular universal, this universal singular could manifest itself—and thus it may not be a world at all" (Hamacher 2004, 355). On the contrary, the question of the right to have rights is the question of how bare life or *zoe* itself makes possible that "place in the world which makes opinions significant and actions effective." There is no avoiding the biopolitical predicament of human rights, just as there is no separating bare life from its legal form of a right to have rights, because the question as to the political meaning of natality is posed by the First Article of the UDHR: "All human beings are *born* free and equal in dignity and rights" (emphasis mine). The real question is: How can nature and world, birth and normative creation, be connected in the form of an originary right to have rights?

In contrast with the previous approaches to Arendt's concept of the right to have rights, Birmingham defends what she calls Arendt's "ontological foundation of human rights" (Birmingham 2006). Her interpretation coincides with several aspects of my biopolitical reading of Arendt's political thought proposed in Chapter 4. Birmingham and I agree that, for Arendt, human rights have a "new guarantee" on earth due to the "law" of plurality and the "law" of natality (or singularity), both of which are not to be reduced to the "law" of equality that structures the distribution of civil and political rights. Birmingham also provides indications that the right to have rights, which is based on the (natural) "laws" of plurality and natality, is linked with the dimension of human life that precedes biography and is tied to *zoe*. However, Birmingham does not see the right to have rights as a *natural* right, more precisely, a *biopolitical* right, despite its internal connection to the givenness (*physis*, nature) of natality. Instead, in a puzzling way, she opposes natality to the very idea of a natural right (Birmingham 2006, 92). The problem with her account of the biopolitical character of the right to have rights is that the connection between biopolitics and the republican conception of right, in Arendt, is absent: Birmingham does not explain why this natural or biopolitical right (to have rights) is republican. Nor does she explain how the right to have rights refers to a biopower of natality, where power is understood according to a republican conception.

Birmingham tries to show that natality already contains within it the principle of publicness or the right to appear in public with others "because the first act, the act of beginning itself—the event of natality—contains both the beginning and its principle within itself. The event of natality that carries within it the principle of publicness, when restated as the law of humanity (understood as the appearance of the actor among a plurality of actors in a public space of freedom) demands that the actor have the right to appear, or, as Arendt succinctly puts it, the right to have rights" (Birmingham 2006, 57). The argument seems to me to be the following: birth is an appearing before others, and this appearance takes place in a constituted political space of plurality where the others are "spectators." This fact makes the one who is the object of the spectator's view an "actor" in a political sense (here comes in the principle of publicness), that is, someone capable of beginning something radically new (here comes in the principle of natality). Thus, natality already entails a right to act and speak in a political space (and hence the right to have rights). But if this is Birmingham's argument, then it contains a leap: natality may give appearance, but this does not mean that the appearance comes under the principle of publicness and, therefore, that the individual who so appears has the right to be treated as a political actor. For Birmingham, what allows the person who appears to be an acting and speaking subject is *the fact* of inclusion in an already constituted political space of appearance: she has not proven that natality gives a *right* to such inclusion. As construed here, natality gives no right to the *constitution* of a political space. At best, it gives the right to be inserted into a space that is *always already constituted by others*. Hence, in the end Birmingham deprives natality of constituent power, just as Ingram had separated constituent power from natality. We still do not know how a republican *zoe* that belongs to the refugee, as bearer of a right to have rights, is possible.

REFUGEES AND HABEAS CORPUS: NATIVITY, NATIONALITY, AND LAW

Agamben's interpretation of Arendt's right to have rights is anterior to that of Benhabib and, in a certain sense, has had more of an impact in applied work on refugees and human rights. The reason is that Agamben boldly posits refugees as the new world-historical political actors rather than as the masses of desperate and indigent stateless people waiting for any nation that is willing to accept and "naturalize" (that is, nationalize) them. Agamben's thesis, which I believe is in the spirit of Arendt's understanding of refugees, is to see their deprivation of the Rights of Man both as the demonstration of the fallacious nature of such Rights and as a more certain and more political basis for developing a new form of politics of human rights: "The refugee is perhaps the only thinkable figure for the people of our time and the only category in which one may see today ... the forms and limits of a coming political community" (Agamben 2000a, 16, 17), which is beyond state sovereignty.

For Agamben, the increasing refugee problem in the late twentieth and early twenty-first centuries is evidence of the fact that "the inscription of the native (that is, of life) in the juridical order of the nation-state" (Agamben 2000a, 18–19) has landed in a cul-de-sac. Agamben's own reading of the eighteenth-century Declarations of the Rights of Man is that they "represent first of all the originary figure for the inscription of natural naked life [bare life] in the political-juridical order of the nation-state.... Nation-state means a state that makes nativity or birth (that is, naked human life) the foundation of its own sovereignty" (Agamben 2000a, 20–21). In other words, far from the idea of the "Rights of Man" referring to a juridical condition of humanity independent of their membership in a nation-state, these Rights function in such a manner as to include the biological lives of people into the juridical order of the nation-state while, at the same time, placing this biological life in a "state of exception," in that zone of indistinction in which the biological lives of people become the object of sovereign life-and-death decisions.

Agamben points to the first two articles of the 1789 Declaration to show how the Rights of Man use birth (natality) in order to link sovereignty to the idea of nation, so that to be born means to be a part of a nation; to be a national to whom the state ascribes some positive rights upheld by popular sovereignty. Put in more pedestrian terms, for Agamben, the Declaration of the Rights of Man holds that being born means one belongs to a nation and has the right to a passport. "If the refugee represents such a disquieting element in the order of the nation-state, this is so primarily because, by breaking the identity between human and citizen and that between nativity and nationality, it brings the originary fiction of sovereignty to crisis" (Agamben 2000a, 20–21). The fact that the refugee problem cannot be resolved by the "concert" of nation-states indicates that the status of the native, of natality and of *zoe*, is not fated to give rise to a "nation" but, on the contrary, may give "birth" (both literally and figuratively) to new political forms of association that escape the grasp of sovereignty. It is in this sense—because of the intimate and necessary relation between nativity or natality and the right to have rights—that the refugee reveals the affirmative biopolitical character of human rights. This, in turn, centers on the problem of what the proper or true legal form of natality is, if it is not the legal form of nationality.

For Agamben, the condition of the refugees should lead to a questioning of the political role of nativity or natality in the state-nation-territory trinity. This, in turn, should lead to an opposition between natality and nationality, as a new ground for the right to have rights. But Agamben stops short of proposing such a new affirmative biopolitics of human rights on the basis of natality and, to date, he has been unwilling or unable to do so. Nonetheless, he does make an important contribution to an affirmative biopolitics of rights by taking into account a feature of the paradoxical political yet state-less "status" of refugees, namely, by thinking about the "extraterritoriality" that characterizes such a "status." His thesis is that the only solution to the problem of refugees is for the nation-state to open up its territory in order to give precedence not to the "security" of those citizens walled inside their national territory, but to a political space that must serve as a "*refugium* (refuge) of the singular" (Agamben 2000a, 24–25). The positive contribution of the problem of refugees, then, is the idea of the primordial political space as a space of refuge for singularity.

Once again Agamben remains faithful—in his way—to Arendt's formulations, for she too had argued that natality ought to give rise to a "place in the world" where the opinion of the singular matters to others. Of course, what this means, both for Arendt and for Agamben, remains rather vague. Agamben seems to concur with Derrida's original suggestion that cosmopolitanism should entail a global network of such cities of refuge "in which the spaces of states have been thus perforated and topologically deformed and in which the citizen has been able to recognize the refugee that he or she is" (Agamben 2000a, 24–25). At the end of this chapter, I return to this hypothesis, which seems to contain the correct position with regard to the deeper (and etymologically more faithful) meaning of *cosmo-polis*, but I shall do so within a more robust conception of republican citizenship than those proposed by either Agamben or Derrida.

Where I part ways with Agamben's critique of modern human rights is in his belief that only the nation-state can provide the legal form for natality. Since nationality or naturalization is a negation of natality, it follows for Agamben that all legal form is also a negation of natality. Agamben's main contention in *Homo Sacer* is that species life (*zoe*) becomes sacred or *sacer*, when it is captured by, or comes under the control of the law, when it becomes included or excluded from *bios politikos*, from "political existence" (Agamben 1998). In *State of Exception*, Agamben argues that this "capture" of life or *zoe* by law or *bios politikos* is made possible only when the law takes exception to itself and a sovereign power declares a state of exception: only in a state of exception can the law apply directly to life.

Agamben's biopolitics is a radicalization and, at the same time, an alteration of Schmitt's axiom according to which only in a state of exception is it possible to decide between chaos and normality or order; law is applicable only in a state of normality, only when social order exists. Agamben turns Schmitt's axiom into a paradox: in order to achieve normality (which is a situation in which law can be applied), a state of exception must be possible or declared. On his reading, this means that there is an application of law only when the law takes exception to itself, that is, when it does not apply (Agamben 2005, 40). Agamben calls "force of law" this characteristic of the law, namely, that it has "validity" (or, is in "force") only when it is in a state of exception to itself. This "force" of law denotes "an anomic space" where bare life is captured "inside" the precincts of the law and yet banned into a space of (legally constituted) anomy, or "pure violence" (Agamben 2005, 68–70). Agamben claims that this "abandonment" of biological life has a specific architectural location: that of the *Lager* or concentration camp.

Agamben argues that the rule of law is nothing other than the means through which an ever-wider network of spaces—states of exception—is established. For him, the greatest and most dangerous illusion is the belief that liberal democratic regimes have defeated totalitarian forms of political life, or, even, that they are the best protection against the return of totalitarianism (Agamben 1998, 10, 121–22, 179). But to argue this point, Agamben is required to show that the modern system of individual liberties, both in its republican and liberal variants (which were explicitly intended to make a sovereign power impossible), are in fact nothing but a variant of sovereign power in the age of democracy.

> The spaces, the liberties, and the rights won by individuals in their conflicts with central powers always simultaneously prepared a tacit but increasing inscription of individual's lives within the state order, thus offering a new and more dreadful foundation for the very sovereign power from which they wanted to liberate themselves. (Agamben 1998, 121)

Liberal democracies, whose constitutional system limits the sovereignty of the state with respect to a system of laws based on inalienable individual human rights, turn out, on this hypothesis, to be in collusion with the capture of biological life by sovereign power. The rights that protect individual *zoe*, at the same time, bring *zoe* under sovereign power and transform every individual endowed with human rights into a potential *homo sacer*. The modern biopolitics of liberal regimes that sees politics as a "decision on life" can no longer be separated from the modern thanatopolitics of totalitarian regimes that sees politics as a "decision on death" (Agamben 1998, 122). The frontier between a politics of life and a politics of death is now "in motion."

Agamben offers two arguments to support his claim that the subject of modern individual rights is a "sacred man" and is thus completely unprotected against the mythical violence of the state (despite any illusions to the contrary that the Declarations of the Rights of Man may harbor). The first argument rests on an interpretation of the 1679 Habeas Corpus Act, one of the foundational sources for modern theories of human rights. According to Agamben, the writ of habeas corpus posits bare life (here identified with the *corpus*, or body, of the accused) as the "new political subject" of rights. Through habeas corpus "nascent European democracy thereby placed at the centre of its battle against absolutism not *bios*, the qualified life of the citizen, but *zoe*—the bare, anonymous life that is as such taken into the sovereign ban" (Agamben 1998, 123). Through the right to habeas corpus, it is the "bare life" of the *homo sacer* that gets "disseminated into every individual being" (Agamben 1998, 124). To clarify this idea, Agamben cites a famous passage from Hobbes's *De Cive*,[14] where the natural equality of all human beings is grounded in their capacity to be killed by anyone: "The absolute capacity of the subject's bodies to be killed forms the new political body of the West" (Agamben 1998, 125). Human rights, on this view, are biopolitical instruments of domination.

Agamben's interpretation of habeas corpus highlights the role played by the idea of *corpus*, but it fails to take into account the full phrase: *habeas corpus cum causa captis et detentionis*, which has its origins in the fourteenth century. "As the name indicated, it required the production of the person in court *along with a showing of the cause of detention*" (Meador 1966, 10).[15] The point is that habeas corpus as Agamben understands it is an interpretation of the writ where only *the body* of the accused, and not *the record* of what law the accused is supposed to have broken, is invoked in court. This omission is of decisive importance because it prevents Agamben from seeing that habeas corpus cannot possibly be an instrument in the "sacralization" of human bare life since the requirement of habeas corpus destroys the very idea of an "original sin," a state of guilt that is conatural to human birth and, thus, deserving of punishment. The writ of habeas corpus, to the contrary, states that "guilt" is only something that can be proven in a court of law, according to artificial laws made by human beings who are equal members of a people, endowed with legislative powers. Thus, "guilt" is not to be determined morally, according to moral codes of divine provenance. The matter of the "record" is essential because it is on this terrain that the battle to inscribe the writ of habeas corpus within sovereignty has unfolded over the past several hundred years. What makes the writ of habeas corpus the foundation of every republican conception of human rights is this original link between body (*zoe*) and the right to a legal opinion. Arendt construes the right to have rights in terms of a connection between natality and the right to have opinions about law.

It is true, of course, that through the writ of habeas corpus, which demands that an inferior court provide the record of charges on which a person stands accused, the superior courts manage to centralize the process of law making and law adjudication, thereby (at first, but only at first) serving the interests of the sovereign power. By contrast, precisely by demonstrating that "a mere order of the King" is not sufficient "legal record" to detain anyone, Selden and other defenders of the writ in the seventeenth century manage to turn habeas corpus into a pure instrument or pure means of resistance against sovereign power, thereby establishing the fundamental "distinction between government under law and government by law" (Meador 1966, 14–15). Where the former nullifies sovereign power, the latter requires it. Agamben is too quick to dismiss the possibility that a discourse on rights, suitably reinterpreted along biopolitical lines, may very well be a "pure means" by which bare or sacred life can "reverse" its domination and acquire a new freedom that no longer stands under a sovereign ban.

A similar shortcoming is found in Agamben's critique of the Rights of Man. He argues that the first article of the French *Déclaration*, in which it is stated that "men are born and remain free and equal in rights," makes birth the "earthly foundation of the state's legitimacy and sovereignty."

Thus, through birth, it is the bare life of individuals that gets taken up by sovereign power. The fact that such a *Déclaration* also clothes these bare individuals with the attire of the *citoyen* is simply a way of repressing the foundation of modern politics on the domination of bare life. When, in the third article of the *Déclaration*, the nation (from *nascio*) is identified as the proper subject of sovereignty, this signals to Agamben that, by way of birth, individual life has fallen prey to the sovereign power of the nation, placing its subjects in a state of exception. This capture of life under the law, in and through the connection of rights to birth, will reveal its hidden, deadly potential through the subsequent birth of nationalism, imperialism and, finally, racism and genocide.

But Agamben's deconstructive reading of the *Déclaration* only works on the false assumption that it is no longer possible to distinguish a republic from a nation-state. Additionally, it relies on the further questionable assumption that the reference to a freedom "from birth," contained in the discourse on human rights, refers to the birth of the nation and the birth of individuals into a nation, and not to another, *political but not national* sense of birth or natality. Both of these assumptions are explicitly rejected by Arendt in her treatment of the idea of right to have rights. First, Arendt ascribes the crisis of the modern republic to the fact that the idea of nation takes over the republican idea of the state.[16] Second, Arendt makes the fact of birth, understood as natality, into the condition for political freedom understood as "the right to action . . . the right to have rights (and that means to live in a framework where one is judged by one's actions and opinions)" (Arendt 1973, 296). The task in what follows, then, is to show why Arendt believes that a conception which *disconnects birth from nationality* (this being the *cosmopolitan* aspect of natality in the right to have rights) may be the sole means through which *a republic without sovereignty* (this being the *republican* aspect of the right to have rights) can become thinkable.

HUMAN RIGHTS AS A RIGHT TO DEMOCRACY

In Shue's understanding of "basic rights" there is a tension between rights to security and subsistence, which are human rights whose addressee is "bare life," and the rights to freedom of movement and participation, which are human rights whose addressee is a protosubject of positive rights, someone actively involved in a "politics" of human rights (Shue 1980, chap. 3 passim). Arendt's formulation of a right to have rights envisages both aspects: through natality, it is bare life and a biopolitical conception of human rights that is being articulated. Through plurality, it is the aspect of a human right to participation in a polity that is being articulated. The importance of Benhabib's interpretation of human rights, on the basis of Arendt's formula of a right to have rights, lies in the notion that human rights are always already rights to a "political" life, a *bios politikos* or, in more recent formulations, that there exists a human right to democracy. For Benhabib, the refugee must always already be considered a potential citizen by virtue of her capacity for communicative action: all human beings are "moral beings capable of communicative freedom" (Benhabib 2011, chap. 5, passim). Benhabib's contribution to the discourse on human rights, therefore, is her application of a discourse-theoretic solution to the perplexing relation between cosmopolitanism and republicanism in human rights outlined above.

Benhabib's innovation consists in reading Arendt's "right to have rights" by separating two senses of the concept of right: the first "right" is moral, while the rights (liberties and entitlements) that this moral right guarantees are juridical. The moral "right" to such civil, political, and social rights belongs to all "humanity," and it means that every human being has a right, by birth, to "membership in some human group." It is this moral, not juridical, idea of a fundamental human right to be part of an organized community that, according to her, ought to ground cosmopolitan law. Now, Benhabib claims that for Arendt the universal moral principle of a right to have rights receives its application, or realization, in the activity of "republican constitution making." But every republican constitution necessarily restricts the universality of the moral right. This belief is premised on her assumption that a particular application of a law would restrict the universality of its meaning (Benhabib 2004, 66).[17] Conversely, for Benhabib cosmopolitanism is defined in opposition to republicanism by linking the former with the "inclusiveness" of the strict universality of the moral right (to have rights) that is innate to all human beings: if cosmopolitanism is moral, then republicanism is ethico-political.

This description of the relation between moral and ethico-political rights does indeed describe the tension between the nominally cosmopolitan Rights of Man and the nominally republican Rights of Citizens. But this is a mistaken reconstruction of Arendt's doctrine. To the contrary, for Arendt, the cosmopolitan right to have rights—in its very form and not just in its application—is always already "republican." Since Benhabib disconnects the human and moral right to have rights from the idea of a republican constitution, she construes an idea of republicanism which is exclusivist of "humanity" and characterized by "civic particularism." But Arendt's "right to have rights" is a formula that was designed to resolve, and not merely to describe, the tension between republicanism and cosmopolitanism that has brought about the "end" of the Rights of Man. As a consequence, applying the distinction between moral and ethico-political rights in order to interpret the meaning of Arendt's formula is the wrong way to go about interpreting it.

Irrespective of whether Benhabib's reading of Arendt is tenable, her own discourse-theoretic interpretation of the right to have rights as a right to democracy is intended to overcome the divide between cosmopolitanism and republicanism. In this way, it envisages how a refugee, despite her condition of statelessness, can nevertheless be considered a citizen. The argument has two distinct parts. In the first part, Benhabib argues that to respect a person as an end in itself, to respect the "human" dignity in that individual, means to recognize her as having a good reason for some action or institution. The individual is a bearer of what Forst calls "noumenal power" or argumentative capability (Forst 2011, 21ff). On this reading, the right to have rights refers to a "basic human right to communicative freedom," which she then parses, following Forst, as a fundamental "right to justification" (Forst 2007).[18] According to this right to justification, one's freedom can only be restricted by a norm that is "generally and reciprocally justifiable." "Our relation to the other is governed by the norms of formal equality and reciprocity: each is entitled to expect from us what we can expect from him or from her" (Benhabib 2011, 69; Forst 2011, 62–63).

The advantage of construing the right to have rights in terms of a "right to justification" is that it necessarily overcomes the tension between being an addressee of a human right and being an author of that right. Benhabib and Forst, after all, are applying the Habermasian notion that subjective and political rights are cooriginal and mutually imply one another, just as Shue argues that it does not make sense to protect the individual's right to subsistence without also recognizing the right to participate in formulating the policies and laws concerning its protection. The point is to bridge the abyss between refugee (who is the addressee of human, moral right) and citizen (who is author of positive rights) at the level of human rights by giving the refugee that "surplus" capability—which she shares with citizens of constituted polities—for publicly arguing for what she considers to be just or right. In Benhabib's and Forst's accounts, thanks to this deliberative surplus, the refugee is always already endowed with a portion of constituent power. Thus, Benhabib states that "the right to have rights then is not only a right to conditions of membership but entails the right to action and to opinion in the public sphere of a polity the laws of which govern one's existence" (Benhabib 2011, chap. 5). Forst puts it this way: the message of human rights is not only the claim to be a member of society but to count as someone with the right to justification means that "there can be no legitimate social or political order if it cannot be appropriately justified to their subjects, and that is why the original meaning of human rights is more a *republican* meaning than a classically *liberal* one" (Forst 2011, 60, translation mine).

The problem with this "republican" reconstruction of human rights in Benhabib and Forst is that the "constituent power" that is ascribed to the refugee, by virtue of her or his capacity for communicative action, is a power that is always already *predetermined by a given legal, positive constitution*. Benhabib follows Habermas by insisting that the right to have rights is analytically tied to its inscription in a legal order. I think this is correct: the right to have rights has no meaning unless it is a right to a legal opinion, an opinion about and of law, as I showed above in my analysis of habeas corpus. But this point does not mean that such a law must assume the form of an already constituted republican legal order, as it does for Habermas and Benhabib.

For Benhabib, the inscription of a right to have rights in the law always means its inscription in a "positive" law, guaranteed by the coercive power of a sovereign state. This is problematic for two reasons. First, Benhabib discounts the fact that Arendt explicitly asserts that natality gives rise to a "new law on earth," and this "law" is undoubtedly the inscription of a right to have rights, but it is not an inscription found in an already given political constitution of a nation-state (nor, a fortiori, of a future world-state). Second, by making the constituent, discursive "power" and the "authority" of the refugee *depend* on its inscription in a positive law backed by the "power" and "authority" of a sovereign state, the refugee is necessarily placed in a situation of asymmetry that betrays the formal requirements of communicative action. Put another way, the "space of reasons" that is presupposed in Forst's construal of the "right to justification" is not homogeneous and suprapolitical. On the contrary, its topography changes depending on whether one is inside or outside of already constituted political spaces. It is not true that simply by speaking or acting all actors and speakers are always already recognized as "an authority": the space of appearance where this can be a reality must be constructed, and this space *does not* match the space of already constituted political spaces. A right to have rights is intended to construct precisely that space where everyone, refugee and citizen, can be equal authorities. However, this space is something that cannot be achieved by inclusion or naturalization into an already existing polity or an already existing democracy. So, the conversion from subject of rights to author of rights is a principle that works only within a constituted space that has been legally framed, without taking into consideration the refugee. If it is going to apply to the refugee, then the refugee must have the right to an opinion about the law of the land that is not given by that law of the land, but by another "law of the earth." Furthermore, the refugee must have this right to another legal opinion from birth.

The problem with the discourse-theoretic reconstruction of the right to have rights is that it inevitably reduces the space of political participation of bare life to the already constituted political space of citizenship.[19] This means that the "law" of natality is collapsed into a (positive) law of equality, where the constitutional determination of this equality is necessarily exclusive of others. Below I will explain in what sense Arendt thinks that a constitution is inherently exclusive: it is due to the fact that every constitution turns the right to have rights, understood as bare life's right to political action, into a right that can be exercised only by the "representatives" of bare life. This is equivalent to saying that, if human rights are rights to democracy, then the only ones who can exercise this democratic privilege are the "representatives" of bare life, the health and security officers of NGOs, and so on. It is impossible to think about the right to have rights unless one deconstructs the idea of a republican constitution and its principle of representation. Natality gives the right to constituent power, but this "constitution" is not in line with the traditional idea of a republican constitution that is presumed normative without further critique by Benhabib and Forst.

Because Benhabib lets the right to have rights depend on its inscription in positive law (that is, because the right to have rights gives access to a political space previously constituted by positive law), her solution to the problem of refugees centers on naturalization. In so doing, she opens herself up to the critique of naturalization mounted by Agamben. Benhabib argues that because the Universal Declaration of Human Rights understands loss of citizenship as a violation of human rights, it follows from the right to justification that liberal democracies have the moral duty to "naturalize"—that is, nationalize—people who have been "denaturalized" by losing their citizenship in some nation-state. According to Benhabib, the nation-state ought to engage in a moral discourse with the stateless person and ought to give reciprocally acceptable reasons why that stateless person should or should not be accepted in the country as a national. She calls for nondiscriminating conditions of naturalization that are to be made public and applied through a clear legal procedure that avoids criminalizing refugees and immigrants. This is her basic "solution" to the problem of refugees.

The fact that a discourse-theoretic approach to the right to have rights needs to fall back on a logic of "naturalization" is indicative of a basic flaw in this approach. The flaw consists in not having thought through how a "right to justification" addresses the second requirement of a "right to have rights," namely, a consideration of the juris-generative power of natality (and not merely the juris-generative power of rational aptitude). This requirement states that, just like *at the level of communication*, the refugee must already be a citizen by virtue of her (constituent) noumenal power, similarly, *at the level of its bare life*, the refugee must already be a citizen, by virtue of what I have called her (constituent) biopower. This constituent biopower is the power that withdraws natality from its sovereign inscription in nationality, such that being born always already means being born into a political status that is not reducible to a national status, that is, to a status granted by a nation-state or any other organized political community. A right to have rights presupposes that the event of being-born gives rise to a people who are without a state, but who are endowed with constituent power.

Considered from the standpoint of this second, biopolitical requirement of the right to have rights, Benhabib's discourse-theoretic solution falls short. As a result, the right to justification—at least as it is construed by Benhabib and possibly by Forst—seems incapable of fulfilling both criteria of the right to have rights.[20] It falls short because Benhabib takes "naturalization" as the solution to the problem posed by refugees. This means that, for her, what is "natural" to the humanity of the human being is the status of being a member of an organized community: "naturalization" means the process whereby someone's humanity is recognized in and through their being returned to the space of a human-made community of "formal equality and reciprocity." In other words, her position is that only by giving someone the right to belong to a community do we recognize their "human dignity" and cease doing violence to the "nature" of humanity which, from this perspective, is a status best captured by citizenship (conversely, withdrawing citizenship status is an attack on the "nature" of humanity). Benhabib's solution to the problem posed by the refugee accepts the very cause of the problem, namely, the belief that nativity or natality contains within it something like a natural right to have a passport, a homeland, a nationality, and a country. For Benhabib, it is not birth, natality, or simply life that gives human beings their "right to have rights." Rather, it is birth-into-community, the always already politically recognized "birth" that gives human beings their "right" to have rights.[21] The function of birth is that one is born a "human" being, where "humanity" is an attribute that can only be granted by inclusion in a community (be this a family, a tribe, a nation, a republic).

This position amounts to denying what could be considered Arendt's "first principle," namely, her claim that the right to have rights is grounded in natality *and is opposed to* nationality. Whereas, for Arendt, all legitimate community is based on the principle of equality (and thus equality lies at the basis of civil and political rights), the right to have rights is neither constructible nor based on the principle of equality. The right to have rights is based on the principles of natality and of plurality, neither of which should be reduced to or understood from a civil-political ("democratic") idea of equality. Benhabib's cosmopolitanism is in fact a communitarianism of humanity: one has rights only because one belongs, by birth, to some human community. The proof that one belongs to this community lies in one's ability to be understood by others who are like oneself and to exchange "good reasons" with them. These "good reasons" are the coin of the realm of humanity (in Kantian jargon, the kingdom of ends). But just as Benhabib's theory of naturalization denies natality a constituent biopower by subsuming birth under a constituted community, so, in Forst, identifying the right to have rights with the right of justification wrongly locates the source of the "authority" that belongs equally to all participants in the communicative process. In Forst, the "authority" of the speaking individual comes from her freedom to move around in the space of reason: to grasp reasons, to criticize arguments, and to offer other or better reasons. But between a refugee and a citizen, it is clear that the space of reason is not homogeneous: the refugee never has the power or "authority" of argument and reason behind her. The public use of reason is always a power of the constituted community and not of the stateless individual. The state always has a surplus of reasons (the reasons of state) to deny the refugee a truly political status: this is what Shue has called the "view that compatriots always take priority" (Shue 1980, 132ff). To analyze the paradoxical political "human status" of the refugee, one must not reduce the "noumenal power" of the refugee to the power or authority generated by justifications. Instead, one must understand this "noumenal power" as the power granted by opinion. The refugee's power comes from a legal opinion, where the law in question is the "new law on earth" of natality and plurality that, like habeas corpus, is a pure means that is not at the disposal of any sovereign power and its reason of state.

ARENDT'S RIGHT TO HAVE RIGHTS AS A BIOPOLITICAL RIGHT TO CONSTITUENT POWER

In the secondary literature, Arendt's critique of Hobbesian-style natural right (on the grounds that it is atomistic) is often understood to mean that Arendt rejects all natural right. I do not think this is the case. Arendt develops a conception of republican natural right while rejecting the Hobbesian doctrine of natural rights. What makes Arendt's conception of natural right "republican" is that in the "state of nature," natality gives rise ipso facto to peoplehood: or, stated another way, for republicanism, the state of nature is not populated by isolated individuals (as in liberal contract theory); by virtue of natality, it is populated by free and equal peoples. In order to appreciate what is at stake in this shift from an apolitical conception of human rights to a republican conception of human rights, one has to work backwards from Arendt's conception of an authentic republican constitution, to its (biopolitical) conditions of possibility.

In *On Revolution*, Arendt develops her version of what Ackerman and Rawls later call the "dualist" conception of constitutional democracy, based on the "distinction between constitutional and normal politics ... it distinguishes the people's constituent power to form, ratify and amend a constitution from the ordinary power of legislators and executives in everyday politics; and it distinguishes also the higher law of the people from the ordinary law of legislative bodies" (Rawls 1996, 405–6). The fourth chapter of *On Revolution* sets out a dualist reading of *constitutio libertatis*. In it, Arendt argues that the term "constitution" is radically ambivalent because it contains a moment of political closure to the outside and freezes a people's freedom into the form of a state; but it also contains a moment of political openness to what is extrapolitical (namely, natality and its "new law") and maintains the connection between freedom and the activity of revolution. Thus, on the dualist reading of constitutionalism, a constitution is an internally divided, antagonistic assemblage or *dispostif* of the following elements: a limited government versus a "new system of power"; a set of negative liberties (as catalogued in the Bill of Rights) versus a new "right to be seen in action"; a safeguard against government versus a new way of sharing in the "government of affairs" (Arendt 1990, 147).

She resumes this point by referring to Montesquieu, her main source for this dualist interpretation of republican doctrine:

> For the main subject of Montesquieu's great work, studied and quoted as an authority on government at least a decade before the outbreak of the Revolution, was indeed 'the constitution of political freedom', but the word 'constitution' in this context has lost all connotations of being a negative, a limitation and negation of power; the word means, on the contrary, that the 'great temple of federal liberty' must be based on the foundation and correct distribution of power. It was precisely because Montesquieu ... had maintained that power and freedom belonged together; that conceptually speaking political freedom did not reside in the I-will but in the I-can. (Arendt 1990, 150)

For Arendt, the republican conception of the power of the people is "federalist" because a powerful people can only be constituted by establishing relations and alliances among politicized individuals, and it is these *foedera* (these alliances) that empower a people. Arendt's expression of the "right to have rights" thus corresponds to the dualist conception of the constitution: the original "right" (to have positive rights) lies at the basis of what Rawls calls "the higher law of the people," whereas the "positive rights" that this law of the people grants all of its citizens lies at the basis of the "ordinary law of legislative bodies." Arendt's fundamental claim, to phrase it otherwise, is that Rawls's "higher law of the people" depends on the (natural, biopolitical) laws of plurality and natality, whereas positive rights depend on the (constructed, democratic) law of equality.

Therefore, on Arendt's republican account of a constitution (in this she does not differ from either Rawls or Schmitt), every legitimate constitution must entail (implicitly or explicitly) a list of civil and political (and possibly social and economic) rights. Ascribing these rights to citizens is what it means to recognize everyone as being "equal." Thus, equality among humans is a political construction; equality is an internal predicate of "citizens." There is no "natural" equality in this sense and, therefore, according to a republican idea of politics, "who" is equal and in what sense is always already an object of contestation. Both Rawls and Arendt share this political constructivism with respect to equality. Following Arendt's usage, I shall call this side of the republican constitution the "civil constitution."

But the republican idea of a constitution also contains a reference to the "higher law of the people," a constituent power of the people that corresponds to the "natural" right to have (positive civil, political, and socioeconomic) rights. My thesis is that this conception of the right to have rights is addressed by Arendt in her texts on republicanism, specifically in relation to the "freedom of opinion" or "public spirit" and in her discussion of "public happiness" and "public freedom."[22] "Public freedom consisted in having a share in public business," and what moved them to this activity was "'the passion for distinction' which John Adams held to be 'more essential and remarkable' than any other human faculty . . . 'every individual is seen to be strongly actuated by a desire to be seen, heard, talked of, approved and respected by the people about him, and within his knowledge'" (Arendt 1990, 119). The correlate of this passion for distinction is the natural right or freedom to form an opinion, and it is in relation to opinion that Arendt refers to the term "public spirit": "The decisive incompatibility between the rule of the unanimously held 'public opinion' and freedom of opinion, for the truth of the matter is that no formation of opinion is ever possible where all opinions have become the same. Since no one is capable of forming his own opinion without the benefit of a multitude of opinions

Biopolitical Cosmopolitanism 245

held by others, the rule of public opinion endangers even the opinion of those few who may have the strength not to share it" (Arendt 1990, 225).

A republic distinguishes itself from a democracy because the former defends the freedom of opinion whereas the latter follows public opinion. "Interest and opinion are entirely different political phenomena. Politically, interests are relevant only as group interests.... Opinions, on the contrary, never belong to groups but exclusively to individuals.... *Opinions will rise wherever men communicate freely with one another and have the right to make their views public*" (Arendt 1990, 227, emphasis mine). In passages such as these, Arendt clearly identifies the right to have rights, that is, the right to appear in public and the right or freedom *to form an opinion*, but not the right of justification. The "authority" that is recognized in every participant in a communicative process, then, is that of making up her own mind about any and every matter of public concern: freedom of opinion here stands at the antipodes of the reason of the state (which, by definition, always restricts this freedom to form an opinion about public matters to a representative of the people or political community) and is, ultimately, destructive of such reason.

From this follows Arendt's belief that the "revolutionary" character of a republican constitution is found in those institutions that are established by the constitution and intended to maintain this *natural* freedom of opinion within a given political society because "[political] authority in the last analysis rests on opinion." The authority of constituted power rests on a freedom of opinion that is rooted in the *natural* condition of humanity (this is natality) and which, thereby, escapes the influence of a constituted public reason. That such a natural or biopolitical freedom of opinion is also the bearer of a constituent power is a truth that "is never more forcefully demonstrated than when, suddenly and unexpectedly, a universal refusal to obey initiates what then turns into a revolution" (Arendt 1990, 228). But can one be more precise as to what kind of opinion does the condition of natality generate, and what institutions can keep it alive?

An answer to this question can be found if one turns to Arendt's discussion of the problem faced by the American Revolution: "how to build a lasting institution for the formation of public views into the very structure of the republic" (Arendt 1990. 228). As is well known, Arendt argues that the Senate and the Supreme Court were, respectively, "a lasting institution for opinion and a lasting institution for judgment" (Arendt 1990, 228). At first glance, this seems like a surprisingly "conservative" choice: Why should the "aristocratic" Senate and the nonelected Supreme Court be the defenders of revolutionary "public spirit" and the "freedom of opinion"?

There are several factors behind Arendt's choice. First among them is that the Senate and the Supreme Court are intended to be the deciding institutions concerning what counts as "law" and they are, at the same time, those institutions in which it is possible to distinguish between an opinion and an interest. In the House of Representatives, not to mention the executive branch of the president, the exchange of opinion is less "free" because it is more often than not mandated by the furtherance of the diverse "interests" represented by its members. In the Senate and the Supreme Court, precisely because their members are more "shielded" from the force of interest (including by such aristocratic measures as property requirements for election), the formation of public opinion has a greater chance of being oriented by law. Arendt's idea, then, is that the Senate and the Supreme Court are institutions in which the natural freedom of opinion receives the force of positive law.

Since she connects the right to have rights with the right to freedom of opinion, one can now say more concretely that this right to have rights is the natural right to the formation of legal opinion or an opinion about law. Since what guarantees the right to opinion is the "new law on earth" of natality and plurality, then the right to have rights means that anyone, by virtue of being born on Earth, has a natural right to have an opinion about what the law should be on Earth. By virtue of the difference between this opinion, which comes from outside a polity, and that opinion which is generated from within a polity, it follows that such a right to have rights is a right to a legal opinion that expresses dissent regarding actual laws.

In this sense, Rancière is correct to argue that the true formula for human rights always entails an "inscription" of rights in law (here the law of natality), on the basis of which people who are not authorized to act or speak by positive law are nonetheless authorized to speak and act, thereby "putting two worlds in one and the same world. A political subject, as I understand it, is a capacity for staging such scenes of dissensus. It appears thus that *man* is not the void term opposed to the actual rights of the citizens. It has a positive content that is the dismissal of any difference between those who 'live' in such or such sphere of existence, between those who are or are not qualified for political life" (Rancière 2004, 304). This is correct if only one adds that the *dissensus* that the right to have rights brings into political life (*bios politikos*) is not the result of "putting two worlds" in one, but rather of joining the *zoe* that comes from the "law of earth" (namely, natality, the condition of exile from any and every world) with a political "world" constituted by power and privilege. The right to have rights is dependent on an inscription of law, but it is not a man-made law, or a Declaration of Rights. If, by their actions and opinions, women in the French Revolution could demonstrate "that they had the rights that the constitution denied them" (Rancière 2004, 304), this was not because the right to these actions and opinions was previously inscribed in the Declaration, as Rancière thinks. Rather, it was because the space in which to manifest these actions and opinions was wrenched open by the counterforce exercised by a law (of the earth) that did not fit in the "one" world of the *polis* and tore it apart from the "inside," that is, from the so-called private sphere of the reproduction of species life.

Only if one understands this internal relation between natality (and the cosmopolitan "new law on earth" that it brings about) and freedom of opinion does it become comprehensible why Arendt, in one and the same gesture, *supports* the institutions of legal, public opinion (Supreme Court, Senate) as opposed to the institutions of public interest (House of Representatives, executive branch), and *rejects* them because of their merely representative character. Arendt is struggling with the following problem: How can the public spirit, which is only kept "alive" in these representative institutions for the representatives themselves, be periodically turned over to the people (such a periodic return of power to the people being the definition of a revolution in republican terminology)?

> What was uppermost in his [Jefferson's] mind... was rather the somewhat awkward attempt at securing for each generation the 'right to depute representatives to a convention', to find ways and means for the opinions of the whole people to be 'fairly, fully, and peaceably expressed, discussed and decided by the common reason of society'. In other words what he wished to provide for was an exact repetition of the whole process of action which had accompanied the course of the Revolution... with the constitution making and the establishment of a new government... those activities which by themselves constituted the space of freedom. (Arendt 1990, 234–35)

The "right to have rights" is the *specifically revolutionary right* according to which "the *opinions* of the whole people to be 'fairly, fully, and peaceably expressed, discussed and decided by the common reason of society'" (emphasis mine). But what does "the whole people" and its "common reason" mean in this context? And what role does enlarging the question of republican freedom to a cosmopolitan perspective centered on human rights play in the project of revolutionizing civil society?

Instead of sealing the "end" of the revolution (as happened in the United States), how can a constitution enable an "exact repetition of the whole process of action" of the revolution? This is Arendt's central dilemma. The problem, according to her, is that "while [the American Revolution] had given freedom to the people, [it] had failed to provide a space where this freedom could be exercised." Arendt's response to this dilemma is to *de-constitute* the republican system of political representation, for it is this system that has deprived the people of "the chance to become temporarily 'a participator in government,'" since "the Constitution itself provided a public space only for the representatives of the people, and not for the people themselves" (Arendt 1990, 238). Arendt's solution entails exchanging, or at least supplementing, the system of representation with what a French revolutionary called "the right to assemble in popular societies" (Arendt 1990, 243). For Arendt, popular societies, or, in more contemporary terms, "communal movements" are the true organs of a republic, and their very name betrays their proximity to the "communist movement," whose "spectre," according to Marx, haunted all republican revolutions in the nineteenth century.

Arendt's understanding of the "communal movement" entails a deconstruction of the process of *constitutio libertatis*. To that end, Arendt introduces a new series of binary oppositions: the communal movement represents the "street" as opposed to the system of representation that represents the "body politic." The "people" exist politically insofar as they are organized by the "new federalism" of popular societies and communes, as opposed to "a mercilessly centralized power apparatus which, under the pretence of representing the sovereignty of the nation, actually deprive[s] people of their power" (Arendt 1990, 244–45). Only these communes or popular societies maintain "the public spirit" over and against the "general will" because they express the "diversity inherent in freedom of thought and speech" (Arendt 1990, 245).

Such diversity of opinion can only exist in a "federal" system of the separation of powers, which is "a true republic," as opposed to a system that centralizes power and corresponds to the "nation-state" (Arendt 1990, 245). Arendt claims that "this communal council system" of the popular societies was eliminated with the rise of the political parties and the party system. She thereby sets up her last and decisive opposition, namely, that between the parliament and the people (Arendt 1990, 248). Montesquieu's republican equation of freedom with power, at the end of the day, boils down to this: every human being has a natural right to the formation of an opinion with any others such that this opinion becomes the basis of a *rapport, foedera,* or relationship (this is the "federalist" component of power) to these others that constitute them in a popular society. These communes or societies are the cells of a political body without organs or central organization (without political parties or government) that constitutes the people's constituent power. This entire process of opinion formation, when considered from the viewpoint of the legal, constituted space of positive law, is carried out "in the state of nature." But this republican conception of nature and life no longer has anything to do with the Hobbesian state of nature as a state of exception and is best understood as its antithesis, as the (natural) space of democracy.

Arendt derives these far-reaching conclusions from Montesquieu's republican equation of freedom with power. But the idea of a natural right to opinion, which Arendt offers as the guiding thread in her deconstruction of republicanism and her theory of the commune, is not to be found in Montesquieu. Rather, Arendt's understanding of the revolutionary role played by the natural right to opinion may have been adopted from Spinoza's republicanism, although, as far as I can tell, she never recognizes a debt to Spinoza. The significance of Spinoza's political thought for republicanism is that it undoes the Hobbesian either/or between state of nature and sovereignty. For Spinoza, in fact, a doctrine of natural right can only mean a doctrine that deduces the essence of right from the laws of nature. The state of nature, therefore, cannot be opposed to the best political form of organization.[23] Now, for Spinoza the fundamental natural right is the right or freedom of opinion: "For no one can transfer to another person his natural right, or ability, to think freely and make his own judgments about any matter whatsoever, and cannot be compelled to do so" (Spinoza 2002, TTP XX). Additionally, the freedom of opinion is an objective limit for the right to sovereignty: "Each one therefore surrendered [to the sovereign] his right to act according to his own resolution, but *not his right to think and judge for himself*" (Spinoza 2002, TTP XX, emphasis mine). Alone among the thinkers of modern natural right, Spinoza considers that a democracy (what Arendt calls a commune) is the form of government that is closest to natural right: "In a democratic state (which is the one closest to the state of nature), all men agree, as we showed above, to act—but not to judge and think—according to the common decision. That is, because people cannot all have the same opinions, they have agreed that the view which gains the most votes should acquire the force of a decision, reserving always the right to recall their decision whenever they should find a better course. The less people are accorded *liberty of judgment*, consequently, the further they are from the *most natural condition*, and hence, the more oppressive the regime" (Spinoza 2002, TTP XX, emphasis mine). Arendt's critique of Hobbesian sovereignty does not affect Spinoza's standpoint since, for Spinoza, the establishment of a sovereign power never occurs at the expense of the natural freedom of opinion or its constitutive plurality.

The hypothesis that Arendt's understanding of the juris-generative power of natality is connected to Spinoza's conception of natural right finds additional support if one considers the way in which Esposito and Foucault have tried to formulate an internal relation between biopolitics and rights. Esposito explicitly refers to Spinoza's theory of natural right in his attempt to construct a biopolitical conception of normativity. Esposito argues that Spinoza, unlike Hobbes, does not subject life to an external norm for the sake of securing life. Rather, he asserts that, for Spinoza, normativity (what is called natural right) is thought to be:

> The immanent rule that life gives itself in order to reach the maximum point of its expansion.... It is for this reason that, when seen in a general perspective, every form of existence, be it deviant or defective from a more limited point of view, has equal legitimacy for living according to its own possibilities as a whole in the relations in which it is inserted.... Spinoza makes the norm the principle of unlimited equivalence for every single form of life. (Esposito 2008, 186)

I shall not further engage Esposito's attempt to read Spinoza's "natural right" in terms of a deduction of juridical norms out of the normativity of biological life, for my purpose here is merely to point out this deep coincidence between Spinoza and Arendt concerning the biopolitical ground of the right to have rights. Where Esposito and I may differ is over the fundamental role played by the *right of free opinion* in this biopolitical conception of rights, which is not expressly found in Esposito's reading of Spinoza.

The public space of this kind of opinion formation is something different from the public political space constituted by positive laws: in Arendt, the law of plurality refers to the *freedom to form relationships*, and these relationships (*rapports* in Montesquieu) generate the space within which opinions are meaningful and effective. By contrast, in Arendt the law of natality refers to *the freedom to be different*. Together, these two rightful and constituent conceptions of freedom form the idea of public happiness and the idea of public freedom, which are definitive for her conception of republicanism.

Another indication that these freedoms or rights (which make up what I have called the "natural" right to have positive rights) are biopolitical is provided by the fact they correspond uncannily to the two kinds of biopolitical rights that Foucault works out toward the end of his life. The claim that biopolitics gives rise to a new biopolitical conception of rights is found at the end of the first volume of *The History of Sexuality*. Foucault presents these rights mostly in his nonacademic writings: in his texts on the struggle for rights in the gay and lesbian movement, he posits the existence of a "right to relationships," and in his writings on life, he posits the existence of a "right to be different." Both are examples of rights that emerge directly in relation to biological life; they correspond to the normativity of natality itself.

Arendt's doctrine of the right to have rights is a synthesis of Montesquieu's and Spinoza's republican ideas: natality gives the right to constituent power because it guarantees the freedom to form an opinion, which comes from another law (of the earth) and is about the law (of the polity). Yet this juris-generative opinion is not one formed in representative institutions of the polity (for example, Supreme Court, Congress, and so on), but instead, according to Arendt, it belongs to the "street," to the "people." It is important to understand what kind of public space Arendt is referring to with this expression of the "street." Since this politics of the street is animated by a law of the earth, the "street" cannot refer to a space that is delimited by the walls of the polity or state: it is a space that is always already cosmopolitan and appeals to the opinion of all those who are born on Earth, to all other citizens of the world.[24] This remarkable aspect of republican revolutions—their capacity to spread outside of national borders with incredible speed—was already identified by Kant with the idea of "enthusiasm," which was then taken up by Arendt. But what does such "enthusiasm" mean? How it is possible that citizens of other polities begin to solidarize and sympathize with perfect strangers fighting for freedom in distant lands and on far away squares, more so than with their "compatriots"?

The first explanation for the cosmopolitan enthusiasm generated by the struggle for the right to have rights is that this biopolitical right (to have positive rights), qua right to form legal opinion in the space of the "street," is neither a "subjective" nor a "political" right. The right to have rights is not the "private possession" of every human being considered as an individual or as an atom of humanity, nor is it a right of the politically constituted citizen: in this sense, the right to have rights is not a right of "compatriots." On my account, the right (to have rights) is not a "subjective" right analogous to the right to private property, for instance, because its existence depends on the existence of a *juridical yet natural "rapport"* between self and others. A right to opinion can, a priori, never be a right to "my" opinion, where such possession would be exclusive of or unshareable with the other's opinion (whereas this is precisely the meaning of a natural right to property). That is why Arendt is perfectly consequent when she argues that the logic of opinion formation has an internal relation to a "commune-ist" form of association, something entirely lacking with the logic of interests. Interests are irremediably individual, and their synthesis into a "common interest" must occur through a sovereign "general will" that Arendt opposes to authentic popular power. Unlike interests, opinions are irremediably common. Interests are exclusive of an open and indefinite relationship to the other, whereas opinions require such a relationship as its condition of possibility. The biopolitical or natural right to opinion is also not equivalent to a "political" right of the citizen; the natural right to opinion is rooted in natality, and natality is the condition of being a stranger or refugee in the human world of equality. The right to have rights is not a political right because it is not a right that is deduced from the law of equality, but rather from the law of natality, and this is what makes it a right to be different.

If the biopolitical right to have rights is the right to form opinions in a communal movement, why is this not equivalent to a right to justification, as Benhabib and Forst assert? It is true that the discourse-theoretic approach, at least as formulated in Habermas, does have at its core a potentially anarchic intuition that comes from Arendt, since, as Habermas acknowledges, the idea of communicative action was a linguistic reformulation of Arendt's republican conception of power. But this anarchic core of discourse theory tends to be downplayed in Forst and Benhabib, and its relation to the normative power of natality is not recognized. Instead, they assume that juris-generativity must presuppose positive law and, thus, must presuppose the fact of belonging to some organized political community. Bare life or natality makes one an addressee of human rights for Benhabib and Forst, but only being born-into-community makes one an author of these rights, a participant in their formulation. There is no internal connection between natality and democracy in their thinking.[25]

For this reason, Benhabib's solution to the problem of refugees must take the form of naturalization, of the inclusion of refugees into the system of nation-states. Agamben correctly assumes that for the right to have rights to have any meaning, it must be the refugee's bare life that is juris-generative by virtue of its exclusion (not inclusion, as in Benhabib) from the constituted political space of states and nations. But Agamben's own solution, namely, that the political space of bare life as juris-generative corresponds to the idea of a city of refuge as the originary content of the cosmopolitical ideal, is rather poor when compared to the kind of spaces that Arendt conceived for her republican right to opinion: the street versus parliament; the people organized in communal movements versus the nation centralized in the state; the "public spirit" of "*rapports*" based on shared opinion versus the "general will" of positive legislation. As a way of concluding this chapter, I propose a different way of conceiving of the political space that corresponds to the biopolitical right to form opinion in a communal movement, or the space of the "street" whose juris-generative power, in Arendt, is opposed to the legitimate power of the national parliaments. In this way, I hope to show how the republicanism of the "street" and of the "commune" is compatible with and inextricable from the cosmopolitan sense of the opposition between natality and nationality with which I began my discussion of the right to have rights.

THE RIGHT TO HAVE RIGHTS AS A NEW *NOMOS* OF THE EARTH

As Birmingham, Parekh, and other interpreters have pointed out, Arendt's call for a new way of analyzing human rights is fundamentally cosmopolitan because these rights must be guaranteed by a "new law on the earth." This expression echoes the title of Carl Schmitt's famous critique of post-WWII international law, the *Nomos der Erde* (law of the earth), a work with which Arendt was familiar. Recently, a few interpreters have pursued the thesis that Arendt's doctrine of human rights was more dependent on Schmitt's critique than was previously thought.[26] Since Arendt claims that a "right to have right" means having a natural right to a political space of appearance, Lindahl, for instance, argues that the new *nomos* of the earth that grounds such a right must refer to a territory delimited by positive law. After all, he claims that this is the "original" meaning of *nomos*. On this reading, Arendt's "right to have rights" would be rather self-contradictory, for it would mean that everyone has a natural right to act according to the logic of one's compatriots (Shue), which makes it effectively impossible to have a "politics" of human rights in any real sense of the term "politics" (that is, where the refugee is as political as the citizen). There is no doubt that Arendt's theory of a right to have rights connects law to the division of territory, as in the archaic sense of *nomos*. But such a division of space cannot be the one that Lindahl associates with Ulpian's maxim of "giving to each their own" (Lindahl 2008, passim). Rather, one would have to understand the Kantian interpretation of the maxim that lies behind Kantian cosmopolitanism, as opposed to the Hobbesian interpretation of the same (to which Lindahl refers), which lies behind the Schmittian critique of cosmopolitanism.

Arendt's expression "law of the earth" clearly refers to Kant's reflections on cosmopolitan law (the law that determines every individual has a right to demand hospitality everywhere in the world, but neither naturalization nor conquest) and its deduction from the contingent distribution of people on a finite, spherical surface like Earth. Benhabib tries to resolve—in principle—the problem posed by refugees by arguing that cosmopolitan right gives all refugees the right to be declined hospitality by a given nation-state only if they can be provided with a "reasonable" justification, a justification that must be given in the terms that the refugee can understand and come to agree with. Interestingly, neither in her nor in Forst's formulation does the right to justification have a logical, internal relation to the fact that human beings inhabit the Earth. It seems to me, on the contrary, that Kant and Arendt both have good reasons for connecting the right to have rights (as a right to constitute a public space) to the concept of the Earth, and to the problem of its partition.

Let me return for a moment to Schmitt's claim that the original sense of law as *nomos* derives from *nemein*, the grabbing and delimiting of territory or land. In *Capital*, Marx argued, before Schmitt, that capitalist primitive accumulation requires the fencing off of the commons.[27] Foucault also describes the constituents of biopolitics through his analysis of pastoral power, whose central categories are again tied to the delimitation of territory on earth: "security, territory, population." What all three—Marx, Schmitt, and Foucault—are pointing to is that a basic source of normative power comes from the original partition or distribution of land. As it turns out, this insight actually lies at the heart of republican thought. Machiavelli tied the fate of republican freedom to the struggles for "agrarian laws" that redistribute the original division of lands; picking up on this point, Harrington argued that legislative power belongs to those who have a more or less equal share of the land, and in so doing, he was consciously going against Hobbes's idea that, in the state of nature, no such appropriation and distribution of land was possible because no sovereignty existed to protect property.[28] But does this mean that Harrington was the founding father of the "republic of property," as Negri and Hardt claim?

Of course, I do not wish to deny that in the Schmittian sense of *nomos*, the partition of land (for example, the closing off of the commons) functions as a biopolitical source of normativity that subsumes the foreignness of natality under the sameness of nationality. It is only because one is born in a specific territory, because one is residing in a specific territory or, lastly, because one has a specific descent (that is itself tied to a territory), that natality is related to and subsumed under nationality. The juris-generative properties of territoriality are thus ultimately responsible for the synthesis between natality and nationality that leaves the refugee problem unresolvable within the framework of the nation-state.

But a more important insight is that the juris-generative character of space need not take the form of territoriality and nationality. In fact, I would argue, it does not take this form in the revolutionary tradition of republicanism to which Arendt belongs, and in the name of which she proposes the idea of a right to have rights. Instead, the challenge for Arendt is to define a *space* for the sharing of opinion that carries no reference to the *demarcation of territory*. Thus, the law or *nomos* that is linked to the "right to have rights" cannot be the law or *nomos* of a polity, not even of a Derridean "city of refuge," because the walls of the city, of every city, demarcate insiders from outsiders, haves from have-nots, and so on.[29] The "new law of the earth" must be a *nomadic* law or *nomos*. I speak of "nomadic" law precisely because Arendt consistently links natality to the condition of being born into "a desert."[30]

But how can natality give rise to a common space without territory? I believe that the idea of a common space of opinion in Arendt must logically be linked to the idea of a *place in which one can exchange places and, from this exchange of places, generate different opinions*—the very difference of opinion to which all human beings have a right by virtue of natality. In other words, while nationality ties birth to a single place surrounded by the walls of positive law, natality always occurs outside these walls: the right to a free opinion is necessarily the right to move beyond the walls of the polity and exchange places with those who are outside its walls. In fact, the very concept of natality entails the idea of taking the place of another: in being born, one stranger takes the place of another stranger. There is something about infants that makes them infinitely exchangeable and, for that reason, adults are infinitely hospitable towards them. It is false to say that one is born into a "family." Phenomenologically, the opposite is the case: the "family" constitutes and reconstitutes itself every time around the hospitality extended towards a perfect stranger who is, by definition, entirely exchangeable for another infant. A "family" would not be such if it were a community that could refuse to accept "whoever" and "whatever" comes out of the womb and onto the face of the earth.

Similarly, as Kant shows in his deduction of private right in the *Metaphysics of Morals*, the space occupied by a thing excludes the possibility of it being occupied by another thing, and that is why each thing must be capable of belonging to someone rather than to someone else or to everyone. But in the case of a space of distinction or opinion, the space becomes "political" not when my occupation of it excludes another (as in private property), but rather when it is constituted by an *exchanging of places* with any other. This is the reason why republicanism is misconstrued as a "republic of property." In reality, as Spinoza, Kant, and Arendt show, the only consistent republicanism is a republicanism of opinion and judgment which opens up the *nomos* based on appropriation and division of land.[31]

This internal connection between natality (as a biopolitical right to free opinion) and the original exchange of place with others, once and for all severs the seemingly "natural" connection between juris-generative power and place of birth (*nascio-/natio/territory*) that leads to the false resolution of the problem of the refugee by prioritizing nationality and naturalization. As I mentioned at the beginning of this chapter and again in relation to Arendt's republicanism, cosmopolitanism need not be construed in such a way as to deny priority to peoples. Arendt connects power (and thus opinion) to peoples, but she distinguishes peoples from both from populations and nations. The difference between a people and a population or nation is that the latter are always linked to an enclosed territory: populations are driven over territories, like herds drawn from one enclosure to another; nations grow out of territories, like the vegetation. Both give rise to images of political government drawn from husbandry and farming. By way of contrast, peoples, at least in the Roman and Jewish republican traditions, are defined by two traits. First, in these traditions a people is a function of the consent to equal law, which presupposes the natural right of opinion or judgment (and both the Roman and Jewish peoples famously reject several law tables handed down to them). Second, the consent to a common and equal law is dependent on the *political space* that generated the equal law. This space, as Rancière has pointed out, is the place in which a profound division between the space of a constituted "people" and the space of a constituent "plebs" comes to light. The "plebs" here refer to those individuals who have no "title to govern" (Rancière 2009), those whom I have been calling "refugees" in this chapter.[32] The republican definition of a people, then, is the following: a law is only "equal" (and can therefore be consented to by a people) when it emerges out of the dissenting opinion of the plebs, or out of the juris-generative right to opinion of the refugees.

The distinction between citizen (or compatriot) and refugee in human rights discourse is structurally identical to the distinction between a people and a plebs in revolutionary republicanism. The right to have rights is the right to live under laws that have been formed in a space where the place of the people and the plebs, or the citizens and the refugees, are exchanged. One can rethink the connection between natality and the right to have positive rights in terms of Kant's idea of an innate right to "external" freedom (or, in Arendt's terms, a space where one's opinion matters to others), so long as one does not take the expression "external" to mean the spatial territory demarcated by a nation. Kant is able to connect his idea of an innate right to external freedom with his idea of cosmopolitanism precisely because he denies that "externality" (that is, belonging to the earth) refers to territoriality. For Kant, one does not have, by birth (*nascio-*), a right to a national territory (*natio-*). Instead, the "space" or exteriority to which human biological life has an innate right is the space of exteriority to government, the space of the absence of state or rule (*an-archy*). This space is not a Hobbesian state of nature but is rather that place occupied by the plebs or refugees and endowed with a constituent power of opinion or judgment. Only if the citizens, included in the positive *nomos* of their polity, exchange places with the refugees in this space of exteriority, can their government count as legitimate. The space of statelessness must not only be understood as a state of lack: it is rather that condition which enables the constituent power of a people.

The cosmopolitan moment of a republican conception of the people, then, is expressed by the idea that a people—unlike a population or a nation—always becomes such *from the outside in*. This is not a process of the assimilation of "foreigners" by "natives," or a process of naturalization.[33] In fact, it is nearly the opposite: it is a paradoxical "incorporation" of the "native" by the "foreigner," which amounts to a process of the de-territorialization of the native from her place of birth and reterritorialization into a space of common opinion. Clearly, this exchange of places between the native and the foreigner could never have a juris-generative effect if these "stateless" strangers were not already innate holders of natural rights. It would therefore be mistaken to believe that, under republicanism, inclusion into a previously constituted community gives strangers their rights: on the contrary, only because they already have, by nature (by the law of natality), this right to constitute a space of common opinion, is it possible for them to repartition every territory and every *nomos*. This gives rise to a people that is irreducible to a tribe or nation and that henceforth governs itself only by consenting (giving opinion) to its laws. Republican citizenship, on this model, is never a status that is assigned from "inside" a territory or of a state—in this it is strictly opposed to "nationality" and nationalism—but it always advenes to those inside by contagion and incorporation from those who live outside of the *nomos*. Ultimately, only the *foedera* or relations established between natives and strangers (or refugees) can turn both into "citizens": prior to the exchange of places between natives and strangers, natives remain merely subjects of their territorial *nomos*, rather than a free collectivity that is governed by laws of its own choice.

The refugee is always already in the right because he or she is born-into-right. There exists no justification that a nation-state could give that would be "reasonable" for the refugee to accept. There is no possible justification for excluding the justified because it is only they (the refugees qua the justified) that make possible the giving of justifications to those inside a territory and, in so doing, give them access to the status of "citizen" once again and yet for the first time. Citizenship and peoplehood always come to a given territory from outside that territory, from nomads and refugees. The real lesson withheld by Arendt's concept of a "right to have rights" is that it is impossible, on juridical grounds, to separate cosmopolitanism from republicanism.

PART IV

Biopolitics of Eternal Life

8

BARE LIFE AND PHILOSOPHICAL LIFE IN ARISTOTLE, SPINOZA, AND HEIDEGGER

CONTEMPLATIVE LIFE AND BIOPOLITICS

Foucault introduced the concept of biopower in order to explain how something like "thanatopolitics," the mobilization of entire populations "for the purpose of wholesale slaughter in the name of life necessity," became the norm in the twentieth century (Foucault 1990, 137). Agamben and Esposito have since offered two paradigms that seek to explain the seemingly inevitable transition from a biopolitics to a thanatopolitics. Yet Foucault had reservations about whether thanatopolitics could really be understood solely from a consideration of the idea of biopower. Indeed, he had recourse to the paradigm of sovereignty (and its sacrificial logic of "blood") to account for the constitution of modern racism and genocidal eugenics. Agamben closed the circle by hypothesizing that biopower is, in reality, a power over bare life that has its origin not in life itself, but in the sovereignty of law.[1] Esposito, for his part, has argued that the distinctive operation of Nazi thanatopolitics consisted of identifying a "lifeless existence," *Dasein ohne Leben*, a form of life (a *bios*) that was entirely lacking in "spirit" and which, as a consequence, was reduced to mere "biological" life (*zoe*) and could be exterminated as a "life not worthy of being lived" (Esposito 2008, 134). In both Agamben and Esposito, therefore, the source of the power over life comes from outside of life (*zoe*) itself. It is as if there is something irreducibly affirmative about the concept of the power of life, of "biopower," that never lets itself be placed at the service of the power over life, which is also a power of death ("thanatopolitics").

If biopolitics can be transformed into thanatopolitics, this may be because the life that is here produced, namely, a *zoe* that is entirely separate from a *bios*, is a life that is destined to die: it has death inscribed on it from the very beginning. Stated positively, this chapter pursues the hypothesis that an affirmative conception of the power of life requires thinking about material life as eternal: as a *zoe aionios* that is not destined to die, but rather stands over mythical fate itself. Esposito suggests that the power of life must be interpreted "philosophically" if it is to escape thanatopolitics (Esposito 2008, 150). I understand this claim in the following sense: philosophy becomes truly political when it provides a conception of life (*zoe*) that is immediately theoretical or contemplative. Philosophy becomes political where biology becomes philosophical. Philosophy here is to be understood in the traditional sense of contemplating what is most real or actual, what never perishes, what is eternal. Thus, by the expression "eternal life" I refer to a conception of a contemplative *zoe* that is at once a political life.

Eternal life is a theme that traverses both Western philosophical and religious traditions. This chapter focuses on two fundamental philosophical conceptions of eternal life, those found in Aristotle and Spinoza. Both thinkers are well known for relativizing the distinction between good and evil to the human domain, placing God and life, and therefore the philosophical life (which is directed to the knowledge of both), above morality. Both Spinoza and Aristotle see, in the idea of eternal life, an aporia. Eternal life corresponds to the life of the mind, or the contemplative life. Yet herein lies a contradiction. The human being is capable of this form of life because, like God, she is endowed with reason: at the same time, the human is incapable of sustaining this form of life because, unlike God, she is endowed with a body or, better, with a *zoe*. Any attempt to think about eternal life needs to contend with this aporia. In order to account for this aporia, philosophy as a form of life must give up the "ascetic ideal" which understands the body and sentient, biological life (*zoe*) as its "tomb" and, instead, consider how it is that the body and sentient life also philosophize.

The path that I pursue in this chapter may appear somewhat circuitous because, at various points, I discuss Heidegger's early philosophy at some length. It has become a commonplace to oppose Spinoza with Heidegger, if only because of the apparent absence of any treatment of the Marrano philosopher by Heidegger himself.[2] Nothing would seem to be more opposed to Spinoza's philosophy of life and joy than Heidegger's "humanistic" defense of the distinction between life and existence, and between animal and human life, which rests on the assumption that only human beings are conscious of the fact that they will die and that death is their most imminent possibility. For Heidegger, to exist is to care about how one is going to live, and such care makes sense only when it is understood that death is always on the horizon. Thus it appears Heidegger's thesis is that a "true life" is a life that affirms its being-toward-death; it is a life that is not lived carelessly, but resolutely. Existing is caring about one's life, not by preserving life, but rather by giving life a kind of meaning that it cannot obtain from within.[3] For that reason, animal life is said by Heidegger to be "poor in world," where world refers to a web of meanings in which *Dasein* exists. Yet I suggest that each of the contemporary thinkers who has dealt with the notion of eternal life and its internal relation to power (from Jonas, through Derrida and Deleuze, to Negri and Agamben), has tried to bring Heidegger and Spinoza together.

SPINOZA, DIVINE PROVIDENCE, AND ETERNAL LIFE

If Heidegger appears keen to separate animal life from human existence, *zoe* from *bios*, Spinoza appears set on reconceiving human *bios* from the naturalistic perspective offered by the idea of conatus, or the effort that all things make in order to persevere in their being, that is, in terms of *zoe*. Perhaps more than any other Spinoza interpreter, Zac has insisted that one of the keys to understanding Spinoza's philosophy is to see that, for him, life is essentially eternal and only secondarily temporal: "According to Spinoza, salvation is eternal existence, on the condition that one disassociate the word 'eternity' from the idea of a future existence in another world ... the principle of eternalization is found in the way in which we exist or more precisely in our 'act of existing'" (Zac 1979, 11, translation mine). The thesis Zac defends, which I believe to be entirely correct, is as follows: if all things are in God, if there is no transcendence in Spinoza's system, if God and all other things share a univocity of being,[4] then these things must be as eternal as their immanent cause. Yet only God is the cause of itself (*causa sui*), so that its essence (what it is: cause) is at the same time its existence (how it is: of itself). All other things have an essence that does not coincide with their existence: how each thing is depends not only on what it is, but also on what other things do to it, and what it does to other things. The problem posed by the eternity of things is this: How can a being whose existence is not infinite also be infinite?[5] Zac's solution is to say that one has to distinguish two senses of existence for finite things: an abstract sense of existence (where each thing depends on something else) and the "very nature of existence" where each thing depends only on the force through which it perseveres in being. As Spinoza says:

> Here by existence I do not mean duration, that is, existence insofar as it is considered in the abstract as a kind of quantity. I am speaking of the very nature of existence, which is attributed to particular things because they follow in infinite numbers in infinite ways from the eternal necessity of God's nature. I am speaking, I repeat, of the very existence of particular things insofar as they are in God. For although each particular thing is determined by another particular thing to exist in a certain manner, the force by which each perseveres in existing follows from the eternal necessity of God's nature. (*Ethics* II,47, scholium)[6]

This force is later designated as "life" (*vita*), and the thesis is that the life of each thing is the *immanent* cause of each thing, that is, life is that whereby each thing remains *within* God, and, likewise, nothing that God causes stands apart from God (this is how Spinoza explains how God is both the cause of itself and the cause of the other without contradiction: what takes away the contradiction is life itself as conatus).[7]

In his *Metaphysical Thoughts* appended to the *Principles of Cartesian Philosophy*, in a chapter dedicated to "the Life of God," Spinoza discusses the meaning of life in Aristotle as "the continuance of the nutritive soul, accompanied by heat" (found in *De respiratione* 474a25, but also *De anima* 415a23–24), only to reject the division of the soul into three kinds (vegetative, sensitive, intellective). He then refers to Aristotle's definition of life "as the operation of the intellect" in *Metaphysics* XII, 7 (1072b27–29), only to question why God's life should be reduced only to the activity of the intellect as opposed to the will. These objections to the Aristotelian conception of life in reality aim at making it possible to attribute life to all things because all things are in God and God is (eternal) life. "Therefore by life we for our part understand the force through which things persevere in their own being. And because that force is different from the things themselves, we quite properly say that things themselves have life. But the force whereby God perseveres in his own being is nothing but his essence, so that those speak best who call God 'life'" (*Metaphysical Thoughts*, chap. 6).

Zac argues that what, in this early work, Spinoza calls *vita Dei* becomes the concept of *potentia Dei* in the *Ethics* (Zac 1979, 13ff). From the perspective of God as absolute substance or immanence, life is power and power is life: this is the "plane" of affirmative biopower as the eternalization of life. The difference between the life of God and the life of things mentioned in the above passage is not a difference in the kind of life, but in its mode of being: "Life is the force that makes things persevere in their being. God is living and all things are living. But while things have life, God is life" (Zac 1979, 14). That beings persevere in their lives is the expression of God's life: this is the doing of God as *essentia actuosa*. But while they persevere in their lives, things will also overpower and be overpowered by other things, and all will eventually encounter something that occasions their destruction (*Ethics* IV, 3–5).

In the *Short Treatise on God, Man, and His Well-Being*, Spinoza defines the second true attribute of God (the first attribute is being the first and immanent cause of everything else) as consisting of "his Providence, which to us is nothing else than the striving which we find in the whole of Nature and in individual things to maintain and preserve their own existence" (*Short Treatise*, chap. 5). I shall therefore call Spinoza's account of life "providential" insofar as the struggle to keep alive that characterizes the duration of every being rests on something other than itself, namely, on the eternal life that perseveres in it and through which it receives what it struggles to preserve. In this context, Spinoza distinguishes between a general and a particular providence: the former is "that through which all things are produced and sustained insofar as they are parts of the whole of Nature"; the latter "is the striving of each thing separately to preserve its existence" (*Short Treatise*, chap. 5). Thus, each thing can be understood either according to general or particular providence.

Spinoza gives the example of organs: as parts of a whole (a living thing) each organ is "provided for, cared for," but considered by itself (as being itself a whole), each organ strives to "preserve and maintain its own well-being" (*Short Treatise*, chap. 5) and can therefore enter into conflict with other organs, thus eventually leading to the death of the entire body. God or life is providential in a general sense insofar as it grants every essence a conatus (that is, insofar as its nature is such that it has the power to preserve its life). God does not show a particular providence in the sense of favoring one aspect of nature over another, in their inevitable struggle. Nevertheless, Spinoza argues that there is a sense in which God can also be a particular providence: "God is the cause of, and providence over, particular things only. If particular things had to conform to some other Nature, then they could not conform to their own, and consequently could not be what they truly are" (*Short Treatise*, chap. 6). In other words, all things will do everything they are capable of in order to preserve their conatus. Virtue is to do what one must in order to preserve and maintain one's power, or to perpetuate the life that perseveres in and through one's own actions. "The more man endeavors and is able to seek his own advantage, that is, to preserve his own being, the more he is endowed with virtue. By contrast, insofar as he neglects to preserve what is to his advantage, that is, his own being, to that extent he is weak" (*Ethics* IV, 20). God's particular providence is to favor the virtuous (as opposed to the weak), that is, God favors those beings that cultivate their power or capacity.[8] Here "virtue" defines that form of life, that *bios*, of a life (*zoe*) that is divine and eternal. Spinoza's "ethics" is entirely dedicated to the proposition that life (*zoe*) does not persevere because it receives a form, a determination by the activity of its faculties (*bios*), but, on the contrary, its form or determination serves to maintain a life (*zoe*) that perseveres in an absolute fashion, that is, without end or limit.

The dependence of each being on God is nothing other than the conatus of each being (Zac 1979, 18). As a force or power of life in each being, the conatus links that being to God and makes it infinite because it was caused by God who is infinite, but the force that each being is given is not infinite because God gives conatus equally to all beings, who express the life of God in their different modes. For this reason, life in finite beings always encounters resistance from the life of other beings, to whom they are opposed. Thus, from the perspective of duration rather than eternity, all beings are in constant resistance and opposition with each other in their effort to maintain themselves in life: this effort to resist and oppose what resists it is the conatus as the *essentia actualis* of each being. Yet the life that each being wants to maintain and persevere in corresponds to conatus as the *essentia actuosa* of God (Zac 1979, 19). "Nor do things effect anything other than that which necessarily follows from their determinate nature" (*Ethics* III, 7 proof). What a being must do is live; what it can do is only what it must: namely, find a way to keep on living. The "must" here is to live or to act; the "can" corresponds to the power to act: no being can avoid expressing all its power in every one of its actions.

The conatus is the indefinite striving in life of any being, which can be put to an end only by the opposite striving of another being. In this sense, each human life is not eternal: it participates in God's life and divides itself against another participant (*Ethics* IV, 4). Yet Spinoza also claims that, in this same participation and because of it, we feel we are eternal: "The human mind cannot be absolutely destroyed along with the body, but something of it remains, which is eternal" (*Ethics* V, 23). Spinoza defines the human mind as the idea of the body (*Ethics* II, 13). It would seem, therefore, that with the destruction of the body, its idea or mind would also be destroyed. But this is so only when considering beings in their relation to other beings, and not when considering a being in relation to its divine or immanent cause: in the latter case, the essence of the body is always already given as an idea in God.

> This idea, which expresses the essence of the body under a form of eternity, is a definite mode of thinking which pertains to the essence of the mind, and which is necessarily eternal. Yet it is impossible that we should remember that we existed before our body, since neither can there be any traces of this in the body nor can eternity be defined by time, or be in any way related to time. Nevertheless, *we feel and experience that we are eternal*. For the mind senses those things that it conceives by its understanding just as much as those which it has in its memory. Logical proofs are the eyes of the mind, whereby it sees and observes things. So although we have no recollection of having existed before the body, we nevertheless sense that our mind, insofar as it involves the essence of the body under a form of eternity, is eternal, and that this aspect of its existence cannot be defined by time, that is, cannot be explicated through duration. (*Ethics* V, 23, scholium, emphasis mine)

There are two important elements in this conception of the eternity of the life of the mind: as the idea of the body, the mind cannot "remember" its existence prior to its life, and yet it "feels" or "senses" that it existed "before" its allotted time; it "feels" and "experiences" itself to be eternal. I take Spinoza's use of the term "feeling" and "experience" here to be significant: it refers to the conatus particular to the mind that invests it prior to any conception it may form and, thus, prior to any "subjectivity" or "self-consciousness." This feeling of the mind for a life that is "earlier" than any duration, this experience of an a priori knowledge of God, is the basis for Spinoza's claim that such knowledge of God is an "intellectual love of God" (*Ethics* V, 32, corollary).

Moreover, it is from this understanding that Spinoza derives the belief that "salvation or blessedness or freedom consists in the constant and eternal love toward God, that is, in God's love toward men. This love or blessedness is called glory in the Holy Scriptures, and rightly so" (*Ethics* V, 35 scholium). Again, Spinoza's conception of eternal life is offered within an account of divine providence: God loves those who love God intellectually, that is, those who know God in the form of eternity. These are people whose life is simultaneously philosophical and political, since the biblical idea of glory (*kabod*) refers both to the presence of God as King of the world and to God's glorification by his people.[9] But, given that Spinoza decidedly rejects the understanding of God as a sovereign who gives laws to his subjects (*Theological-Political Treatise*, chap. 4), the glorification of God which is carried out through the eternal life of contemplation cannot be "political" in the traditional sense of being associated with either the coercive or the spiritual government of a sovereign or a church. What is the inner connection between the life of the mind's capacity to "feel" its eternity and the political meaning of the contemplative life? In order to attempt to answer this question, it is necessary to take a detour through Heidegger's "existentialist" conception of life.

HEIDEGGER AND THE DECONSTRUCTION OF EXISTENTIAL LIFE

Heidegger's doctrine of being-toward-death appears to pose the ultimate challenge to any conception of eternal life. Despite appearances, Heidegger's approach to the conception of biological life offers pathways that lead back to a Spinozist conception of eternal life. This is central to the later development of the thought of Derrida, Deleuze, and Agamben with regard to the possibility of an affirmative biopolitics. The path that leads from Heidegger back to Spinoza was tentatively frayed by a group of French phenomenologists who were influenced by Merleau-Ponty's and Henry's accounts of the "flesh" as the proper locus of intentionality, that is, of a disclosure of the truth of beings. One of the clearest examples of this tendency is found in an essay by Franck that discusses Heidegger's account of the animal in *The Fundamental Concepts of Metaphysics* (Franck 1991) and that anticipates Agamben's later reading of this text.

Heidegger begins his analysis of life (*zoe*) by distinguishing the instrument from the organ (Heidegger 1995, sect. 52): whereas the instrument is "ready for something," the organ is "capable of something." But, additionally, he argues that it is incorrect to say that the eye is capable of seeing; rather, one should say that the organism is capable of seeing through the eye (Franck 1991, 138). Heidegger illustrates how the organism as a whole, and not the single organ, is capable or powerful by giving the example of protoplasmic creatures who make their own organs to fulfill particular needs, only to destroy them once those needs have been satisfied (Heidegger 1995, sect. 53).[10] That the organ is at the service of the organism betrays another fact, according to Heidegger: namely, that the organism is characterized by wanting to actualize its capacity to see through the organ. There is an organ, and so a capacity, because the organism is characterized by a drive (*Trieb*). "Something which is capable ... is intrinsically regulative and regulates itself. In a certain sense it drives itself towards its own capability for.... Capacity is only to be found where there is drive" (Heidegger 1995, sect. 54, 228). As Franck formulates Heidegger's point: "Being-capable-of ... is to be self-driven toward that of which the capacity is capable: toward itself. Capacity therefore implies a relationship to self that one finds in the concepts of self-regulation and self-preservation by which the organism is customarily defined" (Franck 1991, 140). What I wish to highlight here is the relation between drive and capacity: the living being wants to see, and therefore employs its organ of sight; the living being wants to prolong its existence, and therefore goes in search of food. Heidegger speaks of the capacity that characterizes life as a property (*Eigentum*): "In this instinctual 'toward' the capacity as such becomes and remains proper to itself (*sich zu eigen*)—and does so without any so-called self-consciousness or any reflection at all, without any relating back to itself.... The way and manner in which the animal is proper to itself is not that of personality, not reflection or consciousness, but simply its proper being (*Eigentum*). Proper peculiarity (*Eigen-tümlichkeit*) is a fundamental character of every capacity. This peculiarity belongs to itself and is absorbed by itself (*eingenommen*)" (Heidegger 1995, sect. 56, 233). Once one reaches the component of the drive, Heidegger believes he has found the logic of animal "behavior" (as opposed to human action). The drive, which turns life into property, is necessarily what can be captivated by something outside it, by what surrounds it. The surrounding corresponds to what disinhibits the animal's drives and, therefore, allows for the perseverance in being of the living being (Heidegger 1995, sect. 58–61).

Here there is an important distinction with regard to the conatus in Spinoza: the living being is dependent on its "disinhibiting ring" (Heidegger 1995, sect. 60, 255) as a condition for depending on itself by satisfying its wants through its capacities. "It is only if this prior relatedness of what can be stimulated to that which can stimulate it already possesses the character of an instinctual drive which instinctually encounters (*triebhaften Entgegen*) the stimulus, that anything like the eliciting of a stimulus is possible in general" (Heidegger 1995, sect. 60, 256). Heidegger concludes that the unity of the living body is given by the unity of the ring of captivation: "We must say that life *is* nothing but the animal's encircling itself and struggling (*Ringen*) with its encircling ring, a ring by way of which the animal is absorbed without its ever being with itself (*bei sich selbst*) in the proper sense" (Heidegger 1995, sect. 61, 257). One could say that the living being, for Heidegger, "feels" itself alive only in its interaction with its surroundings and not, as Spinoza claims, through the relation between its nature and God.

Franck's interpretation suggests that, on the basis of Heidegger's analysis of the concept of animal life, *Dasein*'s own animal life is more essential than its existence (Franck 1991, 144). Franck's thesis is that precisely where *Dasein*'s existence is meant to transcend its animal life, namely, in the experience of anxiety, Heidegger recognizes anxiety's physiological conditions, and this betrays the fact that *Dasein*'s "truth of its existence" depends on being "firstly a living driven being [*un étant pulsionnel vivant*] whose meaning is neither ecstatical nor categorical" (Franck 1991, 145). The argument is that if there were no drive to keep alive, it would be impossible for *Dasein* to experience anxiety; at the same time, this drive can only lead to the condition of existence (to anxiety or being-toward-death) because there also exists a "death drive." Franck then concludes that "resoluteness being motivated by the drive, we must stop understanding ourselves as *Dasein* and temporality and think ourselves as living, driven flesh [*chair pulsionelle vivant*]" (Franck 1991, 145). Since to be in the mode of *Dasein* means to live by effecting the ontological difference between beings and Being, or, to temporalize temporality, Franck suggests that thinking of ourselves as "living, driven flesh" requires accepting that "life is incarnate without either Being or time." Franck does not himself associate this idea to the essence of the living being as its immanent causality, but, like in Spinoza, Franck also holds that life is "incarnate" to the extent that it escapes duration and is thus a form of eternal life.

Before Derrida embarked on his last works on animality, he had already attempted to subvert Heidegger's priority of existence over life by way of a deconstruction of being-toward-death. Derrida questions Heidegger's famous distinction between *verenden* (perishing) and *eigentlich sterben* (dying), according to which animals are incapable of dying (Derrida 1993, 30). "Life as such does not know death as such" (Derrida 1993, 37). This feature of life as incapable of death can also be phrased affirmatively: life has an internal connection to its eternalization. Franck posed a similar conundrum to Heidegger's account of existence: if *Dasein* has an understanding of Being because it knows death as death, then it must lack an understanding of itself as "incarnated life." Ultimately, Franck argues that in order for *Dasein* to attain an understanding of itself as living, it would have to give up the understanding of Being that defines its very existence. For Derrida, the real reason behind *Dasein*'s grasp on its understanding of Being is as follows: just as life does not have the capacity to die, so *Dasein*'s existence can never "end" or "perish" and therefore "remains immortal in its originary being-toward-death" (Derrida 1993, 39).

The actual deconstruction of Heidegger's being-toward-death, though, passes through the category of possibility or capacity. In section 49 of *Sein und Zeit* (Heidegger 1986), Heidegger lays out the distinctions among *Verenden*, *Ableben* and *Sterben*, where the latter is within the capacity of *Dasein* alone. Dying in this sense is what places *Dasein* at the furthest remove from life, since no living organism has "produced" for itself the capacity or "organ" for dying that (according to Heidegger) *Dasein* possesses, precisely as a condition for the unity or wholeness of itself as an existing being. Death is *Dasein*'s "most proper possibility" because *Dasein* has the power to die at any moment (section 52). Only by assuming or appropriating for itself this faculty or power, does *Dasein* begin to exist "authentically." But what does it mean to press forward and realize this capacity? Heidegger argued that the living being presses on with its capacities, actualizing them within its drive to preserve itself. Clearly, for Heidegger, appropriating the capacity for dying does not mean being driven on by life, but rather somehow disconnecting oneself from this drive, or breaking with the ring of disinhibition, thereby allowing beings to stand as they are for the first time: human freedom and disclosing the world *as world* are equivalent for Heidegger. Here, learning to die is still related to philosophizing, if by this one understands a disclosive engagement with the world.

But this is not the direction of Heidegger's thought which Derrida exploits for his deconstruction of death. Instead, Derrida centers his argument on the second sense Heidegger gives to the capacity for dying: "Death is also for Dasein, Heidegger ultimately says, the possibility of an impossibility" (Derrida 1993, 68), referring to the claim that death is *die Möglichkeit als die der Unmöglichkeit des Existenz überhaupt* (Heidegger 1986, sect. 53, 262). Thus, the capacity for dying is a capacity for the impossible, in the sense that death singularizes the existence of *Dasein* to the point of being an unrepeatable, "miraculous" event (Heidegger 1986, sect. 53, 263). Can something contain the possibility of the impossible, or a power for impotence? "Heidegger does not say 'the possibility of no longer being able to be Dasein' but 'the possibility of being able no longer to be there' or 'of no longer being able to be there' [*die Möglichkeit des Nicht-mehr-dasein-können*]" (Derrida 1993, 68). Death is not the possibility that what exists--*Dasein*--will cease to exist at some point in time. Death is also not an impossibility for *Dasein*, as if it were the simple negation of possibility-for-being (*Seinkönnen*). Rather, death is an affirmative power of existence: dying is a being-able, but what it is able to do in dying is nothing, nothing actual, no action.[11] Dying is therefore not the power not to have power (for this is merely contradictory), but it is the power or ability to be nothing ("being-able-not-to-be-there"). This means that, considered as a possibility, dying gives "nothing" to *Dasein*'s capacity-to-be: dying gives *Dasein* nothing to be. What is impossible is this nothing that *Dasein* is given to be. But the phrase "it is impossible to be nothing" should be understood affirmatively. As such, in a first sense, it can mean that *Dasein* has only its Self to be; it does not have other selves or other things to be. In a second sense, death reveals that for such a Self "nothing is impossible." In both senses, death as the possibility of an impossibility is the ultimate "enabler" of existence.

Derrida, for his part, pushes the Heideggerian interpretation of dying to an extreme, at which point it turns against itself into a conception of eternal life. Derrida claims that dying, as *Dasein*'s most proper and yet most impossible possibility, may also offer it the possibility of not being in the mode of existence, or, in other words, the capacity to be-otherwise-than-existence. On this radical construal of Heidegger's doctrine of being-toward-death, which to be sure finds no explicit textual support in *Sein und Zeit*, dying would constitute the passage from existence back to life, for dying would be the possibility of "the impossibility of being dead" or the "impossibility of existing once one is dead" (Derrida 1993, 73). Dying, in other words, as an impossibility for existence, would be that threshold of existence that is closest, not furthest, from living as conatus. In Derrida, the capacity for dying denotes, so to speak, a zone of indetermination between life and death (which he associates with the strange "existence" of the *revenants*, or the ghosts of the departed who return to visit the living).

Derrida sees in Heidegger this spectral return of *Dasein* back into the plane of immanence: "The impossibility that is possible for Dasein is, indeed, that there no longer be Dasein: that precisely what is possible become impossible. . . . It is therefore the impossibility of the 'as such' that, as such, would be possible to Dasein and not to any form of entity and living thing . . . animals also die" (Derrida 1993, 75). Rather than death being the possibility that uncovers the truth of the fact that *Dasein* is "what has being as its possibility" (*Seinkönnen*), death now becomes the paradoxical possibility that reveals *Dasein* itself, as a pure existing, to be impossible or unattainable. In this extreme sense, the possibility of death undermines the distinction between living and existing, thereby granting animals the possibility of dying and simultaneously granting *Dasein* the knowledge of itself as eternal life.

FEELING OF ETERNITY

Like Derrida, Agamben has also pursued the deconstruction of Heidegger's category of possibility or capacity, but he has done so with the explicit intention of returning existence to the plane of immanence by employing Heidegger in conjunction with Deleuze (Agamben 1999b, 239). Agamben's discourse starts by situating Heidegger's analysis of capacity within the context Aristotle's *De anima* II, 5 in which he asks "why perception of the senses themselves does not occur" (Aristotle 1989, 417a1–3). Why can I see with my eyes but I cannot see my eyes? The question can also be phrased as follows: what is it that makes the organ belong to the organism rather than the other way around? Aristotle's answer, according to Agamben, is that sensing (*aisthesis*) exists as potential in the organs: until that potential is actuated upon by light, the eye is in a state of "anesthesia" (Agamben 1999b, 178).[12] It is through this example that Agamben explains how the organs are not the organism, but instead belong to it; they are a possession of the organism, and as such, they enjoy a potential life. Properly speaking, the eye does not see (because seeing is something an organism does with the eyes); the eye, in its potential or "anesthetized" state, is instead characterized by its potential to not-see. This is not an inability to see (which would make it blind), but an ability to un-see. Aristotle gives the example of darkness: when the eye is not being used for seeing, it is not blind, but it "distinguishes" darkness, or the absence of light (Agamben 1999b, 181). More precisely, one cannot actually see darkness, for there is no light through which to see. This is why Aristotle speaks about the potential to see in terms of "feeling": "We feel ourselves seeing." This distinction between feeling and sensing is crucial because it suggests that, by fulfilling their functions, organs are doing nothing other than feeling for themselves. Potential life, the state of suspended animation or "anesthesia," entails an absence of sensing but the presence of a more fundamental experience of feeling.

My claim is that this presentient self-feeling corresponds to the drive-condition of all capacity theorized by Heidegger, except that Heidegger's notion of excitability leaves no room for the self-reflexivity present in the dimension of feeling. In other words, the dimension of feeling is already a dimension of what phenomenologists call "intentionality," but without reference to any apperception or transcendental self-consciousness. The "intentionality" of feeling lies at the center of what Brague calls the conception of "fleshliness" that characterizes the medieval appropriation of Aristotle's conception of life. In this conception, flesh is what links together the ontological extremes of a life that is prerational (animals and plants) with a reason that is radically lacking body (God and angelic essences).

Brague shows that the medieval account of flesh makes use of Aristotle's general claim that all knowledge is grounded in perception and "every perception occurs through touch" (*De anima* II, 13 435a18ff; Brague 1996, 236). The medium of touch is flesh. This claim, though, occasioned a debate within medieval philosophy as to whether the flesh is also the organ of touch, apart from being the medium of touch (in this last case, the organ of touch would then be the heart). The problem is that the flesh functions as a medium to perceive, for example, hot or cold, but it also has the capacity to become hot or cold itself. Flesh thus appears to be an organ of perception and not just a medium of sensation. Brague resolves this dilemma by claiming that "flesh is in contact with itself before it can perceive" (Brague 1996, 236), in other words, the flesh as organ is in contact (is in touch) with the flesh as the medium of touching. "In touch we perceive what we touch and, at the same time, what makes us touch. We do not see our eye, hear our eardrums, or smell our nostrils: we feel our flesh. We perceive not only the fact but also what makes it possible at the same time. Therefore touch is a transcendental perception of sorts" (Brague 1996, 238). The term "transcendental" is here a synonym for the phenomenological idea of intentionality (what Heidegger calls the disclosure of a world) and, simultaneously, for what Deleuze calls the "field of immanence," which denotes the possibility of an experience of (a) life without any self-consciousness.[13]

Agamben's interpretation of the Aristotelian topos of potentiality does not exploit the above idea of feeling. However, in order to explain the idea of potentiality as the possibility or power of privation, or as a "potentiality-not-to-act," he refers to a passage of the *Metaphysics* IX, 1046a30–32 in which Aristotle says that "impotence or what is impotent is a privation contrary to this potentiality. Thus, for the same thing and according to the same relation, every potentiality is opposed by an impotentiality."[14] Agamben glosses it as follows: "*Dynamis*, potentiality, maintains itself in relation to its own privation, its own *steresis*, its own nonbeing.... To be potential means: to be one's own lack, to be in relation to one's own incapacity. Beings that exist in the mode of potentiality are capable of their own impotentiality" (Agamben 1999b, 182). Agamben's interpretation omits Aristotle's point that not all beings exist potentially. Only "corruptible" beings are things for which it is possible not to be, and only for them is it true that they have the "potential to be and not to be." That is why Aristotle concludes, "None of the things that are absolutely incorruptible is potentially in an absolute sense . . . thus they all exist in act. Neither can necessary beings exist potentially; necessary beings are first beings: in fact, if they did not exist, nothing would exist. And neither is eternal movement . . . potential. . . . That is why the sun, the stars and all the heavens are always in act" (*Metaphysics* 1050b15–25). In general, Aristotle's treatment of potentiality relativizes possibility with respect to actuality: his argument is intended to show that actuality is always anterior to possibility (*Metaphysics* 1049b20–30).

Agamben's interpretation of potentiality is a departure from Aristotle insofar as it is an attempt to understand corruptibility or mortality as a positive, even universal-ontological attribute of being that parallels and shadows the Aristotelian interpretation of being as *energeia*: to every act there corresponds a "fundamental passivity.... A passive potentiality [which] ... undergoes and suffers its nonbeing" (Agamben 1999b, 182). In reality, Agamben seems intent on giving a description of Aristotle's ontology that is as close as possible to Heidegger's doctrine of being-toward-death, understood as revealing not only *Dasein*'s most proper possibility but also the true structure of being as such (qua temporality). Not surprisingly, Agamben gives his account of potentiality the status of an "existential": "Other living beings are capable only of their specific potentiality; they can only do this or that. But human beings are the animals who are capable of their own impotentiality" (Agamben 1999b, 182). This replicates Heidegger's claim that only human beings can die, whereas all other animals merely perish.

But Agamben's construal of the idea of potentiality also has a Deleuzian side to it which reverses the "existentialist" construal of life into what I have called its "providential," Spinozist conception. The Deleuzian side comes into focus when Agamben asks whether the capacity to not-act (to which dying corresponds as the potential of in-existence), might also have a corresponding (and highly paradoxical) "action." Put in other terms, Agamben is asking whether potentiality might correspond to a virtuality (what I have been calling eternal life) that underlies every "actually" lived life (the life that one consciously lives, or one's *bios*, which occupies a certain duration of time). Agamben believes that in Aristotle's *Metaphysics* there is actually a passage that refers to this virtuality. He renders it as follows: "A thing is said to be potential if, when the act of which it is said to be potential is realized, there will be nothing impotential." This phrase is extracted from a passage that, in its entirety, runs thus: "It may be that he who has the potential to walk does not walk, and that he who is not walking have the potential to walk. A thing is potential if the act of which it is said to be capable of implies no impossibility. I give an example: if one has the potential to sit down and can sit down, once they really have to sit down they will not find it impossible to do it" (*Metaphysics* 1047a23–27). Agamben rejects the common sense interpretation of this passage, namely, that if it is not impossible for someone to do X, then it is within their potential to do X. Instead, he claims that the potentiality, which does not remain impotential when the potentiality passes into action, refers to the potential to not-act (the *adynamia*) that shadows every potential action. Thus, on his reading, every potential to do something not only entails having the potential to not do something, but, additionally, to "act" out this potential to not do the action itself. To take Aristotle's example, this would mean that if something has the potential to walk, it also has the potential not-to-walk; when the person acts by walking, the potential not-to-walk does not simply vanish without a trace. Instead, it gets translated into the act in the form of an immanent passivity or suffering from the act of walking.

Nothing that Aristotle says in the *Metaphysics* indicates this interpretation, but Agamben salvages it by referring to a passage in *De anima* where Aristotle refers to "the preservation of what is in potentiality by what is in actuality and what is similar to it" (*De anima* 417b2–16). He glosses: "We are confronted with a potentiality that conserves itself and saves itself in actuality. Here potentiality, so to speak, survives actuality and, in this way, gives itself to itself" (Agamben 1999b, 183). Agamben's point can be exemplified as follows: when I take a walk I am also actualizing the potential not to walk because, by taking a walk, I am at the same time being taken walking. In this sense, one can say that the act is taken care of; it is preserving the actor through its congenital impotence or through the congenital undoing which accompanies all our doings. Through his account of potentiality, Agamben is recovering what I have called the providential idea of life at the heart of Aristotle's conception of life, which Heidegger had rendered in existential terms.

My hypothesis that Agamben's account of potentiality construes a Spinozist Aristotle appears validated when one considers the essay dedicated to Deleuze's last published text, "Immanence: A Life . . . " (Deleuze 2001). At stake in this text, for Agamben, is the connection between the concepts of "immanence" and "a life . . . ".[15] Immanence in Deleuze refers to the Spinozist claim that God is the immanent cause of all things, so that God's being is said in the same way as the being of its modes. Deleuze understands immanent cause in opposition to emanation: the things that are caused by God do not flow from God but "immanate" in him. The central problem for both Deleuze and Agamben is to understand what it means for each and every being to remain within God without being God: how to eternalize one's life without being immortal.

In "Immanence: A Life..." Deleuze illustrates this mortal yet eternal life, this virtual life, by referring to a description found in a novel by Dickens in which a character oscillates "between his life and his death" such that his individual life or *bios* "gives way to an impersonal yet singular life, a life that gives rise to a pure event, freed from the accidents of internal and external life, that is, of the subjectivity and objectivity of what happens. 'Homo tantum' for whom everyone feels and who attains a kind of beatitude" (cited in Agamben 1999b, 229).[16] The "spark of life" that flickers in between life and death is described by Dickens as "instinctively unwilling to be restored to the consciousness of this existence, and would be left dormant... if [it] could." Thus, the immanent life in question, the life or *zoe* Deleuze understands as not-yet incarnated in any individual *bios*, approximates the state of presentient feeling or animated suspension I thematized in the previous section. Dickens's citation also makes it clear that immanent life contains a kind of resistance to consciousness and to existence; in this sense, it approximates that life or *zoe* that is disclosed by dying, understood as the possibility of the impossibility of existence, as a life that flows through *Dasein* without ever finding its unity of purpose in the Self.

Agamben now calls this virtual life "bare biological life" and attempts to give an analysis of it by turning, once again, to Aristotle: this time, to his discussion of the vegetative or nutritive soul in *De anima* II, 2. Generally speaking, Agamben's aim is to construe this immanent, virtual life in terms of an indistinction between "biological life and contemplative life and between bare life and the life of the mind. *Theoria* and the contemplative life ... will have to be dislocated into a new plane of immanence" (Agamben 1999b, 239). The important question in this context is why Agamben, following Deleuze, identifies the point at which biological life touches and fuses into contemplative life in the phenomenon of metabolism and nutrition, rather than in the phenomenon of perception (corresponding to animal life). My hypothesis is that metabolism and contemplation, which are presumed to be entirely opposed capacities, in fact coincide one with one another because they both reflect the dependence of mortal life on God's life, on the basis of which an eternal life is conceivable. Thinking about life from the perspective that metabolism is the fundamental phenomenon of life is the essential feature of what I have been calling the providential conception of life.

At first blush, Aristotle's discussion of the nutritive or vegetative soul as "the first principle [through which] living things have life" (*De anima* 413b1) does not seem conducive to connecting presentient life with contemplation.[17] This is because, for Aristotle, there is a clear separation between the "nutritive life" of plants and the "desiring" life of animals. While animals "have sense-perception" and locomotion, plants lack both of these. As Aristotle writes, "First of all in perception all animals have touch. Just as the nutritive faculty can exist apart from touch and from all sense-perception, so touch can exist apart from the other senses" (*De anima* 413b3–6). Cooper has remarked that in Aristotle's biological treatises he appears anxious to preserve the clear demarcations between the three kinds of souls despite the fact that, as I have shown in the case of touch, the immanent character of life undermines these degrees of internal transcendence (Cooper 2002, 85). As Spinoza said in his *Short Treatise*, if one understands God as life, then it is no longer possible to hold onto the division between kinds of souls, including the division between organic and inorganic matter. Agamben also points out that Deleuze's immanent life "marks the radical impossibility of establishing hierarchies and separations" (Agamben 1999b, 233).

Nonetheless, choosing metabolism or nutritive life as the domain within which to think eternal life acquires some plausibility once it is recognized that, for Aristotle, the nutritive soul is characterized by two functions, nourishment and reproduction, "for it is the most natural function in living things . . . to produce another thing like themselves—an animal to produce an animal, a plant a plant—in order that *they may partake of the everlasting and divine in so far as they can*; for all desire that, and for the sake of that they do whatever they do in accordance with nature" (*De anima* 415a27–415b1, emphasis mine). Thus, nutritive life becomes "eternal" in and through its capacity to reproduce the being of the species that, for Aristotle, is an eternal thing, since only the individuals of a species, and not the species itself, can come into being and disappear from being. Metabolism and reproduction reflect the basic fact that life, all life—even plant life, which is otherwise deprived of desire—is a function of the desire to imitate the life or being of God. Spinoza, for one, argues that all desire, when properly understood, that is, when it is articulated by adequate ideas, is an intellectual love of God.

The crucial question becomes: What is the structure of metabolism or nutritive life such that it makes possible an immanent, bare life which undermines the distinction between life and existence, *zoe* and *bios*, instead offering up a life *sub species aeternitatis*, or an eternal life? Agamben takes up Deleuze's claim that immanent life is "pure contemplation without knowledge" (Agamben 1999b, 233). When Deleuze penned this expression he was surely aware that Aristotle argues in *Nicomachean Ethics* X, 8 that the life of contemplation is a divine and blessed life. Thus, the idea of a "contemplation without knowledge," that is, a contemplation that takes place at the level of presentient, presubjective life, may itself be a conjunction of Aristotelian motifs passed through the filter of Spinozist metaphysics: since immanent life is the life of the one and only immanent being, God, and since the divine life is a contemplative life, as Aristotle argues, then it follows that immanent life, *zoe*, must also be a life of contemplation (a *bios theoretikos*). Agamben's own interpretation of Deleuze, somewhat surprisingly, does not follow this reasoning. Instead, he takes up Deleuze's claim that sensation and habit are both examples of a "contemplation without knowledge" because they are both examples of a "force that preserves without acting." In other words, sensation (or feeling) and habit manifest that affirmative capacity not-to-act that "preserves" or "saves" all of human action, which Agamben already analyzed in his discourse on the category of potentiality. But at this point one still does not know why the force or potentiality that "saves" human life while "preserving" it alive is contained in the phenomenon of metabolism, or how the true nature of metabolism is defined.

GLORY, OR THE METABOLISM OF GOD

The project of turning Aristotelian "contemplative life" into Spinozist "living contemplation" (Agamben 1999b, 234) boils down to understanding the relation between metabolism, or what Aristotle calls the nutritive soul, and the conatus. According to Agamben, there is a deep analogy between the two because the nutritive soul is defined as "a potentiality such as to maintain its possessor as such" (*De anima* 416b18) and the conatus is defined as the desire of each thing to persevere in its being. Yet Aristotle's point is simply that the nutritive soul maintains its body by ingesting food, but this process does not generate the substance itself (that is, the ensouled body) because the metabolism does not generate the soul. Certainly, the link between Aristotle's metabolism and Spinoza's conatus is that both are forms of "self-preservation." However, Agamben's claim that "Deleuze (like Spinoza) brings the paradigm of the soul back to the lower schema of nutritive life" (Agamben 1999b, 236) does not seem to be correct insofar as Aristotle's schema of nutritive life is one that assumes the validity of an ensouled body as the primary substance of what is alive, where the soul is thought to have a body that it needs to preserve by the faculty of metabolism. This picture of the soul-body relation does not correspond at all with Spinoza's metaphysics, where the relation between body and mind is not one of one-sided dependence, as it is in Aristotle. Indeed, for Spinoza, the body is not dependent on the mind at all, just as the mind is not dependent on the body because both are equiprimordially caused by God. God's life, the conatus, does not move from the soul to the body by way of the metabolism, but flows equally through and the body and the mind. The difference between them is that the mind can engage in a process of metabolism with God's life, that is, it can come to know the meaning of its dependence on God's providence, which is qualitatively different from the kind of metabolism that is constitutive of the body.

The meaning of eternal life turns entirely on an adequate understanding of the essence of self-preservation or metabolism. In his essay on Deleuze, Agamben moves from Aristotle to Spinoza: he argues that metabolism in its "original meaning of *trophe* [to nourish] is 'to let a being reach the state toward which it strives' [NB: this is a citation from Benveniste, not Aristotle], 'to let be' then the potentiality that constitutes life in the original sense (self-nourishment) coincides with the very desire to persevere in one's own Being that, in Spinoza and Deleuze, defines the potentiality of life as absolute immanence" (Agamben 1999b, 237). From my perspective, the continuity that Agamben sees between Aristotelian nutritive life and Spinozist conatus is problematic because it is premised on the belief that conatus, as the desire to persevere in its being, has the structure of a Hegelian desire to desire. Only on this assumption can Agamben argue that "potentiality, insofar as it 'lacks nothing' and insofar as it is desire's self-constitution as desiring, is immediately blessed. All nourishment, all letting be, is blessed and rejoices in itself" (Agamben 1999b, 237). I take this to mean that metabolism, or the faculty of nourishment, allows a being to persevere in its state of desire; it thus "satisfies" the basic desire to keep desiring (which is how

Agamben construes the conatus), and for that reason "all nourishment is blessed." This construal of the relation among metabolism, conatus, and contemplation in Spinoza boils down to the following: to live is to want to desire, but when desire is instrumental to need, it is unfree (it is not desire for desire itself); that is why the satisfaction of appetites (self-nourishment) preserves us as desiring beings by freeing desire from need, and is thus essential for blessedness. To paraphrase Hegel: the satisfaction of material needs would already be the realization of God's Kingdom on earth.

This, however, does not seem to be the relation between self-preservation or metabolism and blessedness that Spinoza has in mind. To approximate Spinoza's thought, it may be useful to reflect on the other relation between nourishment and blessedness that is found in many, if not all cultures: the giving of thanks for the gift of food that allows each being to remain alive. Nourishment here serves to remind the living being that its life—which it is charged with maintaining—is not its property and is not, so to speak, in one's hands (it is neither *Vorhandenheit* nor *Zuhandenheit*, to employ Heideggerian categories). Before the meal, one washes one's hands and gives thanks ("blesses" the food) precisely for the "grace" or "glory" of continuing to live, thanks to the nourishment one has found. Here, the food is blessed because it lets the individual preserve the life she has been given—the life which perseveres through her. This entire grammar of blessedness, though, makes very little sense if interpreted along the lines of Aristotle's ontology because, for him, the soul does not *receive* "a life . . . " to live, but *is* the principle of life. In Aristotle, the body that is fed and preserved by the nutritive soul is not blessed because, like the slave in relation to the free man, it is the possession of another without in turn being the possessor of the one who owns it (*Politics* I, 5). For Spinoza, by contrast, the body and the mind both "have" a life to live only to the extent that they nourish it, that is, to the extent that they make it more capable or powerful or virtuous, and thus are authorized to seek whatever is most useful for its preservation. In so doing, they are engaging in a form of worship for "a life" that is God's and, as such, can never truly become their property. Aristotle's ontology is therefore lacking in the reflexivity entailed by the idea of an immanent cause.

But how are we to understand this reflexivity of the immanent cause, of "a life," contained by the idea of a metabolism? Agamben holds that this reflexivity or "beatitude coincides with the experience of the self as an immanent cause, which he [Spinoza] calls *acquiescientia in se ipso*, 'being at rest in oneself'" (Agamben 1999b, 237). Acquiescence is the result of the third kind of knowledge (*Ethics* V, 27, proof). Spinoza's epistemology distinguishes between knowledge and experience based on the imaginative or temporal connection between two things (the first kind of knowledge), knowledge or experience based on the rational (a priori) connection between two things as determined by the eternal laws of nature (the second kind of knowledge), and knowledge or experience that is not based on the connection of each thing to another according to necessary law, but rather is based on the connection of each thing to its divine ground (the third kind of knowledge). This connection, so to speak, justifies the necessity of each singular thing in an absolute way, and not simply in a relative way, as is the case when that thing is understood to follow necessarily from another thing of the same ontological rank. To experience everything according to this third kind of knowledge is to experience "the mind's intellectual love toward God."

Now, Spinoza argues that this love toward God is, at the same time, "the love of God wherewith God loves himself not insofar as he is infinite, but insofar as he can be explicated through the essence of the human mind considered under a form of eternity. That is, the mind's intellectual love toward God is part of the infinite love wherewith God loves himself" (*Ethics* V, 36). This means that God does not know itself to be perfect insofar as it is an absolute substance, but only insofar as it has knowledge of the third kind, that is, of an intuitive knowledge of the infinity of singular modes in which its infinite attributes are expressed. From here follows Spinoza's surprising claim that God loves itself only in the form of the mind of the human being who knows God according to this third kind of knowledge. Only the human being's contemplative living truly immanentizes God's life. That is why Spinoza argues that, insofar as God desires to know itself, it must also desire to love the human species and show particular divine providence: "It follows that God, insofar as he loves himself, loves mankind and, consequently, that the love of God toward men and the mind's intellectual love toward God are one and the same" (*Ethics* V, 36, corollary). But what can it mean that God's providence is only revealed by the practice of "a (philosophical) life"?

It is here that Agamben's intimation that the *acquiescientia in se ipso* takes the same grammatical form as *pasearse* is made explicit. Agamben points out that Spinoza sought an expression to render the idea of "an action in which the agent and patient enter a threshold of absolute indistinction." This is an action that "suffers" itself, and only from out of this suffering is it "saved" or preserved. This structure of action has an obvious application in elucidating the problem of the indistinction between God as the cause of all things and things insofar as they are eternalized in and through the possession of the third kind of knowledge. The term that Spinoza uses to illustrate this relation between God and its infinite modes, in which the latter "immanentize" God, is the Ladino expression *pasearse*, which refers to the act of walking when, at the same time, one is also being taken for a walk. The point here is that in walking, it is not only I that am taking a walk, but—"at the same time" yet without any duration, and *sub species aeternitatis* or "under the aspect of eternity"—it is the walking that has always already taken me along with it. When applied to the problem of immanence, this term suggests that while God's life is producing the essences with conatus, "at the same time" yet without duration and *sub species aeternitatis*, this life is also being taken along by its effects: they are in God to the extent that God is "immanentized" in them.

Beatitude or blessedness is an *acquiescientia in se ipso*, a "being at rest in oneself" in two senses: first, because the third kind of knowledge shows that all the persevering on the part of the finite thing finds its "resting point" in the life that it is nourishing. The *in se ipso* does not refer to the self considered apart from God, but to the mind of the finite self that, in the third kind of knowledge, becomes a part of God's mind. Yet, in a second sense, the reflexivity in the formulation of the *acquiescientia* refers to the fact that, insofar as God loves itself intellectually through the human being's intellectual love of God, it is in the activity of philosophizing that God is being taken along and can therefore be said to provide for God's resting place, just like when one takes a walk, it is also the walking that is taking one along, such that it is possible to say that the self, in walking, is also always resting in itself, and is thus, virtually speaking, unmoved and eternal.

The conclusion of the above analysis of beatitude is that Spinoza teaches that a philosophical life, or the divine living contemplation (for these are the same), is what brings God down from the Height of His Throne, where the tradition said He ruled over the world like a King. A (philosophical) life is providential because in and through such "a life," God has become entirely "immanent" and is wholly "among" things and in no way separate from them. For a (philosophical) life there can be no more sacred precincts like churches or states, spaces and times absolved from the profane, where God's representatives come to stand in judgment over the becoming of life. From this point of view, God's life as the eternal living contemplation refers to the state of things in which everything is connected with everything else in such a way as to allow it to persevere in its most singularizing being. Spinoza conceives of a philosophical life, of the eternal living contemplation, as the Sabbath of God.

In a recent work, *The Kingdom and the Glory*, Agamben returns one more time to the question of metabolism, but unlike in his previous writings on potentiality, he now does so within an explicit discourse on divine providence. Toward the close of the book, Agamben hazards an interpretation of Spinoza's reference to glory in *Ethics* V, 36, the very same passage that has occupied me since the start of this chapter. The circular relation between the human species' intellectual love of God and God's love of itself as a love for the human species is now understood as the climax of a theory of glory. Agamben argues that the theological concept of glory is a transposition into the religious sphere of the political practice of the glorification of a king or emperor (Agamben 2007b, 250ff). Glorification is the acclamation, on the part of an assembly (or synagogue), of a person who is thereby raised onto the throne of sovereignty. Analogously, the prayers and the hymns of the faithful which glorify God make up God's glory or Throne, that is, God's resting place. There is no glory without glorification, just as there is no glorification without glory.

Following a study of Mauss on practices of nourishment in the Vedas, Agamben points out that, in this literature, the practice of sacrificing is considered to be a way of nourishing the gods; the life of the gods, in turn, is nothing but the vital principle that keeps all things living. Thus, by feeding the gods through their glorification, human beings are in turn nourishing themselves from the glory of the gods.[18] If one applies the above conception of glory to the idea of divine metabolism of immanent life in Spinoza, the outcome is a complete revolution of the meaning of glorification upon which rest both the divine and human forms of sovereignty and, therefore, every church and state. From this point of view, God lives its life thanks to the glorification or nourishment provided by all of the living things that persevere in their being by doing everything they must to preserve the life that has been given to them. In other words, God does not live on thanks to the prayers and sacrifices made in His name, but because every living thing pursues its natural right. In turn, God's life and glory are the nourishment for a (philosophical) life: God finds its "rest" as the most blessed of food in the human freedom to think, in that *libertas philosophandi* that Spinoza, in the *Theologico-Political Treatise*, withdraws from the precincts of each and every revealed theology.

But what is the biopolitical significance of the fact that a (philosophical) life is the final resting place, the Sabbath, of God? Agamben theorizes this Sabbath simultaneously in Aristotelian and in Marxist terms: a living contemplation means a life (*zoe*) in which all of our functions and activities, everything that constitutes our *bios*, are rendered un-workable or inoperative (*inoperosità*). This conception of inoperativeness or unworkability is related to Negri's idea of an antinomy between living labor and wage labor (the form in which work is done under capitalist relations of production). For Agamben, such a withdrawal from work would finally "free the living man from its biological or social destiny, and assign him to that undefinable dimension that we are used to calling politics.... Life, which contemplates its (proper) power to act makes itself *inoperosa* [inoperative or unworkable] in all of its actions, it lives only (its) *vivibilità* [livability]. In this *inoperosità*, the life that we live is only the life through which we live, only our power to act and to live, our *ag-ibilità* [capacity to act] and our *viv-ibilità* [capacity to live]. The *bios* here coincides without remainders with the *zoe*" (Agamben 2007b, 274, translation mine).

At the start of this chapter I mentioned Esposito's hypothesis that philosophical practice would become the basis for a politics only once biology, in turn, could be grasped philosophically. I then proceeded to argue that this requirement is found in a Spinozist-Deleuzian conception of eternal life as "a (philosophical) life." Agamben claims that such "a (philosophical) life" is political in the sense that it realizes a communist condition by delivering life from the social division of labor, making every such division "inoperative" and handing over life to its pure capacity to act. But this solution remains caught within an Aristotelian framework that separates thinking from labor. My critique of Agamben's Aristotelianism was intended to lead to a more adequate, because more Spinozistic formulation, of an affirmative politics of life *sub species aeternitatis*. Rejecting primitive communism precisely because it would make women the common property of all, Marx asserts that a truly communist society—in which no one could become the property of anyone else and thus everyone would live according to natural right—would be populated by a political animal who "has his natural existence (*zoe*) become his human existence (*bios*) and nature become human for him" (Marx 1975, 350). From the perspective advanced in this chapter, Marx's requirement that "nature become human" is possible when God has become entirely immanentized as nature (*Deus sive Natura*) and society is so organized that it nourishes itself from God (Nature) in order for every one of its members to be afforded the possibility of leading "a (philosophical) life." To lead such "a life" is to give up on the existentialist conception of life and its fear of death that lies at the basis of every construction of sovereignty; the Spinozist freedom to philosophize makes a meal out of sovereignty and metabolizes this fear into a providential life that cares for others in the form of planned social relations of production.

9

ETERNAL RECURRENCE AND THE NOW OF REVOLUTION

Nietzsche and Messianic Marxism

ECONOMIC THEOLOGY AND THE CRITIQUE OF POLITICAL ECONOMY

An important component of the social imaginary of modern civil society is an image of history as progress into an indefinite future in which the human species keeps perfecting itself. In our age of imminent environmental catastrophe, the belief in progress has reversed itself into the widespread sensation that precious little time remains for the human species to get its relation to its own species-life and that of other living beings right. As the time that remains gets abbreviated, the messianic and the apocalyptic mindsets resurge. Yet all civil societies uphold economic imperatives that keep postponing meaningful political decisions at the global level in the name of social and economic "progress." Economics presents itself as the most objective science of society, and it shares with the rest of modern science a temporal scheme according to which linear, empty time is the form of objectivity. This scheme was secured by the Kantian philosophical legacy and remains foundational for mainstream modern economic science as well. Our "today" is thus torn between a messianic and a scientific mindset where neither one seems capable of overcoming the other.

If Marx is right to say that all economy can be reduced to a question of the "economy of time" (Marx 1974, 173), then a critique of civil society ultimately requires a critique of progress and of the form of linear time. Lukács and Benjamin were among the first to become aware of the need for

Marxism, as a scientific and thus materialist account of history, to develop a conception of time that would constitute a synthesis of the messianic and the scientific mindsets. They shared the intuition that the reification of social relations identified by Marx also affects temporality. When temporality is reduced to an empty progression in linear time, history freezes over, and everything begins to repeat itself eternally. This is why Benjamin thought that Nietzsche's teaching of the eternal recurrence of the same was the ultimate temporal expression of the form of value, of commodity fetishism. Lukács and Benjamin shared the belief that the spell of commodity fetishism could be broken only by radicalizing reification, that is, only when the worker's self-consciousness becomes identical to that of any other, eternally repeated commodity. If the production of identical commodities is symbolized by the doctrine of the eternal recurrence of the same, then attaining class consciousness is the same as living the eternal recurrence. Only the thought of such an eternal life can overcome dialectically the form of the commodity and the "eternity" of the value form. It follows that a revolutionary consciousness depends on a materialist conception of eternal recurrence and of the eternal life capable of bridging the messianic and the scientific approaches to history.

This approach to the problem of temporality in late capitalism distinguishes itself from several recent attempts at an "economic theology" that offer an interpretation of political economy from the messianic mindset, but in so doing leave aside the scientific grounding of modern economics. These attempts depend on a combination of two axioms: first, that Adam Smith's "invisible hand" is a secularized version of divine "providence" or "government;" second, that "credit" is the "form of value" of bourgeois political economy.[1] On the basis of these two axioms, political economy is uncovered as an "economic theodicy" or *Oikodizee* (the coinage of Vogl), a doctrine of the economy as the final tribunal of divine justice, meting out rewards and punishments.

The axiom of economic theology according to which the form of value in capitalism is "credit," and, therefore, that the economy (at least seen from the point of view of money) is ultimately based on "faith," "confidence," and other such affects, comes from philosophies of money (for example, Simmel, Schumpeter, et al.) that gave up on Marx's theory of value. In Chapter 2 I tried to show why the critique of political economy may still require a theory of value. Marx was right to argue that "the economists themselves say that people place in a thing (money) the faith which they don't place in each other. But why do they have faith in a thing? Obviously only because that thing is an objectified relation between persons; because it is objectified exchange-value, and exchange-value is nothing more than a mutual relation between people's productive activities" (Marx 1974, 160). The form of value in bourgeois economics is based on exchange, not on credit, and it is the latter that draws its condition of possibility from the former, not vice versa.

The approach of economic theology to the critique of political economy inscribes the series of unpredictable "events" that compose the fluctuations of prices, that is, the disparity between prices and real value (or "natural" price, the equilibrium point of demand and supply) within a theological metanarrative. This approach does not ask what makes value itself possible or what the conditions of possibility are for achieving equilibrium because its acceptance of the paradigm of secularization directs the economic inquiry either towards "God" (or some representative thereof) or towards the absence of "God" (or some representative of this absent God). Yet the solution to the problem of value may lie beyond the alternative of religion or atheism. Although it is true that a study of the problem of value (which does not just remain at the surface with a pure consideration of prices) leads to the categories of "event" and "tendency," this does not entail that their meaning can be captured through a discourse on secularized conceptions of divine providence. Indeed, the approach of economic theology to the critique of political economy may in the end simply reinforce the old canard according to which Marx's "critique" of bourgeois political economy is nothing but a "theology" of history, and communism is but the latest version of an irrational and nihilist messianism.

In the popularized versions of economics, the "wild" history of market fluctuations gives rise to two opposed accounts or narratives. In one narrative, the market is entirely rational, the most perfect way to gather, transmit, and make use of information about the objective value of anything. Wild swings in prices are caused by external interferences with free market mechanisms and by a lack of competition and communication between economic actors. In another narrative, the free market is essentially characterized by "irrational exuberance," by the equivalent of manic-depressive mood swings, by exorbitant economic cycles, and so on (Vogl 2011, chap. 2 passim). These two, partial perspectives on the problem of price fluctuation seem to correspond to the isolation of objective (or substantive) and subjective conceptions of value, respectively.[2] If one believes that value is an "objective" property of commodities, then one believes that price fluctuations must have a hidden "logic" that expresses this "objectivity" of value. If one believes that value is a "subjective" or "emergent" property linked with the psychology of those who sell or buy commodities, then price fluctuations are at the mercy of the aggregate effects of the beliefs, prejudices, wishes, and hopes of economic agents, and there is thus no "logic" to the market. But neither of these two conceptions, by itself, is thought to account for equilibrium in classical or marginalist economics. Furthermore, Marx's theory of the form of value is intended to go beyond the dualism of objective and subjective theories of value. So, from a Marxist point of view, there would seem to be little interest in reconstructing an "economic theodicy" of prices; more to the point, the critique of such a theodicy would not be the functional equivalent of a critique of political economy.

The belief of economic theologians that credit is the form of value seems to gain in plausibility once finance capitalism is placed center stage and intensifies with the so-called democratization of credit, the (periodic) rise and fall of "supply-side" economics, the invention of derivatives and hedge funds, and so on. What all of these economic phenomena have in common is that they are oriented toward the future, where what determines the "destiny" of prices is not the past course of prices, but the interplay among scenarios of what might happen in an incalculable future (in a future characterized by some or another radically "new" event).[3] It is only a misinterpretation of certain instruments of finance capital that leads economic theologians to mistakenly infer that, since exchanges are now being made with respect to an uncertain and changeable future, and not just a known and unchangeable past, credit takes priority over the form of exchange, making value a function of the credibility of promises and hopes. But what is being exchanged now is simply a prediction of what will be exchanged at a future time. This does not mean, at any time now or in the future, that the rootedness of value in exchange will be abolished: to believe this is the equivalent of believing that anyone (any rational economic actor) would be willing to give someone something in exchange for nothing. If such "pure" credit existed in political economy, then one would be justified in speaking of a theological basis of credit, but it would no longer be the basis of capitalist political economy which, by definition, exists only due to the foundation that all exchanges are equal exchanges (or exchanges of equivalents, that is, values). The point is that credit is a commodity like any other and, therefore, it falls under the law of (exchange-)value.

This is not to deny an important novelty associated with the rise of financial capitalism, namely, the idea that economic laws, previously thought to be invariant forms by economic science, are now starting to be understood in terms of tendencies and events (in terms of chaos, quantum, and complexity theories, for example). But the introduction of event and tendency into economic science is something that Lukács and Benjamin first predicted, and they did so by relying, more or less explicitly, on Nietzsche's critique of linear progress enshrined in the concept of the eternal recurrence.[4] However, the eternal recurrence of the same is the one hypothesis about history that is radically incompatible with every Christian conception of history and with every economic theology. Foucault says at one point that "economy is an atheist discipline; economics is a discipline without God; economics is a discipline without totality" (Foucault 2010, 282). The eternal recurrence of the same is the only hypothesis about history that allows for a critique of political economy because it places itself at the same "atheistic" level of economics and its status as "science" in modern civil society.

CLASS CONSCIOUSNESS AND THE REIFICATION OF TEMPORALITY

The time seems ripe, therefore, to reconsider the first theory of reification, proposed by Lukács in the central chapter of *History and Class Consciousness*: "Reification and the Consciousness of the Proletariat." The concept of reification has recently made a comeback in contemporary social and political theory. After Habermas jettisoned it in the 1970s, Honneth (2005) and Agamben (2007) have both tried to rescue it from oblivion. I suggest that Lukács's theory of reification should be read by placing the phenomenon of temporality, rather than of self-consciousness, at the center of the interpretation. Lukács's fundamental insight is that, whatever else class consciousness may mean, it must be the opposite of the consciousness of a person.[5] Class consciousness is ultimately the self-consciousness of (the worker as) a commodity, and commodities are embodiments of (labor) time. Thus, in Lukács, class consciousness denotes a way of living time or being time: it is not, as in Kant, self-consciousness as a form of time, but a way of acting in which forms of objects dissolve into life-processes. In his critique, Habermas ignored Lukács's theory of temporality (Habermas 1984), and it remains obstructed from view in the recent work of Honneth.[6] This new conception of temporality is the topic of the first part of this chapter. I shall then pass on to discuss Benjamin's radicalization of Lukács, which takes the form of thinking the temporality of commodities in terms of the eternal recurrence of the same.

For Lukács, reification means, in the first instance, that labor-power has become a commodity. The social or common character of labor-power is reduced to something that is separable, assignable to a person, and quantifiable in terms of wages. In short, by being reified, the power of labor loses entirely its social character. In a reified world, what is common or social stands completely outside of the lives of workers and appears in the form of eternal laws of the free market that establish social relations between commodities and rule over the lives of workers like mythical divinities. A reified world is a world in which the only thing everyone has in common is that they are following the laws of economics. Reification refers to a process in which the laws of economics progressively become the laws of all human interaction, colonizing all other life-worlds. To describe reification is to describe the generation process of *homo oeconomicus* and the "methodological individualism" characteristic of modern social sciences.

History itself begins to come to an end, to freeze, once social interaction is conceived in economic terms. Whereas Fukuyama thought that the coming-to-an-end of history is a contingent result of the adoption of liberal civil society all over the globe, Lukács argues that it is a necessary outcome of reification. There is an analytic relation between the absolutization of civil society in neoliberalism and the neoapocalyptic mentality. Indeed, if labor-power is a commodity and is reduced to the capacity of an individual to do his or her assigned job, if, in short, the process of production is deprived of all power over its products, then living labor thereby forfeits all power to change its situation and, thus, all power to make history. When labor-power is a commodity, and society is based on the exchange of such a commodity, history fixates itself in the eternal present of historicism.

The hegemony of economics over social relations and the end of history are the two features of civil society Lukács wants to overcome through the idea of class consciousness. His goal is to describe that standpoint from which the "necessary" laws of economics become contingent because they turn out to be aspects of a process that they themselves do not control. The possibility of turning a permanent "Today" into a revolutionary "Now" such that it makes a difference for history and brings history back to life, depends on giving priority to process over facts, on restoring to history its "effectivity," to use Foucault's expression.

The concepts of reification and alienation in Lukács are often understood as presupposing an originary and reconciled concept of humanity, just like the idea of "false consciousness" presupposes a "true" self-consciousness or authentic existence. This widespread reading is largely a misinterpretation. Lukács was an antihumanist, if by this expression we mean a philosophical discourse that attempts to go beyond the category of the "person" and its "dignity." Lukács's real innovation is showing the fundamental role played by temporality in the constitution of commodity fetishism. As Marx says in *The Poverty of Philosophy* in relation to Ricardo's theory of value: "Time is everything, man is nothing; he is at most time's carcass" (Marx 1973, 47). For civil society, time is the innermost form of things: time is how things become objects for the consciousness of the bourgeois subject, the person who owns private property. For such a subject, temporal form is radically indifferent to material content. In other words, in civil society nothing has its proper time, facts and events are entirely disconnected. Instead, time functions as space, as a way to place or order events so that they appear as facts. Lukács thinks that any consequent historical materialism needs to reverse such an understanding of time, so that each thing gives rise to its own time of manifestation, so that temporal relations emerge from the processes developed from material contents. To be a historical materialist means to disassociate time from the idea of form and instead associate it with what the early Lukács called "soul" or "life," and the later Lukács called an ontology of living labor, or a social ontology. For historical materialism, time becomes the process of a species-life (a common *zoe*) that adopts and discards individual forms of life (*bios*). Such a time no longer belongs to the person; it is not *bio*-graphical time; it is a *zoe*-political time. Its temporal arc is not the birth and death of an individual, but the life-span of the human species-being, that is, the time of the future of humankind.

Kant argued that the time that makes objectivity possible (and thus, that underlies the construction of "laws of nature") is itself not in time; it is a timeless form of appearance. Lukács wants to reverse this postulate and understand the temporality of time, the contingency of time itself, the "process" character of time (since Heidegger, one also speaks of the "event" character of time). Lukács takes this vocabulary of process from sources he did not want to recognize directly: Whitehead's anti-Platonism and Bergson's idea of creative evolution. Bergsonism is the attempt to rescue time from being spatialized or quantified, so that it may be understood as a lived intensity.[7] Lukács's attempt to use temporality in order to establish the priority of life over form (of value) betrays the influence of Simmel (Simmel 2011), who in turn was deeply marked by Nietzsche. If time remains the form of consciousness, as it is for post-Kantian thought, then consciousness can never grasp time as its most proper "object": unable to grasp time, consciousness remains on this side of the object, merely subjective and, thus, remains unable to become life; it remains reified. According to Lukács, to the contrary, the capacity to grasp, to conceive (in German, *begreifen*), to give shape to time itself is exactly what characterizes class consciousness in opposition to individual consciousness. Lukács employs a Hegelian vocabulary, but in reality his theory of class consciousness provides a Marxist elaboration of Nietzsche's investigation into the "use and abuse of history for life." Class consciousness means to use history for the sake of a supratemporal species-life, and not to see life as something that happens in time (ultimately, in the temporal relations of capitalist production). In this sense, class consciousness is consciousness of the eternity of life.

Lukács carries forward this Nietzschean approach to Marxism through a remarkable reading of labor-power and labor time in the fundamental fourth chapter of the first book of *Capital* dealing with commodity fetishism, which, according to him, "contains within itself the whole of historical materialism" (Lukács 1968, 170). In this chapter Marx shows that the products of labor acquire their exchange-value and become commodities only when abstraction is made of their use-value. Products are reified because they are produced by a homogeneous labor-power, an "abstract" social labor. Social labor, in turn, acquires its homogeneity or abstract character by applying labor-power over a homogeneous labor time. Thus, the production of commodities or the reification of labor-power is not possible except through the generation of abstract labor time. Lukács thinks that in order to solve the riddle of commodity fetishism one must provide the equivalent of an "analytic" of abstract time.[8]

All of the laws of economics apply to an abstract reality in the sense that it is composed of facts occurring in empty, linear time. The objective validity of the laws of economics, what makes them seem like "natural" laws, is their basis in abstract (labor) time. Lukács maintains that if abstract, quantitative time can be turned into concrete, qualitative time and if (in the words of Bergson) time as space can be transformed into time as *durée*, then at that point the laws of neoclassical economics lose their veneer of timeless validity.[9] But how does this transformation take place? In what I take to be the central passage of *History and Class Consciousness*, Lukács argues that commodity fetishism is experienced differently by the worker than it is by the capitalist. Reification turns the capitalist into a passive "spectator" or subject of the process of production. Here it is true what Honneth says about all reification, namely, that all activity is reduced to an "unparticipatory and observing conduct" (Honneth 2005, 35). But for the worker who is caught up in the productive process, the passive attitude of spectatorship is impossible. Reification forces the worker

> into becoming the object of the process by which he is turned into a commodity and reduced to a mere quantity. But this very fact forces him to surpass the immediacy of his condition. For as Marx says, 'Time is the place of human development.'[10] The quantitative differences in exploitation which appear to the capitalist in the form of quantitative determinants of the object of his calculation, must appear to the worker as the decisive, qualitative categories of his whole physical, mental and moral existence. (Lukács 1968, 166)

If reification is going to be reversed, everything turns on grasping the distinction between the quantitative experience of time characteristic of the owner and the qualitative experience of time characteristic of the worker.

For the capitalist, labor time is only quantitative; it must be exactly measurable in order that it can be paid for in the form of wages: "Quantification [of time] is a reified and reifying cloak spread over the true essence of objects and can only be regarded as an objective form of reality inasmuch as the subject is uninterested in the essence of the object to which it stands in a contemplative or (seemingly) practical relationship" (Lukács

1968, 166). In drawing the distinction between necessary and disposable time, the capitalist reckons with a "vulgar" concept of time, as Heidegger refers to it. Calculations with respect to a linear concept of time are essential when it comes to the determination of wages in relation to the length of the working day (absolute surplus value) and in relation to the productivity of living labor during the working day (relative surplus value). The exploitation of labor-power under capitalist conditions of production, that is, the extraction of surplus value, depends entirely on the impersonal manipulation of abstract time.[11]

But for the worker, as opposed to the capitalist, *the passage of time* is not merely a quantitative matter. For the worker, the "time that remains," the time that elapses after necessary labor and before the emergence of the product, is a qualitative category for the worker. But how is it possible that, in the process of production itself, time elapses in a qualitatively different way for worker than for capitalist? Lukács gives an example of how a quantitative relation can suddenly turn into a qualitative relation: when one is thirsty, one drinks water, just as when one has a need, one employs a certain amount of labor force in order to satisfy that need, thereby reproducing one's life. But after a certain quantity of water is consumed, if the drinking continues, then one drowns. Here a quantitative change brings about a qualitative change. The same logic applies for the passage of abstract labor time. After a certain amount of labor time has passed (the necessary time), a qualitative change occurs in that living labor ceases to reproduce itself as species-life, but instead begins to reproduce dead or congealed labor (profit, surplus value). That is, the surplus value or the life of capital is generated at the expense of the reproduction, not of the bare life, but of the social life of the worker and the disposable time that ought to constitute the production of an actual social bond within which products acquire their effective meaning, namely, as media of social life, is instead transmuted into the life or self-reproduction of exchange-value.

Can one "measure" exactly the moment in time when the change from a quantitative relation changes into a qualitative one? The law of the falling rate of profit, what Marx calls the fundamental law of capital, reflects the fact that living labor does not turn into dead labor at the moment of selling one's labor-power. Rather the shift occurs at a moment within the process of production itself and is, in a certain sense, an incalculable factor of production. The owner does not know exactly when necessary time ends and disposable time begins since the cost of living labor that the owner pays for as wages buys the owner the use of living labor as a commodity, not as life. The increased productivity of living labor, essentially due to disposable time turned into social knowledge and industry, makes it so that the price paid in terms of wages for living labor always gets the owner less necessary labor than what the owner calculates on, and this inevitably raises his costs of production at a higher rate than his profits, hence the overall lowering of the rate of profit.

The abstraction of labor time splits time into two temporal series that enter into contradiction at some moment in the experience of the worker. This moment corresponds to that *event or Now* in which class consciousness ceases to be the unconscious of the worker and becomes the act of an entire class of workers. This moment of time also necessarily corresponds to the event where the individual loses her personality, loses, above all, her juridical, contractual persona. The first temporal series refers to capital, to the growth or reduction of profit; the second temporal series refers to necessary labor time, to its increase or reduction. The first temporal series remains quantitative, but in the second temporal series, and only for the worker, every change in labor time to increase capital (whether this is change in the absolute surplus value—the length of the working day itself—or a change in the relative surplus value—the increase in productivity that lowers necessary time) is immediately felt qualitatively as a negative change in its time series or lifetime. Exploitation remains invisible to workers at the moment that they are selling or bargaining over the price of their labor-power, for this transaction necessarily takes the form of a fair exchange of use-values between two persons with equal rights. The experience of exploitation appears to the worker only when the labor time gets manipulated, when the worker has to do more in less time (relative surplus value), or when the working hours are extended (absolute surplus value). No changes in labor time ever leave the worker *indifferent*: there is no "contemplative" attitude with respect to time for the worker. Rather, labor time becomes the sole real concern for the worker. For the capitalist, instead, the object of concern is profit, the result of production. This profit, in turn, is of complete indifference to the worker who exercises abstract labor-power.

Here one can see yet another reason why Benjamin Franklin's maxim "time is money" is false from a Marxist perspective. For the capitalist, the passage of time is really no object since the capitalist owns all the time in the world, or, more exactly, because history ended for him with the generation of profit at the time of paying wages. For the worker, by contrast, the time that remains in the world before history comes to an end (before the production of the commodity is finished, and the laws of bourgeois economics come into force) is of *absolute* concern, since the reproduction not of herself as individual, but of her species-life, depends on it. It is as if worker and capitalist lived in accordance to two opposed historical forces: the owner expects labor to be conducted as if it were a vocation, as a profession, in which salvation is achieved in and through the historical progression *ad indefinitum* in linear time. For the worker, every increase in the productivity of labor leads to an acceleration of the "end" of time, which opens up the possibility of "messianic" counter-conducts with respect to the "time that remains" before this end of time.

Negri's theory of the worker's self-valorization, as well as Agamben's concept of *inoperosità*, which I have discussed in previous chapters, are reflections on such messianic counterconducts. But the "self-valorization" of the worker, against the valorization given to her labor capacity by the capitalist and measured in terms of salary, should also be thought beyond the rejection of wage labor and of work characteristic of operaism and postoperaism. Rather, the "self-valorization" of workers should find its realization in "sustainable" forms of production, whereby "sustainable" is not determined in relation to individual human beings, but in relation to the human species-being as one among many species-beings who share the same, transhuman life world. In this context, class consciousness designates a *praxis* that is carried out with consciousness of the "time that remains" for species-life and as care for its "sustainability."

The attitude toward the passage of time for the capitalist is necessarily apocalyptic (positing the end of history as a starting point for its calculus of profit): "*Après moi le deluge*! is the watchword of every capitalist and of every capitalist nation. Capital therefore takes no account of the health and the length of life of the worker, unless society forces it to do so" (Marx 1976, 381). By way of contrast, the attitude toward the passage of the time for the worker, whose concern is the time that remains before the end of time, is messianic. This is the grain of truth that exists in the messianic turn given to post-Marxist thought by Agamben, Badiou, Žižek, and others. But, in truth, there is nothing particularly new here: Lukács's analysis of class consciousness in terms of the duality and contradiction of the temporal series is already a small treatise on the messianic attitude of the worker (which finds parallel developments in the messianic Marxism of Bloch and Benjamin).

Labor-power can be exchanged for wages only if it is understood as the possession of the individual worker, that is, only if it is treated as a commodity. At the same time, capitalist relations of production turn labor into an abstract universality because, on the side of the object, labor under capitalist relations of production produces identical commodities that lack all particularity, and, on the side of the subject, labor is abstract universality because it no longer refers to the individual who accomplishes it (for example, the artisan and her know-how, her experience, and so on). Under capitalist conditions of production, labor is something that, by definition, someone else can also do. In the famous chapter on commodity fetishism, Marx shows that this feature of labor is based on the abstract universality of labor time: "In the problem of labor time, reification [is shown] at its zenith" (Lukács 1968, 167). Wage labor is an activity that fills up time conceived of as a series of instants or "nows": *now* you screw this on, *now* you press that button, and so forth. From the perspective of capital, the essential problem is how human species-life is to be occupied or employed in and through time, how to keep workers busy through time. For the capitalist, it is literally inconceivable that the species-life could make use of time. If one could conceive this, one would thereby cease to be a capitalist. But for the worker, what is of essential importance is the time that remains and how to use this time for the species-life, rather than what to do individually in this time. How to make the best use of time, rather than what to do in time, becomes the decisive paradigm switch that allows the worker to be conscious of the social nature of labor-power.

CLASS STRUGGLE AS A WAR OF TIMES

Capitalism presupposes the worker to be a person (otherwise she could not sell her labor-power) and, at the same time, in its relations of production, it denies the personality of the worker, otherwise no commodity could be produced.[12] This is a simple contradiction of capitalism. The former side of the contradiction, the struggle of workers for inclusion in civil society and for bourgeois rights of the person, is best shown in Marx's historical writings. The latter side of the contradiction, Marx develops in the *Grundrisse* and in *Capital*. It is therefore misguided to see a "tension" between both types of works in Marx, as Honneth has lately argued (Honneth 2011). Rather, the historical and the economic writings together show the fundamental contradiction of capitalism, and this contradiction manifests itself in an analytic of temporality and a theory of the event.

But Lukács did not write *History and Class Consciousness* to prove that capitalism is contradictory, and thus irrational. It was already well known that capitalism necessarily generates crises it is apparently unable to cope with, yet this does not mean that it will collapse. In the *Critique of Pure Reason*, Kant discovered that reason is necessarily self-contradictory as soon as it attempts to transcend the conditions of linear time, of unending progress in time. Kant resolves the antinomy in a contemplative way by displacing the problem onto the future. The marginalist revolution is a neo-Kantian revolution in economics in the sense that it displaces the contradiction of capital into the future. It attempts to neutralize the law of falling rate of profit by thinking of the form of exchange-value as a debt form passed on to the future generations of species-life in an increasing measure (corresponding to the decrease in the rate of profit).[13] Lukács already knew that a mere contradiction was insufficient to destroy capitalism; after all, Nietzsche had already shown that life depends on errors. The point of Lukács's book was to explore another question: How is it possible for the consciousness of the irrational nature of capitalism to turn into *revolutionary action*? "The consciousness of the proletariat must become deed" (Lukács 1968, 178). The problem Lukács faced was the following: What makes an antinomy *the condition of possibility of praxis*? For Lukács, the only way the neo-Kantian scheme of salvation through crisis can be overcome is if the experience of the contradiction of capitalism takes the form of a class consciousness that is no longer merely contemplative but also *praxis*. Class consciousness is not another type of self-consciousness, in that sense, but concrete action. What needs to be thought is how this action is an action in history, in the linear unfolding of time, designed to reverse it, or to break it open. Class consciousness is what breaks history into two; it is an action that is at the same time an event that leaps out of linear time.

Lukács claims that as class consciousness, "consciousness is not the knowledge of an opposed object but is the self-consciousness of the object [thus] the act of consciousness overthrows the objective form of the object"

(Lukács 1968, 178). The "objective form" of the object is abstract time, the time of surplus value, whereas "history is the history of the unceasing overthrow of the objective forms that shape the life of man" (Lukács 1968, 186). Here Lukács appeals to a Nietzschean and Simmelian biopolitical formula that understands life as something that cannot be contained by any form in order to illustrate the paradoxical thesis that the object (the worker as commodity) can overthrow its form by virtue of being living labor. Therefore, class consciousness refers to an action or praxis that counters abstract time; class consciousness is "untimely," to employ a Nietzschean concept. Thus, revolutionary action is best conceived as a war of times, the struggle of the time of the living against capitalist time. Class consciousness is the consciousness that the disposable time of living labor is opposed to the disposable time of capital. The latter time is abstract time, time as linear progression. By way of contrast, the disposable time of living labor is a time that comes from the future back to the past and acts in the "time of the now" (*Jetztzeit*) as Benjamin would later name it.[14] To generate more capital, less time must remain for the worker as the "time that remains" (before the end of the world) gets compressed into the instant of decision, which is the instant when the worker comes to realize her labor-power does not belong to her, but is social. This decision is messianic and existential at the same time. For the worker, continuing in the abstract time of capital generation means having less time to live in common.

This now-time of living labor is what Lukács calls the self-consciousness of the commodity; it is now-time that allows the object to "overthrow the objective form." The object's form is constituted by its relations in time with the other objects that come before-and-after. For the object, overthrowing its objective form would mean wrenching itself out of the linear continuum. This is the task of revolutionary praxis. To illustrate revolutionary action as acting against one's time, Lukács turns to Marx's discussion of the struggle over the length of the labor day in chapter 10 of part 3 of the first volume of *Capital*. Given that labor-power is bought and sold as a commodity, the capitalist has a legal "right" to increase the labor day; the worker, by contrast, by legal right, wants to reduce it: "There is here, therefore, an antinomy, right against right, both equally bearing the seal of the law of exchange. Between equal rights force decides. Hence, in the history of capitalist production, the establishment of a norm for the working day presents itself as a struggle over the limits of that day, a struggle between collective capital, i.e., the class of capitalists, and collective labor, i.e., the working class" (Marx 1976, 344; Lukács 1968, 178). The temporality of class struggle is an event or encounter between disparate times that breaks open the homogeneity and linearity of the temporal series.

This theme of revolutionary action as a struggle between times reappears in Benjamin's *Theses on the Concept of History* as well as in Althusser's theory of the conjuncture of "invisible" temporal series in his concept of "structural causality" in *Reading Capital* (Althusser and Balibar 1979). But in Marx's treatment it is also a struggle in which the juridical mask of the person, the legal equality of the contract, is cast down and the "protracted and more or less concealed civil war between the capitalist class and the working class" appears in the light of day (Marx 1976, 412). The illusion that the work contract is valid for all times ("from now and into the future") vanishes and class struggle faces the problem of violence (*Gewalt*) that has appeared in Marxist and post-Marxist thought from Luxemburg and Lenin, through Benjamin's "Critique of Violence" to Arendt's *On Revolution*, and is today a prominent theme in Badiou and Žižek. But this does not make the concept of class struggle as such antinomian, for Marx explicitly concludes the chapter by calling for workers "to put their heads together and, as a class, compel *the passing of a law, an all-powerful social barrier* by which they can be prevented from selling themselves and their families into slavery and death by voluntary contract with capital" (Marx 1976, 416, emphasis mine). It is interesting to note that Marx's discussion of the struggle over the length of the working day is characterized as a struggle for "a normal working day," one which does not produce "the premature exhaustion and death of this labor-power itself" (Marx 1976, 376). In this sense, one could perhaps say that the legal regulation of working conditions as a result of class struggle is the "normal," but not yet "normative" outcome of such struggle.

How does class consciousness look when considered according to its normative power, that is, when it is oriented not toward keeping capitalist relations of production in check but rather toward overcoming them and creating new conditions of production? Lukács seeks a "dialectical overcoming" of the capitalist antinomy of reason. He is not interested in a revisionist, social-democratic solution that understands the (messianic) idea of living labor as a regulative ideal, thereby transforming the "time that remains" or the absent time (eternity) of living labor into a perpetual progress in the fight for better working conditions. For Lukács, the dialectical solution lies in "the premise that things should be shown to be aspects of processes" (Lukács 1968, 179):

> Thus the knowledge that social facts are not objects but relations between men is intensified to the point where facts are wholly dissolved into processes. But if their Being appears as a Becoming this should not be construed as an abstract universal flux sweeping past, it is no vacuous *durée réelle* but the unbroken production and reproduction of those relations, when torn from their context and distorted by abstract mental categories, can appear to bourgeois thinkers as things. Only at this point does the consciousness of the proletariat elevate itself to the self-consciousness of society in its historical development. (Lukács 1968, 180)

For class consciousness, or for the "self-consciousness" of the commodity itself, objects no longer appear as facts, but as aspects of processes: "If process [is seen as] the truth about things, then this means that the developing tendencies of history constitute a higher reality than the empirical facts" (Lukács 1968, 181). Economics reflects the world of "empirical facts"—that is, the world of abstract time—whereas the world of production, of concrete temporality, by contrast, is a world composed of "tendencies." What does it mean that objective reality is not a reality of facts, but of tendencies? One thing it means is that, from the perspective of class consciousness, the time that remains, the future, is always already prior to the present time— it is more real than the present because it has already happened—and this happening is inherently a repetition: the same returns eternally as commodity and as revolutionary praxis (once the commodity becomes conscious of its eternal recurrence). Another thing it can mean is that the use of time (not the use of labor-power) must become the object of planning, and this planning, this new economy of time, gives rise to the new—to what cannot be planned.

The logic of the argument is this: time is not money because, for capital, time is not my time, and thus, capital pushes me against my time, my life (*zoe*). Capital turns the worker's species life into bare life, as a threshold between life and death, a living death (this is the consciousness of the worker, and this is the moment of taking consciousness qua commodity—class consciousness is born in relation to time, in relation to the idea that time is not my possession in capitalism, and yet time is life, so this awareness is awareness that my life is no longer mine). For me to have disposable time, that is, for me to live the life of the species, neither time nor labor can be "mine." Therefore I no longer have the labor-power to sell as a commodity, with the consequence that capitalist relations need to be overthrown; labor-power is social power and it must become an organized, planned use of social power. Time is gotten hold of, it is not just the condition for consciousness of objects, but is itself the object of class consciousness. Class consciousness is consciousness of the right time; it is the encounter between the *virtù* of planning and the *fortuna* of contingency. Class consciousness is all about the organization of time, the planning of time, as Marx says in the *Grundrisse*. Class consciousness can never be the fulfilling of a pregiven goal or task given by the profession (even if this task is given by professional revolutionaries), but instead consists in freeing oneself from such tasks. Planned production is what gives back disposable time to workers; it is the revocation of abstract labor time.

Class struggle is therefore best understood as a clash, a confrontation, of temporalities. The more workers control their labor time, the more common their use of labor-power becomes, the more objects cease to appear as facts and become aspects of processes, or enabling conditions for events. The laws of economics reflect the world of social facts, that is, the social world of abstraction. This is a world in which nothing "happens" with the commodities; where commodities are "stuck" in a specific time which repeats itself eternally (this is "fashion"); where commodities are simply used up and consumed. To class consciousness, by contrast, the world is composed only of tendencies: objects come into existence as a function of happenings. When commodities are bought and sold purely as a function of "trends," as things to be played with, and when this attitude is prominent in both producers and consumers, then class consciousness is not far off.

To sum up, political action is informed by class consciousness whenever it exhibits at least three features. First, whoever frees up for others the use of those instruments of production that are made available to them by virtue of their profession can be said to exhibit class consciousness. To view life in professional terms, to believe that the point of life is to have a profession, is to view life in sacred terms, as a secularized history of salvation. But class consciousness understands history as a story of increasing profanation of what is sacred, as a history where fall and failure are not synonyms of guilt but of joy. To be communist nowadays means to revoke the vocation of one's profession, to remain an amateur and a beginner within and about one's profession.

Second, to have class consciousness means to be aware of the contradiction between capital and time: more disposable time for the worker is less disposable time for capital accumulation. Thus, every form of struggle for greater freedom in the use of time exhibits class consciousness. Class struggle should privilege the conquest of more disposable time within production at the workplace, rather than being solely a struggle for better wages, better working conditions, or more leisure time. Having class consciousness means living the time that remains creatively, both inside and outside of work; thus, class consciousness is already found in those workers who educate themselves both inside and outside of their jobs. This education needs to be an education that is not oriented professionally, a form of education that does not have as its goal the generation of human capital. It would have to be a transmutation of what is currently called a "liberal" education, which is simply a way of satisfying the capitalist class' need for labor flexibility and cheaper ways to channel workers into professional lives that necessarily get shorter and shorter and must be repeatedly replaced during a lifetime.[15] Class consciousness, by way of contrast, entails understanding a professional life as a means to the end of a free education and not the other way around. The struggle for a universal and free education exhibits class consciousness.

Third, class consciousness is found whenever individuals attempt to organize their time in order to minimize the duration of their working day. All organization of time to generate freedom from the division of labor already recognizes the social nature of labor-power, since it is impossible to organize one's time in such a way without collective action and class solidarity among workers. To see the time of day as an *empty time that needs to be filled* with tasks to be accomplished is a bourgeois consciousness of time. On the contrary, to see the working day as *a time that needs to be socially organized in order to be free from tasks*—that is what it means to exhibit class consciousness. The daily planner or agenda is the metaphor for bourgeois time-consciousness. If one looks at life from the perspective of a daily planner, one is literally organizing one's activity in order to fill up the time table. A calendar written in accordance with class consciousness would look entirely different: everyday tasks could be performed at the most awkward or inappropriate of times, activities that are scheduled in a series of days could be compressed in the span of a few hours in one day, urgent meetings and pressing deadlines could be postponed beyond measure, to the point that all urgency would be lost. Time would be organized in order to build up sufficient creative energy to achieve one action that would burst out of linear time, one event that could never be contained in a daily planner because it could not be planned. The impersonal person of class consciousness is he and she "who is willing and whose mission it is to create the future," "the birth of the new" (Lukács 1968, 203–4).

ETERNAL RECURRENCE AS THE UNITY OF MESSIANISM AND MATERIALISM

In the unpublished notes to his *Theses on the Concept of History*, Benjamin writes, "Marx said that revolutions are the locomotives of world history. But maybe they are something entirely different. Maybe revolutions are the way in which the human species travelling on this train grabs for the emergency break" (Benjamin 1991c, 1232). When Benjamin voiced this idea of revolution, it was considered marginal within the communist movement since communist revolution was thought to be a necessary outcome of the "laws of history," the "goal" toward which all history aims. Recently, Benjamin's combination of messianism with historical materialism has been adopted in the form of the Pauline, antinomian visions of communism advocated by Badiou, Agamben, and Žižek, among others. The reason for such a belated embrace is not surprising; when awareness spreads that the train of world history, in its pursuit of progress, is rapidly approaching the point of no return in the destruction of the planet's environment and consequently of the human species, who in their right mind would not want to pull the emergency break? Still, the question remains whether a messianic vision of history can secure for itself a scientific, materialistic foundation.

In these late fragments, Benjamin argues that Marxism is characterized by three basic concepts: the class struggle of the proletariat, historical progress, and the idea of a classless society. For Benjamin, Marx was wrong to suggest that the idea of the classless society corresponds to an endpoint (*Endziel*) of historical progress. In so doing, Marx missed "the true messianic figure" of classless society, namely, that the interruption of historical progress can happen at any moment. In a word, for Benjamin true class consciousness is the consciousness that the revolution *always* happens in the time of a *now* (which he calls *Jetztzeit*). A Marxist theory of revolution evinces a link to messianism only if it is possible to link the happening of a revolution to an eternal now (which is not, obviously, the "eternal present" of historicism). This concept of an eternal "Today" interrupts the progress of world history and brings it to a halt. But is Benjamin's messianic interpretation of Marxism compatible with Marxism as a rigorously materialist, "scientific" discourse?

The thesis of this chapter is that the link between messianism and historical materialism is preserved so long as one inscribes both within the teaching of eternal recurrence (*das ewige Wiederkunft*).[16] Benjamin discovered that this teaching was not only espoused by Nietzsche, who had no particular sympathies for communism, but also by the most famous revolutionary of the nineteenth century, Louis-Auguste Blanqui.[17] Blanqui is responsible for at least two fundamental ideas of what would later become Marxism-Leninism: first, the idea that a revolution can only be the result of a conspiracy led by a few individuals and not a spontaneous uprising of the masses; second, the idea that without a violent takeover of the state machinery, every revolution is destined to perish at the hands of the counterrevolutionary forces.[18] Hence Blanqui, before Marx, draws from the successes and failures of the communard experience the conclusion that no revolution can succeed without a "dictatorship of the proletariat." At the same time, Blanqui is the author of a bizarre cosmological meditation, *L'Éternité par les astres* (Eternity proven by the stars), in which he tries to show that each one of us has an infinite number of avatars in infinite parallel universes, who are forever living exactly the same life that we are currently living. How does Blanqui's belief in the "now" of communist revolution fit together with the doctrine of eternal return? This was the decisive riddle for Benjamin in his last years.

Sometime between the essay on Goethe and the unfinished study on Baudelaire, Benjamin wrote the *Theologico-Political Fragment* in which eternal life is again at stake. In the secondary literature, the actual dating of the *Fragment* is considered to be of crucial importance for understanding the development of Benjamin's Marxist thinking. Adorno, who first published it, claims that it was written no earlier than 1935; thus, it belongs to the time of Benjamin's work on his Baudelaire book. Scholem, by contrast, claims that the *Fragment*'s explicit use of motifs drawn from the Kabbalah indicates that Benjamin must have written it much earlier, before his "turn" to Marxism in 1924.[19] Since then, the question of dating has become symptomatic of a break in the schools of Benjamin interpretation that divide the author between a "mystical" and a "materialist" phase. The fact that the motif of eternal life, as I have discussed in Chapter 5, is found both in Benjamin's earliest works and in his later work on Baudelaire suggests that Benjamin understood eternal life, and eternal return, in a way that unites the messianic and the scientific or materialist approaches to communism.

Benjamin's *Theologico-Political Fragment* begins within the context of the messianic tradition in Judaism by putting forward the thesis that the messianic age cannot be called forth in and through history, and that is why "the Kingdom of God is not the *telos* of the historical dynamic; it cannot be established as a goal. From the standpoint of history, it is not the goal (*Ziel*) but the terminus (*Ende*)" of the historical process (Benjamin 2002, 305). This thesis resumes in its essentials the conclusion of Rosenzweig's *Star of Redemption*. The *Star* ends with a meditation on Maimonides's fundamental question in *The Guide of the Perplexed*, namely, the relation between the account of the Beginning (Creation) and the account of the Chariot (Redemption). Rosenzweig's surprising thesis is that Redemption is to be found already in Creation. This means, first, that historical progress does not lead to redemption: history is not a history of salvation (*Heilsgeschichte*). Second, and more strikingly, since in Maimonides the account of Creation corresponds to a physics of Nature and the account of Redemption corresponds to a metaphysics of Nature, Rosenzweig's thesis is that redemption is to be found in a materialist account of Nature that denies the illusion of historical development.

For Rosenzweig, and in this he also remains a follower of Maimonides and Spinoza, eternal life is related to knowing God, and the latter is equivalent to establishing the correct relation between the love of the neighbor (that is, politics) and the love of God (that is, religion). This correlation between politics and religion is grounded on the dualism of Creator and creature: "How else could he be conscious of loving God when he loves the neighbor, than because he knows in his core and from the start that the neighbor is God's creature.... Being created by God and being in the image of God are the foundations set down in him by Creation and upon this foundation he can build for himself the house of his eternal life in the temporal current of love going back and forth between God and love for the neighbor" (Rosenzweig 2005, 278). The distinction between human species and world with respect to their potential eternity is that the eternity of the human species is determined at Creation: "Man was created into the supra-man."[20] The world, by way of contrast, becomes "supra-world" in and through the revelation at Sinai (Rosenzweig 2005, 279). God is always eternal, that is, He is always in Redemption. The fundamental problem of the third part of *The Star* is, then, how can human beings attain eternal life by establishing God's Kingdom on earth. Rosenzweig's solution is that the Kingdom is established in an "untimely" movement of return to the origin, to Creation.

Since "Creation is really already Redemption," Rosenzweig argues that Jewish messianism ultimately stands for a "strange inversion" of temporality, whereby the end of Redemption becomes the beginning, becomes Creation: "In this reversal it [the life of the eternal people] denies time as resolutely as possible and places itself outside of it" (Rosenzweig 2003, 443). In other words, from the messianic perspective "progress" toward Redemption, or God's Kingdom, requires going against historical "progress" and turning time back toward Creation. Judaism must be understood as an "active denial" of the Christian *saeculum* and thus of the process of secularization: "The active denial would take place solely in the reversal" of time and the denial of history. As Rosenzweig says, "To reverse a between [the Christian *saeculum*] means to make its after into the before, and its before into the after, the end into the beginning, the beginning into the end. And the eternal people does that" (Rosenzweig 2003, 443). Anyone who has read Nietzsche's description of the eternal return in the second section of Part 3 of *Thus Spoke Zarathustra*, "On the Vision and the Riddle," will be struck by how similar it is to Rosenzweig's messianic inversion of time.

Benjamin's *Fragment* takes up Rosenzweig's thesis that the messianic age cannot be called forth in and through history and makes it the basis of his critique of those socialists and communists who understand the classless society or messianic kingdom as the endpoint of the historical process. Since history cannot bring about salvation, Benjamin postulates that "the secular order should be erected on the idea of happiness." This is the unmistakable Epicurean-Marxist signature of his adherence to messianism. The problem for Benjamin is finding the common term between Epicurean secularism and Jewish messianism. In the *Fragment* he opts to address this problem by presenting the messianic through a famous yet obscure image of an encounter of natural forces, very much in the spirit of Epicureanism whose philosophy of history depends on the cosmology of the swerve of atoms. Benjamin takes up the idea of the counterhistorical force of the messianic and gives it—unsurprisingly given the Maimonidean idea of Creation as the physics of Nature—a cosmological formulation, that is to say, a formulation in terms of physics:

> If one arrow points to the goal toward which the secular dynamic acts, and another marks the direction of messianic intensity, then certainly the quest of free humanity for happiness runs counter to the messianic direction. But just as a force, by virtue of the path it is moving along, can augment another force on the opposite path, so the secular order [*die profane Ordnung*]—because of its nature as secular—promotes the coming of the Messianic Kingdom. (Benjamin 2002, 305)

Commentators have not paid much attention to this strange attempt to figure a supernatural process (namely, that of salvation in the World to Come) through an image that comes from cosmological forces. What theory of physics is Benjamin thinking about?

In the Newtonian universe, there is one force at work in nature, and that is the force of gravity. This is the force of attraction between bodies. Benjamin and Scholem were both interested in the mathematical revolutions of the late nineteenth and early twentieth centuries, and I think it is safe to assume they also followed the revolutionary developments in physics, beginning with Einstein's discovery of special relativity, which shattered the Newtonian view of the universe. In particular, what must have struck their imagination was Einstein's attempt to apply relativity theory to the entire universe (theory of general relativity), thereby giving rise to the first truly scientific cosmology.[21] After all, in a letter to Scholem concerning Kafka's "cosmology," Benjamin cites from the work of the famous twentieth-century physicist Eddington, who sought to explain the new world picture revealed by Einstein's discoveries to a lay public.

For my purposes here, I shall not employ Eddington but American theoretical physicist Greene's more recent attempt at explaining the cosmology of general relativity to a lay public.[22] To make a long and complicated story short, when Einstein wanted to apply special relativity to the cosmos at a macrolevel, he had to presuppose that the universe is everywhere homogeneous. But this assumption generated a mathematical result that indicated the universe was not static but instead that space was always either expanding or shrinking. In order to compensate for this result, Einstein introduced a cosmological constant which represents the energy of space itself and which essentially consists in a "repulsive gravity" that can balance out the attractive kind of gravity exerted by the mass found in space.

Following Einstein's theory of general relativity, according to Greene, recent findings in cosmology have shown that the universe is in fact expanding and that it began with a Big Bang. However, there is still no consensus as to the shape of the expanding universe or whether it is finite or infinite: Does the universe curve outward, inward, or remain flat? The answer to this question depends on the overall density of matter in the universe. The discovery that energy also exists in space as so-called dark energy, makes it likely, when added to the density of matter, that space is expanding in a flat shape. Assuming that space is flat and infinite, then it could shrink to the point at which it "begins" in an event like a Big Bang and then expand again, and, if space is infinite, then it could "shrink" to attain that Big Bang density of matter without thereby ceasing to be infinite. The result is that the universe looks like an eternal and infinite space that shrinks and expands in a kind of cosmological rhythm, and this rhythm corresponds to "the turning on and then shutting off the inflationary burst" of repulsive gravity (Greene 2011, 51ff).[23] This is not unlike the Kabbalistic hypothesis of Tsimtsum (God's initial self-contraction that led to Creation).

It is conceivable that Benjamin's reference to two opposed forces at work in the universe (the historical and the messianic) appeals—however obscurely—to the interaction of two forces of this kind (and not simply to the action and reaction of one force exerted by two masses). This hypothesis is significant because contemporary cosmology tends to argue that the inflationary universe is in reality most likely a multiverse, that is, infinite space necessarily makes room for an infinite amount of parallel universes and corresponds uncannily with the hypothesis of the eternal return conceptualized by Nietzsche and Blanqui and recovered by Benjamin.

The first formulation of eternal recurrence appears in the *Gay Science* in the aphorism entitled: "The Greatest Weight" (Nietzsche 1974, 341). The "greatest weight" is an ambiguous expression; it can refer to the idea of gravity and to the vision of a universe dominated by the necessity of its force as the only force in it.[24] But it can also refer to the teaching of the eternal recurrence as a vision of the cosmos in which there is room for another force that makes all things or beings "lighter" and more joyful, a kind of repulsive gravity. It is striking that Nietzsche considers the eternal return as a cosmological hypothesis before he gives it what some commentators have called an "existential" formulation, namely, as "a test for life affirmation (or life denial)" (Hatab 2005, 66).[25] This latter formulation appears in the aphorism through the words of a "demon" who conjures the possibility that one's life, as it has been lived thus far, will repeat itself exactly the same way, forever: "There will be nothing new in it." The aphorism then suggests that the initial reaction of despair at the prospect of a life without novelty would be followed by enthusiastic acceptance for having lived "a tremendous moment" (and indeed, every moment could be such a tremendous moment) for the sake of which one would "desire nothing more than this ultimate eternal confirmation and seal" (Nietzsche 1974, 341). In this first, full-blown formulation, the notion of the eternity of every moment appears as "the greatest weight," which can either transform or destroy one; again, the analogy with the experience of reification in modern civil society as understood by Marx and Lukács is striking. Below we shall see that this ambivalent relation to the thought of eternal recurrence is also found in Blanqui.

In the second section of Part 3, "On the Vision and the Riddle," of *Thus Spoke Zarathustra*, the prophet Zarathustra again confronts the "spirit of gravity." Here, the cosmological context is placed in relief because Nietzsche has the taunting dwarf say to Zarathustra that no matter how far one throws a stone, it will eventually be dragged down by the force of gravity. What Zarathustra opposes to gravity is the vision of the eternal recurrence of every moment. This "vision" consists of two paths stretching out into an eternal past and an eternal future which meet under the gateway called the "moment" (*Augenblick*). In other words, every moment can be seen as the meeting point of an eternal past and an eternal future, in the sense that what will happen in the future has already happened an infinite number of times (in the past) and everything that has happened in the past will happen again an infinite number of times (in the future). The hypothesis of the eternal recurrence is that the future can be known by looking into the past and, conversely, by looking into the past one shall be led to the future. This formula is general enough to explain both astrology and cosmology where in both practices, one peers at the stars, the (eternal) past, because they contain the (eternal) future. Benjamin therefore says that "the [materialist] historian is a prophet turned backwards" (Benjamin 1991c, 1235).

In his last notebooks collected under the title *The Will to Power* Nietzsche tried to offer physical arguments for the doctrine of eternal recurrence.[26] These have usually not been taken very seriously. Yet the recent cosmology of a multiverse (that is, the idea that there exist an infinity of parallel universes in infinite space) may provide Nietzsche's cosmological hypotheses with some degree of vindication. According to such a cosmology, there are an infinite number of regions in infinite space that lie beyond the cosmic horizons (that is, beyond the reach of light) of any given universe and that they evolved without the possibility of any interchange of light or information between them. This has led cosmologists to speak of a "patchwork" of universes spread out in limitless space where "each patch represents a single cosmic horizon" (Greene 2011, 29). Given this assumption, Greene argues that eternal return is a physical necessity because "collectively, a finite number of particles, each of which can have finitely many distinct positions and velocities, means that within any cosmic horizon only a finite number of different particle arrangements are available. . . . By the same reasoning, the limited number of particle arrangements ensures that with enough patches in the cosmic quilt—enough independent cosmic horizons—the particle arrangements, when compared from patch to patch, must somewhere repeat" (Greene 2011, 33). If one is a consistent materialist, then one must hold that "a physical system is completely determined by the arrangement of its particles," from which it follows that

> if the particle arrangement with which we're familiar were duplicated in another patch—another cosmic horizon—that patch would look and feel like ours in every way. This means that if the universe is infinite in extent, you are not alone in whatever reaction you are now having to this view of reality. There are many perfect copies of you out there in the cosmos, feeling exactly the same way. And there's no way to say which is *really* you. All versions are physically and hence mentally identical. . . . And so every possible action, every choice you've made and

every option you've discarded will be played out in one patch or another. (Greene 2011, 34)

The most recent advances in cosmology seem to give credence to the belief that the doctrine of the eternal recurrence of the same is a scientific doctrine perfectly compatible with the most rigorous materialism.

Having presented the structure and logic of the eternal recurrence as a scientific hypothesis, I am now in a position to return to Benjamin's *Fragment* in order to explain how this same teaching represents the highest formulation of a messianic thought. The central messianic claim found in the *Fragment* is the following:

> The spiritual *restitutio in integrum*, which introduces immortality, corresponds to a worldly restitution that leads to the eternity of downfall, and the rhythm of this eternally transient worldly existence, transient in its totality, in its spatial but also temporal totality, the rhythm of messianic nature, is happiness. For nature is messianic by reason of its eternal and total passing away. (Benjamin 2002, 306)[27]

Nature is redeemed or attains its messianic state (which now simply means that nature or the universe is brought back to its state at creation, at the moment of the Big Bang) in the form of a "worldly restitution that leads to the eternity of the downfall" because it eternalizes every one of its contingent and fleeting moments. In my opinion, the most likely referent for such a "worldly restitution" is the eternal repetition of every world in the (messianic) rhythm of this eternal life which consists in the eternal rebirth of universes found in the cosmology of parallel universes. As Rosenzweig shows, the Jewish (but not the Christian) messianic doctrine holds that Redemption is not found at the "end" of History, but in a return to the beginning, a return to Creation. From the perspective of the eternal recurrence, Creation *is* Redemption because Creation means the *eternal* creation and decreation of parallel universes that make up the eternally repeated life of the universe. The eternal life of Redemption, viewed messianically, is this very same eternally repeated, worldly and utterly profane life.

According to Benjamin, such an "eternally transient" existence is the counterpart to the immortality of the soul because it effects a *restitutio in integrum*, it restores the lost integrity. The term employed by

Benjamin is of legal origin, referring to cases of negligence where damages sought are not punitive, but rather restore what was lost by rescinding the contracts or agreements that caused harm, and thus returning the parties to their original position. From a messianic perspective, in particular, it is the Mosaic covenant and its introduction of the idea of sin and guilt in relation to life (*zoe*) and natality (symbolized by the Fall of Adam and Eve) that caused harm to the human species as a living species. A restoration of original innocence, that is, of eternal life prior to the Fall, can only occur by rescinding the terms of this covenant (and, by extension, the terms of all religious covenants). In so doing, the human species falls back on the eternal repetition of every moment of its fleeting, animal life, caught up in a rhythm of destruction and recreation that is the worldly order of happiness. Why the happiness of the human species coincides with its "downfall" to an eternal, animal life remains unsaid in Benjamin's *Fragment*, but one thing now appears clearly, namely, that the messianic age must be thought of in terms of the eternal recurrence, and not against it.

Benjamin concludes the *Fragment* by adding that "the task of world politics" consists in striving towards such an eternal "passing away" of nature, "whose method must be called nihilism" (Benjamin 2002, 305–6). Based on the above interpretation, the term "world politics" should be understood as a cosmo-politics or cosmopolitanism, a politics based on the cosmology of the eternal recurrence that strives to eternalize life in this world, rather than seeking to redeem or transcend it in a World to Come.[28] Such a cosmo-politics is "nihilistic" because it does not aim to make the world "better," because it does not posit a "true" world beyond this eternally transient world. Such a cosmo-politics affirms that what there is in this world—everything that constantly rushes to its destruction—is all that there is. Yet, the eternal "Yes" addressed to every fleeting instant—that from one point of view is the depth of nihilism—is also a secret invocation of the messianic kingdom, which can only enter the world through the narrow door provided by each and every one of its fleeting moments. Here, therefore, is already *in nuce* the critique of progress and the preoccupation with the "now-time" of revolution that characterizes Benjamin's later *Theses on the Concept of History*.[29]

ETERNAL LIFE AND HAPPINESS IN DOWNFALL

In all likelihood, Benjamin had already penned the *Theologico-Political Fragment* prior to 1938, when he communicated to Horkheimer that he had found a copy of Blanqui's *L'éternité par les astres* in a Parisian second-hand bookstore. Still, the joy of recognition upon reading Blanqui's meditation must have been great for it seems to incorporate a worldly nihilistic politics, together with the vision of eternal recurrence, that Benjamin had already formulated in his *Fragment*. Just like Nietzsche's, Blanqui's theory of eternal recurrence relies on a principle of physics. Blanqui follows Laplace's spectral analysis which gave the result that sixty-four chemical elements composed the entirety of the stars in the infinite universe. (Blanqui was aware that more elements could be discovered in the future, but his point is that this new number would still be finite.) He then reasoned, like Greene, that given a finite set of elements in a finite number of combinations, an infinite number of iterations will eventually have to recombine in exactly the same way, not once but an infinite number of times, in order to fill the infinity of the universe. Like in Greene's multiverse, Blanqui also deduces from the eternal recurrence the consequence of "infinite Doppelgängers."[30] Thus "each man possesses in the infinite extension an indefinite number of doubles who live one's life in exactly the same way that he lives it. He is infinite and eternal in the person of other himselves. [*Il est infini et étérnel dans la personne d'autres lui-meme*]" (Blanqui 2003, 45, translations mine). This is a first sense in which the materialist doctrine of the eternal recurrence of the same entails a conception of eternal life; we eternalize ourselves not in our personal self-consciousness, but in and as our impersonal avatars.

In the preparatory fragments of the *Baudelaire* book, Benjamin offers a dialectical interpretation of Blanqui's vision of eternal recurrence. Undoubtedly, as many commentators have pointed out, Benjamin sees it as a picture of Hell, "the most terrible indictment against a society" (Benjamin 1991c, 1071), which projects into its cosmology the situation of late capitalism characterized by the eternal recurrence of the same commodities, each one an identical avatar of the other (Benjamin 1991c, 1153).[31] He writes, "The idea of eternal recurrence transforms the historical event itself into a mass-produced article" (Benjamin 2006, 140). Benjamin speaks of Blanqui's vision as a mythical example of the *Urgeschichte* of the nineteenth century (Benjamin 1991c, 1174). Thus, in an unpublished fragment, he writes that in every myth the existence of the world is conceived as punishment. In the case of the eternal recurrence, where "the universe is cast in bronze and copies incessantly the same page" (Blanqui 2003, 46) the punishment becomes the eternity of *Nachsitzen*, where humanity is forced to copy the same lesson forever (Benjamin 1991c, 1234).

Furthermore, as interpreters have clarified, Benjamin also identifies in Blanqui's vision the work of "spleen," the modern form of melancholia that reduces history to a fossilized landscape, representing human history as "natural history." Blanqui's text voices this melancholia explicitly: "This eternity of humankind determined by stars is melancholic, and even sadder is that our brother-worlds are sequestered from us by the inexorable barrier of space" (Blanqui 2003, 48). This melancholia is the other side of the consciousness that there is no progress: "Always and everywhere in the terrestrial arena, the same drama, the same setting, on the same narrow stage—a noisy humanity infatuated with its own grandeur, believing itself to be the universe and living in its prison as though in some immense realm, only to founder at an early date along with its globe, which has borne with deepest disdain the burden of human arrogance" (Blanqui 2003, 48). For Benjamin, Blanqui's vision of eternal return is a destruction of progress, which shows that what is most "modern" is also what is most ancient, simply repeated, innumerable times.

Yet this radical destruction of the ideal of historical progress cannot be separated from the revolutionary possibility contained in every present instant, something for which Blanqui always stood.[32] Lukács closes his central essay on reification in *History and Class Consciousness* with the claim that class consciousness is demonstrated in whoever "is willing and whose mission it is to create the future," "the birth of the new" (Lukács 1968, 203–4). It is this Lukácsian reference to the "new" as emerging from the dialectical overturning of commodity fetishism, of eternal repetition, that is explicitly recovered in Benjamin's reading of Blanqui. Taking an idea from Löwith's interpretation of the eternal recurrence in Nietzsche (Löwith 1997), Benjamin hypothesizes that "the new" that is supposed to jump out of the spleen and its eternal return, is the very thought of the eternal recurrence, which breaks with repetition insofar as it confirms it (Benjamin 1991c, 1152). Thus, Benjamin concludes that "the true messianic face" of a classless society is the interruption of history that can happen at any instant (Benjamin 2006, 1231–32) when one understands that the structure of the present, or every "today," is given by its eternal recurrence.

Benjamin, Arendt, and Blücher (Arendt's husband to be) briefly coincided in Paris during their exile from Nazi Germany. Benjamin recorded some conversations between them on the political meaning of Blanqui's cosmology and, specifically, on the point of whether such cosmology expressed Blanqui's hopelessness about the revolution. Blücher—who had himself been a member of the German Communist Party before going into exile—defended the hypothesis that the cosmology and the conspiratorial activities of Blanqui shared a secret continuity and were aspects of one and the same political thought (Benjamin 1991c, 1154). Is the eternal recurrence the affirmative thought of Blanqui as the leader of the proletarian party (as Marx calls him), or is it the "desperate" meditation of a failed, jailed conspirator who wanted to artificially create the revolution before its historical conditions of possibility were realized? For Marx, Blanqui's belief in the revolutionary "Now-time" was an "alchemy of revolution" while, for Benjamin, it was an indication of an allegorical view of history (Benjamin 1991c, 1157; Benjamin 2006, 51–52). This disparity is fundamental and is taken up in nearly the same terms by Foucault in his late essay "What is Enlightenment?" where the crucial question appears to be identical to that shared by Blanqui and Benjamin: What difference can "Today" make for history? Only within the framework of a theory of eternal recurrence, of the destruction of all illusions of progress and teleology in human history, can this question really assume a critical dimension.

For Benjamin, the goal of a communist politics can only be the worldly happiness of the human species once it rejoins all other living species. Such a politics requires rescinding the covenant with God as Creator and wiping clean the guilt (the debts) and the "bad conscience" of the debtor (the workers) accrued in relation to this Creation.[33] Such an idea of worldly happiness is tied to the idea of the eternal recurrence because, as a late fragment in *Central Park* claims, "eternal recurrence is an attempt to combine the two antinomical principles of happiness: that of eternity, and that of the 'yet again'" (Benjamin 2006, 161).[34] Benjamin does not oppose undialectically the messianic "now" of revolution to the eternal recurrence of the same in capitalist commodity production. For Benjamin, our happiness is made up of events that could have happened to us in our lives, but which did not happen during our transient, worldly existence. As he says in the second of the *Theses on the Concept of History*, "The kind of happiness that could arouse envy in us exists only in the air we have breathed, among people we could have talked to, women who could have given themselves to us" (Benjamin 1968, 254). We do not envy people who are completely other than ourselves, but the personal impersonality of other ourselves who we think are happy.[35]

Blanqui expresses a similar intuition: despite the fact that "every human being is eternal in every second of its existence" (Blanqui 2003, 47) because its life is being lived an infinite number of times on parallel planets and by parallel avatars, the eternally recurring universe is constantly changing; avatars that die at one point of the infinite universe are being produced, exactly the same, in another part of the infinite space, beyond our cosmic horizon. Blanqui calls this process "an alternation, a perpetual exchange of renaissances through transformations" (Blanqui 2003, 46). I would argue that this eternal rhythm of destruction and rebirth is what Benjamin's *Theologico-Political Fragment* identifies as the only possible form of a happy life because each of our lives is not only lived exactly like we live it forever, but it is also lived, by another avatar, in a slightly different way than we live it, and that happy version is also lived like that forever: "Let us not forget that everything that we could have been here on earth we actually are somewhere else" (Blanqui 2003, 47).[36] Referring to Kafka, Benjamin also speaks of a hope which exists only for the hopeless, for those who have abandoned all belief in progress.

Thus, the happy life that could have been ours, but was not, does exist; it is the life of avatars in parallel universes where every possible variation of what did not happen, but could have happened, is actually alive and present. If our present is really the "today" that some past has been expecting in the hopeless hope of being redeemed by it, as Benjamin theorizes in the *Passages* and in the *Theses on the Concept of History*, then such an expectation is grounded in Blanqui's cosmological proof of the eternal recurrence of the same. The encounter with the past that constitutes the messianic moment on this earth, in Benjamin, already exists and has always existed in some parallel universe. Cosmologically speaking, the messianic is that "little door" or "wormhole" that opens up between two infinitely separate universes allowing for their communication and interaction. The doctrine of the eternal recurrence of the same is a cosmological proof of the existence of a messianic life.

Benjamin diverges from Blanqui's melancholic vision because he does not exclude the possibility that avatars may encounter one another. Blanqui's idea of repetition misses the possibility of repetition within history itself, that is, the return of the past as and into the present that brings to a halt the empty progression of time. But this is a consequence that follows from Benjamin's conception of happiness. In order to recapture those events that could have happened to us, but did not, it must be possible to relive our past life, to recapitulate it, so to speak (this corresponds to the other idea that Benjamin connects with *restitutio*, namely, the idea of *apokatastasis*). This, in turn, constitutes the messianic interruption of historical becoming or the "now" of revolution. In the essay "On Some Motifs in Baudelaire," Benjamin argues that involuntary memory is that organ which recaptures this happy past that never was a present, and he opposes it to the shock-encounters in modern civil society that destroy the aura of natural things and their ability to look back into our eyes (Benjamin 1991b, 645–46).[37]

What Blanqui never managed to conceptualize, according to Benjamin, is the paradoxical way in which the eternal recurrence of the same interrupts the eternal repetition of the identical cosmic drama. Benjamin relies on a suggestion made by Löwith according to which the doctrine of the eternal recurrence in Nietzsche has two senses, an "anthropological" and a "cosmological" interpretation. According to the first, "the eternally same recurrence appeared as an ethical task, renewing itself in every moment, for the willing man for whom this teaching is to replace the Christian belief in immortality" (Löwith 1997, 156–57). Löwith had identified this last aspect of the eternal recurrence in Nietzsche as its hidden "Christian" heritage, in the sense that, for Christianity, a single event (in this case, the resurrection of Jesus Christ into eternal life) is enough to break the "eternal circles" of pagan cosmology. But Benjamin does not adopt this interpretation of the eternal recurrence, if only because his messianism is radically non-Christian and his materialism is cosmological. Benjamin's fundamental belief that past historical events are the potential meeting points of opposed profane and messianic forces is a conception antithetical to the Pauline belief that a single event (for example, the resurrection of Jesus the Christ) can save the whole of history and direct it beyond itself (to God's Kingdom). The notion of eternal recurrence destroys every conception of progress: for Benjamin, this destruction of progress is a necessary response to the fact that all of history is one catastrophe, every event a ruin, a fragment. What counts for Benjamin, as for Nietzsche, is the "use" that can be made of this destruction of history "for life," that is, for human happiness.

In the *Theologico-Political Fragment* Benjamin claims that everything on earth seeks its happiness in its decadence or going under. "For in happiness all that is earthly seeks its downfall [*im Glück erstrebt alles Irdische seinen Untergang*], and only in happiness is its downfall destined to find it" (Benjamin 2002, 305). The thesis is drawn from the *Birth of Tragedy* where Nietzsche relates the Dionysian destruction of the illusion of individualism to the Chtonic (and not the Olympian) conception of divinity; thus, it is no coincidence that in the *Fragment* Benjamin uses the expression of "*das Irdische*" ("the earthly") when speaking of this profane happiness in clear allusion to the Dionysian-tragic context in which the *Fragment* and the problem of eternal life must be placed.

Tragic wisdom, according to Nietzsche, is a Dionysian affirmation of life that both adopts and adapts to a higher purpose the wisdom of Silenus, according to which "not to be born, not to be, to be nothing" is the best, and "second best for you is—to die soon" (Nietzsche 1993, sect. 3). Nietzsche believes that the wisdom of Silenus applies to the self-destructive hero who represents the principle of individualism; the individual *bios* must perish so that species-life (*zoe*) may eternalize itself and give rise to ever new creations. With the doctrine of eternal recurrence, the tragic destruction of individualism finds support in a cosmological principle. As Löwith formulates the "cosmological" interpretation, "the recurrence appeared not as a 'plan for a new way to live' and a 'will to rebirth' but as *destruction and rebirth that happens by nature* and that is completely indifferent to all plans made by man out of his thrownness" (Löwith 1997, 157, emphasis mine). Nothing is unique, everything that exists has already existed an infinite amount of times, and everything is its own copy. In this way, the Dionysian appropriation of this destruction of individualism experiences the eternal recurrence also as the hieroglyph of the circle of redemption itself,[38] the *restitutio in integrum* through which each life is eternally returned to the moment of beginning anew. As Löwith correctly puts it, shifting the accent on the centrality of eternal life (*zoe*) in Nietzsche: "The eternal recurrence is a recurrence of what is always the same, that is: of life that is uniform and of equal power in everything living" (Löwith 1997, 189). "And what overcomes itself to affirm the eternal recurrence is—in case *all* life is self-overcoming—also not man ... but life, which is homogeneous and of equal power and significance in all that is" (Löwith 1997, 191). Understood from this perspective, the eternal recurrence of the same is a doctrine that redeems natality, the happiness of creation, as part and parcel of the self-destructive (because self-overcoming) drives of impersonal, eternal life on earth.[39]

Only the connection of eternal recurrence as a cosmological principle to life and natality explains why Nietzsche always associated the idea of eternal recurrence with the true nature of a happy life. The first time that the concept of eternal recurrence appears in his corpus, it is in the context of Nietzsche asking himself for the conditions of "the greatest fruitfulness and the greatest enjoyment," that is, the conditions in which creativity coincides with pleasure, natality with happiness. Not unlike Hegel who saw in Antigone's divine law of natality a redemption of war in the punishment it imposes on the violence exerted by sovereignty and state-hood in the name of their political *bios*, so here Nietzsche associates the Dionysian principle of natality with leading a "dangerous" life, capable of desiring "the eternal recurrence of war and peace" (Nietzsche 1974, 285).[40] Given that Blanqui's avatars nullify the bourgeois illusion of self-ownership, revealing the sense in which each one is exactly the same as everyone else, and thus making possible the coincidence of class consciousness with the messianic now-time of revolution, is it far-fetched to think Benjamin saw in Blanqui's revolutionary life (*bios*), always defeated and always ready to give it one more try, the true reflection of happiness in eternal life (*zoe*)?

NOTES

INTRODUCTION

1. In the current literature one finds at least three distinct approaches to biopolitics. For the sociological approach to Foucault's discourse on governmentality and biopolitics, see Lemke 2007. Agamben's and Esposito's body of work perhaps is best understood as a political philosophy of life. For an approach that connects the sociological with the ethical aspects of biopolitics, see N. Rose 2007; Fassin 2009. The trilogy of Negri and Hardt (2001, 2005, 2011) contains many illustrations of a trajectory of thought that traverses the field of biopolitics from the standpoint of a political philosophy of life to a theory of subjectivity. In general, this subject-oriented interpretation of biopolitics is associated with Deleuze 1988.

2. For a preliminary discussion of this term, see Vatter 2009.

3. For the current discussion on the "idea of communism," see Douzinas 2010. For the "communist horizon" as articulated within the perspective of Badiou and Žižek, see Bosteels 2011; J. Dean 2012. For the relation between republicanism and communism in the sense employed here, see Vatter 2007, 2004a.

4. For a previous reading of Hegel's *Phenomenology of Spirit* from a Foucaultian perspective, see Butler 2000, chap. 1, but neither political economy nor biopolitics feature centrally in this interpretation. For the current critical theory approach to Foucault, see the articles in Honneth and Saar 2003. On how Foucault's studies of governmentality connect to Marxist concerns, see Marzocca 2008; Legrand 2004; Lemke 2004; Nigro 2001.

5. "If the great Cartesian break posed the question of the relations between truth and subject, the 18th century introduced with respect to the relation between truth and life, a series of questions of which *The Critique of Judgment* and the *Phenomenology of Spirit* were the first great formulations. . . . Must not the entire theory of the subject be reformulated once knowledge, instead of opening itself to the truth of the world, roots itself in the 'mistakes' of life?" (Foucault 2001a, 1595, translation mine).

6. Although Kouvelakis (2003) and Abensour (2010) rescue a "republican" or "radical democrat" Marx, they avoid the task of finding this republicanism in Marx's mature works on economics and, in particular, in his theory of value.

Honneth (2011) argues that it is a hopeless task to join Marx's critique of political economy with his "democratic" politics and proposes to discard the former while keeping Marx's historical analyses of working class struggles as more or less acceptable descriptions of the importance of "events" in the normative self-understanding of "struggles for recognition." The arguments in this book both with regard to the critique of political economy and to the theory of revolutionary events cast into doubt Honneth's strategy.

7. For an interpretation of Hayek as the master thinker of neoliberalism, see Mirowski and Plehwe 2009.

8. For some examples, see Agamben 2005; Badiou 2003; Žižek 2003. For recent discussions of messianic politics critical of the above literature, see Butler 2012; Martel 2012.

1. THE TRAGEDY OF CIVIL SOCIETY AND REPUBLICAN POLITICS IN HEGEL

1. On these concepts, see now Esposito 2010.

2. See d'Hondt 1990.

3. One of the best treatments of the problem of *Natural Law* is found in Dickey 1987, 213–27. But Dickey does not see how the combination of Plato and Greek tragedians in *Natural Law* orients Hegel's political thought on an orbit that is far beyond any "Christian" way of dealing with political economy (Dickey speaks of a "theology of divine economy" that is supposed to counteract political economy) (Dickey 1987, 229).

4. See G. Rose (1981) and Dickey (1987) on Hegel's critique of Kant and Fichte being ultimately motivated by his critique of political economy. For a less political, more philosophical approach to Hegel's critique of Kant and Fichte, see, in general, Siep 1992.

5. I discuss the problem of legal exception in Benjamin, Agamben, and Foucault further in Chapters 3, 6, and 7.

6. On Hegel's liberalism and antiliberalism, see Ruggiero 1944; Habermas 1987; Smith 1989; Honneth 1992; Cristi 2005; Kervégan 2005.

7. For variations on this interpretation, see Taylor 1979; Bobbio 1981; Riedel 1982; Heller 1999; Dallmayr 2002.

8. On honesty as bourgeois virtue, see Hegel 1979, 149/468ff. On bourgeois virtues in a sense that is not incompatible with Hegel's view, see now McCloskey 2010.

9. I have modified the English translation of the passage where necessary to clarify its meaning.

10. For a brief recapitulation of Hegel's mature conception of freedom, see Wood 1990, 36–52.

11. Both G. Rose (1981) and de Boer (2010a) have tried to understand Hegel's *Logic* from his early conception of tragedy, but neither have emphasized as I do

here the crucial role played by the mechanism of sacrifice and its critique in Greek tragedy in Hegel's political thought.

12. "The form of reason which takes shape here as a tragic one is political, namely, republican, since the equilibrium between Kreon and Antigone, between the formal and counter-formal, is kept too equal" (Hölderlin 1988, 115).

13. As already foreshadowed, I discuss the "sociality of reason" from a Freudian angle rather than from a more rationalistic approach found in recent Hegelian scholarship (Pinkard 1994; Pippin 1989, 1997, 2011; Habermas 2004, 186–229).

14. This does not detract from Butler's point that, for example, "opposing Antigone to Creon as the encounter between the forces of kinship and those of state power fails to take into account the ways in which Antigone has already departed from kinship, herself the daughter of an incestuous bond, herself devoted to an impossible and death-bent incestuous love of her brother, how her actions compel others to regard her as 'manly' and thus cast doubt on the way that kinship might underwrite gender, how her language, paradoxically, most closely approximates Creon's, the language of sovereign authority and action" (Butler 2000, 6). However, it is undeniable that Hegel's understanding of Antigone, and in general of tragic conflict, is also attuned to the ways in which the tragic hero breaks with the logic of taboos (a logic that structures, at once, both kinship and the communal power based on it—at least if one goes by Freud's hypothesis).

15. See here the work on sacrality in Agamben 1998, 2005.

16. See the long discussion of war as battle of revenge in Hegel 1979, 133–42/451–60. Somewhat later Hegel specifically distinguishes between a war "of families against families" from the *sittlich* sense of war, "of peoples against peoples" (Hegel 1979, 149/468).

17. In Greek tragedies, the presence of a sacrificial meal is signaled by the use of metaphors of the hunt and eating of savage animals through which a "sacrifice" is adorned. See Vidal-Naquet's essay on "Chasse et sacrifice dans l'*Orestie* d'Eschyle" in Jean-Pierre Vernant 2001, 133–59. On the blending of sacrifice and hunt, see Girard 2005; Segal 1982, 27–53; and especially Detienne 1977.

18. On the importance in Hegel's conception of freedom of *Freigabe* (in difference from *Autonomie*), see the excellent points made by Siep 1992, 166–71.

19. On Antigone's "incestuous" *philia* and its subversive role, see now Butler 2000, although I disagree that "there is no justification for the claim Antigone makes. The law she invokes is one that has only one possible instance of application and is not, within any ordinary sense, conceptualizable as law" (33). If Antigone is referring herself to the law of natality, then there may be a way in which natality and legality fit together, as I explain further in Chapters 3 and 7 dedicated to Arendt's conception of natality. For other attempts at defending the

political sense of Antigone's appeal to divine law, see Weber 2004; Honig 2013, chaps. 5 and 6.

20. As Girard also argues, the *dispositif* of the sacrifice is always already set aside once a mechanism of civil justice is at hand because civil justice puts an end to the threat of revenge (Girard 2005, chap. 1, passim).

21. On Athena's rejection of "femininity" and her embodiment of the virtue of warriors, see Vernant 1974, 169–77. The classical reading of the sexual politics underlining the *Oresteia* trilogy remains in my opinion that of Winnington-Ingram 1948, who brings out the features of Clytemnestra as an Amazon-manqué and understands Athena as a counterpart to Clytemnestra precisely due to their shared masculinity: "Everything, then, that Clytemnestra's nature demanded and her sex forbade or hampered, Athena is free to do, by virtue of her godhead" (Winnington-Ingram 1948, 144). Winnington-Ingram is also careful to show that Athena, because she is neither born of woman nor is she married, is the only one who can overcome the conflict between the (matriarchical) claims of kinship voiced by the Furies and the claims of (patriarchical) marriage voiced by Orestes as justification for the murder of his mother (Winnington-Ingram 1948, 145–47).

22. The importance of the antimonarchic reference is picked out in Harris 1973.

23. On *Hestia* from a philosophical perspective, see Benvenuto 1993.

24. On the problem of the *Pöbel* in Hegel, see the wide-ranging reconstruction in Losurdo 2004.

25. "Society was now based on complicity in the common crime; religion was based on the sense of guilt and the remorse attaching to it; while morality was based partly on the exigencies of this society and partly on the penance demanded by the sense of guilt" (Freud 1950, 146).

26. Acosta (2009) and de Boer (2010a, 21–29) have proposed that Hegel's shift from his reading of the *Eumenides* in *Natural Law* to his reading of *Antigone* in the *Phenomenology of Spirit* reveals a shift in his understanding of tragedy itself. For Acosta, Hegel defends Greek *Sittlichkeit* as a successful model of reconciliation in his reading of the *Eumenides* only to later criticize Greek ethical substance in his reading of *Antigone*. For de Boer, the original "entanglement" of opposite principles found in the *Eumenides* is discarded by Hegel in his later interpretation of *Antigone*, which more traditionally follows the self-subversion of each principle due to the very fact of abstract opposition. I argue below that the *Phenomenology* (and thus Hegel's reading of *Antigone*) adheres to the logic of (self-)sacrifice already found in *Natural Law* (and its reading of *Eumenides*).

27. On the limitation of civil courts of justice to account when "the people becomes the criminal" in and through "singular individuality," see also Hegel 1979, 175/497.

28. In the *Genealogy of Morals* Nietzsche will argue that all moral conscience originates in the experience of being punished for a debt incurred.

29. Bienenstock's analysis of Hegel's idea of *sittliche Macht* (political power) in its difference from *Gewalt* as violence or coercion has captured well the same intuition. In this sense, I agree with her thesis that for Hegel "it is culture, not force, which invests the state with power" (Bienenstock 1983, 143).

30. See Kojève 1969; Honneth 1992. For attempts at relativizing the importance of the struggle for recognition between master and slave, see Smith 1992; Faes 1995; Bluhm 2004.

31. On the relation between discipline, "polished" social conduct and "civil" society, see now Taylor 2004.

32. I refer to Strauss's discussion of the master-slave dialectic already to be found in Hobbes (Strauss 1952, chap. 2).

33. Rousseau roots all ethical virtue in the "natural virtue" of pity, and of this latter says that it "will be all the more energetic as the witnessing animal identifies itself more intimately with the suffering animal. Now it is evident that this identification must have been infinitely closer in the state of nature than in the state of reasoning. Reason is what engenders egocentrism [*amour propre*] and reflection strengthens it" (Rousseau 1992, 37). Later, Rousseau also is careful to distinguish "savage society" or what Hegel calls "natural *Sittlichkeit*" from "civil society": in the former, "each one began to look at the others and to want to be looked at himself, and public esteem had a value. The one who sang or danced the best, the handsomest, the strongest, the most adroit or the most eloquent became the most highly regarded" (Rousseau 1992, 49); in civil society, by way of contrast, inequality depends exclusively on wealth and poverty.

34. "For example fish are determined by nature to swim and big fish to eat little ones, and therefore it is by sovereign natural right that fish have possession of the water and that big fish eat small fish.... For the power of nature is the very power of God who has supreme right to do all things" (Spinoza 2007, chap. 16). "Everything that occurs in the organic world consists of overpowering, dominating, and in their turn overpowering and dominating consist of reinterpretation, adjustment, in the process of which their former 'meaning' and 'purpose' must necessarily be obscured.... The form is fluid, the 'meaning' even more so.... It is no different inside any individual organism: every time the whole grows appreciably, the 'meaning' of the individual organs shifts" (Nietzsche 1994, Essay 2, sect. 12).

35. See Heidegger 1988, 141–48, in which he places life at the center of Hegel's conception of self-consciousness, correctly perceiving Hegel's reliance on Aristotle's *De anima*. On this point, see Bienenstock 1989. I take up Heidegger's and Aristotle's conceptions of life in Chapter 8.

36. On the human being as the animal that classifies, and on the paradox that the classifying animal falls under no classification, see now Agamben 2004, 23–27.

37. For the complications attached to the idea of desiring the Other's desire, see now Butler 2010.

38. On Schmitt's relation and debt to Hegel as well as of the question of how "Schmittian" Hegel really was, see Kervégan 2005; Cristi 2005.

39. For Strauss's Kojevian reading of Hobbes, I refer to Vatter 2004b. For Pippin's own discussion of Strauss, Kojève, and Schmitt, see Pippin 1997.

40. See also Markell's claim that the slave's self-consciousness is characterized by "a self-negation, an abdication of self-consciousness' own claim to absolute independence" (Markell 2003, 107).

41. In *Natural Law* Hegel speaks about "the necessity of war. In war there is the free possibility that not only certain individual things but the whole of them, as life, will be annihilated and destroyed for the Absolute itself or for the people; and therefore war preserves the ethical health of peoples in their indifference to specific institutions, preserves it from habituation to such institutions and their hardening. Just as the blowing of the winds preserves the sea from foulness which would result from a continual calm, so also corruption would result for peoples under continual or indeed 'perpetual' peace" (Hegel 1975, 93). I think the reference here is to the "winds" of republican warfare that swept into Germany with the French Revolution and Napoleon's campaigns. See Lukács's discussion of this point in Lukács 1975; and now Dotti 2009.

42. On the tribunal of world history, see now Nuzzo 2012, 129–35.

43. For a recent discussion of the long and complicated relation between these passages in Hegel's work and feminist thought in the twentieth century, see Hutchings 2010. For a very interesting argument that Hegel is not referring to Sophocles at all, but instead to Aristophanes's "feminist" comedies, see de Boer 2010b.

44. For a reading of Machiavelli along these lines, see Vatter 2013.

45. Hence I differ from Butler's thesis that "Hegel's writing moves to suppress Antigone and to offer a rationale for suppression: 'the community . . . can only maintain itself by suppressing this spirit of individualism'" (Butler 2000, 36). Markell, by contrast, has given an ingenious reading of this passage in which "womankind" is said to refer to the depiction in Polyneices's shield which portrays "a woman leading modestly a man, conducts him, pictured as a warrior . . . She claims she is justice" (Markell 2003, 116). But Markell's reading cannot account for the fact that in Hegel's text womankind is associated with luck (*fortuna*) rather than justice, and the brave youth (*virtù*) is not "modestly" led by the feminine power.

46. I discuss this other economy of desire in Chapter 5 in relation to the problem of marriage in civil society.

47. "In this way Theseus founded Athens, and the French Revolution preserved the state, the whole, through horrible violence. This violence is not despotism but tyranny, pure dreadful domination, but it is necessary and justified, because it constitutes and preserves the state as this real individual. This state is the simple absolute spirit [*Dieser Staat ist der einfache absolute Geist*] . . . no concept of good

and bad, infamy and baseness, craftiness and trickery; it is itself all of this but elevated, because evil is reconciled with itself in the state—Machiavelli's *The Prince* was written in this great sense" (Hegel 1987, 258–59, translation mine).

2. LIVING LABOR AND SELF-GENERATIVE VALUE IN MARX

1. For the history of composition, see the still excellent foreword by Nicolaus in Marx 1974. See now also Bellofiore 2009, in relation to the new critical edition (MEGA) of Marx's work.

2. On Marx's critique of constitutionalism, see Abensour 2010; Kouvelakis 2003; Brunkhorst 2007.

3. The citation is found in the *Erstausgabe des Kapitals*, MEGA, vol. M/II.5, Berlin: Dietz, 37.

4. I discuss this motif in the next chapter. For the problem of animality in Adorno and Horkheimer, see also Lemm 2010.

5. On the paradigm break occasioned by Habermas's *Theory of Communicative Action* within the Frankfurt School, see Brunkhorst 1983.

6. In 1997 was published in German a collection of the most significant writings Backhaus 1997. I shall be mostly referring to a representative essay in Backhaus 1992. The ideas of Backhaus were influential in the volumes of *Open Marxism* edited by Bonefeld, Gunn, and Psychopedis; they are also influential on the approach represented by Bellofiore; see also Bellofiore 2004. Bidet 2007 is structured around a critique of Backhaus's interpretative paradigm.

7. A precursor to Backhaus's ideas on the form of value can be found in the Russian economist Rubin 1978.

8. See Brunkhorst 1983, for an attempt to show how the categories of Habermas's theory of communicative action take over from the categories of a Marxist theory of value in an attempt to break the impasse identified by Adorno.

9. It seems to me that the approach to Marx proposed by Wolff and Resnick is unable to disentangle itself from this aporia: they offer more of a (sociological) interpretation of class and of surplus value without giving sufficient weight to the (economic-legal) problem of the form of value. But see Gibson-Graham 2001; Wolff 1998.

10. I place "abstract" in parentheses because Ricardo did not have a concept of average social labor, that is, a concept of abstract labor. Marx believed that this was one of his innovations in economics.

11. In marginalist theory, this amounts to the claim that the surplus is a result of the owner cutting down on costs of production, not on exploiting the labor-power of the worker.

12. For another view point on the "eternity" of value, see Kordela 2002.

13. In general, on immaterial labor, see Lazzarato 1997.

14. On the problem of measure in relation to Negri's reading of Marx, see now Cooper 2010; Caffentzis 2010.

15. Bidet's recent work on *Capital* also proposes to understand the internal relation that capitalist economy has with the system of law; to that end he appeals to the concept of "organization" to understand the essence of law (Bidet 2007). In my opinion, this effort is misguided principally because the neoliberal conception of a system of law is antithetical to the idea of "organization," as I discuss in Chapter 6. In any case, Bidet does not mention the possibility of a biopolitical analysis of capital.

16. "Money is the physical medium into which exchange-values are dipped, and in which they obtain the form corresponding to their general character" (Marx 1974, 167).

17. "All commodities are perishable money, money is the imperishable commodity.... Money is originally the representative of all values ... in practice the situation is inverted, and all real products and labors become the representative of money [that is, capital]" (Marx 1974, 149).

18. "The truth is that the exchange-value relation—of commodities as mutually equal and equivalent objectifications of labor time—comprises contradictions which find their objective expression in *a money which is distinct from labor time*" (Marx 1974, 169).

19. In Chapter 9 I discuss the ways in which Lukács and Benjamin understand this point and what follows from this in relation to class consciousness and class conflict.

20. On the connection between poverty and form of life in the Franciscan movement, which is common to both Negri and Agamben, see now Agamben 2011.

21. Negri refers to Marx 1974, 287: "The worker's participation in the higher, even cultural satisfactions ... is economically possible only by widening the sphere of his pleasures." Here the crucial importance of the earlier works of Rancière on disposable time, see above all Rancière 2012.

22. "Rather the exchange of objectified labor as value, as self-sufficient value, for living labor as its use-value, as use-value not for a specific, particular use of consumption but as use-value for (exchange) value" (Marx 1974, 469).

23. I refer here on recent work dedicated to the "precariat," for instance, Lorey 2012.

24. See Lemke 1997, 2007, 2011; Bröckling 2011.

25. This is the dimension of biopolitics that lies at the centre of Rose's investigations into "the politics of life itself" and "ethopolitics." See N. Rose 2007, 24–27, 39–40.

26. On the biopolitics of production in relation to Foucault's thought, see now also Revel 2008; Marzocca 2008.

27. Negri makes his "autonomist" idea of living labor dependent on the axiom that it is possible to return to a "purity" of use-value: "All multiplication of wealth and life is linked to this type of value: there is no other source of wealth and power"; "Marx characterizes the working class as a solid subjectivity ... its use-value is creative; it is the unique and exclusive source of wealth" (Negri 1991, 70, 73).

28. As Cooper puts it, "Life, as mobilized by regenerative medicine, is always in surplus of itself.... What regenerative medicine wants to elicit is the generative moment from which all possible forms can be regenerated—the moment of emergence" (Cooper 2008, 127).

3. REIFICATION AND REDEMPTION OF BARE LIFE IN ADORNO AND AGAMBEN

1. The concept of bare life does not play a central role in other commentaries of Benjamin's essay, see for example Derrida 1994, 124–26; Honneth 2007, 154–56. For Butler, divine violence has the finality of manifesting the "sacred in life," which coincides with a dissolution of the bond between guilt and the rule of law (but not with a dissolution of guilt). The sacred in life, on her reading, is the permanent transience of bare life (Butler 2006, 216–17).

2. Most of the secondary literature dedicated to Agamben's political thought is centered on his conception of sovereignty, not on his affirmative politics of bare life. See, for instance, Norris 2005; Geulen 2005; Sinnerbrink 2005; Fox 2007; Passavant 2007.

3. See Negri and Hardt's claim that "capitalist prehistory comes to an end ... when naked life is raised up to the dignity of productive power, or really when it appears as the wealth of virtuality" (Hardt and Negri 2001, 366).

4. Compare with Heidegger's basic definition of *Da-sein* in *Sein und Zeit*: "In its Being this entity is concerned about its very Being [*diesem Seienden in seinem Sein um dieses Sein selbst geht*]" (Heidegger 1986, 12, translation mine).

5. On the fundamental opposition between life-world and system that stands at the basis of Habermas's version of critical theory, see Habermas 1975, 1984b.

6. Only through the "anthropological machine" do animals become beasts. For the attempt to overturn this perspective, and show the "bestiality" of men from the point of view of the animal, see Derrida 2006; Lemm 2009.

7. See Heidegger 1995. I discuss Heidegger's conception of animal life further in Chapter 8.

8. In Agamben's discourse, the term "the Open" (*das Offene*) has two, opposite meanings. In one sense, *das Offene* refers, in the manner of Rilke or Nietzsche, to what surrounds the animal and keeps it "in" without dominating or excluding it. In another sense, *das Offene*, in the manner of Heidegger, is a synonym for what only a world-disclosure is able to obtain, namely, access to the Being of beings.

Agamben wants to argue that the authentic world-disclosure occurs only when one is made aware of the animal Open. For an attempt to apply Agamben's discourse to understand life in the "German-Jewish" tradition from Kafka through Rosenzweig and Benjamin to Celan, see Santner 2006, 10–15.

9. This is the kind of conception of nature that Benjamin appeals to in *Thesis XI* when he envisages "a kind of labor which, far from exploiting nature, is capable of delivering her of the creations which lie dormant in her womb as potentials" (Benjamin 1968, 259).

10. On the concept of form-of-life, see Quintana 2006.

11. See Adorno's injunction: "Try to live in such a way that one may believe to have lived life like a good animal [*versuchen, es so zu leben, dass man glauben darf, ein gutes Tier gewesen zu sein*]" (Adorno 2003, 294, translation mine).

12. The concept of fetishism, and its relation to facticity, characterizes Agamben's thought from his earliest publications, see Agamben 1979b, 1999a, 1999b.

13. On this passage, see the commentary in Buck-Morss 1991, 110–58; Marinas 2001.

14. On the disputed paternity of the idea of commodity fetishism as a dialectical image, see Hillach 2000, 186–229.

15. In Adorno's criticism to Benjamin there resonates Horkheimer's theory of labor and rationality found in Horkheimer 2005, 215 and 244.

16. In his exposé Benjamin speaks of things being "freed from the drudgery of being useful" (Benjamin 1999a, 9).

17. On such creatures in Benjamin and Kafka, see Hanssen 2000; Santner 2006, 26–27.

18. Horkheimer and Adorno argue that the family is not only an essential moment of individuation, but also perhaps the only place where the individual experiences that happiness he or she longs for during the rest of his or her life, but only on condition that the family be liberated from the father's authority over the household (Horkheimer 2005, 191). See also the recent rehabilitation of the family in Honneth 2001, 94–101.

19. On this point, see also Butler 2005, 105; Kaufmann 2001, 166–69.

20. Rhetorically, Agamben sets out to defend Benjamin from Adorno's charge of being undialectical and skipping over the necessary mediations between economic structure and cultural superstructure. Thus, Agamben responds to Adorno that "Marx abolishes the metaphysical distinction between *animal* and *ratio*, between nature and culture, between matter and form, in order to assert that, in praxis, animality is humanity, nature is culture, matter is form. If this is true, the relation between structure and superstructure can be neither a causal determination nor a dialectical mediation, but an immediate identity" (Agamben 1979a, 123). But in his subsequent work, notably in *The Open*, Agamben gives an interpretation of the above mentioned identities between man and animal,

nature and culture, precisely in the sense of Adorno's "rational identity," as I have indicated above.

21. On reification in Lukács, Heidegger, and Adorno, see Goldmann 1977; Honneth 2005; G. Rose 1978; García-Düttmann 2004. I return to discuss reification in Chapter 9.

22. See also the account of the common found in Hardt and Negri 2005, 103–15, 202–8.

23. See the decisive third footnote of chapter 3 of *The Protestant Ethic* (207–10).

24. "The bourgeoisie cannot exist without constantly revolutionizing the instruments of production, and thereby the relations of production, and with them the whole relations of society.... All that is solid melts into air, all that is holy is profaned" (Marx 1978b, 476).

25. For recent interpretations of this text, see Weber 2005; Steiner 2006.

26. Agamben's explanation of capitalism's immunity against revolutionary consciousness (that is, its immunity against profanation) recalls the theses of Marcuse on consumer society and its ability to nullify social contradictions in *One-Dimensional Man*.

27. The idea of the "rest" or "remainder" is fundamental to Agamben's thought, and it appears in the Italian titles of his books *Ciò che resta di Auschwitz, Homo Sacer III* (Agamben 1999c) and in *Il tempo che resta* [*The Time that Remains*].

28. On the discussion of Kafka's relation to Judaism and theology, see Biale 1985; Horwitz 1995; Kaufmann 2001; Weigel 2008.

29. On the parable as a meditation on violence "before" the law, see Derrida 1985, which Agamben discusses in Agamben 1998, 49–54. On the relation between Agamben and Derrida, see Thurschwell 2005, 173–97.

30. On the Führer as "living law," see Agamben 1998, 173; 2005, 137–43. On terror as "realization of the law of movement of some suprahuman force, Nature or History," see Arendt 1973, 465.

31. Cited in Moses 1999, 159. Agamben renders the thought as follows: "It does not signify, yet still affirms itself by the fact that it is in force" (Agamben 1998, 51).

32. As Moses and others have shown, Scholem's formula of a law that is in force without signifying is meant as a positive description of the "negative theology" that he identifies in Kafka (Moseș 1999, 150).

33. Benjamin states that "it is our task to bring about a real state of emergency" in *Thesis* VIII (Benjamin 1978, 257). For the distinction between "willed" and "real" state of emergency, see Agamben 2005, 55–57.

34. "The kind of happiness that could arouse envy in us exists only in the air we have breathed, among people we could have talked to, women who could have given themselves to us" (Benjamin 1968, 254). I return to this idea in Chapter 9.

35. Motifs found in *Theses* XVI through XVIII (Benjamin 1968, 262–63).

36. See *Thesis* II. Agamben renders this idea as follows: "What cannot be saved is what was, the past as such. But what is saved is what never was,

something new.... So in historical redemption what happens in the end is what never took place. This is what is saved.... But this—what has never happened—is the historical and wholly actual homeland of humanity" (Agamben 1999b, 158).

37. For another interpretation of this conception of study in Agamben, Benjamin, and Kafka, see Weber 2008, 198–210.

38. Kaufmann (2001, 158) argues that in Benjamin's reading of Kafka there is a separation of theology from revelation, and Benjamin keeps the former and discards the latter in order to advocate an antinomian, Pauline reading of the messianic. In this sense, Kaufmann is much closer to Agamben's Benjamin interpretation than the one I offer here. Kaufmann interprets the idea of study as turning "existence into Scripture, life into doctrine," and entailing a "dream of a redeemed law ... a code that takes the distinctions out of judgment and the judgment out of law." He even identifies this new law with Kafka's story of Sancho Panza. There is in Kaufmann the attempt to read Sancho Panza in directly Pauline terms. As Kaufmann says, Benjamin uses Sancho Panza in order to "imagine Scripture without commandment, revelation without the law" (2001, 160). This position ultimately leads Kaufmann to see Benjamin's position and Adorno's as much closer than they are in reality, coinciding on their purportedly common "theology" just where I see them diverging most strongly.

39. Kafka's prose poem is cited completely in Benjamin 1999b, 816, but Benjamin leaves the text without an interpretation.

40. "Every epoch, in fact, not only dreams the one to follow but, in dreaming, precipitates its awakening. It bears its end within itself and unfolds it—as Hegel already noticed—by cunning" (Benjamin 1999a, 13).

41. The ironical sense of *Thesis* I is pointed out by Wohlfarth 2006, 268: "Benjamin draws very different consequences from his theologico-political model than Adorno.... Where Adorno believes that he is defending Benjamin's own theology against its author, Benjamin gives up the kind of 'Esotericism' Adorno subscribes to him.... Adorno's standpoint in this sense is no less '*plump*' than Brecht's.... No matter whether we are dealing with theology or with autonomous art, Adorno's credo is the same: the more one contributes to historical materialism, the less one follows it" (translation mine).

42. Agamben mentions this citation once, as far as I can tell, but leaves it without interpetation (Agamben 1999b, 154).

43. See *Thesis* IX in Benjamin 1968, 257.

4. NATALITY, FERTILITY, AND MIMESIS IN ARENDT'S THEORY OF FREEDOM

1. Arendt is often, and in a sense rightly, seen as an antibiologistic thinker in the secondary literature, see Ricoeur 1983; Heller and Feher 1994; Savarino 2003; Beiner 2004. But this assumption has also often had the unfortunate consequence of leading interpreters to abstract Arendt's concept of natality from her complex theory of life (Kristeva 2000).

2. "The human condition of labor is life itself" (Arendt 1958, 7). See also Arendt 1958, 98–99.

3. Arendt defines "the human condition of plurality" as "the fact that men, not Man, live on the earth and inhabit the world" (Arendt 1958, 7).

4. At the time of writing and publishing this article, Birmingham (2006) was not yet available to me and so I could not take into account her reading of natality. I discuss her interpretation in Chapter 7 in relation to Arendt's theory of human rights. Geulen (2008) seems unaware of previous scholarship on Arendt and biopolitics.

5. Arendt cites Augustine in connection with the idea that natality is the condition of human freedom in Arendt 1977, 167; 1978, II, 217; 1973, II, 108–10; 1990, 212–13, 215.

6. The best account of the significance of these lacunae for the interpretation of Arendt's system as a whole remains Forti 1996; see also Savarino 1997.

7. There is a brief, but important discussion of the possible Heideggerian origin of the concept of natality in Schürmann 1996, 68n33. Collin discusses Schürmann's interpretation, and in general takes up the paradox of Arendt's concept of natality, seemingly embedded in nature yet antinatural (Collin 1999, 99). Bowen-Moore also thinks that Arendt's treatment of "natality as a philosophical theme" is of Heideggerian provenance (Bowen-Moore 1989, 2), and is intended to counteract Heidegger's emphasis on mortality. Szankay problematizes the "philosophical" understanding of the concept of natality, but nonetheless also separates it from both "anthropological" and "biological" category (Szankay 1995, 6). Brunkhorst (1999) mentions that the term "natality" seems to correspond to Heidegger's discussion of birth found in section 72 of *Sein und Zeit* (Heidegger 1983, 374). Villa (1996) and Taminiaux (1985) ignore this Heideggerian origin in their discussions of Arendt's relation to Heidegger's thought.

8. On the philosophical importance of the suffix—*barkeit* for a theory of capacity or faculty, see Weber 2008.

9. On Voegelin's understanding of modernity as a return of gnosticism, see Voegelin 1994, 1952. On Blumenberg's response and later correspondence with Schmitt on these matters, see Blumenberg 1996, 2007.

10. It is no coincidence, therefore, that Arendt's first mention of natality occurs in her article on "Ideology and Terror" where she equates totalitarianism with the

"tyranny of logicality" (Arendt 1973, 473) and opposes it to "the great capacity of men to start something new" because "over the beginning, no logic, no cogent deduction, can have any power because its chain presupposes, in the form of a premise, the beginning." It is also no coincidence that in her book on Eichmann Arendt would later argue that the "radical evil" of totalitarianism was precisely its "banality," understood as the "thoughtlessness" with which Hitler's executioners proceeded in applying his commands.

11. For a discussion of the analogy between Nazism and gnosticism, see in general the treatment of Nazi thanatopolitics in Esposito 2008.

12. This is also what Voegelin believes, and that is why it was especially important for Arendt to refute Voegelin's critique of her totalitarianism book (Arendt 1994, 401–9). For Voegelin, in fact, the solution to the nonseparation of life from thought could only be Platonist, that is, based on a conception of the soul or *psyche* whose most proper object of desire (*eros*) are the ideas, pure and eternal objects of thought. For Arendt and Jonas, on the contrary, the only possible solution to the nonseparation of thought from life consists in rejecting their absolute transcendence, in making thought inhere in life. That is why Arendt's last work is entitled *The Life of the Mind*: "life" here is to be taken as a fundamental basis for "mind."

13. See, for example, his essay "Evolution und Freiheit" (Jonas 1994, 11–33) where Jonas argues that metabolism, even in one-celled organisms, provides the "fundamental sense in which the concept of freedom can serve as the thread of Ariadne to come to an understanding of what we call 'life'" (Jonas 1994, 13, translation mine).

14. Jonas compares Heidegger to gnosticism in his article "Gnosticism and Modern Nihilism" published in *Social Research* in 1952. The text appears as the epilogue to (Jonas 1958). Arendt identifies the fundamental experience on the basis of which totalitarianism emerges as "loneliness," which translates directly Heidegger's *Einsamkeit* as a fundamental feature of human existence, an analysis of which is given in (Heidegger 1995). Crucially, this is the text (based on the lectures he gave in 1929–30) where Heidegger goes to great lengths to separate human existence, which is "weltbildend," world-forming, from animal life, which is famously characterized as being "weltarm," lacking in world. I discuss further Heidegger's conception of animal life in Chapters 3 and 8. Jonas rejects Heidegger's claim that human *Dasein* is "lowered" by being placed, qua "animal rationale," in continuity with animality (Jonas 1958, 333).

15. A particular important statement is found in Benjamin's *Theological-Political Fragment* (Benjamin 2002, 305–6), which I discuss at length in Chapter 9. The most condensed formulation of this motif in Benjamin appears in the second of his *Theses on the Concept of History*, a typed manuscript of which Arendt brought with her from Paris to New York: "Our image of happiness is indissolubly bound up with the image of redemption. The same applies to our view of the past, which is the concern of history. The past carries with it a temporal index by which it is

referred to redemption. There is a secret agreement between past generations and the present one. Our coming was expected on earth" (Benjamin 1968, 254). On the foundation of political philosophy on the "happy life" in this Benjaminian sense, see also (Agamben 2000a, 113). Villa's claim that "the spirit of Benjamin, not Heidegger, informs her search for hidden treasures," though true, remains completely undeveloped and indeed stands in unresolved tension with his principal thesis according to which Arendt's "ontological approach to human freedom . . . points unequivocally toward Heidegger and specifically toward *Being and Time*" (Villa 1996, 119). On Arendt's relation to Benjamin in Berlin and Paris and her efforts to publish his posthumous work, see Schoettker 2006.

16. In her 1929 discussion of Augustine's theory of Creation, Arendt emphasizes Augustine's idea that "man is something so long as he adheres to him by whom he was made a man." To which Arendt glosses: "This adhesion is not a matter of will and free decision; it expresses a dependence inherent in the fact of createdness" (Arendt 1996, 51). The English translation is not quite exact because the phrase "fact of createdness" is not in the original: Arendt says, "Diese Bezogenheit ist keine willkürlich gestiftet, sondern der Ausdruck der *Abhängigkeit* der *creatura qua* creatura" (Arendt 1929). She does speak of a "Tatsache der Kreatürlichkeit" or "fact of creatureliness" (Arendt 1929). The point, for Arendt, is to distinguish a false "dependence" of human beings to their desired objects, which orients action toward death and the future, from a true "dependence" of human beings on an "origin," that is, divine Creation, that "relies exclusively on rememberance and refers back to the past" (Arendt 1996, 51). It is only the latter dependence that "frees" human action from teleology and allows it to be *novitas*. Only in the 1964–65 revision of her old manuscript does she add, "To put it differently, the decisive *fact* determining man as a conscious, remembering being is birth or 'natality', that is, the *fact* that we have entered the world through birth. The decisive fact determining man as a desiring being was *death or mortality* [clear allusion to Heidegger's standpoint in *Sein und Zeit*]. . . . In contrast, *gratitude for life* having being given at all is the spring of rememberance, for a life is cherished even in misery. . . . This will to be under all circumstances is the hallmark of man's attachment to the transmundane source of his existence" (Arendt 1996, 51). Here one sees the decisive shift between the original version of 1929 and the revised version thirty years later: the "fact" of "creatureliness" has becomes the "fact" of "natality." Both facts determine a condition of human existence that is not the object of the will because it depends on creation, but whereas in 1929 Arendt interprets "life" from the status of being a creature (thus she speaks of "der Art des kreatürlichen Lebens" in Arendt 1929), by the time of her revision creatureliness comes to be defined in terms of life: "gratitude for life having being given at all" is the crucial fact. There follows Arendt's revised conclusion: "Hence, it was for the sake of *novitas*, in a sense, that man was created. Since man can know, be conscious of, and remember

his 'beginning' or his origin, he is able to act as a beginner and enact the story of mankind" (Arendt 1996, 55).

17. In the published article I was misled by the English translation into believing that Arendt used the expression "human condition" already in her dissertation. This is not the case. I take this opportunity to correct that mistake.

18. In *Sein und Zeit* Heidegger writes "Das 'Wesen' des Daseins liegt in seiner Existenz" (Heidegger 1986, 42). Arendt will discuss and criticize these positions immediately after the war, in her essays "What Is Existential Philosophy?" and "French Existentialism" (Arendt 1994, 163–96).

19. Parts of which are now found in Arendt 2005.

20. "What radical evil is I do not know, but it seems to me it somehow has to do with the following phenomenon: making human beings as human beings superfluous (not using them as means to an end, which leaves their essence as humans untouched and impinges only on their human dignity, rather, making them superfluous as human beings). This happens as soon as all unpredictability—which, in human beings, is the equivalent of spontaneity—is eliminated. And all this in turn arises from—or, better, goes along with—the delusion of the omnipotence (not simply with the lust for power) of an individual man. If an individual man qua man were omnipotent, then there is in fact no reason why men in the plural should exist at all" (Arendt and Jaspers 1992, March 4, 1951). The idea that "making men superfluous" is definitive for the totalitarian phenomenon is also found in (Arendt 1973, 459).

21. On the importance of biopolitics as the central avenue to the interpretation of totalitarianism, see Forti 2003, 2006. For an attempt to read Arendt's political theory as a response to biopolitics, see Duarte 2004. But on Duarte's interpretation, Arendt stands clearly outside the discourse of biopolitics and offers an external critique thereof. Duarte modifies his earlier views, also in response to my interpretation, in his recent treatment of the question in Duarte 2010. See also the discussions of Arendt's importance for contemporary biopolitics in Braun 2007; Bazzicalupo 2006.

22. On the concept of "target" and "targeting" in relation to Benjamin, see Weber 2005.

23. I use this expression from Deleuze and Guattari to indicate that aspect of life insofar as it escapes, or avoids, being the "target" of domination (Deleuze and Guattari 1987).

24. This does not mean that natality corresponds to Heidegger's concept of *Geworfenheit* (thrownness) (Heidegger 1986, 135), as claimed, all too quickly, in Benhabib 1996, 109; Villa 1996, 141.

25. That the "living death" of the Muselmänner was achieved in the Lager in part through forced labor, that is, through a practice of laboring with no end or purpose in sight (Arendt 1973, 444f), is further evidence, for Arendt, that the way

toward a totalitarian politics of death is prepared by the universalization of the condition of *animal laborans* in a society of "jobholders," a society in which whoever is so unlucky as to fall into unemployment runs the risk of literally being left to die (Arendt 1973, 126–35, 322).

26. This is the basic dualism that Ricoeur, among many others, sees at the basis of Arendt's "philosophical anthropology" (Ricoeur 1983, 22). For a recent interpretation of Arendt's theory of natality entirely based on the neo-Aristotelian dualism between *bios* and *zoe*, see Durst 2004. For a discussion of the biopolitical significance of Aristotle's distinction between *bios* and *zoe*, see Agamben 1998. For a critique of this distinction in contemporary biopolitical discourse on the grounds that it does not correspond to Aristotle's usage, see Dubreuil 2006; Finlayson 2010. Both seem to miss the evident point that, for Aristotle as for just about every philosopher in the Western tradition, there is a crucial and politically relevant distinction to be made between the individual form of life and the life of the species. But see now Romandini 2010, for a detailed analysis of the relevant texts in Plato and Aristotle that modifies Agamben's interpretation while maintaining its central thrust.

27. This is the path variously pursued, for example, by Foucault and Deleuze. It is also the path defended in Lemm 2009.

28. Already in the last part of her dissertation Arendt shows that in Augustine the idea of "community" or "society" of the faithful (that is, the city of God) cannot escape reference to a common descent of the "human race" from one progenitor (Arendt 1996, 111). Arendt's point is precisely that such a common descent makes it impossible to think of forming a political society based on the plurality of individuals: the society of the faithful (the church) is a society of a plurality of individuals "isolated" in God's presence, but it is not, for all that, a political society. I disagree with Collin's reading of the dissertation, for whom Arendt's conception of plurality signals the "conjunction" of Augustine's two cities (Collin 2000, 86).

29. Arendt's "humanist" position, prior to her discovery of the category of natality, is crystallized in the following claim: "Actually the experience of the concentration camps does show that human beings can be transformed into specimens of the human animal, and that man's 'nature' is only 'human' insofar as it opens up to man the possibility of becoming something highly unnatural, that is, a man" (Arendt 1973, 455). It is interesting that in her analysis of totalitarian domination, which tries to transform "the human personality into a mere thing that even animals are not," Arendt claims that "under normal circumstances this [goal] can never be accomplished, because spontaneity can never be entirely eliminated insofar as it is connected not only with human freedom but with life itself, in the sense of simply keeping alive" (Arendt 1973, 438). Here Arendt clearly wants to link human freedom to a biological condition, but has not yet identified natality as this condition.

30. See Arendt's ambiguous description and attitude toward the racism of Boers: "The Boers were never able to forget their first horrible fright before a species of men whom human pride and the sense of human dignity could not allow them to accept as fellow-men.... What made them [African peoples that according to Arendt belong to 'tribes of which they have no historical record and which do not know any history of their own'] different from other human beings was not at all the color of their skin but the fact that they behaved like a part of nature, that they treated nature as their undisputed master, that they had not created a human world, a human reality.... They were, as it were, 'natural' human beings who lacked the specifically human character" (Arendt 1973, 192).

31. "Not the loss of specific rights, then, but the loss of a community willing and able to guarantee any rights whatsoever, has been the calamity which has befallen ever-increasing numbers of people. Man, it turns out, can lose all the so-called Rights of Man without losing his essential quality as man, his human dignity. Only the loss of a polity itself expels him from humanity" (Arendt 1973, 297).

32. In *Origins of Totalitarianism* Arendt speaks of "the assumed existence of a human being as such" as the doubtful basis of "the conception of human rights" (Arendt 1973, 299). A similar scepticism about the existence of a "human nature," or, should it exist, about the possibility of coming to know it, opens *The Human Condition* (Arendt 1958, 10–11). Arendt, instead, opts for speaking about the "conditions," as opposed to the "nature," that make a "human" life possible.

33. "Not only did loss of national rights in all instances entail the loss of human rights; the restoration of human rights, as the recent example of the State of Israel proves, has been achieved so far only through the restoration or the establishment of national rights" (Arendt 1973, 299).

34. "The result of understanding is meaning, which we originate in the very process of living insofar as we try to reconcile ourselves to what we do and what we suffer" (Arendt 1994, 309). Here the accent must fall in the radical refusal to separate "understanding" from "process of living," and, equally, on the need to reconcile oneself to the limitations of action by recognizing "what we suffer."

35. Such a reading of Arendt characterizes the early reception of *The Human Condition* and still weighs on interpretations like the one suggested by Benhabib (1996), who sees, precisely in the presumed attachment of Arendt to the *polis*-experience, the root of her "reluctant" modernism. In this context it is interesting to consider the exchange between Jaspers and Arendt occasioned by her biography of Rahel Varnhagen, in the letters from August 23, 1952, and September 7, 1952. Arendt responds to Jaspers as follows: "You're absolutely right when you say this book 'can make one feel that if a person is a Jew he cannot really live his life to the full.' And that is of course a central point. I still believe today that under the conditions of social assimilation and political emancipation the Jews could not 'live.' Rahel's life seems to me a proof of that precisely because she tried out everything on herself

without attempting to spare herself anything and without a trace of dishonesty. What always intrigued me about her was the phenomenon of life striking her like 'rain pouring down on someone without an umbrella'" (Arendt and Jaspers 1992, 198). What is interesting in Arendt's response, in my terms, is her attempt to think the negation of life, the "lack" of life as experienced by an assimilated Jew in the eighteenth and nineteenth century, by referring to "the phenomenon of life" itself, rather than by appealing to some value or sphere beyond life itself. That is why Arendt both picks up on Jaspers intention, but changes its meaning by dropping his idea of a "full" life not accessible to Jews as Jews. By this time, Arendt had begun to find the way out of the impasse at the end of *The Origins of Totalitarianism*.

36. On Arendt's messianism and its connection to Benjamin's idea of a "weak messianic force," see now Gottlieb 2003, 135–60.

37. In "Ideology and Terror" she defines totalitarianism as a movement akin to a "sandstorm" started by "teaching and glorifying the logical reasoning of loneliness where man knows that he will be utterly lost if ever he lets go of the first premise from which the whole process is started" (Arendt 1973, 478).

38. The idea that we are born into a world that is primordially a "desert" is very old in Arendt. In her dissertation she speaks of "the particular strangeness in which the world as a 'desert' preexists for man" (Arendt 1996, 67). In a fragment of 1955 she speaks of the "threat" posed to the world as in-between by natality, then adds, "in its need for beginners that it may be begun anew, the world is always a desert" (Arendt 2005, 203).

39. Examples of the tendency of thinking natality as always already contained within the world abound: "A birth happens to the being who is born.... It is invariably already human because it is always welcomed by human beings, caught in a narrative which questions it.... It is immediately the child of words—the child of the Word as much as of the flesh" (Collin 1999, 107); "The question of beginning, of natality, is ultimately linked to one's sense of communal identity, that is to say, linked to one's sense of belonging and to one's way of comporting oneself in a world inhabited by and shared with others" (Bowen-Moore 1989, 9); "The world which receives us into it and makes us feel welcome is not the world objectified by natural science but a phenomenological world, a world of human doings, of affairs of men in association with one another, of sights and sounds appropriate to a fitting human dwelling" (Beiner 1984, 362); "The weakness of the parvenu and the strength of the pariah depend on how much they received or did not receive with birth, that is, having or not having had the possibility to benefit from the experience of 'feeling at home.' *Heimatgefühl* constitutes the intimate nucleus of the personal identity that functions as 'first root'" (Durst 2004, 785); "Natality is the condition through which we immerse ourselves into a world at first through the goodwill and solidarity of those who nurture us.... The condition of natality involves inequality and hierarchies of dependence" (Benhabib 1996, 196).

A welcome exception is Tassin (1999), who clearly sees the tension between natality and world building. That natality does not "destine" the individual to a given world is what Tassin refers as the "acosmism" of Arendt's conception of freedom. But Tassin does not relate this "acosmism" further to Arendt's theological foundation of her concept of natality.

40. Dietz (1995) and Pitkin (1998) both reject, against some previous feminist readings of Arendt, the claim that her concept of action and of politics is "gendered," in the sense that the public sphere would be predetermined as masculine in opposition to the feminine private sphere. By contrast, both seem to argue that Arendt's concept of labor is gendered because of the strong association Arendt makes between labor and giving birth (Pitkin 1998, 166). Whatever Arendt may have thought about the family, she never associates natality with the household or with child rearing. Natality is the reason for the existence of politics; it is not the reason for the existence of the family. This is clear from her rejection of all attempts to root the political in the presumed "need" that human beings have to live together in order to take care of necessities. If natality is associated to labor in Arendt, it is only in the sense that the politicization of labor should emancipate it from the strictures of the family. "The great, enormously great and entirely unrecognized merit of Marx: having grounded public life and the being of man on labor and not on the family. The emancipation from the spell of labor and the tyranny of the family. The emancipation of property as a basis of political life is merely a consequence of the emancipation of the political from the family" (Arendt 2002, 71). I pursue further this theme in Chapter 5.

41. In a note from December 1952, Arendt comments on Aristotle's passage that distinguishes "living" from "living well" and asks herself, "Marx: what happens if instead of *logon echon* one places the 'laboring' (=producing) living being? Marx never doubted about the animality (*das Animalische*) in the definition 'animal rationale.' Through the concept of labor he attempts to connect immediately what is specifically human to the animal. That means, mutatis mutandis, to derive freedom from necessity. . . . The Greeks do the opposite: they 'derive' freedom out of the 'rational' or violent domination of the necessary. This is one of the reasons why the *logos* becomes tyrannical. . . . *Eu zen*= to live in freedom= to dominate tyrannically over necessity" (Arendt 2002, 280–81). If one recalls that Arendt always opposes freedom to the "tyranny" of logic, it becomes clear that in the above passage she sides with Marx's attempt to politicize life through a new conception of labor, against the Greek solution.

42. On this reading, the old debate as to whether Arendt is "nostalgic" for the Greek *polis* or, instead, merely a "reluctant" modernist is shown to be completely besides the point. Conversely, her attack on Marx for having politicized labor and life can be analyzed as an attempt to distinguish her own position from someone with whom she felt herself uncomfortably close—this closeness is manifest in

Arendt's defense of the communes as the form of government of the future (of a democracy to-come, Derrida would say), opposed to the present form of government, that is, totalitarian government (Arendt 1990).

43. See Heidegger's definition of world as referential totality in *Sein und Zeit*: "The relational totality of this signifying we call significance. It is what makes up the structure of the world" (Heidegger 1986, 87, translation mine). Obviously the question of the "meaning of politics" that structures Arendt's *Was ist Politik?* mimics Heidegger's pursuit of the "Frage nach dem Sinn von Sein" in *Being and Time*. Yet for Arendt this pursuit of the "Sinn" (meaning) of politics is also and explicitly carried on against existentialism, as shown by her critical essays on French and German existentialism of the same period (Arendt 1994). The crucial difference between the Heideggerian-existentialist pursuit of meaning, and the Arendtian one, is that Heidegger still has in *Sein und Zeit* a prelinguistic, subjectivistic conception of meaning, as shown now by Lafont (2000, 11–84), whereas for Arendt the question of meaning is always already linguistic and so intersubjective: there is no revealing or appearing of something as something prior to and without speech.

44. On the conditions of phenomenalization and singularization, and their internal limits, see Schürmann 1996. But Schürmann interprets Arendt's natality as a principle of phenomenalization only; whereas he follows Heidegger in the belief that mortality, not natality, is the counterprinciple of singularization. I argue, instead, that Arendt's natality also serves as a principle of singularization. Plurality, rather than mortality, functions for her as principle of phenomenalization.

45. For Kant, freedom as a fact of reason has no phenomenality. Arendt struggles throughout her *Denktagebuch* in the 1950s to find a way in which to reconcile Kant's definition of freedom as spontaneity with his claim that freedom is an idea of reason.

46. Arendt speaks of dramatic *mimesis* as the only way in which "the living flux of acting and speaking can be represented" (Arendt 1958, 187). But my use of "mimetic" in this context is derived from the sense that Benjamin, and then Adorno, gave to this term, where *mimesis* stands for a nonrepresentational relation, that Benjamin calls a "nonsensuous similarity" (Benjamin 1999b, 696). It is interesting to note that Benjamin associates the "mimetic faculty" to natality: "If, however, mimetic genius was really a life-determining force for the ancients, then we have little choice but to attribute full possession of the gift, and in particular its perfect adaptation to the form of cosmic being, to the newborn. The moment of birth, which is decisive here, is but an instant. This directs our attention to another peculiarity in the realm of similarity. The perception of similarity is in every case bound to a flashing up" (Benjamin 1999b, 695).

47. In a recent article on natality, Markell has provided an interesting interpretation of what I call the mimetic relation between natality and action, one that emphasizes the "responsive" character of action to its condition of natality. His

claim is that "we can also understand the relationship of beginning to birth in Arendt by seeing 'birth' as the paradigmatic case of an 'event' to which the actor responds" (Markell 2006, 7). Natality "is that in virtue of which the actuality of events acquires its weight" (Markell 2006, 7). For Markell, the crucial character of action lies in its being always already a "response" to the givenness of an event, a response that signals the significance of this event for the actor. That is why Markell, somewhat surprisingly, argues that "nothing about beginning requires a break with the terms of an existing order, or resistance to regularity as such." All that beginning reflects is "a stance of practical engagement with events" (Markell 2006, 7). Thus action or beginning is always already "our attunement to its [the event's] character as an irrevocable event, which also means: as an occasion for response" (Markell 2006, 10). The problem with this reading is twofold: it seems to deprive natality of its status as "ontological root" of action because it turns action into a matter of taking or not taking an intentional "stance" toward the actuality of events, and thus something that we can choose to adopt or not to adopt. Arendt's theory of action receives in this way an occasionalist interpretation. The second problem with Markell's reading is that natality comes to represent, in the life of the individual, merely its openness to "the constellation of circumstances, events and forces, to which each new act is a response" (Markell 2006, 10). Natality here loses the crucial feature of being the condition of human life that pulls, in and through its reference to the absolute past of creation, every actor out of its captivation to the present circumstances. In Markell natality becomes the source of a "latent self" found in the present circumstances of our life that we can only make "patent" through our actions. Action would then merely reflect what one understands to be one's "place in the world," where this place is pregiven with respect to the in-between individuals constitute in and through their actions and words.

5. THE HEROISM OF SEXUALITY IN BENJAMIN AND FOUCAULT

1. In this context, it is customary to refer to the passage from John 17:3, "This is eternal life [*zoe aionios*], that they may know Thee the only true God," which harkens back to the prophetic beliefs in an age in which all peoples will have access to the vision of God. In both the Jewish and the Christian traditions, eternal life does not refer to the pagan conception of the immortality of soul as much as to that form of life that will prevail in the age (*aion*) to come, when human beings shall return to the Garden of Eden. The main distinction between these two traditions is that for the Christian eternal life is already accessible through faith in Jesus Christ, whereas for Judaism eternal life presupposes the advent of a messianic time which precedes the Last Judgment.

2. For a thoroughgoing discussion of the problem of guilt and myth in Benjamin's early work, see now Greiert 2011, 83–142.

3. For a general discussion of Bachofen's and Morgan's hypotheses, see Wesel 1980.

4. I have not come upon any discussion in the secondary literature of Benjamin's remarkable use of this term. The term, especially in connection with its later Thomistic usage in the form of a supernatural order, refers to the doctrine of the human being's return to his or her original status of "divine sonship," a status which was lost with the fall of Adam. Such a return is only possible as a function of a "supernatural gift" of God that "elevates" human beings to the vision of God's "glory." The term "supernatural life" may also refer to the "supernal world" of the highest sphere (Sephiroth) in kabbalistic mysticism.

5. Rosenzweig's discussion of Jewishness and consanguineity in the last part of *The Star of Redemption* dedicated to the eternal life of the Jewish people is clearly a fundamental chapter of the story. For a discussion of Jewish "political theology" starting with the orientation toward family in the Jewish "social contract," see Novak 2005. Novak does not give a biopolitical reading of these themes.

6. Or Plato's God: one needs only recall that in the *Statesman* (309a–311e) marriage is seen as the key regulation by the statesman who needs to warp and weave together the two species of courageous and moderate men. In 261c, Plato makes clear that politics is about breeding and nurturing the human species.

7. For another interpretation of Benjamin's critique of original sin, see Weber 2010; on Benjamin's related concept of "afterlife," see Weber 2008, 79–94.

8. On some of the Christian and Jewish motifs of redemption from sin in the *Elective Affinities* essay, see in general Weigel 2008. But Weigel offers neither a biopolitical reading of these motifs, nor does she address the idea of eternal life in this essay.

9. Abrahamic religions do not share this fidelity to the same sex because they place the reproduction of the *ghenos* above fidelity to the person one has sex with in marriage. In these religions, it is not unusual for prophets to have more than one wife, and Catholic dogma cites the barrenness of marriage as ground for its dissolution. The absence of fidelity to sex in their conceptions of marriage may also explain their deep-seated rejection of homo-sexual marriage (whether the one sex is gay, lesbian, trans-, and so on) in principle. It appears that Jesus himself profanated traditional marriage codes, and that may be the reason why in early Christian communities something like homosexual marriage seemed to be permitted (Boswell 1996). In any case, and generally speaking, fidelity to the sex of the person that one marries was never central to patriarchical conceptions of marriage, but, quite the reverse, one never married for sex, but for money, procreation, social advancement, and so on. One can perhaps argue that the more women achieve equality with men, the more so-called heterosexual marriage takes the form of

Kantian homo-sexual marriage. It is interesting to point out in this context that for Kierkegaard marriage seems to be a problem only for men rather than women: it is men who are interested in marriage as a philosophical problem. In fact, in *Either/Or* both the seducer and the judge seem to speak about marriage to women as a roundabout way of speaking about their love for each other. In Kierkegaard, in this sense, Christian marriage is always already framed around a homosexual discourse of love. Perhaps this is also the reason why Kierkegaard never discusses the question of sex in marriage. Marriage for him is never about sex, but only about love, and the image of love is the love of and for the Father.

10. I thank Andreas Greiert for pointing this out to me. On the Benjamin-Klages connection, see Pauen 1999.

11. See the expressions "reconciliation exists only with God" and "each one [is] wholly alone for himself before God" (Benjamin 1996, 342).

12. Benjamin argues at length that these two ways are described in the novella that Goethe inscribes within the second part of the novel.

13. The reference is to *Mutterrecht* (Bachofen 1943, III593).

14. We also know that Arendt was aware of Scholem's interpretation of the sect of Sabbatianism from early on, roughly around the same time that she begins to use Augustine's vocabulary for natality. See her review of Scholem's 1948 book, "Jewish History, Revised" (Arendt 2007, 303–11).

15. Scholem's strong interest for Nietzsche is documented in his early diaries, and must have been a topic of discussion with Benjamin in their youthful conversations, although apparently Benjamin never got to read a copy of "Redemption Through Sin." This does not exclude the possibility that Benjamin could have heard from conversations with Scholem of the general thesis of a redemption through sin. I thank Enrico Lucca for this indication.

16. Unfortunately I have not been able to consult the study in Hebrew by Rapoport-Albert 2010 on women in Sabbatianism. For a contemporary, slightly ludicrous and New Age attempt at reestablishing the doctrines and practices of Sabbatianism, see the website of the movement at www.donmeh-west.com.

17. "Could one even say that, in historical context, Zarathustra's courtship of life yearns for a 'remarriage,' considering the tradition's nihilistic 'divorce' from life?" (Hatab 2005, 82). In other words, an allegorical interpretation of *Thus Spoke Zarathustra* would place this work amongst the genre of comedies of remarriage, just like the *Elective Affinities* and *Either/Or*. An entirely different question, which I cannot entertain here, is the nature of the comedy at stake.

18. On the political imaginary of the George Circle, see now Norton 2002.

19. On these motifs in Nietzsche, see now Lemm 2009.

20. The structure of Benjamin's unfinished book on Baudelaire is discussed in Jennings (2003, 91–93), and in Jennings's introduction to the collection of Benjamin's writings on Baudelaire (Benjamin 2006, 1–25).

21. Bajorek 2009 is a recent attempt to make sense of Benjamin's connection to Marxism by analyzing Benjamin's reading of Baudelaire as allegorist and ironist (24).
22. On modernity as "marche funèbre," see Heller 1993.
23. See Plaut and Anderson 2001.
24. For a study of "queer" motifs in Benjamin, see Chisolm 2002.
25. On phantasmagoria in Benjamin, see now Berdet 2013.

6. FREE MARKETS AND REPUBLICAN CONSTITUTIONS IN HAYEK AND FOUCAULT

1. For a discussion of this reception of the late Foucault, see Lemke 2004; Brown 2005; Demirovic and Henry 2008; among others.
2. For the definition of governmentality, see M. Dean 1999, 10–27; Lemke 2007.
3. For this point, see Tellmann 2011, 287–94.
4. For a classic formulation, see M. Dean 1999, 118–23.
5. On this point, see Dillon and Neal 2011.
6. For the centrality of Hayek in the creation of neoliberal hegemony, see now Mirowski and Plehwe 2009.
7. For examples of this approach to cosmopolitanism, see Benhabib 2004; Brunkhorst 2005; Eberl 2011.
8. Post-Marxist thought has long identified the "juridification" of politics as a neoliberal temptation. For an example, see Brown and Halley 2002.
9. For a recent discussion of this other sense of normative order, see now Teubner 2012.
10. The discussion of why the modern construction of the phenomenon of life (whether in Darwin, Nietzsche, Whitehead, Bergson, Jonas, Luhmann to name just a few) allows for the derivation of value from fact would take me too far afield here.
11. See Canguilhem 1966, 1983, 1994.
12. For another reading of Hayek through Foucault's categories, see now Spieker 2013. Spieker concentrates on Hayek's "evolutionary account of order" (311) according to which the free market is the result of a process of "natural selection" between "disciplined" actors and those who are not. But this idea of "discipline" is not connected to Hayek's discourse on law. Spieker in fact concentrates on Foucault's idea of politics as war in *"Society Must be Defended"* rather than in the lectures on governmentality proper. His picture of Hayek is Hobbesian, while mine will turn out to be that of a (modified) Kantian.
13. This critique of classical assumptions of equilibrium is already found in the essay "The Meaning of Competition" in Hayek 1949. According to Foucault, the

"free and responsible" subject generated by the order of the market is just a condition for its "normal" functioning (Foucault 2010, 144, 150, 172–77). See here in general Lemke 2007, on this kind of normativity in the conception of power.

14. See the discussion of this point in Valverde 2011.

15. For detailed discussion of Foucault's conception of norms, see Napoli 2003; and Legrand 2007. Both of these works, though, do not consider the possibility that Foucault recovers a discourse of the law, as opposed to the norm, in an affirmative sense, as I shall argue here.

16. For another argument, with which I find myself in broad agreement, concerning Foucault's alternative and affirmative understanding of law, see now Golder and Fitzpatrick 2009, chap. 2.

17. Not even in such texts where he comes closest to identifying law with ideology, for example, in Foucault 1995, 2003.

18. For a discussion of this view, see Gehring 2007.

19. See Agamben 1998; Esposito 2008.

20. For some examples, see Patton 2005; N. Rose 2007; Fassin 2009.

21. I do not mean that Foucault is "republican" in the sense in which this term is commonly used, for instance, in French political discourse, a use which has been recently criticized in Rancière 2009. Foucault is "republican" in a more anarchic sense of the term, a sense that has been developed by Rancière since Rancière 1995 and is also found in Balibar 2010.

22. On Canguilhem and Foucault, see now Muhle 2008.

23. See Canguilhem 1994, 370; Blanc 1998, 91.

24. I follow here the interpretation proposed by Muhle 2008.

25. It must be added that Hayek also rejects all organicism—usually opposed to organization—but he does so in ways that do not affect the substantial agreement that his idea of spontaneous order shares with Canguilhem's notion of life's internal normativity.

26. I do not have space here to discuss at greater length how this notion of individualization by way of speciation, and vice versa, depends on the close relation between biopolitical norms and the constitution of a "milieu" or "environment" (*Umgebung/Umwelt*) in which a species can maximize its "standard of life." See here the discussion of "milieu" in Foucault 2009.

27. I refer here to my discussion and critique of Weber's formula in Chapters 3 and 9.

28. On Marsilius, see Syros 2012; on Machiavelli, see Skinner 2002; on Spinoza, see del Lucchese 2011.

29. For a discussion of this principle as well as the idea of freedom as *sui iuris* status, see Skinner 1998; Vatter 2011.

30. On the appeal to Scholasticism in the Austrian School of economics, see Crespo 2002, 2006.

31. It is only if one accepts Schmitt's conception of "political theology" that it becomes plausible to think that both law and economics are "secularized" versions of theology. But in my opinion it is a mistake to begin from Schmitt's political theology if one wishes to understand the political economy of neoliberalism. This does not mean, obviously, that one cannot compare productively Schmitt with Hayek, as has been done by Cristi 1998.

32. For examples, see the essays "Two Pages of Fiction: The Impossibility of Socialist Calculation" and "The Use of Knowledge in Society" in Hayek 1984. On the question of the evolution in Hayek's thought from what Mirowski calls the "Abuse of Reason" phase to the "Evolutionary proto-cyberneticist" phase, see Mirowski 2007. But Mirowski downplays the importance of jurisprudence in Hayek's development and abstracts from biopolitics entirely. He has now reconsidered this last point after reading Foucault work on governmentality, as evidenced by Mirowski and Plehwe 2009. In the last chapter of the book, I explain in what sense Marx's historical materialism need not be interpreted as a secularized idea of divine providence.

33. See the chapter entitled "Nomos: The Law of Liberty," in volume I, "Rules and Orders" in Hayek 1982, 94–124.

34. I here follow Caldwell 1988 on the genesis of Hayek's mature thought. Mirowski, instead,argues that "for Hayek, the proposition that 'Markets do the thinking that people cannot' was extricated from its relatively Mysterian status in Phase (ii) to assume its more concertedly Naturalistic status in Phase (iii) by means of an endorsement of the proposition that 'Matter can think'. . . . [Hayek] was concurrently describing the individual mind equally as a machine for registering change" (Mirowski 2007, 366). Whereas Caldwell sees Hayek's switch to the problem of useful knowledge as distributed along networks as being a switch toward a truer depiction of human action, Mirowski understands this switch as a radicalization of the "reification" of consciousness characteristic of bourgeois political economy. Both are in a sense correct: Caldwell's reading of Hayek helps to explain the biopolitical ground of neoliberal political economy, while Mirowski is right insofar as biopolitics denotes a form of power and control that can also be understood with the vocabulary of reification as I showed in previous chapters.

35. "The Principles of a Liberal Social Order" was a conference originally pronounced at the "Tokyo Meeting of the Mont Pélerin Society" in 1966 in Japan.

36. There is an ambivalence on the part of Hayek with regard to Kant: as a republican thinker of political self-organization and revolution, Kant is rejected by Hayek. However, as the thinker of the purposelessness of legal system, he is approved by Hayek. Lastly, he also meets Hayek's approval as a liberal thinker of law as noninterference in the liberty of others.

37. It is crucial that Hayek assigns government only one role, namely, the enforcement of norms; thus police action is central for him. All other functions of

government, basically providing for needs that individuals or corporations cannot provide for (for example, public services) is secondary to the state's function of providing security. Both of these functions, when considered together, belong to the meaning of *Polizei* (police) as Foucault understands it. On this meaning of the term, see the essays found in Dubber and Valverde 2008; Purtschert and Meyer 2008.

38. On security and insurance from a biopolitical perspective, see now Dillon 2007; Dillon and Neal 2011; Lobo-Guerrero 2010.

39. I would place in this context the importance of the interpretation given by Lemke of the relation between Foucault and the project of a critique of political economy. See Lemke 2004, 2007.

40. One need only to think about how this insecurity of the working classes, their slide into abject poverty and death, is thematized from Malthus and Ricardo to Marx. Nowadays this insecurity is understood in terms of "precariety" and in the shift from the "proletariat" to the "precariat." On the new insecurity of neoliberal capitalism, see Boltanski 1999; Lorey 2012; Tellmann 2013.

41. See Foucault 2010, 118–21, on neoliberal regulation of competition. In general, risk and insurance go together with instability and financial capital, see also Cooper 2011.

42. Here Foucault's analysis of neoliberalism rejoins Walter Benjamin's critique of *Gewalt* and his unmasking of the police as the "rotten core" of bourgeois systems of law.

43. In this sense, I agree with Patton (2005, 270) and Golder (2010) that Foucault has a positive discourse with respect to rights, but for me this basis is to be understood from the distinction between pastoral and political power, the latter espousing the ideal of self-mastery as *sui iuris*.

7. BIOPOLITICAL COSMOPOLITANISM: THE RIGHT TO HAVE RIGHTS IN ARENDT AND AGAMBEN

1. See the "progressive" narratives contained in Hunt (2008) and Glendon (2002); for a critical, revisionist vision of this history, see now Moyn 2012.

2. I am referring to the categories of Shue 1980.

3. For the idea of normative power, see Forst 2011, 21–24; for life itself as basis of legitimacy, see Fassin 2009; N. Rose 2007.

4. For a demonstration of this point in relation to Maritain and the UHDR, see Vatter 2013.

5. See the interesting discussion of this Article and the meaning of "dignity" in Menke 2007, 147–63, which points to the theological background of its assumptions, but not to its biopolitical ones.

6. I have discussed at length the Freudian connection between sacredness and taboo in Chapters 1 and 3.

7. An example of this slippage is found in Dworkin's treatment of the right to abortion. Dworkin proposes that we think about the right to abortion from a standpoint that is shared by both the proponents and opponents of this right. This standpoint, for Dworkin, does not center on when the fetus acquires a human personality, but is given by the belief in the sacredness of life which, according to him, is a belief that is held by both sides of the debate, although it is differently interpreted (Dworkin 1994, 64–101). The defenders of the rights of the fetus argue that what is at stake is the defence of the sacredness of human life understood as *zoe*, the biological life of the human species, whose sacredness comes from having been created by God or by a divinized conception of nature, and whose "value" is thus not at the disposal of human free choice. Dworkin calls this the "natural" determination of the sacredness of life. The defenders of the rights of the mother, instead, argue that what is at stake is the defence of the sacredness of human life understood as *bios*, the life of the individual of the species, who is capable of giving its biological life a "form" and a "value" by its own free choice of activities. Dworkin calls this the "autonomous, individual-based" determination of the sacredness of life (Dworkin 1994, 82–83, 90–91). In both cases, Dworkin is referring to a form of life that carries in it a "surplus" of life, an excedence of value, which is designated by its "sacredness." It is a remarkable coincidence that although Dworkin wrote his book prior to the appearance of Agamben's *Homo Sacer*, he nevertheless employs exactly the same distinction between *zoe* and *bios* that Agamben mobilizes in order to understand the essence of biopolitics.

8. For an exaggerated portrayal of this thesis, see Hamacher 2004, 348: "The universal rights of man are the rights of the policeman. . . . Politics is essentially national and international police politics."

9. See Esposito's critique of the presuppositions of the modern discourse of human rights found in Esposito 2012; for Negri and Hardt's critique of the contemporary politics of human rights, see now Hardt and Negri 2000. I discuss in detail Agamben's theory of human rights below.

10. On Foucault's idea of human rights, see now Golder 2011. On Rancière's defense of human rights, see Rancière 2004.

11. For different formulations of this view of human rights, see Isaac 1996; Cohen 2006; Ingram 2008. For more general discussion of this "political, not metaphysical" standpoint with respect to human rights, see Parekh 2008, chap. 5; Menke 2007, chap. 1.

12. See Balibar 2002a, 2010.

13. A right to have rights does not "spring immediately from the 'nature' of man" and, in that sense, is not "metaphysical" because it depends on "human plurality" (Arendt 1973, 298), and the "human dignity" that is linked to human rights, for Arendt, is tied to a "polity" because "only the loss of a polity itself expels him from humanity" (Arendt 1973, 297). See the clear treatment in Parekh 2008, 123–35.

Parekh, though, points out that the problem of human nature as a foundation for human rights was very much in the mind of the drafters of the UDHR, while at the same time they also wanted to "find a formula that did not require . . . to take sides on the nature of man and society, or to become immured in metaphysical controversies" (Cassin, cited in Glendon 2002, 68). On the unavoidability of an account of human "nature" when speaking of human rights, see in general Griffin 2008.

14. I leave aside for a moment the fact that Agamben assumes a continuity between Hobbes and the principle of habeas corpus that I do not see and is perhaps nonexistent.

15. I rely throughout on the brilliant discussion of these points in Meador 1966.

16. On the difference between republic and nation-state in Arendt, see Brunkhorst 1999; Forti 1996.

17. This is a neo-Kantian idea of application. For a different solution to the problem of application, see my discussion of Hegel in Chapter 1.

18. "To respect the dignity of a person means to recognize her as someone who is owed appropriate reasons when actions or norms affect her in relevant ways. . . . In the space of reasons every person counts as an 'authority'" (Forst 2011, 84, translation mine).

19. Thus Forst criticizes the prevalent use of human rights to pose limits to the sovereignty of states in international politics because such a practice tends to "overlook the primary *intra-state* role of human rights," and leads to "skewed conclusions" (Forst 2011, 73, translation mine). This confusion between an inter-national and a intra-national use of human rights is avoided by Menke 2007, 749, who stresses that "only a right that does not already presuppose the status of membership in a political community, but has this very status as its object, is a real human right." But Menke withdraws from the obvious consequence of seeking a biopolitical or natural ground to such a human right, and instead, paradoxically, argues that "the foundation for each human being's right to membership in a political community cannot be found outside of or below his or her existence within such a community [*sic*], but rather in the experience of the significance of this political existence, and experience that can only be made from inside this political existence" (Menke 2007, 754). Menke nowhere mentions the connection between natality and the right to have rights.

20. I therefore disagree with Forst that the "right to justification" is prior to the "right to have rights." On the contrary, the former is a subspecies of the latter. Or, more precisely, only for an individual who is always already part of a polity, is it true that a right to justification occupies the role of a right to have (civil and political) rights. But for those individuals who have no polity, who are bare life, then the basic meaning of a right to have rights cannot possibly be the right to justification.

21. Indeed, the very definition of a right to justification carries a reference to naturalization, as if every being born is the very process of being "naturalized"

into a pregiven community: "The capacity to formulate goals of actions does not precede the capacity to be able to justify such goals with reasons to others. Reasons for actions are not only grounds which motivate me: they are also accounts of my actions through which I project myself as a 'doer' on to a social world which I share with others, and through which others recognize me as a person capable of, and responsible for, certain courses of action" (Benhabib 2011, ibid.). Here it is clear that "justification" is an activity of projection; it is an essential part of the project of constructing for oneself a *bios*, a biography. But for that very reason it has no relation to natality, which is tied to *zoe*. I refer to the Arendtian sense of this distinction discussed in Chapter 4.

22. The importance of Arendt's analysis of republican "public happiness" for her idea of human rights is brought out by Parekh 2008, chap. 4, but, like Birmingham, she fails to connect natality with opinion in her formulation of the right to have rights.

23. On these themes, the best treatment remains Lazzeri 1998. See also Saar 2009, for a reading of Spinoza's theory of government from a biopolitical perspective.

24. For another reading of the "street" in Arendt, see Butler 2012, chap. 6.

25. This is why both Forst and Benhabib, ultimately, share Habermas's conclusion that natural (or subjective) rights are only cooriginal with political rights—a thesis, as I have shown, that Arendt rejects because for her political rights are always rights to equality and equality is a political construction, it is not something "natural," unlike natality and plurality. Natality and plurality, though, are not features of an individual subject, and therefore the right to have rights that is grounded on them cannot be a "subjective" right.

26. I refer to the work of Lindahl 2006, 2008; Keedus 2011. These readings, though, refer mainly to Arendt's notion of positive law as *nomos* and not to her conception of a "right to have rights" nor to its connection with natality, which is entirely absent in their treatment of the problem of law and rights in Arendt.

27. This argument is taken up in an expanded sense by Hardt and Negri in *Commonwealth* (Hardt and Negri 2011). I disagree, though, with their description of republicanism as the ideology of *homo proprietarius* and of Kant as "a prophet of the republic of property" (Hardt and Negri 2011, 3–22).

28. "[Harrington] did, however, hold that only a democracy of landholders—that is, only a society where a *demos*, or many, of landed freemen held land in relative equality—possessed the human resources (Machiavelli might have said the *materia*) necessary to distribute political authority in the diversified and balanced ways that created a self-stabilizing *politeia*" (Pocock 1975, 387–88).

29. On the study of walled states as a symptom of the crisis of sovereignty, see Brown 2010.

30. This line of interpretation of Arendt's right to have rights as a right to a space of opinion that is not territorialized brings her political thought in relation with

the concept of de-territorialization in Deleuze and Guattari. On this concept, see now Patton 2010.

31. For a reading of Kant's theory of law along these lines I refer the reader to Vatter 2011.

32. For recent formulations of the idea of a people along these terms, see Nasstrom 2007; Vatter 2012.

33. For a deconstruction of assimilatory practices, see Honig 2003. On the other hand, I am not sure whether Honig's idea that foreignness is the necessary "supplement" of the foundation of a nation-state extends as far as the claim I wish to make here, namely, that a republican people constitutes itself from the outside inward.

8. BARE LIFE AND PHILOSOPHICAL LIFE IN ARISTOTLE, SPINOZA, AND HEIDEGGER

1. "Life . . . can in the last instance be implicated in the sphere of law . . . only in an *exception*. There is a limit-figure of life, a threshold in which life is both inside and outside the juridical order, and this threshold is the place of sovereignty" (Agamben 1998, 27). On the permanence of sovereign power in Foucault's construction of biopower, see Esposito 2008, chap. 2.

2. For a discussion of the "absence" of a formal discussion of Spinoza in Heidegger, see "Heidegger and Spinoza" in Balibar 2002b, 169–88; Barash 1994.

3. For a recent study of the Heideggerian idea that life must be thought starting from death and lack, see now Garrido 2012.

4. On this thesis, see Deleuze 1992.

5. This is also the question posed in Negri 1994, where Negri revises the interpretation of eternal life in Spinoza that he offered in Negri 1999. Negri now argues that "Man is not born free but he becomes free through a metamorphosis in which his body and his spirit, acting in concert, recognize love in reason. Eternity is thus lived in the constitutive praxis; praxis constitutes us as eternal" (Negri 1994, 146).

6. All further quotations from Spinoza are taken from the Shirley translation in Spinoza 2002.

7. "God is a cause of all things. . . . God is a being of whom all attributes are predicated; whence it clearly follows that all other things can by no means be, or be understood, apart from or outside him" (*Short Treatise*, chap. 3). Here is also the definition of God as "an immanent, and not a transeunt cause, since all the he produces is within himself, and not outside him, because there is nothing outside him" (ibid.).

8. I disagree here with Zac's interpretation which claims that Spinoza only defends general, not particular providence (Zac 1979, 15). For another view according to which Spinoza denies the existence of particular providence, see James 2012.

9. This definition of glory is given by Maimonides (1963, I, 64), and is probably what Spinoza had in mind. Agamben (2007b, 220ff) gives an extended interpretation of glory to which I return below.

10. The amoeba and one-celled organisms are also exemplary for the analysis offered in Jonas 2001, which I cannot treat here in the detail it deserves.

11. "Der Tod als Möglichkeit gibt dem Dasein nichts zu 'Verwirklichendes' und nichts, was es als Wirkliches selbst *sein* könnte [Death as possibility gives nothing to Dasein to realize and nothing for it to *be* as a reality]" (Heidegger 1986, sect. 53, 262, translation mine).

12. For an excellent discussion of the problems associated with anesthesia or "dormant perceptiveness" in Aristotle and Agamben, see Cooper 2002. In this article, Cooper is also pursuing the theme of the eternalization of life, but she does so in relation to the possibility of "unnatural" growth of life, whether it be in recent biomedical technology or in relation to the "immortal life of value" in capitalism (Cooper 2002, 94).

13. For another approach to the medieval problem of the medium and organ of perception in view of the current discussion of biopolitics, see now Coccia 2011.

14. All following citations from the *Metaphysics* refer to the edition found in Aristotle 1993 and are translated by me.

15. On the Deleuzian conception of life and its relation to Agamben's biopolitics, see now Luisetti 2011.

16. On the idea of *homo tantum*, see Hardt and Negri 2001, 203–4; Esposito 2008; Campbell 2006.

17. All citations of *De anima* are drawn from Aristotle 1989.

18. Mauss and Agamben allude to the possibility that the Eucharist, where God becomes the food of the holy assembly of the faithful, may find its model in this Vedic understanding of a divine metabolism.

9. ETERNAL RECURRENCE AND THE NOW OF REVOLUTION: NIETZSCHE AND MESSIANIC MARXISM

1. On economic theology, see the contributions by Agamben 2007b; Milbank 2006; Goodchild 2009; M. C. Taylor 2008; Connolly 2008; Weber 2009; Vogl 2011.

2. On the history of these two conceptions of value, see Mirowski 1991.

3. On the temporalities of financial markets and financial crises, see Cooper 2011; Ayache 2010.

4. For an interpretation of the logic behind derivatives based on philosophies of the event, and which gives an important role to the hypothesis of eternal recurrence in a pluriverse, see now Ayache 2010.

5. Esposito argues that the juridical category of person is the fundamental category of reification, and thus de-reification must orient itself toward the "impersonal" (Esposito 2012). In this sense, what Lukács means by class consciousness belongs to the "impersonal."

6. According to Honneth, reified consciousness is a consciousness of the subject-object division which distances us from others and distorts intersubjectivity (Honneth 2005, 27). There is no mention in his analysis of the problem of temporality. The importance of temporality in Lukács's critique of Kant is also missed in G. Rose (1981, 24–36), who argues that Lukács and Habermas together belong to a "neo-Kantian" Marxism.

7. On the Lukács-Bergson relation, see Colletti 1973. On Bergson from a biopolitical perspective which on several points intersects with my analyses of biopolitics in this book, see Luisetti 2011. For an analysis of capitalism from the perspective of Whitehead, process philosophy, and theory of temporality, see now Connolly 2011.

8. On Lukács as precursor to Heidegger's analytic of *Dasein*, see Goldmann 1977; Villegas 1996.

9. In this sense, Althusser's critique of Lukács as putting forth a Hegelian form of historicism is misguided: Lukács is far closer to Althusser's critique of historicism than the French thinker believed (Althusser 1979).

10. The citation is from *The Poverty of Philosophy*.

11. See Postone 1993 and the critical discussions of Postone's thesis collected in *Historical Materialism* 12:3 (2004). For Postone, the conflict between living labor and capital is a conflict between the capitalist relation of production and the advances in productivity, or the increase in the forces of production (what he calls "the social character of the use-value dimension of labor" [Postone 1993, 293]): this he projects onto the antagonism between concrete (what he calls "historical") and abstract time. Nonetheless, Postone's idea of "historical" time is still based on a historicist conception of time: it presupposes a linear "development" of productive forces in and through history (Postone 1993, chap. 9, passim). This belief in historical development makes Postone discount the crucial importance that the struggle over the length of the working day has for Marx. This is because, in Postone's opinion, these struggles are always already subsumed by capitalism as a struggle for better wages, which reasserts the domination of wage labor (Postone 1993, 317ff). As I show below, Postone's interpretation discounts what Marx says about the struggle over the duration of the working day, namely, that it is the real barrier to capital self-reproduction.

12. "In the market, as owner of the commodity 'labor-power' he stood face to face with other owners of commodities, one owner against another owner . . . But when the transaction was concluded, it was discovered that he was no 'free agent', that the period of time for which he is free to sell his labor-power is the period of time for which he is forced to sell it" (Marx 1976, 415).

13. Thus, Postone's criticism of Lukács on the grounds that the latter's suggestion to breakdown the "eternal" present of the capitalist's temporality into a "historical flow" (Postone 1993, 300) is also part of capitalist development misses the point: all assumptions concerning the temporality of capital formulated from within economics (for example, the theses that punctuated equilibrium subsumes crises; that chaos theory and nonlinear temporality are part and parcel of capitalism, especially of finance capital, and so on) remain neo-Kantian and thus do not affect Lukács's basic critique of neo-Kantianism. For a reconstruction of the historical presupposition of abstract time from a Marxist point of view, see Alliez 1996. On the lack of events in capitalism historical development, on business cycles and crises from this Lukácsian perspective, see now Sewell 2008.

14. On this point, Benjamin found himself very close to the basic intuitions of *History and Class Consciousness* and Benjamin says he owed to this text his conversion to Marxism. On Benjamin's reception of Lukács, see Greiert 2011, 451–77.

15. For the critique of neoliberal education from a post-Marxist point of view, I refer to Aronowitz 2008; Giroux 2007. I thank Michael Pelias for these indications.

16. "For your animals know well, O Zarathustra, who you are and must become: behold, *you are the teacher of the eternal recurrence*—that is your destiny! . . . Behold, we know what you teach: that all things recur eternally [*dass alle Dinge ewig wiederkehren*] , and we ourselves too; and that we have already existed an eternal number of times, and all things with us" (Nietzsche 1995, "The Convalescent," 220).

17. See Schoettker 2005, for a discussion of Benjamin's progressive shift from his earlier attempts at working out a "theology of capitalism" to his later, much more Nietzschean attempt to see in the eternal return the crucial figure of capitalism.

18. On Blanqui's political innovations, see Dommanget 1972.

19. See the discussion of this point in Nieraad 1990; Hamacher 2006. I tend to agree with Nieraad's considered judgment that the *Fragment* probably stems from Benjamin's later period, but my argument turns on the "Nietzschean" background of the *Fragment*, which he mentions quickly but does not entertain. The absence of any mention of the eternal recurrence or of Nietzsche in Hamacher's reading of the *Fragment* is bewildering. On the importance of eternal recurrence in Benjamin's *Fragment* as brought out in Agamben's reading, see De la Durantaye 2000.

20. Rosenzweig's notion of a "supra-man" contains an unmistakeable echo of Nietzsche's ideal of the *Über-mensch* ("over-man") defined as those forms of life that can greet the eternal recurrence with joy rather than nausea.

21. On the interest by Scholem and Benjamin with regard to mathematics, and in particular the new mathematics that would be important for Einstein's general relativity, see now Fenves 2011, chaps. 4, 5, and 6.

22. In what follows I rely on the discussion in Greene 2011, especially chap. 2.

23. "In many versions of the inflationary theory, the burst of spatial expansion is not a onetime event. Instead, the process by which our region of the universe is formed—rapid stretching of space, followed by a transition to a more ordinary, slower expansion, together with the production of particles—may happen over and over again at various far-flung locations throughout the cosmos" (Greene 2011, 54).

24. See Nietzsche's notebooks of spring to fallall 1881 (Nietzsche 1988, KSA 9); this cosmological reading is also central to the interpretation of Klossowski 1969.

25. In general, Hatab's book is a useful review of these three schools of interpretation of the doctrine of eternal recurrence.

26. "The law of the conservation of energy demands eternal recurrence" (Nietzsche 1968, 1063). And again: "If the world may be thought of as a certain definite quantity of force and as a certain definite number of centers of force . . . it follows that, in the great game of dice of existence, it must pass through a calculable number of combinations. In infinite time, every possible combination would at some time or another be realized; more: it would be realized an infinite number of times . . . the world as a circular movement that has already repeated itself infinitely often and plays its game in infinitum" (Nietzsche 1968, 1066).

27. For another reading of this complex passage which does not rely on cosmology, I refer to Butler 2006.

28. "Let us stamp the image of eternity on *our* life! This thought withholds more than all religions, which despise life as something fleeting and teach to look after an indeterminate *other* life [*Drücken wir das Abbild der Ewigkeit auf unser Leben! Dieser Gedanke enthält mehr als alle Religionen, welche dies Leben als ein flüchtiges verachten und nach einem unbestimmten anderen Leben hinblicken lehrten*]" (Nietzsche 1988, KSA 9, 11 [159], 503, translation mine).

29. For an entirely different reading of Benjamin's relation to Nietzsche's eternal recurrence, see Moses 1996, who refers neither to the *Theologico-Political Fragment* nor sees the connections between Benjamin's turn to Nietzsche and his adoption of historical materialism and of communism. My reading of the *Fragment* is also opposed to Hamacher's recent interpretation of the text who separates the messianic from the materialist in Benjamin (Hamacher 2006, 179). Hamacher explains Benjamin's nihilism by appealing to Böhme's mystical idea that God's Oneness can only be attained by negating everything natural or positive because everything living is decadent (181). Given that Hamacher radically separates the profane life from the dimension of eternal life and eternal return, he is unable to give any sense to the idea of *restitutio in integrum*, which is hardly mentioned in his reading.

30. One of the best readings of the Benjamin-Blanqui relation is to be found in Loeschenkohl 2010, in the sense that she also points out the affirmative possibilities withheld in Blanqui's vision of the eternal return and of the Doppelgängers, although she strangely misses its relevance to the problem of eternal life. For an

excellent discussion of the meaning of Blanqui's thought and life in relation to Benjamin, see Abensour 2007. For a different reading of Benjamin's interpretation of Blanqui, see Miller 2008.

31. According to Jennings, the eternal recurrence would merely be "a nightmare vision of a cruelty sufficient to awaken the dead" (Jennings 2003, 104). But this clearly does not do justice to the way in which Nietzsche and Blanqui see something in the eternal return that figures the promise of happiness, and not just the horror of the choking shepherd.

32. "This firm resolve to snatch humanity at the last moment from the catastrophe looming at every turn is characteristic of Blanqui—more so than of any other revolutionary politician at the time. He always refused to develop plans for what comes 'later'" (Benjamin 2006, 166).

33. For a recent discussion of the relation between Benjamin's Marxism and messianism as a form of anarchism, see Martel 2012.

34. Nieraad points to two other occasions in Benjamin's work where this motif of the coincidence of repetition and novelty define the very idea of happiness: in a 1928 fragment, "Spielzeug und Spielen," and in the second version of the 1933 fragment *Agesilaus Santander* (227). In De la Durantaye's discussion of Agamben's take on Nietzsche's eternal recurrence, he claims that Agamben distinguishes between the return of the same and the return of the new: Nietzsche would fall into the first, Benjamin and Agamben into the latter (De la Durantaye 2000, 14–17). This is not to see the emancipatory aspect of eternal recurrence of the same, even in Benjamin.

35. Again, I refer to Esposito's discussion of "impersonality" in Foucault and Deleuze in Esposito 2012, 133–51.

36. Blanqui speaks of this vision as a consolation: "Isn't it better to think that we are currently, on another earth, being together with a dear beloved who is dead; or that one is eternally, in the figure of an avatar, enjoying this bliss" (Blanqui 2003, 48, translation mine).

37. Motifs found in *Theses* XVI through XVIII (Benjamin 1968, 262–63).

38. Klossowski is one of the few interpreters to have seen the connection between the eternal recurrence of the same and the idea of the *circulus vitiosus deus* of *Beyond Good and Evil*. See now Loeb 2010, for a reading of Nietzsche's eternal recurrence tied to the problem of eternal life.

39. In the *Twilight of the Idols* Nietzsche connects eternal recurrence to an affirmation of natality: "What did the Hellene guarantee to himself with these mysteries? *Eternal* life, the eternal recurrence of life; [Das *ewige* Leben, die ewige Wiederkehr des Lebens] the future promised and consecrated in the past; the triumphant Yes to life beyond death and change; *true* life as collective continuation of life through procreation, through mysteries of sexuality [das *wahre* Leben als das Gesamt-Fortleben durch die Zeugung, durch die Mysterien der Geschlechtigkeit]" (Nietzsche 1990, 120).

40. The same intuition is repeated in *Ecce Homo*: "The affirmation of passing away and destroying, which is the decisive feature of a Dionysian philosophy; saying Yes to opposition and war; becoming, along with a radical repudiation of the very concept of being—all this is clearly more closely related to me than anything else thought to date. The doctrine of the 'eternal recurrence,' that is, if the unconditional and infinitely repeated circular course of all things" (Nietzsche 1989, 273–74).

WORKS CITED

Abensour, Miguel. 2010. *Democracy Against the State: Marx and the Machiavellian Movement*. London: Blackwell.
———. 2007. "W. Benjamin entre mélancholie et révolution. Passages Blanqui." In *Walter Benjamin et Paris : Colloque international 27–29 juin 1983*, ed. H. Wismann. Paris: Les Editions du Cerf.
Acosta, María del Rosario. 2009. "From *Eumenides* to *Antigone*: Developing Hegel's Notion of Recognition, Responding to Honneth." *Philosophy Today* 34: 190–200.
Adorno, Theodor W. 2003. *Negative Dialektik. Jargon der Eigentlichkeit*. Ed. R. Tiedemann. Vol. 6 of *Gesammelte Schriften*. Frankfurt: Suhrkamp.
Aeschylus. 1953. *Oresteia*. Trans. R. Lattimore. Chicago: University of Chicago Press.
Agamben, Giorgio. 2011. *The Highest Poverty. Monastic Rules and Form-of-Life*. Stanford: Stanford University Press.
———. 2007a. *Profanations*. Trans. K. Attell. New York: Zone Books.
———. 2007b. *Il Regno e la Gloria. Per una genealogia teologica dell'economia e del governo*. Rome: Neri Pozza Editore.
———. 2005. *State of Exception*. Trans. K. Attell. Chicago: University of Chicago Press.
———. 2004. *The Open: Man and Animal*. Trans. K. Attell. Stanford: Stanford University Press.
———. 2000a. *Means Without End: Notes on Politics*. Trans. V. Binetti; Cesare Casarino. Vol. 20, *Theory out of Bounds*. Minneapolis: University of Minnesota Press.
———. 2000b. *Il tempo che resta [The Time that Remains]*. Turin: Bollati Boringhieri.
———. 1999a. *The Man Without Content*. Stanford: Stanford University Press.
———. 1999b. *Potentialities*. Stanford: Stanford University Press.
———. 1999c. *Remnants of Auschwitz. Homo Sacer III. The Witness and the Archive*. New York: Zone Books.
———. 1998. *Homo Sacer: Sovereign Power and Bare Life*. Trans. D. Heller-Roazen. Stanford: Stanford University Press.

---. 1990. *La comunità che viene*. Turin: Einaudi.
---. 1979a. *Infanzia e storia*. Turin: Einaudi.
---. 1979b. *Stanze: La parola e il fantasma nella cultura occidentale*. Turin: Einaudi.
Alliez, Eric. 1996. *Capital Times: Tales from the Conquest of Time*. Minneapolis: University of Minnesota Press.
Althusser, Louis, and Étienne Balibar. 1979. *Reading Capital*. London: Verso.
Arendt, Hannah. 2007. *The Jewish Writings*. New York: Schocken Books.
---. 2006. *Eichmann in Jerusalem*. New York: Penguin.
---. 2005. *The Promise of Politics*. New York: Schocken Books.
---. 2003. *Was ist Politik? Fragmente aus dem Nachlass*. Munich: Piper.
---. 2002. *Denktagebuch: 1950 bis 1973*. Munich: Piper.
---. 1996. *Love and Saint Augustine*. Chicago: University of Chicago Press.
---. 1994. *Essays in Understanding 1930–1954: Formation, Exile, and Totalitarianism*. Ed. Jerome Kohn. New York: Schocken Books.
---. 1990. *On Revolution*. New York: Penguin.
---. 1982. *Lectures on Kant's Political Philosophy*. Chicago: University of Chicago Press.
---. 1978. *The Life of the Mind*. New York: Harcourt, Brace and Jovanovich.
---. 1977. *Between Past and Future: Eight Exercises in Political Thought*. New York: Penguin Books.
---. 1973. *The Origins of Totalitarianism*. New York: Harcourt, Brace & Company.
---. 1958. *The Human Condition*. Chicago: University of Chicago Press.
---. 1929. *Der Liebesbegriff bei Augustin. Versuch einer philosophischen Interpretation*. Berlin: Verlag von Julius Springer.
Arendt, Hannah, and Jaspers, Karl. 1992. *Hannah Arendt and Karl Jaspers Correspondence 1926–1969*. New York: Harcourt Brace & Company.
Aristotle. 1993. *Metafisica*. Ed. G. Reale. 3 vols. Milan: Vita e Pensiero.
---. 1989. *A New Aristotle Reader*. Ed. J. L. Ackrill. Princeton, NJ: Princeton University Press.
---. 1988. *Politics*. Cambridge: Cambridge University Press.
Aronowitz, Stanley. 2008. *Against Schooling*. New York: Paradigm Publishers.
Augustine, Saint. 1984. *The City of God*. New York: Penguin.
Ayache, Elie. 2010. *The Blank Swan: The End of Probability*. Chichester, UK: Wiley.
Bachofen, Johann Jakob. 1943–67. *Gesammelte Werke*. Ed. K. Meuli. Basel: Schwebe & Co.
Backhaus, Hans-Georg. 1997. *Dialektik der Wertform. Untersuchungen zur marxschen Ökonomiekritik*. Freiburg: ca ira.
---. 1992. "Between Philosophy and Science: Marxian Social Economy as Critical Theory." In *Open Marxism: Dialectics and History*. Vol. 1, ed. W. Bonefeld, R. Gunn, and K. Psychopedis. London: Pluto Press.
---. 1980. "On the Dialectics of the Value-Form." *Thesis Eleven* 1: 99–120.

Badiou, Alain. 2003. *Saint Paul: The Foundation of Universalism*. Stanford: Stanford University Press.
Bajorek, Jennifer. 2009. *Counterfeit Capital: Poetic Labor and Revolutionary Irony*. Stanford: Stanford University Press.
Balibar, Étienne. 2010. *La proposition de l'egaliberté*. Paris: PUF.
———. 2002a. *Droit de cité*. Paris: PUF.
———. 2002b. *Spinoza: Il transindividuale*. Milan: Edizioni Ghibli.
Barash, Jeffrey Andrew. 1994. "Saint Paul, Spinoza et l'absence de l'éthico-politique chez Heidegger." In *Spinoza: Puissance et Ontologie*. Paris: Kimé.
Baudelaire, Charles. 1992. *Critique d'art*. Ed. C. Pichois. Paris: Gallimard.
Bazzicalupo, Laura. 2006. "The Ambivalences of Biopolitics." *diacritics* 36, no. 2: 109–16.
Beiner, Ronald. 1984. "Action, Natality and Citizenship: Hannah Arendt's Concept of Freedom." In *Conceptions of Liberty in Political Philosophy*. Ed. J. Pelczynski and J.Gray, 349–75. London: Athlone Press.
Bellofiore, Ricardo, and Roberto Fineschi. 2009. *Re-reading Marx: New Perspectives After the Critical Edition*. London: Palgrave.
Bellofiore, Ricardo, and Nicole Taylor. 2004. *The Constitution of Capital: Essays on Volume I of Marx's Capital*. London: Palgrave.
Benhabib, Seyla. 2011. *Dignity in Adversity: Human Rights in Troubled Times*. Cambridge: Polity
———. 2004. *The Rights of Others*. Cambridge: Cambridge University Press.
———. 1996. *The Reluctant Modernism of Hannah Arendt*. London: Sage.
Benjamin, Walter. 2006. *The Writer of Modern Life: Essays on Charles Baudelaire*. Ed. M. W. Jennings. Cambridge, MA: Harvard University Press.
———. 2002. *Selected Writings. Volume 3 1935–1938*. Trans. H. Eiland. et al.; ed. H. Eiland and M. W. Jennings. Cambridge, MA: Harvard University Press.
———. 1999a. *The Arcades Project*. Cambridge, MA: Harvard University Press.
———. 1999b. *Selected Writings. Volume 2 1927–1934*. Trans. R. Livingstone et al.; ed. M. Bollock and M. W. Jennings. Cambridge, MA: The Belknap Press of Harvard University Press.
———. 1996. *Selected Writings. Volume 1: 1913–1926*. Ed. M. Bollock and M. W. Jennings. Cambridge, MA: Harvard University Press.
———. 1994. *The Complete Correspondence of Walter Benjamin, 1910–1940*. Ed. G. Scholem and T. W. Adorno. Chicago: University of Chicago Press.
———. 1991a. *Abhandlungen*. Ed. H. Schweppenhauser and R. Tiedemann. Vol. I.1, *Gesammelte Schriften*. Frankfurt: Suhrkamp.
———. 1991b. *Abhandlungen*. Ed. H. Schweppenhauser and R. Tiedemann. Vol. I.2, *Gesammelte Schriften*. Frankfurt: Suhrkamp.
———. 1991c. *Abhandlungen*. Ed. H. Schweppenhauser and R. Tiedemann. Vol. I.3, *Gesammelte Schriften*. Frankfurt: Suhrkamp.

———. 1991d. *Aufsätze, Essays, Vorträge*. Ed. H. Schweppenhaeuser and R. Tiedemann. Vol. II.3, *Gesammelte Schriften*. Frankfurt: Suhrkamp.

———. 1985. *The Origin of German Tragic Drama*. London: Verso.

———. 1968. *Illuminations*. Trans. H. Zohn; ed. H. Arendt. New York: Schocken Books.

Benjamin, Walter, and Theodor Adorno. 1999. *The Complete Correspondence 1928–1940*. Ed. Henri Lonitz. Cambridge, MA: Harvard University Press.

Benvenuto, Sergio. 1993. "Hermes/Hestia: The Hearth and the Angel as a Philosophical Paradigm." *Telos: A Quarterly Journal of Critical Thought* 96: 101–18.

Berdet, Marc. 2013. *Fantasmagories du capital. L'invention de la ville-marchandise*. Paris: Éditions La Découverte.

Biale, David. 1985. "Gershom Scholem's Ten Unhistorical Aphorisms on Kabbalah: Text and Commentary." *Modern Judaism* 5, no. 1: 67–93.

Bidet, Jacques. 2007. *Refundación del marxismo. Explicación y reconstrucción de El Capital*. Santiago: LOM.

Bienenstock, Myriam. 1989. "Zu Hegels Erstem Begriff des Geistes (1803/1804): Herdersche Einfluesse oder Aristotelisches Erbe?" *Hegel-Studien* 24: 27–54.

———. 1983. "Macht und Geist in Hegel's Jena Writings." *Hegel-Studien* 18: 139–72.

Birmingham, Peg. 2006. *Hannah Arendt and Human Rights: The Predicament of Common Responsibility*. Bloomington: Indiana University Press.

Blanc, Guillaume Le. 1998. *Canguilhem et les normes*. Paris: PUF.

Blanqui, Louis Auguste. 2003. *L'Éternité par les astres*. http://www.uqac.uquebec.ca/zone30/Classiques_des_sciences_sociales/index.html [cited June 15, 2011].

Bluhm, Harald. 2004. "Herr und Knecht - Transformation einer Denkfigur." In *Hegels „Phenomenologie des Geistes" heute*. Ed. E. Müller and A. Arndt. Berlin: Akademie Verlag.

Blumenberg, Hans. 1996. *Die Legitimität der Neuzeit*. Frankfurt: Suhrkamp.

Blumenberg, Hans, and Carl Schmitt. 2007. *Briefwechsel 1971–1978*. Frankfurt: Suhrkamp.

Bobbio, Norberto. 1981. *Studi hegeliani*. Turin: Giulio Einaudi editore.

Böhm-Bawerk, Eugen, and Rudolf Hilferding. 1975. *Karl Marx and the Close of His System: Bohm-Bawerk's Criticism of Marx*. London: Merlin Press.

Boltanski, Luc, and Eve Chiapello. 1999. *Le nouvel esprit du capitalisme*. Paris: Gallimard.

Bosteels, Bruno. 2011. *The Actuality of Communism*. London: Verso.

Boswell, John. 1996. *The Marriage of Likeness: Same-Sex Unions in Pre-Modern Europe*. New York: Fontana.

Bowen-Moore, Patricia. 1989. *Hannah Arendt's Philosophy of Natality*. New York: St. Martin's Press.

Brague, Rémi. 1996. "A Medieval Model of Subjectivity: Toward a Rediscovery of Fleshliness." In *The Ancients and the Moderns*, ed. R. Lilly. Bloomington: Indiana University Press.

Braun, Karen. 2007. "Biopolitics and Temporality in Arendt and Foucault." *Time and Society* 16, no. 1: 5–23.

Bröckling, Ulrich, Susanne Krasmann, and Thomas Lemke, eds. 2011. *Governmentality: Current Issues and Future Challenges*. London: Routledge.

Brown, Wendy. 2010. *Walled States, Waning Sovereignty*. New York: Zone Books.

———. 2005. "Neoliberalism and the End of Liberal Democracy." In *Edgework: Critical Essays on Knowledge and Power*, 37–59. Princeton, NJ: Princeton University Press.

Brown, Wendy, and Janet Halley, eds. 2002. *Left Legalism/Left Critique*. Durham, NC: Duke University Press.

Brunkhorst, Hauke. 2007. *Karl Marx. Der achtzehnte Brumaire des Louis Bonaparte*. Frankfurt: Suhrkamp.

———. 1999. *Hannah Arendt*. Munich: Beck.

———. 1983. "Paradigmkern und Theoriendynamik der Kritischen Theorie der Gesellschaft - Personen und Programme." *Soziale Welt. Zeitschrift fuer sozialwissenschaftliche Forschung und Praxis* 3, no. 1: 22–56.

Buck-Morss, Susan. 1991. *The Dialectics of Seeing: Walter Benjamin and the Arcades Project*. Cambridge, MA: MIT Press.

Butler, Judith. 2012. *Parting Ways: Jewishness and the Critique of Zionism*. New York: Columbia University Press.

———. 2010. "Longing for Recognition." In *Hegel's Philosophy and Feminist Thought: Beyond Antigone?*, ed. T. Pulkkinen and K. Hutchings, 109–32. New York: Palgrave Macmillan.

———. 2006. "Critique, Coercion, and Sacred Life in Benjamin's 'Critique of Violence.'" In *Political Theologies: Public Religions in a Post-Secular World*, ed. L. E. Sullivan and H. de Vries. New York: Fordham University Press.

———. 2005. *Giving an Account of Oneself*. New York: Fordham University Press.

———. 2004. *Precarious Life: The Powers of Mourning and Violence*. London: Verso.

———. 2000. *Antigone's Claim: Kinship Between Life and Death*. New York: Columbia University Press.

———. 1997. *The Psychic Life of Power*. Stanford: Stanford University Press.

Caffentzis, George C. 2010. "Immeasurable Value? An Essay on Marx's Legacy." In *Reading Negri*, ed. P. Lamarche, M. Rosenkrantz, and D. Sherman, 101–26. Chicago: Open Court.

Caldwell, Bruce J. 1988. "Hayek's Transformation." *Journal of Political Economy* 20, no. 4: 513–41.

Campbell, Tim. 2006. "Bios, Immunity, Life: The Thought of Roberto Esposito." *Diacritics* 36, no. 2: 2–22.

Canguilhem, Georges. 1994. *A Vital Rationalist: Selected Writings from Georges Canguilhem*. Ed. François Delaporte. New York: Zone Books.

———. 1983. *Etudes d'histoire et de philosophie des sciences*. Paris: Vrin.

———. 1966. *Le normal et le pathologique*. Paris: PUF.
Canovan, Margaret. 1994. *Hannah Arendt: A Reinterpretation of Her Political Thought*. Cambridge: Cambridge University Press.
Cavarero, Adriana. 2000. *Relating Narratives: Storytelling and Selfhood*. London: Routledge.
Cavell, Stanley. 1999. "Benjamin and Wittgenstein: Signals and Affinities." *Critical Inquiry* 25, no. 2.
Chisolm, Diane. 2002. "A Queer Return to Walter Benjamin." *Journal of Urban History* 29, no. 1: 25–38.
Coccia, Emanuele. 2011. *La vita sensibile*. Bologna: Il Mulino.
Cohen, Joshua. 2006. "Is There a Human Right to Democracy?" In *The Egalitarian Conscience: Essays in Honor of G.A. Cohen*, ed. C. Sypnowich, 226–48. Oxford: Oxford University Press.
Colletti, Lucio. 1973. *Marxism and Hegel*. London: Verso.
Collin, Francoise. 2000. "Nacer y tiempo: Agustín en el pensamiento arendtiano." In *Hannah Arendt: El orgullo de pensar*, ed. by F. Birulés. Barcelona: Gedisa.
———. 1999. "Birth as Praxis." In *The Judge and the Spectator: Arendt's Political Philosophy*, ed. J. Herman and D. Villa, 97–110. Belgium: Peeters.
Connolly, William. 2011. *A World of Becoming*. Durham, NC: Duke University Press.
———. 2008. *Capitalism and Christianity, American Style*. Durham, NC: Duke University Press.
Cooper, Melinda. 2011. "Turbulent Worlds: Between Financial and Environmental Crisis." *Theory, Culture and Society* 27, nos. 2–3: 167–90.
———. "Marx Beyond Marx, Marx Before Marx. Negri's Lucretian Critique of the Hegelian Marx." In *Reading Negri*, ed. P. Lamarche, M. Rosenkrantz, and D. Sherman, 127–48 . Chicago: Open Court.
———. 2008. *Life as Surplus: Biotechnology and Capitalism in the Neoliberal Era*. Seattle: University of Washington Press.
———. 2002. "The Living and the Dead: Variations on *De anima*." *Angelaki* 7, no. 3: 81–104.
Crespo, Ricardo. 2006. "The Ontology of the 'Economic': an Aristotelian Analysis." *Cambridge Journal of Economics* 30, no. 5: 767–81.
———. 2002. "Reappraising Austrian Economics' Basic Tenets in the Light of Aristotelian Ideas." *The Review of Austrian Economics* 15, no. 4: 313–33.
Cristi, Renato. 2005. *Hegel on Freedom and Authority*. Cardiff: University of Wales Press.
———. 1998. *Carl Schmitt and Authoritarian Liberalism: Strong State, Free Economy*. Cardiff: University of Wales Press.
d'Hondt, Jacques. 1990. "Der junge Hegel und Benjamin Constant." In *Der Weg zum System: Materialen zum jungen Hegel*, ed. H. Schneider and C. Jamme. Frankfurt: Suhrkamp.

Dallmayr, Fred. R. 2002. *G. W. F. Hegel: Modernity and Politics*. Lanham, MD: Rowman & Littlefield Publishers.

de Boer, Karin. 2010a. *On Hegel: The Sway of the Negative*. Basingstoke, UK: Palgrave Macmillan.

———. 2010b. "Beyond Tragedy: Tracing the Aristophanian Subtext of Hegel's *Phenomenology of Spirit*." In *Hegel's Philosophy and Feminist Thought. Beyond Antigone?*, ed. T. Pulkkinen and K. Hutchings, 133–52. New York: Palgrave Macmillan.

Dean, Jodi. 2012. *The Communist Horizon*. London: Verso.

Dean, Mitchell. 1999. *Governmentality: Power and Rule in Modern Society*. London: Sage.

Del Lucchese, Filippo. 2011. *Conflict, Power, and Multitude in Machiavelli and Spinoza: Tumult and Indignation*. London: Bloomsbury Academic.

De la Durantaye, Leland. 2000. "Agamben's Potential." *Diacritics*. 30, no. 2: 3–24.

Deleuze, Gilles. 2001. *Pure Immanence: Essays on A Life*. New York: Zone Books.

———. 1992. *Expressionism in Philosophy: Spinoza*. New York: Zone Books.

———. 1988. *Foucault*. Minneapolis: University of Minnesota Press.

Deleuze, Gilles, and Felix Guattari. 1987. *A Thousand Plateaus: Capitalism and Schizophrenia*. Minneapolis: University of Minnesota Press.

Demirović, Alex, and Michael Henry. 2008. "Gesellschaftstheorie nach Marx und Foucault." *Prokla 151. Zeitschrift für kritische Sozialwissenschaft* 38, no. 2.

Derrida, Jacques. 2006. *L'animal que donc je suis*. Paris: Galilée.

———. 1994. *Force de la loi*. Paris: Galilée.

———. 1993. *Aporias*. Stanford: Stanford University Press.

———. 1985. "Devant la loi: Préjugés." *Critique de la faculté de juger*. Paris: Minuit.

Detienne, Marcel. 1977. *Dionysos mis à mort*. Paris: Gallimard.

Dickey, Laurence. 1987. *Hegel: Religion, Economics, and the Politics of Spirit. 1770–1807*. Cambridge: Cambridge University Press.

Dietz, Mary. 1995. "Feminist Receptions of Hannah Arendt." In *Feminist Interpretations of Hannah Arendt*, ed. Bonnie Honig, 17–50. University Park: Pennsylvania State University Press.

Dillon, Michael. 2007. "Governing Through Contingency: The Security of Biopolitical Governance." *Political Geography* 26: 41–47.

Dillon, Michael, and Andrew Neal. 2011. *Foucault on Politics, Security and War*. London: Palgrave Macmillan.

Dommanget, Maurice. 1972. *Auguste Blanqui et la révolution de 1848*. Paris: Mouton.

Dotti, Jorge. 2009. "El problema de la guerra en el sistema hegeliano." In *Hegel, pensador de la actualidad*, ed. V. Lemm and J. Ormeño Karzulovic, 285–314. Santiago, Chile: Ediciones Universidad Diego Portales.

Douzinas, Costas, ed. 2010. *The Idea of Communism*. London: Verso.

Dreyfus, Hubert, and Sean Dorrance Kelly. 2011. *All Things Shining: Reading the*

Western Classics to Find Meaning in a Secular Age. New York: Free Press.

Duarte, André. 2010. *Vidas em risco: Critica do presente em Heidegger, Arendt e Foucault.* Rio de Janeiro: Forense Universitaria.

———. 2004. "Biopolitics and the Dissemination of Violence: The Arendtian Critique of the Present." *Pasajes de Pensamiento Contemporáneo* 13. (An English version can be accessed online at HannahArendt.net, Research Notes [April 2005].)

Dubber, Markus, and Mariana Valverde. 2008. *Police and the Liberal State.* Stanford: Stanford University Press.

Dubreuil, Laurent. 2006. "Leaving Politics: Bios, Zoe, Life." *diacritics* 36, no. 2: 83–98.

Durst, Margarete. 2004. "Birth and Natality in Hannah Arendt." *Analecta husserliana* 79: 777–97.

Düttmann, Alexander García. 2004. *So ist es.* Frankfurt: Suhrkamp.

Dworkin, Ronald. 1994. *Life's Dominion: An Argument About Abortion, Euthanasia, and Individual Freedom.* New York: Vintage Books.

Eberl, Oliver. 2011. *Transnationalisierung der Volkssouveraenitaet. Radikale Demokratie diesseits und jenseits des Staates.* Stuttgart: Franz Steiner Verlag.

Esposito, Roberto. 2012. *Third Person: Politics of Life and Philosophy of the Impersonal.* Cambridge: Polity Press.

———. 2010. *Communitas: The Origin and Destiny of Community.* Trans. T. Campbell. Stanford: Stanford University Press.

———. 2008. *Bios: Biopolitics and Philosophy.* Minneapolis: University of Minnesota Press.

Faes, Hubert. 1995. "L'esclave, le travail et l'action. Aristote et Hegel." *Archives de Philosophie* 58: 97–121.

Fassin, Didier. 2009. "Another Politics of Life is Possible." *Theory, Culture and Society* 26, no. 5: 44–60.

Fenves, Peter. 2011. *The Messianic Reduction: Walter Benjamin and the Shape of Time.* Stanford: Stanford University Press.

———. 2005. "Marital, Martial, Maritime Law: Toward Some Controversial Passages in Kant's 'Doctrine of Right.'" *Diacritics* 35, no. 4: 101–20.

Finlayson, James Gordon. 2010. "'Bare Life' and Politics in Agamben's Reading of Aristotle." *The Review of Politics* 72, no. 1: 97–126.

Forst, Rainer. 2011. *Kritik der Rechtfertigungs-verhältnisse. Perspektiven kritischen Theorie der Politik.* Frankfurt: Suhrkamp.

———. 2007. *Das Recht auf Rechtfertigung.* Frankfurt: Suhrkamp.

Forti, Simona. 2006. "The Biopolitics of Souls. Racism, Nazism, and Plato." *Political Theory* 34: 9–32.

———. 2003. *Il totalitarismo.* Roma-Bari: Laterza.

———. 1996. *Vita della mente e tempo della polis: Hannah Arendt tra filosofia e politica.* Milan: Franco Angeli.

Foucault, Michel. 2010. *The Birth of Biopolitics: Lectures at the Collège de France, 1978–1979*. New York: Picador.

———. 2009. *Security, Territory, Population: Lectures at the Collège de France 1977–1978*. New York: Picador.

———. 2003."*Society Must be Defended*": *Lectures at the Collège de France, 1975–1976*. New York: Picador.

———. 2001a. *Dits et Écrits. 1954–1988*. Vol. 2. Paris: Gallimard.

———. 2001b. *L'herméneutique du sujet. Cours au College de France. 1981–1982*. Paris: Gallimard Seuil.

———. 2000. *Power: Essential Works of Foucault 1954–1984. Vol. 3*. Ed. J. Faubion. New York: The New Press.

———. 1997. *Ethics: The Essential Works of Michel Foucault 1954–1984. Vol 1*. Ed. P. Rabinow. New York: The New Press.

———. 1995. *Discipline and Punish*. New York: Vintage Books.

———. 1990. *The History of Sexuality. Volume I: An Introduction*. Trans. R. Hurley. New York: Vintage Books.

Fox, Christopher. 2007. "Sacrificial Past and Messianic Futures." *Philosophy and Social Criticism* 33, no. 5: 563–95.

Franck, Didier. 1991. "Being and the Living." In *Who Comes After the Subject?*, ed. E. Cadava and J.-L. Nancy. London: Routledge.

Freud, Sigmund. 1961. *Beyond the Pleasure Principle*. New York: W. W. Norton & Company.

———. 1950. *Totem and Taboo*. New York: W. W. Norton & Company.

Garrido, Juan Manuel. 2012. *On Time, Being and Hunger: Challenging the Traditional Way of Thinking Life*. New York: Fordham University Press.

Gasché, Rodolphe. 2005. "Sublimely Clueless: On the Foundation of Marriage in Statutory Law." *Cardozo Law Review* 26, no. 3: 921–42.

Gehring, Petra. 2007. "Foucaults 'juridischer' Machttyp, die *Geschichte der Gouvernamentalitaet* und die Frage nach Foucualts Rechtstheorie." In *Michel Foucaults 'Geschichte der Gouvernementalitaet' in den Sozialwissenschaften*. ed. M. Volkmer and S. Krasmann. Bielefeld: transcript Verlag.

Geulen, Eva. 2005. *Giorgio Agamben zur Einführung*. Hamburg: Junius.

Geulen, Eva, Kai Kaufmann, and Georg Mein. 2008. *Hannah Arendt und Giorgio Agamben. Parallelen, Perspektiven, Kontroversen*. Munich: Fink.

Gibson-Graham, J. K., Stephen Resnick, and Richard Wolff. 2001. *Re/Presenting Class: Essays in Postmodern Marxism*. Durham, NC: Duke University Press.

Girard, René. 2005. *Violence and the Sacred*. London: Continuum Publishers.

Giroux, Henry. 2007. *The University in Chains*. New York: Paradigm Publishers.

Glendon, Mary Ann. 2002. *A World Made New: Eleanor Roosevelt and the Universal Declaration of Human Rights*. New York: Random House.

Golder, Ben. 2011. "Foucault's Critical (Yet Ambivalent) Affirmation: Three Figures of Rights." *Social and Legal Studies*: 1–30.

———. 2010. "Foucault and the Unfinished Human of Rights." *Law, Culture and the Humanities* 6, no. 3: 354–74.

Golder, Ben, and Peter Fitzpatrick. 2009. *Foucault's Law*. London: Routledge.

Goldmann, Lucien. 1977. *Lukács and Heidegger*. London: Routledge

Goodchild, Philip. 2009. *Theology of Money*. Durham, NC: Duke University Press.

Gossman, Lionel. 1983. "Orpheus Philologus. Bachofen vs. Mommsen on the Study of Antiquity." *Transactions of the American Philosophical Society* 73, no. 5.

Gottlieb, Susannah. 2003. *Regions of Sorrow*. Stanford: Stanford University Press.

Greene, Brian. 2011. *The Hidden Reality: Parallel Universes and the Deep Laws of the Cosmos*. New York: Alfred A. Knopf.

Greiert, Andreas. 2011. *Erlösung der Geschichte vom Darstellenden. Grundlagen des Geschichstdenkens bei Walter Benjamin 1915–1925*. Munich: Wilhelm Fink.

Griffin, James. 2008. *On Human Rights*. Oxford: Oxford University Press.

Habermas, Juergen. 2004. *Wahrheit und Rechtfertigung*. Frankfurt: Suhrkamp, 2004.

———. 1987. *The Philosophical Discourse of Modernity*. Cambridge, MA: MIT Press.

———. 1984a. *The Theory of Communicative Action. Volume 1. Reason and the Rationalization of Society*. Trans. T. McCarthy. Boston: Beacon Press.

———. 1984b. *The Theory of Communicative Action. Volume 2: Lifeworld and System: A Critique of Functionalist Reason*. Trans. T. McCarthy. Boston: Beacon.

———. 1975. *Legitimation Crisis*. Trans. T. McCarthy. Boston: Beacon.

Hamacher, Werner. 2006. "Das Theologisch-politische Fragment." In *Benjamin-Handbuch. Leben - Werk - Wirkung*, ed. B. Lindner. Stuttgart: Verlag J. B. Metzler.

———. 2004. "The Right to Have Rights. (Four-and-a-Half Remarks)." *South Atlantic Quarterly* 103, nos. 2/3: 343–56.

Hanssen, Beatrice. 2000. *Walter Benjamin's Other History: Of Stones, Animals, Human Beings, and Angels*. Berkeley: University of California Press.

Hardt, Michael, and Antonio Negri. 2011. *Commonwealth*. Cambridge, MA: Harvard University Press.

———. 2005. *Multitude: War and Democracy in the Age of Empire*. Cambridge, MA: Harvard University Press.

———. 2001. *Empire*. Cambridge, MA: Harvard University Press.

Harris, Grace. 1973. "Furies, Witches, and Mothers." In *The Character of Kinship*, ed. J. Goody. Cambridge: Cambridge University Press.

Hatab, Lawrence J. 2005. *Nietzsche's Life Sentence: Coming to Terms with Eternal Recurrence*. New York: Routledge.

Hayek, Friedrich. A. 1984. *The Essence of Hayek*. Edited by C. Nishiyama and K. Leube. Stanford: Hoover Instutition Press.

———. 1973. *Law, Legislation and Liberty.* 3 vols. London: Routledge.
———. 1949. *Individualism and Economic Order.* London: Routledge and Kegan Paul.
Hegel, Georg Wilhelm Friedrich. 2005. *Die Philosophie des Rechts. Vorlesung von 1821/1822.* Frankfurt: Suhrkamp.
———. 2004. *Ueber die Reichsverfassung.* Hamburg: Felix Meiner Verlag.
———. 1987. *Jenaer Systementwuerfe III. Naturphilosophie und Philosophie des Geistes.* Hamburg: Felix Meiner Verlag.
———. 1986. *Vorlesungen ueber die Philosophie der Geschichte.* Vol. 12, Werke in 20 Bd. Frankfurt: Suhrkamp.
———. 1979. *System of Ethical Life (1802/1803) and First Philosophy of Spirit.* Trans. H. S. Harris. Albany: State University of New York Press.
———. 1977. *Phenomenology of Spirit.* Trans. A. V. Miller. Oxford: Oxford University Press.
———. 1975. *Natural Law.* Trans. T. M. Knox. Philadelphia: University of Pennsylvania Press.
———. 1971. *Early Theological Writings.* Trans. T. M. Knox. Philadelphia: University of Pennsylvania Press.
———. 1967. *Philosophy of Right.* Oxford: Oxford University Press.
Heidegger, Martin. 1995. *The Fundamental Concepts of Metaphysics: World, Finitude, Solitude.* Trans. W. McNeill and N. Walker. Bloomington: Indiana University Press.
———. 1988. *Hegel's Phenomenology of Spirit.* Tran. K. Maly and P. Emad. Bloomington: Indiana University Press.
———. 1986 [1968]. *Sein und Zeit.* Tuebingen: Max Niemeyer Verlag.
———. 1978. *Wegmarken.* Frankfurt: Vittorio Klostermann.
Heller, Agnes. 1999. *A Theory of Modernity.* Oxford: Blackwell Publishers.
———. 1993. *A Philosophy of History in Fragments.* Cambridge: Blackwell.
Heller, Agnes, and Ferenc Feher. 1994. *Biopolitics.* Vienna: European Centre.
Hillach, Ansgar. 2000. "Dialektisches Bild." In *Benjamins Begriffe,* ed. E. Wizisla and M. Opitz, 1:186–229. Frankfurt: Suhrkamp.
Hölderlin, Friedrich. 1988. *Essays and Letters on Theory.* Trans. T. Pfau. Albany: State University of New York Press.
Honig, Bonnie. 2013. *Antigone, Interrupted.* Cambridge: Cambridge University Press.
———. 2003. *Democracy and the Foreigner.* Princeton, NJ: Princeton University Press.
Honneth, Axel. 2011. "Die Moral im 'Kapital.' Versuch einer Korrektur der Marxschen Oekonomiekritik." *Leviathan* 39, no. 4: 583–94.
———. 2007. *Pathologien Der Vernunft.* Frankfurt: Suhrkamp.
———. 2005. *Verdinglichung. Eine anerkennungstheoretische Studie.* Frankfurt: Suhrkamp.

———. 2001. *Leiden an Unbestimmtheit*. Stuttgart: Philipp Reclam.
———. 1992. *Kampf um Anerkennung*. Frankfurt: Suhrkamp.
Honneth, Axel, and Martin Saar. 2003. *Michel Foucault. Zwischenbilanz einer Rezeption*. Frankfurt: Suhrkamp.
Horkheimer, Max. 2005. *Traditionelle und Kritische Theorie*. Frankfurt: Suhrkamp.
Horkheimer, Max, and Theodor W. Adorno. 1972. *Dialectic of Enlightenment*. New York: Continuum.
Horwitz, Rivka. 1995. "Kafka and the Crisis in Jewish Religious Thought." *Modern Judaism* 15: 21–73.
Hunt, Lynn. 2008. *Inventing Human Rights: A History*. New York: W. W. Norton & Company.
Hutchings, Kimberly, and Tuija Pulkkinen. 2010. *Hegel's Philosophy and Feminist Thought: Beyond Antigone?* New York: Palgrave Macmillan.
Ingram, James. 2008. "What Is a 'Right to Have Rights?' Three Images of the Politics of Human Rights." *American Political Science Review* 102, no. 4: 401–16.
Isaac, Jeffrey C. 1996. "A New Guarantee on Earth: Hannah Arendt on Human Dignity and the Politics of Human Rights." *The American Political Science Review* 90, no. 1: 61–73.
James, Susan. 2012. *Spinoza on Philosophy, Religion, and Politics: The Theologico-Political Treatise*. New York: Oxford University Press.
Jennings, Michael. 2003. "On the Banks of a New Lethe: Commodification and Experience in Benjamin's Baudelaire Book." *boundary 2* 30, no. 1: 89–103.
Jonas, Hans. 2001. *The Phenomenon of Life*. Evanston, IL: Northwestern University Press.
———. 1994. *Philosophische Untersuchungen und metaphysische Vermutungen*. Frankfurt: Suhrkamp.
———. 1958. *The Gnostic Religion: The Message of the Alien God and the Beginnings of Christianity*. Boston: Beacon Press. (Original edition, Gnosis und spaetantiker Geist, 1934.)
Kafka, Franz. 1986. *Erzählungen*. Ed. M. Brod. Frankfurt: Fischer.
Kant, Immanuel. 1996. *Practical Philosophy*. Ed. M. Gregor. Cambridge Kant Works ed. Cambridge: Cambridge University Press.
Kaufmann, David. 2001. "Beyond Use, Within Reason: Adorno, Benjamin, and the Question of Theology." *New German Critique* 83: 151–73.
Keedus, Liisi. 2011. "'Human and Nothing but Human': How Schmittian Is Hannah Arendt's Critique of Human Rights and International Law?" *History of European Ideas* 37: 190–96.
Kervégan, Jean-Francois. 2005. *Hegel, Carl Schmitt: la politique entre spéculation et positivité*. Paris: PUF.
Kierkegaard, Soren. 1987. *Either/Or. Part II*. Trans. H. V. Hong and E. V. Hong. Princeton, NJ: Princeton University Press.

———. 1983. *Fear and Trembling. Repetition.* Trans. H. V. Hong and E. V. Hong. Princeton, NJ: Princeton University Press.
Klossowski, Pierre. 1969. *Nietzsche et le circle vicieux.* Paris: Mercure de France.
Koch, Getrud. 2003. "Man liebt sich. Man liebt sich nicht. Man liebt sich. Stanley Cavells Lob der Wiederverheiratung." *Texte zur Kunst* 52, no. 13: 110–18.
Kojève, Alexandre. 1969. *Introduction to the Reading of Hegel: Lectures on the Phenomenology of Spirit.* Ithaca, NY: Cornell University Press.
Kordela, Kiarina. 2002. "Capital: At Least It Kills Time." *Rethinking Marxism* 18, no. 4: 539–63.
Kouvelakis, Stathis. 2003. *Philosophy and Revolution: From Kant to Marx.* London: Verso.
Kristeva, Julia. 2000. *El genio femenino. 1 Hannah Arendt.* Buenos Aires: Paidós.
Lafont, Cristina. 2000. *Heidegger, Language, and World-Disclosure.* New York: Cambridge University Press.
Lazzarato, Maurizio. 1997. *Lavoro immaterial. Forme di vita e produzione di soggettività.* Verona: Ombre Corte.
Lazzeri, Christian. 1998. *Droit, pouvoir et liberté: Spinoza, critique de Hobbes.* Paris: PUF.
Legrand, Stéphane. 2007. *Les normes chez Foucault.* Paris: PUF.
———. 2004. "Le marxisme oublié de Foucault." *Actuel Marx* 36.
Lemke, Thomas. 2011. *Biopolitics. An Advanced Introduction.* New York: New York University Press.
———. 2007. *Gouvernementalitaet und Biopolitik.* Wiesbaden: VS Verlag fuer Sozialwissenchaften.
———. 2004. «Marx sans guillemets. Foucault, la gouvernamentalité et la critique du néo-libéralisme.» *Actuel Marx* 36.
———. 1997. *Eine Kritik der politischen Vernunft. Foucaults Analyse der moderne Gouvernementalität.* Hamburg: Argument Verlag.
Lemm, Vanessa. 2010. "Critical Theory and Affirmative Biopolitics: Nietzsche and the Domination of Life in Adorno and Horkheimer." *Journal of Power* 3, no. 1: 75–95.
———. 2009. *Nietzsche's Animal Philosophy: Culture, Politics and the Animality of the Human Being.* New York: Fordham University Press.
Levi, Primo. 1996. *Survival in Auschwitz: The Nazi Assault on Humanity.* New York: Simon and Schuster.
Lindahl, Hans. 2008. "The *Anomos* of the Earth: Political Indexicality, Immigration, and Distributive Justice." *Ethics and Global Politics* 1, no. 4: 193–212.
———. 2006. "Give and Take: Arendt and the *Nomos* of Political Community." *Philosophy and Social Criticism* 32, no. 6: 785–805.
Loeb, Paul S. 2010. *The Death of Nietzsche's Zarathustra.* Cambridge: Cambridge University Press.

Lobo-Guerrero, Luis. 2010. *Insuring Security: Biopolitics, Security and Risk.* London: Routledge.
Loeschenkohl, Birte. 2010. "Entweder/Und, Wiederkunft/Erloesung." *Benjamin-Studien* 2. Ed. D. Weidner and S. Weigel. Paderborn: Wilhelm Fink.
Lorey, Isabell. 2012. *Die Regierung der Prekaeren.* Vienna/Berlin: Turia+Kant.
Losurdo, Domenico. 2004. *Hegel and the Freedom of the Moderns.* Durham, NC: Duke University Press.
Löwith, Karl. 1997. *Nietzsche's Philosophy of Eternal Recurrence of the Same.* Berkeley: University of California Press.
Luisetti, Federico. 2011. *Una vita. Pensiero selvaggio e filosofia dell'intensità.* Milan: Mimesis.
Lukács, Georg. 1975. *The Young Hegel. Studies in the Relations between Dialectics and Economics.* Cambridge, MA: MIT Press.
———. 1968. *History and Class Consciousness.* Cambridge, MA: MIT Press.
Maimonides, Moses. 1963. *The Guide of the Perplexed.* Trans. S. Pines, ed. L. Strauss. 2 vols. Chicago: University of Chicago Press.
Marcuse, Herbert. 1991. *One-Dimensional Man: Studies in the Ideology of Advanced Industrial Society.* Intro. Douglas Kellner. Boston: Beacon.
Marinas, José-Miguel. 2001. *La fábula del bazaar: Orígenes de la cultura del consumo.* Madrid: A. Machado.
Markell, Patchen. 2006. "The Rule of the People: Arendt, Arche, and Democracy." *The American Political Science Review* 100, no. 1: 1–14.
———. 2003. *Bound by Recognition.* Princeton, NJ: Princeton University Press.
Martel, James. 2012. *Divine Violence: Walter Benjamin and the Eschatology of Sovereignty.* New York and London: Routledge.
Marx, Karl. 1998. *The Communist Manifesto.* New York: Penguin Putnam.
———. 1978a. *Capital: The Marx-Engels Reader.* Ed. R. Tucker. New York: W. W. Norton.
———. 1978b. *The Communist Manifesto: The Marx-Engels Reader.* Ed. R. Tucker. New York: W. W. Norton.
———. 1978c. *German Ideology. The Marx-Engels Reader.* Ed. R. Tucker. New York: W. W. Norton.
———. 1976. *Capital: A Critique of Political Economy.* Vol. 1. London: Penguin Books.
———. 1975. *Early Writings.* Ed. L. Colletti. New York: Vintage Books.
———. 1974. *Grundrisse: Foundations of the Critique of Political Economy (Rough Draft).* Trans. M. Nicolaus, ed. M. Nicolaus. Harmondsworth, UK: Penguin Books.
———. 1973. *The Poverty of Philosophy.* Moscow: Progress Publishers.
Marzocca, Ottavio. 2008. "Biopolitica, sovranità, lavoro. Foucault tra vida nuda e vita creative." In *Foucault oggi,* ed. M. Galzigna. Milan: Feltrinelli.

McCloskey, Deirdre N. 2010. *Bourgeois Dignity: Why Economics Can't Explain the Modern World*. Chicago: University of Chicago Press.

Meador, Daniel John. 1966. *Habeas Corpus and Magna Carta*. Charlottesville: University Press of Virginia.

Menke, Christoph. 2007. "The 'Aporias of Human Rights' and the 'One Human Right.'" *Social Research* 74, no. 3: 739–62.

———. 1996. *Tragoedie im Sittlichen. Gerechtigkeit und Freiheit nach Hegel*. Frankfurt: Suhrkamp.

Menke, Christoph, and Arnd Pollmann. 2007. *Philosophie der Menschenrechte*. Hamburg: Junius Verlag.

Milbank, John. 2006. *Theology and Social Theory. Beyond Secular Reason*. London: Wiley-Blackwell.

Miller, Tyrus. 2008. "Eternity No More: Walter Benjamin on the Eternal Return." In *Given World and Time: Temporalities in Context*. ed. T. Miller. Budapest: Central European University Press.

Mirowski, Philip. 1991. *More Heat than Light: Economics as Social Physics, Physics as Nature's Economics*. Cambridge: Cambridge University Press.

———. 2007. "Naturalizing the Market on the Road to Revisionism: Bruce Caldwell's 'Hayek's Challenge' and the Challenge of Hayek Interpretation." *Journal of Institutional Economics* 3, no. 3: 351–72.

Mirowski, Philip, and Dieter Plehwe. 2009. *The Mont Pelerin Society: The Making of the Neoliberal Thought Collective*. Cambridge, MA: Harvard University Press.

Moses, Stéphane. 1999. "Gershom Scholem's Reading of Kafka: Literary Criticism and Kabbalah." *New German Critique* 77: 149–67.

———. 1996. "Benjamin, Nietzsche et l'idée de l'éternel retour." *Revue Europe* 804: 140–51.

Moyn, Samuel. 2012. *The Last Utopia: Human Rights in History*. Cambridge, MA: Harvard University Press.

Muhle, Maria. 2008. *Eine Genealogie der Biopolitik. Zum Begriff des Lebens bei Foucault und Canguilhem*. Bielefeld: transcript Verlag.

Napoli, Paolo. 2003. *Naissance de la police moderne: pouvoir, normes, société*. Paris: La Découverte.

Nasstrom, Sofia. 2007. "The Legitimacy of the People." *Political Theory* 35, no. 5: 624–58.

Negri, Antonio. 1999. *Savage Anomaly: The Power of Spinoza's Metaphysics and Politics*. Minneapolis: University of Minnesota.

———. 1994. "Démocratie et éternité." In *Spinoza: Puissance et Ontologie*. Paris: Kimé.

———. 1991. *Marx Beyond Marx: Lessons on the Grundrisse*. Ed. J. Fleming. London: Pluto Press.

Nieraad, Juergen. 1990. "Walter Benjamins Glueck im Untergang: Zum Verhaeltnis von Messianischem und Profanem." *The German Quarterly* 63, no. 2: 222–32.

Nietzsche, Friedrich. 1995. *Thus Spoke Zarathustra*. Trans. W. Kaufmann. New York: Modern Library.

———. 1994. *On the Genealogy of Morals*. Ed. K. Ansell-Pearson. Cambridge: Cambridge University Press.

———. 1993. *The Birth of Tragedy*. Trans. S. Whiteside, ed. M. Tanner. New York: Penguin.

———. 1990. *Twilight of the Idols. The Anti-Christ*. Trans. R.J. Hollingdale, ed. M. Tanner. New York: Penguin.

———. 1989. *On the Genealogy of Morals: Ecce Homo*. Trans. W. Kaufmann. New York: Vintage Books.

———. 1988. *Nachgelassene Fragmente 1880–1882*: Kritischen Studienausgabe (KSA) 9. Berlin: de Gruyter.

———. 1974. *The Gay Science*. Trans. W. Kaufmann. New York: Vintage.

———. 1968. *The Will to Power*. Trans. W. Kaufmann and R. J. Hollingdale. New York: Vintage Books.

Nigro, R. 2001. "Foucault lecteur et critique de Marx." *Dictionnaire Marx contemporain*. Ed. J. Bidet and E. Kouvelakis. Paris: PUF.

Norris, Andrew, ed. 2005. *Politics, Metaphysics, and Death: Essays on Giorgio Agamben's* Homo Sacer. Durham, NC: Duke University Press.

Norton, Robert E. 2002. *Secret Germany: Stefan George and His Circle*. Ithaca, NY: Cornell University Press.

Novak, David. 2005. *The Jewish Social Contract: An Essay in Political Theology*. Princeton, NJ: Princeton University Press.

Nuzzo, Angelica. 2012. *Memory, History, Justice in Hegel*. Basingstoke, UK: Palgrave Macmillan.

Parekh, Serena. 2008. *Hannah Arendt and the Challenge of Modernity: A Phenomenology of Human Rights*. New York: Routledge.

———. 2004. "A Meaningful Place in the World: Hannah Arendt on the Nature of Human Rights." *Journal of Human Rights* 3, no. 1: 41–53.

Passavant, Paul. 2007. "The Contradictory State of Giorgio Agamben." *Political Theory* 35, no. 2: 147–74.

Patton, Paul. 2010. *Deleuzian Concepts: Philosophy, Colonization, Politics*. Stanford: Stanford University Press.

———. 2005. "Foucault, Critique and Rights." *Critical Horizons* 6, no. 1: 267–87.

Pauen, Michael. 1999. "Eros der Ferne. Walter Benjamin und Ludwig Klages." In *Global Benjamin: Internationale Walter-Benjamin-Kongress 1992*, ed. L. Rehm and K. Garber. Munich: Wilhelm Fink.

Pinkard, Terry. 1994. *Hegel's Phenomenology: The Sociality of Reason*. Cambridge: Cambridge University Press.

Pippin, Robert. 2011. *Hegel on Self-Consciousness: Desire and Death in the Phenomenology of Spirit*. Princeton, NJ: Princeton University Press.

———. 1997. *Idealism as Modernism: Hegelian Variations*. New York: Cambridge University Press.

———. 1989. *Hegel's Idealism: The Satisfactions of Self-Consciousness*. Cambridge: Cambridge University Press.

Pitkin, Hannah Fenichel. 1998. *The Attack of the Blob: Hannah Arendt's Concept of the Social*. Chicago: University of Chicago Press.

Plaut, Eric, and Kevin Anderson. 2001. *Karl Marx: Vom Selbstmord*. Cologne, Germany: ISP Verlag.

Pocock, J. G. A. 1975. *The Machiavellian Moment*. Princteon, NJ: Princeton University Press.

Pogge, Thomas. 2005. "World Poverty and Human Rights." *Ethics and international Affairs* 1, no. 19: 1–7.

———. 2002. *World Poverty and Human Rights*. Cambridge: Polity Press.

Postone, Moishe. 1993. *Time, Labor, and Social Domination: A Reinterpretation of Marx's Critical Theory*. Cambridge: Cambridge University Press.

Purtschert, Patricia, Katrin Meyer, and Yves Winter. 2007. *Gouvernementalität und Sicherheit. Zeitdiagnostische Beiträge im Anschluss an Foucault*. Berlin: Transcript.

Quintana, Laura. 2006. "De la nuda vida a la forma-de-vida. Pensar la política con Agamben desde y más allá del paradigma del biopoder." *Argumentos: Revista de la Universidad Metropolitana de México* 52: 213–60.

Rancière, Jacques. 2012. *The Nights of the Proletariat*. London: Verso.

———. 2009. *Hatred of Democracy*. London: Verso.

———. 2004. "Who Is the Subject of the Rights of Man?" *South Atlantic Quarterly* 103, nos. 2/3: 297–310.

———. 1995. *La Mésentente. Politique et Philosophie*. Paris: Galilée.

Rapoport-Albert, Ada. 2010. "On the Position of Women in Sabbatianism." In *The Sabbatian Movement and its Aftermath: Messianism, Sabbatianism, Frankism*, ed. R. Elior. Jerusalem: Modern Institute of Jewish Studies.

Rawls, John. 2001. *The Law of Peoples*. Cambridge, MA: Harvard University Press.

———. 1996. *Political Liberalism*. New York: Columbia University Press.

Revel, Judith. 2008. "Identità, natura, vita: tre deconstruzioni biopolitiche." In *Foucault oggi*, ed. M. Galzigna. Milan: Feltrinelli.

Ricoeur, Paul. 1983. "Préface." In *Hannah Arendt. Condition de l'homme modern*, 5–39. Paris: Calmann-Lévy.

Riedel, Manfred. 1982. *Zwischen Tradition und Revolution: Studien zu Hegels Rechstphilosophie*. Stuttgart: Klett-Cotta.

———. 1973. "Fortschritt una Dialektik un Hegels Geschichtsphilosophie." In *System und Geschichte: Studien zum historischen Standort von Hegels Philosophie*. Frankfurt: Suhrkamp.

Romandini, Fabián Ludueña. 2010. *La comunidad de los espectros: I. Antropotécnia*. Buenos Aires: Miño y Dávila.

Rose, Gillian. 1981. *Hegel Contra Sociology*. London: Athlone.

———. 1978. *The Melancholy Science: An Introduction to the Thought of Theodor W. Adorno*. London: Macmillan.

Rose, Nikolas. 2007. *The Politics of Life Itself: Biomedicine, Power, and Subjectivity in the Twenty-First Century*. Princeton, NJ: Princeton University Press.

Rosenzweig, Franz. 2005. *The Star of Redemption*. Translated by B. Galli. Madison: University of Wisconsin Press.

———. 2003. *Confluences: Politique, Histoire, Judaisme*. Ed. M. Crepon, G. Bensussan and M. de Launay. Paris: Vrin.

Rousseau, Jean-Jacques. 1992. *Discourse on the Origin of Inequality*. Trans. J. Miller. Indianapolis, IN: Hackett.

Rubin, Isaak Illich. 1978. "Abstract Labor and Marx's Theory of Value." *Capital and Class* 5. Trans. K. Gilbert. http://www.marxists.org/archive/rubin/abstract-labour.htm (accessed on May 26, 2012).

Ruggiero, Guido de. 1944. *Historia del liberalismo europeo*. Madrid: Ediciones Pegaso.

Saar, Martin. 2009. "Politik der Natur. Spinoza's Begriff der Regierung." *Deutsche Zeitschrift für Philosophie* 57, no. 3: 433–47.

Santner, Eric. 2006. *On Creaturely Life: Rilke, Benjamin, Sebald*. Chicago: University of Chicago Press.

Savarino, Luca. 2003. "Hannah Arendt e l'antropologia filosofica." *Discipline filosofiche* 13: 215–37.

———. 1997. *Politica ed estetica*. Turin: Silvio Zamorani editore.

Schmitt, Carl. 2003. *The Nomos of the Earth*. New York: Telos Press.

Schoettker, Detlev. 2005. "Kapitalismus als Religion und seine Folgen." In *Theologie und Politik: Walter Benjamin und ein Paradigma der Moderne*, ed. C. Morgenroth and K. Solibakke. Berlin: Erich Schmidt Verlag.

Schoettker, Detlev, and Erdmut Wizisla. 2006. *Arendt und Benjamin: Texte, Briefe, Dokumente*. Frankfurt: Suhrkamp.

Scholem, Gershom. 1971. *The Messianic Idea in Judaism*. New York: Schocken Books.

Schürmann, Reiner. 1996. *Des hégémonies brisées*. Mauvezin: Trans-Europ-Repress.

Segal, Charles. 1982. *Dionysiac Poetics and Euripides' Bacchae*. Princeton, NJ: Princeton University Press.

Sewell, William H. 2008. "The Temporalities of Capitalism." *Socio-Economic Review* 6: 517–37.

Shue, Henry. 1980. *Basic Rights: Subsistence, Affluence, and U.S. Foreign Policy*. Princeton, NJ: Princeton University Press.

Siep, Ludwig. 1992. *Praktische Philosophie im Deutschen Idealismus*. Frankfurt: Suhrkamp.

Simmel, Georg. 2011. *The View of Life: Four Metaphysical Essays with Journal Aphorisms*. Chicago: University of Chicago Press.

Sinnerbrink, Robert. 2005. "From Machenschaft to Biopolitics: A Genealogical Critique of Biopower." *Critical Horizons* 6, no. 1.

Skinner, Quentin. 2002. *Visions of Politics: Volume II. Renaissance Virtues*. Cambridge: Cambridge University Press.

———. 1998. *Liberty Before Liberalism*. Cambridge: Cambridge University Press.

Smith, Steven B. 1992. "Hegel on Slavery and Domination." *The Review of Metaphysics* XLVI, no. 181: 97–124.

———. 1989. *Hegel's Critique of Liberalism: Rights in Context*. Chicago: University of Chicago Press.

Sophocles. 1991. *Greek Tragedies*. Ed. D. Greene and R. Lattimore. Vol. 1. Chicago: University of Chicago Press.

Spieker, Jörg. 2013. "Defending the Open Society: Foucault, Hayek, and the Problem of Biopolitical Order." *Economy and Society* 42, no. 2: 304–21.

Spinoza, Baruch. 2002. *The Complete Works*. Trans. S. Shirley. Indianapolis, IN: Hackett Publishing Company.

Spinoza, Benedict de. 2007. *Theologico-Political Treatise*. Ed. J. Israel. Cambridge: Cambridge University Press.

Steiner, Uwe. 2006. "Kapitalismus als Religion." In *Benjamin Handbuch*, ed. B. Lindner, 167–74. Stuttgart: Metzler.

Strauss, Leo. 1963. *The Political Philosophy of Hobbes*. Chicago: University of Chicago Press.

Syros, Vasileios. 2012. *Marsilius of Padua at the Intersection of Ancient and Medieval Traditions of Political Thought*. Toronto: University of Toronto Press.

Szankay, Zoltán. 1995. "Arendtsche Denkungsart und Oeffnungsweisen der 'Demokratischen Frage.'" http//polylogos.org/philosophers/arendt/arendt-democratic.html (accessed December 11, 2006).

Taminiaux, Jacques. 1985. "Arendt, disciple de Heidegger?" *Etudes phénoménologiques* 2: 111–36.

Tassin, Étienne. 1999. "L'azione 'contro' il mondo. Il senso dell'acosmismo." In *Hannah Arendt*, ed. Simona Forti, 136–54. Milan: Bruno Mondadori.

Taylor, Charles. 2004. *Modern Social Imaginaries*. Durham, NC: Duke University Press.

———. 1979. *Hegel and Modern Society*. Cambridge: Cambridge University Press.

Taylor, Mark C. 2008. *Confidence Games. Money and Markets in a World Without Redemption*. Chicago: University of Chicago Press.

Tellmann, Ute. 2013. "Catastrophic Populations and the Fear of the Future: Malthus and the Genealogy of Liberal Economy." *Theory, Culture and Society* 30, no. 2: 135–55.

———. 2011. "The Economic Beyond Governmentality: The Limits of Conduct." In *Governmentality: Current Issues and Future Challenges*, ed. U. Bröckling, S. Krasmann, and T. Lemke, 285–303. London: Routledge.

Teubner, Guenther. 2012. *Constitutional Fragments: Societal Constitutionalism and Globalization*. New York: Oxford University Press.

Thurschwell, Adam. 2005. "Cutting the Branches for Akiba." In *Politics, Metaphysics, and Death: Essays on Giorgio Agamben's* Homo sacer, ed. A. Norris, 173–97. Durham, NC: Duke University Press.

Valverde, Mariana. 2011. "Law Versus History. Foucault's Genealogy of Modern Sovereignty." In *Foucault on Politics, Security and War*, ed. M. Dillon and A. Neal, 135–50. Hampshire: Palgrave Macmillan.

Vatter, Miguel. 2013a. *Machiavelli's* The Prince: *A Reader's Guide*. London: Bloomsbury, 2013.

———. 2013b. "The Politico-Theological Foundations of Universal Human Rights: The Case of Maritain." *Social Research* 80, no. 1: 1–27.

———. 2012. "The Quarrel Between Populism and Republicanism: Machiavelli and the Antinomies of Plebeian Politics." *Contemporary Political Theory* 11, no. 3: 242–63.

———. 2011. "The People Shall Be Judge: Reflective Judgment and Constituent Power in Kant's Philosophy of Law." *Political Theory* 6, no. 39: 749–76.

———. 2009. "Biopolitics: from Surplus Value to Surplus Life." *Theory and Event* 12, no. 2.

———. 2007. "Resistance and Legality: Arendt and Negri on Constituent Power." In *The Philosophy of Toni Negri, Vol.2*, ed. T. Murphy and A.-K. Mustapha, 52–86. London: Pluto Press.

———. 2006. "Natality and Biopolitics in Hannah Arendt." *Revista de Ciencia Política* 26, no. 3: 137–59.

———. 2005. "Pettit and Modern Republican Political Thought." In *Political Exclusion and Domination. NOMOS XLVI*, ed. M. Williams and S. Macedo, 118–63. New York: New York University Press.

———. 2004a. "Machiavelli After Marx: The Self-Overcoming of Marxism in the Late Althusser." *Theory and Event* 7, no. 4.

———. 2004b. "Strauss and Schmitt as Readers of Hobbes and Spinoza: On the Relation Between Liberalism and Political Theology." *The New Centennial Review* 4, no. 3: 161–214.

Vernant, Jean-Pierre, and Marcel Detienne. 1974. *Les ruses de l'intelligence*. Paris: Flammarion.

Vernant, Jean-Pierre, and Pierre Vidal-Naquet. 2001. *Mythe et tragédie en Grèce ancienne*. Vol. 1. Paris: La Découverte.

Villa, Dana. 1996. *Arendt and Heidegger: The Fate of the Political*. Princeton, NJ: Princeton University Press.

Villegas, Francisco Gil. 1996. *Los profetas y el Mesías: Lukács y Ortega como precursores de Heidegger en el Zeitgeist de la modernidad (1900–1929)*. México: Fondo de Cultura Económica.

Voegelin, Eric. 1994. *Les religions politiques.* Trans. J. Schmutz. Paris: Les Éditions du Cerf.
———. 1952. *The New Science of Politics.* Chicago: University of Chicago Press.
Vogl, Joseph. 2011. *Das Gespenst des Kapitals.* Berlin: diaphanes.
Weber, Max. 1958. *The Protestant Ethic and the Spirit of Capitalism.* New York: Charles Scribner's Sons.
Weber, Samuel. 2010. "Drawing—the Single Trait: Toard a Politics of Singularity." In *Crediting God: Sovereignty and Religion in the Age of Global Capitalism,* ed. M. Vatter. New York: Fordham University Press.
———. 2009. *Geld ist Zeit. Gedanken zur Kredit und Krise.* Berlin: diaphanes.
———. 2008. *Benjamin's-abilities.* Cambridge, MA: Harvard University Press.
———. 2005. *Targets of Opportunity: On the Militarization of Thinking.* New York: Fordham University Press.
———. 2004. *Theatricality as Medium.* New York: Fordham University Press.
Weigel, Sigrid. 2008. *Walter Benjamin: Die Kreatur, das Heilige, die Bilder.* Frankfurt: Fischer.
Wesel, Uwe. 1980. *Der Mythos vom Matriarchat.* Frankfurt: Suhrkamp.
Winnington-Ingram, R. P. 1948. "Clytemnestra and the Vote of Athens." *The Journal of Hellenic Studies* 68.
Wohlfarth, Irving. 2006. "Die Passagenarbeit." In *Benjamin Handbuch,* ed. B. Lindner, 251–74. Stuttgart: Metzler.
Wolff, Richard, Antonio Callari, and Bruce Roberts. 1998. "The Transformation Trinity: Value, Value Form, and Price." In *Marxian Economics: A Reappraisal, vol. 2.* Ed. R. Bellofiore. London: Macmillan.
Wood, Alen W. 1990. *Hegel's Ethical Thought.* Cambridge: Cambridge University Press.
Zac, Sylvain. 1979. *Philosophie, théologie, politique dans l'oeuvre de Spinoza.* Paris: Vrin.
Žižek, Slavoj. 2003. *The Puppet and the Dwarf: The Perverse Core of Christianity.* Cambridge, MA: MIT Press.

INDEX

Abensour, Miguel, 327n6, 333n2
abortion, 355n7
Abrahamic traditions: conceit of, 160; social contract of marriage, 159
abstract labor, 72–3, 297–9
Acosta, Maria del Rosario, 330n26
Adorno, Theodor, 68; communism, 109–10; *Negative Dialectics,* 119–20
Aeschylus: *Eumenides,* 32–4; *Oresteia* trilogy, 24–5
aesthetic view of life, 162
affection, passion and, 168
affirmative biopolitics, 4–5, 205–6; thanatopolitics and, 7
Agamben, Giorgio, 334n20, 335n8, 336n20, 337n26, 337n27: acquiescence, 285; affirmative biopolitics, 4, 100–1, 270; bare life, 81–2, 99–101, 140; bios, 103–4; commodity fetishism, 106–7, 111–14; form of life, 205; freedom and animal life, 105; *Homo Sacer,* 99–101; life-world, 103–5; messianic life, 115–23; nihilism, 122–3 *The Open,* 102–4; pornography, 118; potentiality, 275–87; profanation, 116–17; providence, 280–9; sacred life, legal order and, 18; right to have rights, 254, 343n26, 355n7, 356n14; rights of refugees, 230–6; vocation, 114–15; zoe, 103–4, 263.
alienation, bourgeois society, 62, 65
Althusser, Louis, 305
animality/animal species, 66–7, 105–6
animal life, 42–6, 272–3. See also zoe; species-life. happiness and, 318; versus humanized life, 47–9, 142–3
Antigone, divine law, 54–9, 105–6
antinomianism, Kafka, 119–20
antinomy of law and order, 200–9; of right, 304–5
Aristotle, 65, 264, 280–4
Arendt, Hannah, 5–6, 350n14, 355n13, 357n22, 357n25–26, 357n30; Blücher, Heinrich, 321; human condition, 135–6; human rights, 137, 222–5; humanism, 141–8; ideological humanism, 145–6; love, 133–4; memory, 133–4; men *versus* Man, 136–7; natality, use of concept, 129–9, 339–40; *On Revolution,* 244–50; *Origins of Totalitarianism,* 136, 146–7; public space, 143; zoe and bios, 141–8
Aronowitz, Stanley, 361n15
artistic creation, 189
Athena, people's court of justice, 33–4
Augustine, 131–2; Creation beliefs,

137–8, 144–5; double origin for human being, 136; love, 133–5; natality, 153–4
Austrian School of economics, neoliberalism and, 211
Ayache, Elie, 359n3

Bachofen, Johann Jakob, 165–6
Backhaus, Hans-Georg, 68–72, 333n6
Bachofen, Johann Jakob, 350n13
Badiou, Alain, 5, 13, 301, 305, 309
Bajorek, Jennifer, 351n21
Balibar, Étienne, 70 224, 226, 352n21, 358n2; bare life, 82–3. *See also* Odradek; Agamben, 99; dualism, 83; facticity and, 101–2; fetishism and, 101; guilt and, 100; messianic condition, 121; nihilism and, 101; power over, 263–4; profanation and, 101; proletariat and, 102; right to have rights and, 241; sovereignty and, 99–102; as wealth of society, 91; work of art and, 174–5
Barash, Jeffrey Andrew, 358n2
Baudelaire, Charles, 179–87, 108, 113.
Bazzicalupo, Laura, 342n21
Before the Law (Kafka), 119–20
Beiner, Ronald, 345n39
being-toward-death, 270–1, 273–4
Bellofiore, Ricardo, 333n6
Benhabib, Seyla, 228, 237–42, 254, 342n24, 344n35, 345n39, 351n7, 357n21
Benjamin, Walter, 336n, 337n, 340n15, 346n, 350n, 363n; Baudelaire and, 179–87; bourgeois marriage, 158–9; commodity fetishism, 178, 182–3; *Elective Affinities* (Goethe), and, 158–71; eschatological dimensions of Judaism, 170–2; haeterism, 165; messianic politics, 118–19, 122–3; reconciliation with God, 167–8; shock, 166–7, *Theological-Political Fragment*, 311–18.
Bergson, Henri, 298
Biale, David, 337n28
Bidet, Jacques, 334n15, 334n16
Bienenstock, Myriam, 331n29, 331n35
biological life: caesura and, 141–2; politics and, 220; sacredness of, 222–4; thanatopolitics and, 156–7; in truth, 170–1
biologization: of capitalism, 88; of the political world, 198
biopolitics, 2; affirmative, 4, 205–6; Arendt, 139–48; Athena's people's court of justice, 33–4; of capital, 81–8; constituent power, 243–54; contemplative life and, 263–5; governmentality and, 195–8; human rights and, 221–4; neoliberalism and, 199–200; political economy and, 196–7; republicanism and, 2; sacredness of biological life, 222–4; thanatopolitics, 156; transition to, 263–4
biopower, 263; conduct for individuals, 207–8; Foucault, 204, 206–7; potentiality, 4; power, 4
bios, 3, 102; capital and, 67, 82, 86; conatus, 265–6; desire and, 43; duality with zoe, 9; metabolism and, 282; sacrifice and, 31, 43; self-consciousness and, 43, 47–51; sexuality and, 157–8; social life, 178; sovereignty, 30, 49–50; of the worker, 86–93; virtue, 268; zoe and, 5, 46, 49, 104–5, 141–8
bios politikos, 142–3, 175, 233, 237
biotechnology, surplus life and, 94–5
Birmingham, Peg, 222, 339n4
The Birth of Biopolitics (Foucault), 2–3, 91

388 *Index*

The Birth of Tragedy (Nietzsche), 175–6
Blanqui, Louis-Auguste, 319, 362n30, 363n31, 363n32, 363n36
Bluhm, Harald, 331n30
Blumenberg, Hans, 339n9
Böhm-Bawerk, Eugen, 69–70
Boltanski, Luc, 354n40
boredom, 105–6
Bosteels, Bruno, 327n3
Boswell, John, 349n9
bourgeoisie, 23, 35, 82; class consciousness, 24; exchange-value and, 64; marriage, 158–9, 179; punishment, 38; sacrifice and, 35; theory of value, 79–80; value reification and, 68; time-consciousness and, 308
Bowen-Moore, Patricia, 339n, 345n39
Brague, Rémi, 276–7
Braun, Karen, 342n21
Brown, Wendy, 351n1, 357n29
Brunkhorst, Hauke, 333n3, 339n7, 351n7, 356n15
Buck-Morss, Susan, 336n13
Butler, Judith, 26, 223, 327n4, 328n8, 329n14, 329n,19, 331n37, 332n45, 335n1, 336n19

Caffentzis, George C., 334n14
Caldwell, Bruce J., 353n34
calling, *versus* profession, 115
Canguilhem, Georges, 47, 198, 203–6; Hayek opposition, 204–5; normative order, 203–5
capital: biopolitics of, 81–8; class consciousness and, 306–7; exchange-value, living labor and, 85–6; fecundity of, 62; labor, subsumption, 82; law of, 89, 93, 299; living labor and, 83; sexual reproduction, 178–87

capitalism: biologization of, 88; class struggle and, 302–9; economic theology, 291–2; knowledge and, 92–3; marriage and, 179; money and, 75–6; pathos-formula, 79; production, sexuality and, 185; profanation and, 116–17; professionalization of activity, 114–15; Protestant ethic and, 114–16; as religion, 116; temporality, 290–1
catallaxy, 94, 209, 212
Cicero, 208, 211
citizens, refugees, 258–9
civil rights, human rights and, 225
civil society: class consciousness, 22–4; class struggle, 302–3 as a crime, 38; depoliticizing, 200; direct democracy, 219; freedom, 205; global, 221–2; guardians, 23–4; Hegel, 17–8; history and, 290, 294–6; homosexual sex, 191; human dignity, 223; individualism and, 29–30; insecurity, 216; law, 20; liberalism, 201; life and, 90; macroeconomics, 93; money in, 68, 76; neoliberalism, 201; pastoral power, 207, 210; profanation, 31–2, 34–5; property and law, 22–3; reconciliation with state, 24–5; republicanism and, 5; sacredness, 223–4; as sacrifice of the sacrifice, 31–2; self-sacrifice and, 19; self-regulation, 206; *Sittlichkeit*, 29; social relations, 161; state and, mutual self-sacrifice, 34–6; risks in, 217; temporality, 296; value, sovereignty of, 60–7
class: bourgeoisie, 23; Plato's *Republic*, 22–4; reconciliation of inequalities, 36
class consciousness, 22–4, 65; abstract

Index 389

time and, 304; bourgeoisie, 24;
  capital and, 306–7; normative
  power and, 305–6; objective form
  of the object, 303–4; political
  action and, 307–9; reification
  of temporality, 294–302; self-
  consciousness of the commodity,
  304–6; time and, 306–8
class struggle, 302–9
Coccia, Emanuele, 359n13
coercion: freedom and, 20;
  punishment as, 38
Cohen, Hermann, 160
Cohen, Joshua, 355n11
Collin, Francoise, 339n7, 343n28, 345n39
comedy of the Hegelian state, 31–6
commodities: as exchange-value, 76–8;
  money and, 76; self-consciousness,
  304–6; sociality of, 75–6
commodity fetishism, 62, 73–4,
  182–3; bare life, 101; dialectical
  character, 106–9, 111–14; exchange-
  value, 62; exhibition value,
  112–13; profanation and, 116–17;
  temporality and, 296
communism: Adorno, 101, 109–10;
  absence of sovereignty and, 123;
  biopolitics and, 4; humanization
  of nature and naturalization of
  humanity, 67; money and, 75–6;
  primitive, 165; sexual, 190–1
conatus, 265–9
conduct of conduct, 206–9
Connolly, William, 359n1
consciousness, 42–3
constituent power, right to have rights,
  243–54
contemplation, metabolism and, 280–1
contemplative life: and biopolitics,
  263–5; living contemplation and,
  282–9

Cooper, Melinda, 94–6, 281, 334n14,
  335n28, 354n41, 359n12
coordination, law and order and,
  209–15
cosmopolitanism: human rights,
  republicanism and, 225–30; right to
  have rights, 238
Creation beliefs, 95–6, 133–5, 143, 311–18;
  Arendt, 137–8, 144–5, 153–5
credit, economic theology and, 292–4
Crespo, Ricardo, 352n30
crime, 37–41
crime and punishment, 20; tragedy,
  26–7
Cristi, Renato, 328n6, 332n38, 353n31
crowds, 181
Critique of Hegel's Philosophy of Right
  (Marx), 63
cunning, feminine and, 55–9; of
  reason, 54–5

Dean, Jodi, 327n3
Dean, Mitchell, 351n2, 351n4
death, 273; eternal life and, 274–5; spark
  of life and, 280
de Boer, Karin, 328n11, 330n26, 332n43
Declarations of the Rights of Man, 231
Decisionism, 54, 58, 169
De la Durantaye, Leland, 361n19
Deleuze, Gilles, 279–80, 282, 327n1,
  342n23, 343n27, 357n30
del Lucchese, Filippo, 352n28
Démar, Claire, 186–7
Derrida, Jacques, 232, 273–5, 335n1,
  337n29, 346n42
Demirović, Alex, 351n1
democracy, 236–43; constitutional,
  244–5; public opinion, 245–6;
  republic comparison, 246;
  republican constitution, 245–6
dependence on God, 268–9

desire: human *versus* animal, 45–6; self-consciousness, 43–4; subject to life, 43
Detienne, Marcel, 329n17
dialectical character of commodity fetishism, 106–9, 111–14
dialectical image, 108–9
Dickey, Laurence, 328n4
Dietz, Mary, 346n40
Dillon, Michael, 354n38
Dionysian life as work of art, 173–8
Dionysian *versus* Apollinian, 166–7
divine law, Antigone and, 54–9; 325
divine providence, eternal life and, 265–70
divine violence, 100, 127
Dommanget, Maurice, 361n18
Dotti, Jorge, 332n41
Douzinas, Costas, 327n3
dream image of society, 107–9
drive-condition of capacity, 276–7
dualist constitutional democracy, 244–6
Duarte, André, 342n21
Dubber, Markus, 354n37
Dubreuil, Laurent, 343n26
Durst, Margarete, 343n26, 345n39
Dworkin, Ronald, 355n7

Eberl, Oliver, 351n7
economic order, law and order and, 210–11
economic theology, political economy and, 290–4
Economic-Philosophical Manuscripts (Marx), 65
economics: coordination and, 207; equilibrium and, 212–13; Marx, Karl, 60–1; neoliberalism and, 211; political economy, 62–3
economy. *See* political economy

economy of time, 290–1
Einstein, 313
Either/Or (Kierkegaard), 162
Elective Affinities (Goethe), 158–71
entrepreneur, 34 , 91–2, 196, 199, 204, 214, 217–19
equilibrium, economics and, 198–9, 212–13
Esposito, Roberto, 4, 18, 29, 31, 141, 251, 263, 352n19, 355n9
eternal life, 7, 264. *See also* metabolism; being-toward death, 270–1, 273–4; downfall and, 118, 319–325; divine providence and, 265–70; happiness, 123, 319–25; marriage and, 161–73; salvation, 265; of sexuality, 168–9, work of art and, 177
eternal recurrence, 173, 317–25
ethical life: tragedy of, 25–6
ethico-political rights, 237–8
Eumenides (Aeschylus), 32–4
exception to law. *See* legal exception; state of exception
exchange-value: bourgeois commercial society, 64; as capital, living labor and, 85–6; commodity as, 76–8; as commodity fetishism, 62; labor as, 75; normativity, 60–1; social bond and, 74; universality, 68–9
exhibition value, 112–13; pornography, 118
existential life, 270–5

facticity: bare life and, 101–2, 111
Faes, Hubert, 331n30
family: political society and, 34; structure, tribal community and, 28
Fassin, Didier, 327n1, 352n20, 354n3
federalism, 244, 249–50
feminism, Claire Démar, 186–7
Fenves, Peter, 361n21
fertility, natality and, 150–1

Index 391

festival, 27–9
fetishism of commodities, 62, 73–4, 178, 182–3; bare life, 101; dialectical character, 106–9, 111–14; exchange-value, 62; exchange-value and, 62; exchange-value as, 62; exhibition value, 112–13; profanation and, 116–17; temporality and, 296
Finlayson, James Gordon, 343n26
Fitzpatrick, Peter, 352n16
flanerie, 181–2, 187
fortuna, 55–8
Forst, Rainer, 238, 254, 356n18, 356n19, 356n20, 357n25
Forti, Simona, 148, 339n6, 342n21, 356n16
Foucault, Michel, 327n1, 327n4, 328n4, 351n13, 352n15, 352n21, 352n26, 353n32, 353n37, 354n39, 354n42, 354n43: biopolitics, 2, 7–11; biopower, 204, 206–7; *The Birth of Biopolitics*, 91; *Courses at Collège de France*, 1, 90, 202, 208; gay life, 189–91; genealogy, 179–80; governing *versus* political action, 1; heroization of the present, 180; law and order: antinomy of, 200–9; economic order and, 210–11; Marxists and, 195; neoliberalism, 199–200; queer life, 190–1; rights, 252; surplus of life, 3–4; thanatopolitics, 7
Fox, Christopher, 335n2
Franck, Didier, 271–2
Frankfurt School, theory of reification, 68, 101
fraternity, 32; homosociality, 26; state as, 30
free market, 18–19; catallaxy, 93–4, 209, 212; economic theology and, 292–3;

neoliberalism, 210–15; pastoral power and, 210
free use of the common, 114–19, 307–8
freedom, 19; beginning, and, 138, 152, 229; coercion and, 20; conditionality, 152; Hegel's definitions, 25–6; ironic freedom, 21–2; law and, 202; ; natality and, 129, 148–55; of opinion, 250–2; natality and, 248; republic and, 250; right to have rights and, 247–9; polis and, 25–6; restoration through punishment, 38–9; rights and, 226; as *sui iuris*, 209; spontaneity and, 149–51; tragic, 26, 121
Freud, Sigmund, 27–9, 36, 107, 122, 136

Garcia-Düttmann, Alexander, 337n21
Garrido, Juan Manuel, 358n3
gay life, heroism of modern life, 187–91
Gehring, Petra, 352n18
genealogy, 179–80; of governmentality, 207–8
Geulen, Eva, 335n2, 339n4
Gibson-Graham, J.K., 333n9
Girard, Réné, 26–7, 329n17, 330n20
Giroux, Henry, 361n15
Glendon, Mary Ann, 354n1, 356n13
glory, 48; metabolism of God and, 282–9
gnosticism, 131–3
Goethe, Johann Wolfgang *Elective Affinities,* 158, 165–70; von Gundolf and, 173–5; marriage, 164
Golder, Ben, 352n16, 354n43, 355n10
Goldmann, Lucien, 113, 337n21
Goodchild, Philip, 359n1
Gottlieb, Susannah, 345n36
governance, neoliberalism and, 197–8
governing *versus* political action, 1
governmentality: biopolitics

and, 195–8; of discipline, 203; genealogy of, 202–3, 207–8; of security, 203
Greek tragedy, 19–22; cunning of reason, 54–5; freedom and, 25; messianic redemption of biological life, 160–1; sacrifice and, 30; transition from tribal to political society, 29
Greene, Brian, 361n22, 362n23
Greiert, Andreas, 349n2
Griffin, James, 356n13
Grundrisse: Foundations of the Critique of Political Economy (Marx), 62, 72–81
guardians in civil society, 23–4
Guattari, Felix, 342n23
guilt context of life, 100–1, 156–7; debt and, 116; law and, 235

habeas corpus, refugees and, 230–6
Habermas, Juergen, 5, 68, 295, 328n6, 329n13, 333n5, 333n8, 335n5, 357n25; *Legitimation Crisis*, 103
haeterism, 165, 172; homosexual sex and, 191
Halley, Janet, 351n8
Hamacher, Werner, 228, 355n8, 361n19, 362n29
Hanssen, Beatrice, 336n17
happiness, 123, 133, 177, 321–5; public happiness, 245
Hardt, Michael, 327n1, 335n3, 337n22, 355n9, 357n27, 358n16
Harrington, 256
Hatab, Lawrence, 350n17
Hayek, Friedrich, 351n6, 351n12, 352n25, 353n31, 353n32, 353n34, 353n36, 353n37; Marx and, 93–4; Canguilhem and, 204–6; coordination: economics and, 207; jurisprudence, 211–12; law and order, 209–15; neoliberal hegemony, 197–8; normative order, 198–9; planning society, 204
Hegel Georg Wilhelm Friedrich, 17–18, 329n14, 329n,16: art of kingship, 23–4; bourgeoisie, 23–4; civil society, 17–18; decisionism, 50, 53, freedom, 19; Greek tragedy, 28–30; Hegelian state, 21–36; life, 46–8; *Natural Law*, 18, 24–5; natural *Sittlichkeit*, 26–8, 30; police state, 20; public law, 19–20; sacrifice, 30–1; science of political economy, 18–19; self-consciousness and animality, 42–50; sovereignty and, 63–5; state of nature, 26–7; tragedy, 22–3; tragedy in ethical life, 22, 25–6; tragic freedom, 26
Heidegger, Martin, 331n35, 335n4, 335n7, 337n21, 339n7, 340n14, 340n15, 340n16, 342n18, 342n24, 347n43, 358n3, 359n11; animals and, 105, 271–5; being-toward-death, 130–1, 264–5, 273–5; facticity, 102; gnosticism, 133; historicity, 134; natality, 130–1
Henry, Michael, 351n1
heroism, 173–5; gay life and, 187–91; modern, 179–87; proletariat's, 184
Hilferding, Rudolf, 69–70
Hillach, Ansgar, 336n14
Hobbes, 44, 50, 143, 234, 256
Hölderlin, 25, 58, 170
Homo Sacer (Agamben), 99–102, 104
Honneth, Axel, 5, 65, 294–5, 298, 303, 327n4, 327n6, 328n6, 331n30, 335n1, 336n18, 337n21
hope, hopelessness, 147, 169, 322
Horkheimer, Max, 178, 319, 336n18
Horwitz, Rivka, 337n28
Hugo, Victor, Baudelaire comparison, 183–4

human condition, Arendt, 135–6
human desire *versus* animal desire, 45–6
human life *versus* animal life, 103–6, 142–3. *See also* bios; zoe
human rights, 137. *See also* right to have rights; biopolitics and, 221–4; cosmopolitanism, 225–30; democracy and, 236–43; habeas corpus and, 234–5; legal opinion, 247–8; natality, 228–30; personal dignity and, 222–3; republicanism, 225–30; sacredness and, 222–4; universal human rights, 221–2
human status, 227, 243
humanism, 141–8
humanity, law of, 227
humanization of nature and naturalization of humanity, 67
Hunt, Lynn, 354n1
Hutchings, Kimberly, 332n43

identity thinking, reification and, 113
immaterial labor, 72–3, 92
individualism, civil society and, 29–30, 177, 215–17, 324
individuality: life and, 206–7; state of nature, 26–7
Ingram, James, 226, 355n11
ironic freedom, 21–2, and irony, 180, 187–9
irony, of womankind, 59

James, Susan, 358n8
Jaspers, Karl, 342n20, 344n35
Jennings, Michael, 363n31
Jonas, Hans, 132–3, 340n14
judge-made law, rule of law and, 211–12
juridical monarchy, 207–8
juridical regression, neoliberalism and, 199–200

juridification of politics, neoliberalism and, 209
justice: 23–4; biopolitics, 33–4, 58; courts, 37–40; decisionism, 58–9; distributive, 214–15; fiction and, 126; legal rights and, 150; nomos and, 196–7

Kabbalah, sexual life and, 170–1
Kafka, Franz: antinomianism, 119–20; Bucephalus, 124–5; *Before the Law*, 119–20; Sancho Panza, 122–3, 125–7; theological aspect, 124–5
Kant, Immanuel, 347n45, 353n36; consciousness, 42; right and coercion, 20, 37, 214, 259; freedom, 149–51; marriage and, 165; time and, 297, 303
Kaufmann, David, 336n19, 337n28, 338n38
Keedus, Liisi, 357n26
Kervégan, Jean-Francois, 328n6, 332n38
Kierkegaard, Søren, 349n9; aesthetic view of life, 162; marriage, 161–5; religious view of life, 162–3; repetition, 163
knowledge: capitalism and, 92–3; perception and, 276–7
Kojeve, Alexandre, 331n30, 332n39
Kordela, Kiarina, 333n12
Kouvelakis, Stathis, 327n6, 333n2
Kristeva, Julia, 339n1

labor. *See also* living labor: abstract, 72–3; average social labor time, 79; dead, 85; disposable living labor, 85; as exchange-value, 75; immaterial, 72–3, 92; machines and, 92–3; as original money, 79; productive and unproductive, 84; real subsumption under capital, 82; self-valorization

of the worker, 91–2, 301; services, 72; unproductive, 84; value and, 69–70; wage labor, 75–6
labor time, 297–309; calculating, 10; capitalism and, 85, 92–3; commodity and, 71; reducing, 89; surplus, 89; value and, 71–82
labor-power: commodities and, 78; as commodity, 295; commodity fetishism, 297; community, 114; needs, 36; as property of worker, 65, 85, 91, 113; reified, 102, 295; selling one's, 299–300; as social power, 306–9
Laclau, Ernesto, 65
Lafont, Cristina, 347n43
law. *See also* rule of law: of capital, 89, 93, 299; class struggle and, 305; general intellect, 93; civil society and, 20, 22–3; divine law, 53–5 of earth, 255–6; freedom and, 202; of humanity, 227; judge-made, 211–12; marriage and, 164; mastery of self, 208–9; messianic and, 125; as nothingness, 120–1; nomocratic and telocratic conceptions of, 213; power as, 200–2; as resistance, 218–20; republicanism and, 21, 202; as resistance, 218–20; right to have rights, 226–7; state and, 20; of value, 77; violence over life and, 99–100, 120
law and order: antinomy of, 200–9; coordination and, 209–15; economic order and, 210–11; neoliberalism and, 200–1, 218–20
Lazzarato, Maurizio, 334n13
Lazzeri, Christian, 357n23
legal application, 39–41, 233
legal exception, Plato, 20. *See also* state of exception

Legitimation Crisis (Habermas), 103
Legrand, Stéphane, 327n4, 352n15
Lemke, Thomas, 93, 327n1, 351n1, 352n13
Lemm, Vanessa, 333n4, 335n6, 343n27
liberalism, 1. *See also* neoliberalism. biopolitics and, 2; legislation in, 216; nomos and, 213; political economy and, 196–7; versus republicanism, 5, 202; social planning and, 204
life. *See also* biological life; surplus of life: aesthetic view, 162; as conatus, 266; conception of, 46–7; existential, 270–5; form of life, 105, 190, 205; individuality and, 206–7 ; inseparability from spirit, 132–3; nutritive, 281–2; plants *versus* animals, 281; private property and, 65; power over, 139–40, 231–6; religious view, 161–3; repetition in, 163; self-consciousness, 47–9; spark of life, 180; supernatural, 159, 165; virtual, 280–1; as work of art, as literature, 125–8, 173–8, 188
life-world, 103–5
Lindahl, Hans, 255–6, 357n26
literature, sovereign power and, 122–8
living contemplation, 282–9
living labor: autonomy of, 83; capital and, 73, 83, 88–92; class consciousness and, 82, 304–6; commodity fetishism and, 82, 113; cost of, 299–300; dead labor and, 85, 102, 299; disposable, 85; emancipation of, 101; entrepreneurship of, 92; exchange-value as capital, 85–7; forfeit of power, 295; immaterial labor, 92; labor-power as property of worker, 85; natality and, 3; ontology of, 296; political economy and, 6; private

Index 395

property, 102; productivity increase, 89; self-consciousness and, 52–4; social networks, 92; sovereignty and, 64; subjectivity, 91–2; surplus life and, 9, 90; surplus value and, 69, 82, 85; time and, 81, 299; use-value, 84–5; value and, 61–2, 82–3; wage labor antinomy, 288; zoe and, 51
Lobo-Guerrero, Luis, 354n38
Loeb, Paul, 363n38
Loeschenkohl, Birte, 362n30
Lorey, Isabell, 334n23, 354n40
love, 133–5, 167–8
Ludueña Romandini, Fabián, 343n26
Luisetti, Federico, 359n15
Lukács, Gyorgy, 22, 54, 68, 102, 332, 360n5; *Class Consciousness and History*, 294–309, 320
lyrical poetry, 176–7

Machiavelli, Antigone and, 54–9
machines, labor and, 92–3
Maimonides, 311
Marinas, José-Miguel, 336n13
Markell, Patchen, 332n45, 347n47
marriage: bourgeoisie, 158–9, 179; capitalism and, 179; disconnect from reproduction, 165–6; divinity of, 169–70; eternal life and, 161–73; Goethe, 164; Kierkegaard, 161–2; law and, 164; matriarchical impulse, 165; philosophical problem, 161; religious approach, 163–4; sexual contract, 164–5; social contract of Abrahamic traditions, 159
Martel, James, 328n8, 363n33
Marx, Karl, 337n24; commons, 256; *Critique of Hegel's Philosophy of Right*, 63, 76; development of ideas, 61–2; *Economic-Philosophical Manuscripts*, 65; *Grundrisse: Foundations of the Critique of Political Economy*, 62, 72–81; human/animal production comparison, 65–7; labor theory, 69–70; political economy, 62–3; primitive communism, 165; profanation of the sacred, 31–2; proletariat, 102; repressive hypothesis, 195; theory of value, 9, 10, 60–1, 68–81, 291, 296; social ontology, 68–72; surplus, 3, 9–10, 61, 69–73, 80–2, 87–95, 217, 299–300; time and, 71–93, 290–325, value theory as sociology, 70; worker suicide, 185–6
Marxism: Foucault and, 195; basic concepts of, 101, 309–10
Marzocca, Ottavio, 327n4, 334n26
masculinity, modern hero, 186–7
master/slave dialectic of Hegel, 49–53
mastery of self, law and, 208–9
materialism, messianism and, 309–18
Maturana, Humberto and Varela, Francisco, 198
McCloskey, Deirdre, 328n8
Meador, Daniel John, 356n15
memory, 133–4
men *versus* Man, 136–7
Menke, Christoph, 20, 22, 354n5, 355n11, 356n19
messiah, *versus* tragic hero, 160–1
messianic kingdom, 122, 170–2, 287–8, 311–22
messianic politics of Benjamin, 118–19, 122–3, 321–3
messianic reversal, 122–3, 125–8
messianism, materialism and, 309–18
metabolism: contemplation and, 280–1; of God, 282–9; nutritive life, 281–2

Meyer, Katrin, 354n37
mind: eternity of, 269–70; as idea of the body, 269–70
Milbank, John, 358n1
Mill, John Stuart, 216
Miller, Tyrus, 363n30
mimesis, 347–8
Mirowski, Philip, 328n7, 351n6, 353n32, 353n34, 359n2
modernity, Baudelaire, 180
money, 334; capitalism and, 75–6; commodities and, 76; communism and, 75–6; distribution, 75; free circulation, 74–5; labor as original, 79; representative character of, 78–9; time, and, 79–81, 297–302; sovereignty and, 64; value and, 73–4
Moses, Stéphane, 337n32
Moyn, Samuel, 354n1
Muhle, Maria, 352n24
mythical violence, 100

Napoli, Paolo, 352n15
Nasstrom, Sofia, 358n32
natality, 5–6, 339, 345–6; Arendt, 129–55, 339; Arendt's Gauss Lectures, 138–9; Augustinian, 153–4; as condition of freedom, 148–55, 230; creation and, 152–3; definition, 3; fertility and, 150–1; freedom and, 129; freedom of opinion, 248; guilt context of life, 156–61; Heidegger, 130–1; juris-generative power, 251–2; law of, 229; mimetic relation, action and, 347–8; nationality and, 232–4; negligence and celebration, 159; normativity and, 222, 228; political space and, 230, 257–8; right to have rights, 226–7, 229–30, 237; constituent power, 252–4; social organization, 159; sovereignty, 231–2; supernatural life, 159; surplus of life, 5–6, 95; nationality, natality and, 232–4; territory and, 256–9
Natural Law (Hegel), 18–28, 31–41, 45
natural right, 243–4
naturalization of refugees, 241–3, 254
Neal, Andrew, 354n38
Negative Dialectics (Adorno), 119–20
Negri, Antonio, 4, 61, 73–6, 83–4, 90–2, 327n1, 334n14, 334n20, 334n21, 335n27, 335n3, 337n22, 355n9, 357n27, 358n5; Hardt and, 91–2, 256, 301
neoconservatism, 95–6
neoliberalism: Austrian School of economics, 211; biopolitics and, 195–200; free market, 210; governance and, 197–8; government and, 1; juridical regression, 199–200; juridification of politics, 209; law and order and, 200–1, 218–20; *nomos* and, 213, 215–17; police in, 215–16; political economy and, 211–12; surplus life, 218–19
Nieraad, Juergen, 361n19
Nietzsche, Friedrich, 171, 173, 297, 315–6, 325, 361n16, 361n17, 361n19, 361n20, 362n26, , 362n29, 363n31; *The Birth of Tragedy*, 175–6
Nigro, Roberto, 327n4
nomos, 88, 196–8, 211–12; legal conception, 207, 213; neoliberalism and, 213, 215–17; right to have rights, 255–60
normality: definition, 3, biopolitics, and, 7, 34; state of exception and, 233, normalization, political rationality, 206–7
normative order: Canguilhem, 203–5; governance and, 197–8; social order, 198; spontaneous, 198–9
normative structure of value, 72–81

Index 397

normativity: Athena and, 34; biological life and, 42–3; Canguilhem, 203–6, 218; capital, reproduction, 187; creativity and, 210, 218; the dandy and, 188; definition, 3; exchange-value and, 60–1, 84; law and, 53; life and, 198; living labor and, 62; money and, 76; natality and, 6–10, 86, 222, 228, 252; neoliberal, 217; nomos and, 256; recognition and, 50; self-consciousness and, 53–4; thanatopolitics, 49; tragic freedom and, 32; ; zoe and, 190, 228; norms, social regulation and, 206–7
Norris, Andrew, 335n2
Norton, Robert E., 350n18
Novak, David, 349n5
nutritive life, 281–2

Occupy Wall Street, 74
Odradek, 101, 109–11
The Open (Agamben), 102–3
opinion, 245–7; interest and, 153–4
Oresteia trilogy (Aeschylus), 24–5
organs, sensing and, 276–7
The Origins of Totalitarianism (Arendt), 136, 139, 146–7

Parekh, Serena, 355n11, 355n13
Parsons, Talcott, 197
Passavant, Paul, 335n2
passion, affection and, 168
pastoral power, 207–8; free market, 210
Patton, Paul, 352n20, 354n43, 358n30
Pauen, Michael, 350n10
Paul, Saint, vocation and, 115; theology and, 119, 128
peoples, 227–8, 249–50, 252, 258–60, 312
Phenomenology of Spirit (Hegel), spirit and sovereignty, 41–54
Pinkard, Terry, 329n13

Pippin, Robert, 43, 49, 329n13, 332n39
Pitkin, Hannah, 346n40
planning, 203–5; 306–7
plant life *versus* animal life, 281
Plato: class analysis, 22–3; legal application and, 39–40; legal exception, 20
Plehwe, Dieter, 328n7, 351n6, 353n32
plurality, 137; right to have rights and, 237
Pocock, J.G.A., 357n28
police: neoliberalism and, 215–16; science of, 2, 215; shift from politics, 2, 91, 202; and human rights, 222–3
polis, freedom and, 25–6
political action: class consciousness and, 307–8; *versus* governing, 1
political economy, 2, 17–18; biopolitics and, 196–7; critique of, 294; economic theology and, 290–4; Marx, 62–3; neoliberalism and, 211–12; rule of law and, 196
political organization, 213–14
political power, 207–8
political rationality, normalization and, 206–7
political society: family in, 34; transition to, 29
political space: natality and, 230, 257–8; right to have rights, 239–40
politicization: of philosophy, 264; of sexuality, guilt context of life and, 157
politics. *See also* biopolitics: biological life and, 220; freedom of life, 129; government and, 1; juridification, neoliberalism and, 209; police shift, 2; right to, 226; self-sacrifice and, 27
population; Arendt, 258; Foucault, 195–7, 218–20, 256; norms, 206–7, 215; versus people, 259; thanatopolitics, 263

pornography, exhibition value, 118
Postone, Moishe, 360n11, 361n13
potentiality, 277–80
power, 200–2; biopower, 204, 206–7; pastoral, 207–8; political, 207–8
profanation: Agamben, 117–18; bare life and, 101; capitalism and, 116–17; of civil society, 31–2, 34–6; commodity fetishism and, 116–17; fetishes, 116; profession/vocation, 117–18; redeemed nature, 118–19; of the sacred, 31–2, 34–5
profession: *versus* calling, 115; profanation, 117–18; vocation as, 114–15; 307–9
professionalization of activity, capitalism and, 114–15
profit, 70–1, 300–1
proletariat: heroism, 184; Marx, 102; women and, 185
Protestant ethic, capitalism and, 114–16
Proudhon, Pierre Joseph, 75
provisional right, 213–14
public law, 19–20
punishment: bourgeoisie, 38; as coercion, 38; as conquest, 38–9; purpose of state, 38; restoration of freedom, 38–9; theory of, 37; mythical violence and, 100
Purtschert, Patricia, 354n37

queer life, 190–1
Quintana, Laura, 336n10

race, politicization, 157; as *ghenos*, 159, 187
Rancière, Jacques, 55, 70, 224, 247–8, 258, 352n21, 355n10
Rawls, John, 244–5
real subsumption, 83–90
reason: contemplative life and, 264; sociality of reason, 27

reconciliation between civil society and the state, 24–5
reconciliation with God, 167–8
redemption, 340–1; through sin, 171–2
refugees: *versus* citizens, 258–9; habeas corpus and, 230–6; naturalization, 241–3, 254; rights, 222
reification, 5–6, 360; bourgeois economics, 68; consciousness, 360; facticity and, 102; identity thinking and, 113; temporality, class consciousness and, 294–302; value and, 62
relativity, cosmology, 313–14
religious approach to marriage, 163–4
religious view of life, 162–3
Repetition (Kierkegaard), 163
republic: communal movements, 249; *versus* democracy, 246; freedom of opinion, 250
Republic (Plato), 22–4
republican constitution, 245–6
republicanism: biopolitics and, 2; civil society and, 5; commune-ism and, 5; constitutional democracy, 245–6; dualist interpretation, 244–5; free market, 18–19; Hayek, *nomos* and, 211–12; human rights, cosmopolitanism, 225–30; law and, 21, 202; of opinion, 258; politics and, 1; republican laws and liberal norms, 212; right to have rights, 238–9
resistance, law as, 218–20
Revel, Judith, 334n26
revenge: taboos and, 32–3; totemism, 28–9
revolutionary praxis, 102, 116, 119–128, 304, 306
Ricoeur, Paul, 343n26
right to have rights, 219, 222–6;

Index 399

constituent power and, 243–54; cosmopolitanism, 238; freedom of opinion, 247–52; human nature and, 228; human status and, 227; law and, 226–7; law of humanity, 227; natality and, 226–7, 229–30, 236–7; constituent power, 252–4; *nomos*, 255–60; plurality and, 237; political space, 239–40; republicanism, 238–9; right to politics, 226
right to justification, 238–9
rights. *See also* human rights: basic rights, 221; Declarations of the Rights of Man, 231; ethico-political, 237–8; freedom and, 226; individual, 19–20; moral, 237–8; natural, 243–4; refugees and, 222; subjective, 19–20
Rose, Gillian, 328n4, 328n11, 337n21, 360n6
Rose, Nikolas, 327n1 334n25, 352n20, 354n3
Rosenzweig, Franz, 173, 311–12
Rousseau, Jean-Jacques, 44, 331n33
Rubin, Isaak Illich, 333n7
Ruggiero, Guido de, 328n6
rule of law. *See also* law: judge-made law, 211–12, 218; political economy and, 196; states of exception and, 232

Saar, Martin, 327n4, 357n23
Sabbatianism, 171–3
sacred: profanation, 31–2; taboos and, 28–9; life, 222–3
sacrifice. *See also* self-sacrifice: bourgeoisie, 35; civil society and the state, 34–6; civil society as sacrifice of sacrifice, 31–2; festival and, 27–8; Freud, 27–8; Greek tragedy and, 30; of the sacrifice, 30–1; self-reflection, 30; tribal community and, 26–7
sacrificial meal, 30–2, 63
Sancho Panza, 122–7
Santner, Eric, 336n17
Sartre, Jean-Paul, 188–9
Savarino, Luca, 339n1
Schmitt, Carl, 50, 63, 167, 197, 214, 255–6
Schoettker, Detlev, 361n17
Scholem, Gershom, 119–20, 171, 313, 337n32, 350n14, 350n15, 361n21
Schürmann, Reiner, 339n7, 347n44
science: of economics, 2; of police, 2; of policy, 215–16; of political economy, 18; social sciences, 2; of social systems, 2
security, and insurance, 215–19
Segal, Charles, 329n17
self-consciousness, 42–3, 306; of the commodity, 304–5; desire, 43–4; life and, 47–9; master/slave dialectic, 49–53; normativity, 53–4; object of consciousness, 43–4
self-sacrifice: civil society and, 19; civil society and the state, 34–6; politics and, 27
self-valorization of the worker, 91, 301
Sewell, William H., 361n13
sexual communism, 190–1
sexual contract of marriage, 164–5
sexual relationships, social relations and, 157–8
sexual reproduction of capital, 178–87
sexuality. *See also* homosexuality: eternal life of, 168–9; guilt context, 170–1; male impotence, 191; Kabbalah and, 170–1; politicization, 157; production in capitalism, 185; redemption through sin, 171–2
shock, 166, 181–2; 323
Siep, Ludwig, 328n4, 329n18

singularity, fertility and, 150–1
Sinnerbrink, Robert, 335n2
Sittlichkeit, 22, 26; civil society, 29; family as natural, 28; dissolution, 55; marriage, 164; sacrifice and festival, 27; sovereign and, 63; tragedy in, 31–2; totemic, 35–6; tribal bond and, 26–7
Skinner, Quentin, 352n28, 352n29
Smith, Adam, 75, 291
social bond, exchange-value and, 74
social contract of marriage, Abrahamic traditions, 159
social ontology of value, 68–72
social order: normative order, 198; spontaneous, 198–9; political organization and, 213–14
social organization of natality, 159
social regulation, norms, 206–7
sociality of commodities, 75–6
sociality of reason, 27
society's dreams, 107–9
sovereignty: art of kingship, 23; bare life and, 99–102; first born and, 64; human rights and, 356; literature and, 122–8; money and, 64; natality and, 231–2; *Sittlichkeit*, 63; sovereign's will *versus* general will, 63–4; spirit and, 41–54; of value, 60–7
Smith, Steven, 328n6, 331n30
species life, 2–7, 47, 65, 87, 93, 150, 331. *See also* biopolitics; natality. alienation, 183; Aristotelian division, 142; capital and, 82, 87–8, 93–4, 306; class consciousness, 51–2, 297; economics, equilibrium and, 207; *Gattungswesen*, 3; Greek tragedies and, 8; Heidegger, 12; individual and, 324; living labor and, 299; neoliberalism and, 217; police activity, 90; private property and, 65; production and, 65; sacredness, 232–3; self-consciousness, 43, 49; singularity and, 150; species-being, 66; time and, 296, 301–2; totalitarianism and, 139; time and, 296; zoe and, 9; zoe aionios and, 160
Spinoza, 250–1, 264–285, 331n34
spirit: inseparability from life, 132–3; objectification, 62; sovereignty and, 41–54
spontaneity, freedom and, 151
spontaneous social orders, 198–9; catallaxy, 209; political organization and, 213–14
state: civil society and, mutual self-sacrifice, 34–6; punishment as purpose, 38; reconciliation with civil society, 24–5; as sacrificial meal of civil society, 63
state of exception, 4; emancipation of life, 100; neoliberalism and, 224; Plato and, 20; rights and, 231; sovereign power and, 236; as space of democracy, 250; *State of Exception* (Agamben), 233; zoe in, 49
Steiner, Uwe, 337n25
Strauss, Leo, 50
subjective rights, 19–20
subjectivity: life and, 207; of value, 81–8
suicide: black suits and, 183–4; of workers, 185–6
supernatural life, 159
surplus of life, 3–4: biotechnology and, 90–5; commodity fetishism and, 107; economic production and, 205; entrepreneurial conduct and, 219; natality, 95; neoliberalism and, 217–19; surplus value and, 88–96

surplus value, 61; living labor and, 69; neoliberalism and, 94–5; possibility, 80; profit, 70–1; subjectivity and, 81–2; surplus life and, 88–96
Syros, Vasileios, 352n28
Szankay, Zoltán, 339n7

taboo, 28–9; festival and, 29; profanation of the sacred and, 32; revenge and, 32–3; sacralization and, 28–9
Taminiaux, Jacques, 339n7
Tassin, Étienne, 346n39
Taylor, Mark C., 359n1
Tellmann, Ute, 351n3, 354n40
temporality, 361. *See also* time: capitalism and, 290–1; class consciousness and, 294–302; class struggle and, 307–8; commodity fetishism and, 296
Teubner, Guenther, 351n9
thanatopolitics, 7; biological life and, 156–7; biopolitics transformation, 156, 224; politicization of sexuality and race, 157; transition to, 263–4
Thurschwell, Adam, 337n29
time. *See also* temporality: economy of, 290–1; labor and, 79–81; value, 82; necessary and disposable, 88, 93, 301–2, 308–9
totalitarianism, 132–3
totemism, 27–8; revenge and, 28–9
tragedy, 22–3; allegorical nature, 175–6; crime and punishment, 26–7; refined hypocrisy, 36; sacrificial crisis, 26; in *Sittlichkeit*, 31–2
tragedy of civil society, 17–18, 63
tragedy of ethical life, 25–6
tragedy of the Hegelian state, 21–31
tragic freedom, 26, 32; ironic freedom, 21
tribal community: family structure and, 28; Freud, 27–8; sacrifice and, 26–7; transition to political society, 29

Universal Declaration of Human Rights, 145, 222, 241
universal human rights, 221–2
use value, 72; free exchange and, 112; living labor, 84–5; loss, 109–10

value. *See also* exchange-value; eternity of, 80; exhibition value: class consciousness and, 65; fear of, 70–1; form of, 61; labor and, 69–70; labor time and, 82; of law, political economy and, 77; Marx on, 60–1; social ontology of, 68–72; Marx's theory as sociology, 70; money and, 73–4; normative structure, 72–81; objectivist theory, 71; profit, 70–1; reification, 68; sovereignty of, 60–7; subjectivist theory, 71–2; substance, 81–8; use value, 72
Valverde, Mariana, 352n14, 354n37
Vernant, Jean-Pierre, 329n17, 330n21
Villa, Dana, 339n7, 342n24
violence: divine, 100; law and, 99, 120; mythical, 100
virtual life, 280–1
vita Dei, 267
Vitalpolitik, 92
vocation: messianic, 115–16; profanation, 117–18
vocation as profession, 114–15
Voegelin, Eric, 339n9, 340n12
Vogl, Joseph, 291–2, 359n1

wage labor, 75–6, 82–3; as activity to fill time, 302; exploitation of individual, 71; class consciousness and, 90; living labor and, 84, 86–7, 288; self-valorization of worker and, 301

war: Antigone and divine law, 54–9; Hegel, 54
Weber, Max, 68, 114–5, 207
Weber, Samuel, 337n25, 338n37, 339n8, 342n22, 349n7, 359n1
Weigel, Sigrid, 337n28, 349n8
Wesel, Uwe, 349n3
Wohlfarth, Irving, 338n41
Wolff, Richard, 333n9
Wood, Allen W., 328n10

Zac, Sylvain, 265–7, 358n8

Zizek, Slavoj, 5, 301, 305, 309
zoe, 3, 102; bare life, 105; bestial, 104; bios and, 67, 141–8; conatus and, 265; contemplative, 264; creativity and, 178; duality, 9; eternal, 189; ethical life and, 45; normativity and, 228; opposite, 7; sacrifice, 43–4, 49; sacrilege, 30–1; self-consciousness, 43, 46–52; sovereignty, 42, 234; republican, 230; rights and, 234
zoe aionos, 12, 264

COMMONALITIES

Timothy C. Campbell, series editor

Roberto Esposito, *Terms of the Political: Community, Immunity, Biopolitics.* Translated by Rhiannon Noel Welch. Introduction by Vanessa Lemm.

Maurizio Ferraris, *Documentality: Why It Is Necessary to Leave Traces.* Translated by Richard Davies.

Dimitris Vardoulakis, *Sovereignty and Its Other: Toward the Dejustification of Violence.*

Anne Emmanuelle Berger, *The Queer Turn in Feminism: Identities, Sexualities, and the Theater of Gender.* Translated by Catherine Porter.

James D. Lilley, *Common Things: Romance and the Aesthetics of Belonging in Atlantic Modernity.*

Jean-Luc Nancy, *Identity: Fragments, Frankness.* Translated by François Raffoul.

Miguel Vatter, *Between Form and Event: Machiavelli's Theory of Political Freedom.*

Miguel Vatter, *The Republic of the Living: Biopolitics and the Critique of Civil Society.*

Maurizio Ferraris, *Where are You? An Ontology of the Cellphone.* Translated by Sarah De Sanctis.